For our children and future generations – may they enjoy growing prosperity, as previous generations have done.

Incentives matter.

PROSPERITY THROUGH GROWTH

PROSPERITY

Boosting Living Standards

THROUGH

in an Age of Autocracy and AI

GROWTH

DR ARTHUR B. LAFFER,
MATTHEW ELLIOTT,
MICHAEL HINTZE AND
DOUGLAS McWILLIAMS

Biteback Publishing

First published in Great Britain in 2025 by
Biteback Publishing Ltd, London
Copyright © The Jobs Foundation 2025

ISBN 978-1-78590-946-7

10 9 8 7 6 5 4 3 2 1

A CIP catalogue record for this book is available from the British Library.

Set in Minion Pro

Printed and bound in Great Britain by
CPI Group (UK) Ltd, Croydon CR0 4YY

FSC
www.fsc.org
MIX
Paper | Supporting
responsible forestry
FSC® C013604

CONTENTS

PREFACE *BY LORD HINTZE*

'Knowledge is the basis of all good decision-making.'

This is not the Britain I came to from my home in Australia via Harvard Business School in 1984. That Britain was first and foremost a place of opportunity. It encouraged me to work hard and to become successful and to create wealth. I hope that the welcome it gave me has been repaid by the significant taxes I have contributed and the philanthropic donations I have made in the four decades I have been here.

It is nothing short of tragic that the young wealth creators of today – men and women like me all those years ago – are being driven to emigrate, not just to the obvious hubs such as the United Arab Emirates but also to destinations like Italy, Portugal and even France, which welcome them with open arms.

Innovators and employers are optimising their potential by moving offshore. It has been suggested that 10,800 millionaires quit the country in 2024 alone. We live in an age of remote working. Leaving the UK is an easy option. Looking back, I wonder if I would have chosen to build my career here if I had encountered the economic climate that exists now.

What do I see when I look at the UK in 2025?

The planning system for property and infrastructure development seems to have been designed deliberately to disincentivise – with poor pay-offs and minimal accountability. Recent inheritance tax changes have broken farms and family businesses and are contributing to the mass exodus of wealth creators. The recent increase in employers' National Insurance and the prospect of the Employment Rights Bill are driving up joblessness.

It makes no sense to me. A growing economy comes about thanks to the thousands of small businesses and charities within local communities, all of which have struggled under increasing burdens in the past few years. These are the organs of growth that our recent governments seem determined to punish one way or another.

This book first took shape in November 2024, when I was talking to an old friend of mine, Dr Arthur B. Laffer, the renowned American economist and, of course, the originator of the Laffer curve. He suggested that we should work together to develop a 'North Star' for economic policy in the UK, a guide that would be both theoretical and practical, giving the country a blueprint for economic growth.

We were later joined by my fellow peer Matthew Elliott, co-founder of the TaxPayers' Alliance and a well-known political strategist with a long track record executing complex policy research projects. The UK economist Douglas McWilliams then joined us, bringing an in-depth knowledge of the British economy and his editorial and writing skills, and the team was complete. He is the founder of the well-respected Centre for Economics and Business Research.

We believe that if we are to encourage growth and prosperity in the UK, then our economy requires a transformational reset structured around three essential tenets: principles, policy and politics.

For too long, the economy has been dominated by political ideology. In his essay, which opens the first section of this book, Arthur Laffer cuts through the dogma to produce a roadmap for growth.

This is followed by a section explaining how it might be applied to the UK – a '24/7 Growth Plan' for the economy.

The final section looks at the political obstacles to growth, and how they might be overcome. This is based on a series of interviews conducted with some of the major influencers of our time. They come from different sectors and from across the political spectrum. I am enormously grateful to them for agreeing to share their views:

- Former Prime Ministers: Sir Tony Blair, Lord Cameron of Chipping Norton, Rishi Sunak MP, Boris Johnson and Liz Truss.
- Former Chancellors: Lord Lamont of Lerwick, Lord Clarke of Nottingham, George Osborne, Lord Hammond of Runnymede, Sir Sajid Javid, Nadhim Zahawi, Kwasi Kwarteng and Sir Jeremy Hunt MP.
- Former ministers: Sir Vince Cable and Lord O'Neill of Gatley.

- Faith leaders: The Rt Rev. and the Rt Hon. Lord Chartres.
- Senior civil servants: Lord Macpherson of Earl's Court, Lord O'Donnell, Sir Tom Scholar and Lord Stevens of Birmingham.
- Former Bank of England officials: Andrew Bailey, Clare Lombardelli and former chief economist Andy Haldane.
- Senior government advisers: Rupert Harrison, Lord Petitgas and Lord Walney.
- Senior business leaders: Jamie Dimon, David Giampaolo, Richard Gnodde, Sir John Rose and Lord Wolfson of Aspley Guise.
- Major business group leaders: Jonathan Geldart, Anna Leach, Stephen Phipson and Rupert Soames.

The authors of this book have no intention of forcing a particular agenda on our readers, but it is true to say that we have found common ground in the belief that the effective pursuit of growth is beyond politics and benefits the whole of society. It is clear to us that without proper economic principles and a basic understanding of what they mean, growth and prosperity are choked from the very start.

We must understand what makes economies and therefore societies work and accept that incentives – both actual and aspirational – are critical. The policies and political practicalities that flow from them are crucial to achieving prosperity through growth. A bad structure with bad incentives makes it impossible to achieve value and create wealth and opportunity.

I hope the economic framework outlined in these pages will encourage people of all political persuasions to consider the basic principles – the North Star – that once fuelled our wealth and growth in the UK and can do so again.

This prosperity can and indeed should be used to support our whole society – but in a way that is focused on absolute value and not on the politics of envy, class war or any other ideology.

I am deeply proud to call the UK my home.

This is a country blessed with incredible assets in its education, law and language, as well as world-beating innovation in areas such as financial services, life sciences, artificial intelligence (AI) and film production.

It is home to world-leading theatres, museums, fashion creatives and culture.

Britain is a truly great country with great opportunity for all: it is an inclusive society that has historically had room for immense diversity of thought and endeavour. But that endeavour needs to be nurtured, encouraged and rewarded if it is going to pay dividends to the country as a whole.

We need to restate the obvious. Incentives matter – and not just to those involved in tax policy. People respond to rewards and penalties and adjust their behaviours accordingly. The decisions that they make affect the success of the entire nation, and that is why this book has been written.

I sincerely hope it will help to refocus minds for the broader benefit of the country which will, in turn, lead us to enjoy prosperity through growth.

The Lord Hintze, Kt., AM, GCSG
September 2025

INTRODUCTION

This book represents not only the views of its authors but also ideas gleaned from an extensive series of interviews with a wide range of those with experience in politics, government and business about what is going wrong with the United Kingdom and especially the UK economy.

To many of our interviewees, especially those closest to the business sector, not only is the UK economy near a state of economic collapse but also the current state of politics is likely to be incapable of rescuing the country. Our interviewees referenced especially the flow of talented people, both of international and of British descent, deciding to leave the UK and operate elsewhere (Figure 1 shows a visualisation of data from Henley & Partners giving projections of net movements of millionaires) and the likely departure of many of the remaining manufacturing businesses if UK energy costs continue to be uncompetitive. Our analysis also suggested that with technology increasingly dependent on AI, data centres and big data, the location of this sector would more and more be driven by the cost of energy.

Forecasts specially commissioned for this study from world economic league table specialists the Centre for Economics and Business Research (Cebr)* show the UK on unchanged policies slipping down the league table of gross domestic product (GDP) per capita at purchasing power parity from its current position of thirtieth in 2024 to forty-sixth by 2050, being overtaken by Poland, Slovenia, Lithuania, the Czech Republic, Croatia, Bahrain, Hungary and Saudi Arabia by 2040 and by Turkey, Latvia, Serbia, Romania, Georgia, Moldova, Estonia, Panama, Israel and the Slovak Republic by 2050.

---

* More details are provided in Annex 2.

FIGURE 1: HENLEY & PARTNERS' PROJECTIONS
OF NET MOVEMENT OF MILLIONAIRES 2025*

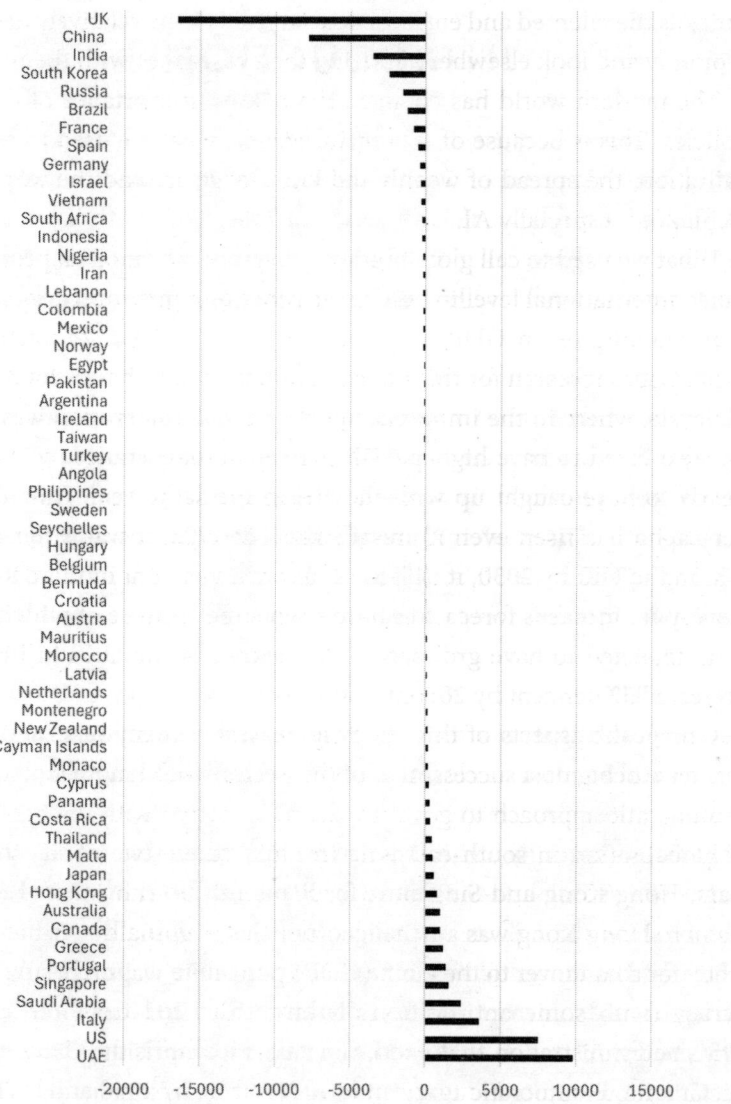

Source: Henley & Partners

---

* This data, provided by Henley & Partners, is controversial and includes estimates. The Tax Justice Network has criticised elements of the methodology and apparent inconsistencies in https://taxjustice.net/press/millionaire-exodus-did-not-occur-study-reveals/, though its own conclusions are also controversial. The Henley & Partners data is much more consistent with the impressions we received in our interviews and from our own research.

And even such projections of a gentle decline down the league table may be too good to be true. Slips have an unhealthy tendency to turn into slides as the talented and entrepreneurial react to the relatively declining economy and look elsewhere, moving their resources with them.

The modern world has changed the relative importance of different policies. This is because of two major trends: what we used to call globalisation, the spread of wealth and knowledge around the world; and technology, especially AI.

What we used to call globalisation, probably now more appropriately called international levelling up, is the process of previously poor countries catching up in GDP per capita terms with the traditionally rich West. Cebr's research for this book in Annex 2 shows how a country like Malaysia, where in the immediate post-war years starvation was rife, is now expected to have higher GDP per capita than France by 2050 and nearly to have caught up with the UK in the same year. China's GDP per capita has risen even more quickly – in 1998, it was 8 per cent of that in the UK; by 2050, it is forecast to be 87 per cent of the UK's GDP per capita. India's is forecast to have risen slightly more slowly but even so is expected to have grown from 7 per cent of the UK's in 1998 to a projected 52 per cent by 2050.

One of the aspects of this levelling up is that many of the countries that have been most successful at prioritising growth have adopted a fairly autocratic approach to government. This started with the beginnings of globalisation in south-east Asia in 1968,* where two of the shooting stars, Hong Kong and Singapore, happened to be run in an autocratic fashion. Hong Kong was a British colony that eventually was being kept ready for a handover to the Chinese, and Singapore was originally a democracy (with some anti-democratic laws inherited from the colonial British administration that had faced an armed uprising) that gradually became more autocratic under the remarkable personality of Lee Kuan Yew. By 2050, Singapore is forecast to be the richest non-energy-based economy in the world in GDP per capita terms, twice as rich as the United States and not far short of three times as rich as the UK (see Annex 2).

---

* The moving of electronics factories from the developed world to Asia is generally considered to have started with Fairchild's investment in Hong Kong in 1968.

Countries that are not autocratic themselves increasingly have to compete with other countries that are and which can therefore avoid the politics of envy, whereby they are forced to redistribute from those who work hard to those whose economic contributions are lower.

This results in movement of economic activity, people, talent and resources. In economic terms, it changes the elasticities of response to, for example, taxes or regulations. Countries that adopt business-unfriendly taxes or regulations are increasingly likely to lose their businesses much more quickly to those countries more insulated from pressures to be anti-business than in earlier years. In the UK, the Office for Budget Responsibility has admitted that it has had to revise up its elasticity of migration response to tax changes for the so-called non-doms,[1] and private discussions indicate that the UK authorities have been surprised at the extent of the impact of the Autumn 2024 Budget on the movement of people.

Paradoxically, because such governments have been successful in achieving growth, many of the autocratic governments are not in fact unpopular – their populations in many cases have accepted the trade-off between lack of democratic accountability and the huge relative gains in economic growth. In Singapore, for example, the party that has ruled since independence in 1965 still won 65 per cent of the vote in 2025, in elections that independent observers have largely accepted as fair.[2]

Technology and especially AI, meanwhile, are also changing the rules of the game. The main reports on the economic implications of AI[3] indicate: 1) a boost to productivity and GDP, though the estimates of the scale of this boost differ wildly; 2) a huge churn in jobs, with around 40 per cent of current jobs being changed or replaced as a result of AI; 3) a probable increase in inequality as more easily automated jobs which tend to be less skilled disappear while more senior jobs are enhanced; and 4) a probable boost to mobility as the world's economic landscape realigns.

Most studies predict substantial job destruction, which is often presented as a negative. While it is true that job destruction without any compensating gains would not be a desirable outcome, since most Western economies are suffering from a productivity malaise, a development that has the potential to boost productivity should be seen in potentially a more positive light. Most past technological changes have created more jobs than they have destroyed and no one has made a strong case that AI is in any way different except in scale and speed.

In many ways, the micro effects of AI may be very much more important than the macro effects, since looking at a macro level, many of the potential effects offset each other. At a micro level, these offsets do not exist. If, as seems likely, job content will be affected for as many as 40 per cent of existing jobs, new skills and possibly different people will be needed to do them. If a significant proportion of jobs will be done by different people, the churn will have to be encouraged to move people from one set of jobs to another. It is therefore important that incentives can perform their normal role of reallocating people in the labour market.

AI will increase the premium placed on skills. The seminal study by the UK Department for Education on the impact of AI[4] showed that whereas much of the previous generations of technology and automation had affected manual jobs, AI is likely to affect most the more routine non-manual jobs most, while at the same time placing a premium on human intervention to guide the use of the AI. One consequence will be the need continuously to upgrade the UK educational system to help develop the skills most required by AI. Our plans for public expenditure take this into account.

In addition, the heavy data needs of AI (e.g. big data) will almost certainly place demands on UK infrastructure, both for communications and energy in addition to security. Again, ensuring that this infrastructure is fit for purpose will be critical in ensuring that the best AI-related jobs are located in the UK.

The redistribution of jobs that is likely to be associated with AI places a premium on incentives.

The UK has actually done relatively well with tech, mainly through its so-called Flat White Economy.* The UK's particular advantage has been in its strength in using tech, rather than producing tech. The UK's e-commerce market is claimed to be $196 billion, the third largest in the world,[5] while the government claims that it is also the world's third largest AI economy.[6]

---

* Named after the eponymous book *The Flat White Economy* by co-author Douglas McWilliams, Duckworth, 2015.

The future of the UK tech economy will depend heavily on the extent to which AI develops. Worldwide, there appears to be a race to attract AI talent and skills. Clearly, the UK will need to focus on relevant skills but also will need to be attractive to entrepreneurs and to those with the relevant talents. This heightens the focus on incentives. The success of AI in the UK will also be dependent on the size of the market, so the issue becomes circular: make the economy successful and it will succeed in AI, which will make it more successful.

Since the end of the 1980s, governments in the Western world have shied away from the economic approach of promoting growth through incentives.

Yet both social and technological developments since then have greatly amplified the importance of incentives. One social development is massively increased mobility and especially international mobility. Many talented people now operate in a range of economies – often having more than one passport, they have a choice about where to do their business. Where they do their business generates substantial spin-off benefits for the local economy. Young people, too, see the opportunity of moving to get a better life. The British Council's Next Generation 2024 report[7] shows that 72 per cent of UK-based eighteen- to thirty-year-olds would consider moving to another country. We have used the analysis of the impact of local taxation on migration between different states and localities in the US to help understand the scale of the impact of tax differentials in a world where the obstacles to migration decline.

A second social development reflects the technological changes including AI – specific talented and entrepreneurial people have become relatively more important in driving growth, which has been reflected in increased inequality of incomes. Economist Thomas Piketty[8] has highlighted the growth in inequality, though his explanations have been controversial; more recent authors have associated this growth with technology and to a lesser extent globalisation.[9] Insofar as growth has been biased towards the talented and entrepreneurial, incentivising them to operate in their own economy rather than in someone else's becomes increasingly important.

The technological development that has most increased the role of incentives as an economic policy is the increasing ability to become a digital nomad. In earlier periods, you potentially had to change your job and possibly your occupation if you wanted to move to a different location. This was a severe handicap and restrained mobility. Now, technology often makes it possible to do the same job from different locations. Yet the knock-on effects of your spending depend critically on where you have chosen to operate.

While incentives have become increasingly important in choice of location, competition between locations has also increased. At one point, the realistic range of options for someone who wanted to emigrate from the United Kingdom was mainly other English-speaking countries like the United States and the former dominions. But economic development around the world and increased language skills mean that there is a much wider range of alternative places to do business. Indeed, one of our interviewees claimed that 'Dubai is now the nineteenth largest British city'.

The Cebr analysis shows that after taking account of purchasing power, UK GDP per capita had risen by a tiny 7.3 per cent, about 0.4 per cent per annum, between 2008 and 2024 compared with 24.4 per cent in the US. Not surprisingly, the weekly poll by pollsters More in Common shows the cost of living and, by implication, the standard of living as far and away the most important issue for British people in May and June 2025, with 61 per cent placing it at the top of their list (compared with 38 per cent for the NHS; 29 per cent for immigration and 28 per cent for asylum seekers crossing the Channel).

The growth of autocratic states is also relevant. While autocracy has many disadvantages and for most people these disadvantages will outweigh any economic advantages, for those who are especially financially motivated, the ability of autocratic states to pursue low-tax policies that promote growth without the democratic pressure to 'soak the rich' can be an important growth driver.

So, while promoting incentives might have become culturally less fashionable, especially in Europe, economically its importance has never been greater.

New research described in this book has shown how the post-communist 'transition economies' have performed since settling down after communism. The research has looked at all the states for which data is available and shows that those states that have kept taxes low have grown significantly faster than those that have adopted a high-tax policy. The book also contains research looking at different localities and states within the US and shows how much better low-tax states have performed in an economy with a high degree of labour mobility.

Some of our interviewees have commented that people in places like China now look down on the West as decadent societies, condemned to failure because of giving too much priority to the weak and the lazy and insufficient priority to the talented or entrepreneurial. Yet democracy also dislikes economic failure, as is shown in the increasing numbers shunning the traditional political parties that voters perceive to have failed.

We have devised here a programme to restore the UK economy, drive prosperity and hence grow living standards. We start by setting out the five grand kingdoms of the macro economy: taxation, government spending, monetary policy, regulation and free trade. For each of the grand kingdoms, there is an optimal policy which all point to the North Star of economic growth. We then use this North Star to devise a 24/7 Growth Plan (twenty-four proposals that will deliver 7 per cent additional GDP in five years – and 29 per cent additional GDP in twenty years).

The 24/7 Growth Plan has been carefully costed and the sums add up. We put this programme forward as an offering so that the UK political class can show leadership and hence bring the UK economy back to life rather than slipping down the world economic league table as implied by the Cebr forecasts commissioned for the book.

Such projections are not set in stone, but should be seen as a challenge. It is up to the UK's politicians to show that democracy can work and that such predictions can be proved wrong. It is up to them to restore belief in the UK as a growing economy and encourage the most entrepreneurial and brightest in the world to come to this country.

In our interviews, one of the most successful of all UK political leaders pointed out that the political difficulties in reviving the UK are not insurmountable. 'All it takes is leadership,' he commented. We think that there are other institutional changes that may need to be made to help revive the country. They are discussed in Part III.

Part I of this book describes the North Star, set out by one of the co-authors, Dr Arthur B. Laffer, by which those navigating economic policy can set their sextant. It then describes the five kingdoms of macroeconomic policy that comprise the North Star for achieving economic growth.

Part II applies these principles to specific economic policies for the UK, costs their impact on growth and their fiscal impact and sets out the 24/7 Growth Plan.

Part III describes the results of thirty-three interviews with political leaders and other opinion formers about what they believe needs to be done and especially how the measures could be implemented.

The country is running out of choices. The choice of muddling through, further slipping down the GDP per capita league table, may not even exist – failure tends to breed further failure, and a slip may turn into a slide. We are confident that changing UK policy to follow the North Star and the five kingdoms of economic growth and implementing the 24/7 Growth Plan will turn the economy round and will start to restore the UK to its rightful place. Now is the time for the political class to show leadership, so we can all enjoy prosperity through growth.

PART I

THE PRINCIPLES OF ECONOMIC GROWTH: THE FIVE KINGDOMS

CHAPTER 1

DR ARTHUR B. LAFFER'S NORTH STAR OF ECONOMIC GROWTH

*'We're in a situation of genteel decline – people just putting up with
1 per cent growth. We're effectively getting poorer, but we're pretending we
aren't, and we need to convince people it doesn't have to be that way. But
we need to convince people we've got a very clear plan.'*
– Lord Cameron of Chipping Norton

The United Kingdom is but one country in a world of slightly fewer than 200 countries. But what a country it is. Its past history of economic prowess could well be the single best of the lot. The United Kingdom and the industrial revolution are synonymous. Its present state of economic affairs, however, is not as distinguished as we think it should be, and its future, if left unattended, is far from bright. To turn the country back to its exceptionalism, much needs to be done. If what the United Kingdom wants is what other countries don't have, it must do things that other countries won't do. This how-to template is based on my vision of macro-economics, including salient facts which have convinced me of its efficacy.

Economics is about incentives and how people respond to incentives. People like doing things they find attractive and avoid things they find off-putting. Government actions affect both the attractiveness and repulsiveness of activities. And, as such, the messages sent by government to people and markets make activities more or less attractive. Just how government interacts with the world at large determines economic destiny.

By way of example, if you feed a dog, you know where the dog will be at feeding time. However, if you beat a dog, you know where the dog *won't* be (anywhere near you), but you'll have no idea where the dog *will* be. Positive incentives tell people what they should do while negative incentives tell people what not to do. The conceptual difference between the two incentives is of the essence, and the behavioural consequences are significant.

FIGURE 2: UK GDP AS A SHARE OF THE WORLD
(annually, 1950–2025)

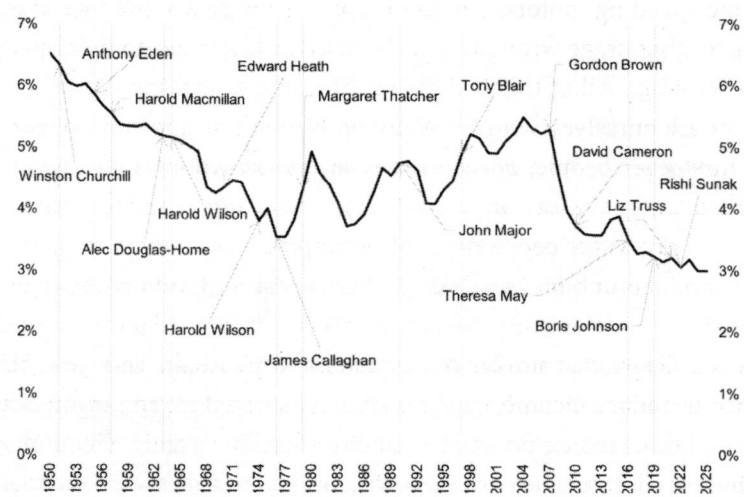

Source: World Bank, Historical National Accounts

OVERVIEW

For the purpose of this template, I frame macroeconomics into five major categories, which I call grand kingdoms. My selection of ordering is not intended to reflect that kingdom's degree of importance. The first grand kingdom is taxation. The second grand kingdom is government spending, followed by monetary policy. I list regulation as number four. And finally, we have international trade.

Organising macroeconomics, as I do, into these five kingdoms allows me to describe what I believe to be the ideal policy for each kingdom. Once optimal policies are defined, it's easier to evaluate policies by determining whether they move us towards or away from the North Star of economic growth. What follows is my description of each kingdom and a powerful example or two of the evidence supporting my selection.

We go into greater detail on each element of the five kingdoms in the chapters that make up Part I of this book.

I. TAXATION (SEE CHAPTER 3)

We fine speeding motorists to get them to slow down. We fine wrong-doers to discourage wrongdoing. We also tax cigarettes to deter people from smoking. All of this is done in the name of making life safer. But then we ask ourselves: why do we tax people who earn income, or people who hire other people, or businesses that make wonderful products at low costs and have lots of profits? The answer for these latter taxes, of course, is not to get people to earn or employ less, or even to make inferior products at high cost. We tax these entities to fund government.

But don't think for a minute that just because our stated purpose for taxation is different that similar consequences won't result. They will. Taxes on income reduce income, taxes on employment reduce employment and taxes on profits reduce profits, the quality of products and increase costs.

All taxes constitute negative incentives and damage the taxed activities – sometimes this is intentional, as in so-called 'sin taxes', where we want people to engage less in the taxed activities. Pound for pound of tax revenues, some taxed activities do more damage to the economy than others. The goal of taxation is to have a tax system that collects the requisite revenues to fund government while doing the least damage to the economy. James Mirrlees is a Nobel Prize-winning British economist who is famed for his work on optimal tax theory.[1] His key insight was the case for a flat tax of about 20 per cent.[*] Mirrlees wrote, 'I must confess that I had expected the rigorous analysis of income taxation in the utilitarian manner to provide arguments for high tax rates. It has not done so.'[2] Mirrlees's early work supports the general principle regarding the best structure of taxation, which is to have the lowest possible tax rate on the broadest possible tax base.[†]

---

[*]   Mirrlees started with no presumption against high marginal tax rates. Indeed, he has been an adviser to the Labour Party, which for decades imposed marginal tax rates in excess of 80 per cent. But Mirrlees found that the top marginal tax rate should be only about 20 per cent; and moreover, it should be about the same 20 per cent for everyone. In short, Mirrlees's work justified what is now known as a 'flat tax'.

[†]   It is true that in later work he muddied the waters on this subject. But it is his earlier work, building on the insights of William Vickrey, for which he received the Nobel Prize.

The lowest possible tax rate provides the least incentives for people and businesses to avoid, evade or otherwise not report taxable income. And the broadest possible tax base – eliminating as it should deductions, exemptions, exclusions, credits and other omissions and preferences – provides taxpayers with the least amount of opportunity to place income in tax-advantaged categories to avoid paying taxes. This is the golden rule for taxation – the key to achieving the North Star of economic growth.

EVIDENCE FROM THE DIFFERENT US STATES

One of the themes of this book is that a key change in the twenty-first century is the heightened mobility of labour and capital and especially that of talented and entrepreneurial people. Because of that, we have looked particularly closely at the relative performance of different parts of the US, to provide hard evidence of what happens in a highly mobile world. The results show how much better low-tax regimes perform; this backs up our analysis of the impact of different policies in the post-communist 'transition' economies.

The actual power of taxation and its consequences is demonstrated convincingly by looking at the different tax and spend policy regimes in the various states and localities of the United States.* This section sum-marises a more extended section in Chapter 3, which looks not only at local income taxes but also at local property and estate taxes.

The US Constitution prohibits any state from placing barriers on in-terstate commerce or movements of people. The US has one language, one set of federal laws, one federal tax system and one currency. When it comes to state and local policies, however, each entity is on its own to do what its voters and/or its government chooses. And, in many instances, there are wide gaps in just what these entities choose to do. There exists a vast comprehensive database over many, many years which allows us to assess what the actual consequences are from the data of this cauldron of experimentation. It is the best example of how tax policies actually affect behaviour.

And to extrapolate from these data points, we form a set of principles

---

* In Chapter 3 on taxation, we also look at the evidence from all the twenty-seven states that have transitioned from communism. The story is similar – those with lowest tax have grown fastest; those with highest tax slowest.

applicable to the modern British economy. I can only say policies should be designed from actual data and only the data. We use the past to infer the future.

From 1960 to the present, the United States has run a shockingly illuminating experiment in the effects of taxation on the economy. In 1960, nineteen of the fifty American states lacked a state income tax. The only income tax that residents of those states owed every year was to the federal government. The remaining thirty-one states taxed incomes on top of the federal income tax. At various points from 1961 to 1991, eleven of the income-tax-free states adopted an income tax. Eight states stayed the course and have remained zero-income-tax states to this day. One state, Alaska, had a long-standing income tax and dropped it, in 1980. All the states other than Alaska that had an income tax in 1960 still have one today.

The set-up of the experiment was serendipitously masterful: what happens over the two-generation period beginning with the time of each state's adoption of an income tax, when an approximately equal number of states, scattered around the country, adopt an income tax? Rarely in economic policy and development are such natural experiments set up so well – as a laboratory researcher might do, controlling for size, duration, insertion and the policy variable, in this case the adoption of an income tax.

From this near-perfect natural experiment, we have the results – and they could not be clearer. The states that held firm in not adopting an income tax totally outperformed the states that added an income tax – in terms of all the major metrics of economic performance and well-being.

The ten states that adopted the income tax from 1961 to 1976 were a string of contiguous states in a geographical line running from east to west – New Jersey, Pennsylvania, West Virginia, Maine, Ohio, Indiana, Michigan, Illinois, plus Nebraska and Rhode Island. Connecticut was the eleventh and last of the adopting group, taking on an income tax in 1991. Since these states adopted an income tax, their share of the national economy has dropped rapidly, while that of the remaining thirty-nine states has risen. Not only have these states' share of national GDP and population fallen but their total state and local tax revenue has also diminished sharply. Table 1 highlights this, comparing the shares for each of the eleven states with the share of the remaining thirty-nine states.

TABLE 1: PERFORMANCE METRICS OF THE ELEVEN STATES THAT ADOPTED AN INCOME TAX FROM 1961–1991

| States | First Year of Tax | Maximum Tax Rate[†] | | Share of Remaining Thirty-Nine States[*] | | | | | |
| | | | | Population | | | GSP | | |
		Initial	Current	5 Years Before	2023	% Change	5 Years Before	2023	% Change
Connecticut	1991	1.5%	7.0%	1.8%	1.4%	-23.4%	2.4%	1.6%	-33.4%
New Jersey	1976	2.5	11.8	4.9	3.6	-27.9	5.4	3.7	-30.5
Ohio	1972	3.5	6.0	7.6	4.5	-40.5	8.0	4.1	-49.2
Rhode Island	1971	5.3	6.0	0.7	0.4	-38.2	0.6	0.4	-43.5
Pennsylvania	1971	2.3	6.9	8.5	5.0	-41.6	8.5	4.5	-46.8
Maine	1969	6.0	7.2	0.7	0.5	-27.7	0.6	0.4	-26.5
Illinois	1969	2.5	5.0	8.1	4.8	-40.5	9.8	5.1	-48.4
Nebraska	1968	2.6	5.8	1.1	0.8	-31.1	1.0	0.8	-19.0
Michigan	1967	2.0	6.7	6.3	3.8	-39.2	7.9	3.1	-60.8
Indiana	1963	2.0	5.1	3.8	2.6	-30.8	3.8	2.3	-39.0
West Virginia	1961	5.4	5.1	1.5	0.7	-55.9	1.2	0.5	-60.9

| Total State and Local Tax Revenue | | |
5 Years Before	2021	% Change
2.4%	2.1%	-10.4%
5.4	4.7	-12.1
6.1	3.9	-36.2
0.7	0.4	-32.5
7.7	5.0	-34.5
0.6	0.6	-3.9
7.8	5.7	-26.0
0.9	0.8	-17.3
6.6	3.1	-53.4
3.4	2.3	-33.2
1.1	0.5	-52.6

Source: US Census Bureau, Bureau of Economic Analysis, Laffer Associates

The '5 Years Before' in the table refers to the yearly average in each case of five years before the adoption of the state's income tax.

---

[*] Due to data limitations, shares of personal income have been substituted for Indiana and West Virginia's shares of GDP

[†] Maximum tax rate is top combined state and local tax rate in each state

TABLE 2: ECONOMIC PERFORMANCE OF THE ZERO-INCOME-TAX STATES AND THE HIGHEST INCOME TAX RATE STATES

State	As of 1/1/2023 Top Marginal PIT Rate*	Ten-Year Growth				2010–2020
		2012–2022				
		Population	Employment	Personal Income	Gross State Product	State & Local Tax Revenue†
Alaska	0%	0.3%	1.4%	28.8%	9.2%	-10.3%
Florida	0%	15.4	22.5	76.7	78.4	25.2
Nevada	0%	16.0	21.4	78.1	67.0	49.1
New Hampshire‡	0%	5.1	6.7	53.5	53.9	31.2
South Dakota	0%	9.2	8.5	58.2	53.9	41.7
Tennessee	0%	9.1	13.6	61.5	66.1	24.7
Texas	0%	15.3	19.5	61.5	65.8	58.6
Washington	0%	12.8	19.3	80.4	81.1	54.9
Wyoming	0%	1.0	-2.0	32.9	22.1	22.7
Nine Zero Earned Income Tax Rate States§	**0.0%**	**13.9%**	**19.0%**	**67.6%**	**68.9%**	**41.5%**
US§	**5.7%**	**6.0%**	**11.4%**	**55.7%**	**56.7%**	**34.5%**
Nine Highest Earned Income Tax Rate States§	**11.2%**	**2.8%**	**9.2%**	**55.7%**	**59.1%**	**33.9%**
Delaware	7.9%	11.1%	14.4%	54.8%	40.4%	50.9%
Vermont	8.8	2.6	-1.1	43.2	38.9	39.6
Maryland	9.0	4.2	5.6	39.7	41.4	36.2
Minnesota	9.9	6.1	7.6	51.2	49.7	38.3
Hawaii	11.0	2.5	6.6	43.1	36.6	44.9
New Jersey	11.8	3.7	10.1	49.5	44.1	19.6
California	13.3	2.8	11.5	65.2	70.3	43.8
Oregon	14.7	8.7	16.5	73.3	71.3	48.5
New York	14.8	-0.4	4.9	46.5	54.6	19.9

Source: Laffer Associates, US Census Bureau, Bureau of Labor Statistics, Bureau of Economic Analysis

---

*   Top Marginal PIT Rate is the state top marginal rate on personal earned income imposed as of 1 January 2023 plus local rates from each state's largest city. Deductibility of federal taxes from state tax liability included where applicable.

†   State & Local Tax Revenue is the growth in state and local tax revenue from the Census Bureau's State & Local Government Finances survey. These data are from 2010 to 2020 due to data release lags.

‡   New Hampshire interest and dividend ('unearned') income tax not included.

§   PIT rates are equal weighted average, growth rates are group totals.

In stark contrast, the nine states that kept their zero-income-tax status (joined by Alaska in 1980) gained a share of the national economy in all the same metrics. States that have stayed out of the income tax game have become the unquestioned leaders in all the growth drivers of the American economy.

Their populations, employment rates, personal incomes and gross state products (GSP) have grown exceptionally as these states have confirmed their lack of interest in adopting an income tax. Table 2 shows their growth in several key metrics compared to that of the nine highest personal income tax rate states.

Perhaps the most piquant of the statistics from these tables concerns state- (and local-) level tax revenue. States that have added tax domains – namely the domain of the income tax – have underperformed in terms of tax collections. States that have not added tax domains – namely the domain of the income tax – have had exceptional tax revenue growth. The point is worth repeating, and the evidence is unambiguous. States that have not adopted income taxes have achieved gains in tax revenue at a much faster rate than states that have added this supposed workhorse of tax revenue generation.

There most certainly was a better way. Washington State – no income tax the whole while – attracted start-up entrepreneurialism that defined the new age (Microsoft, Amazon, Starbucks). Nevada inhaled population and income from California. Texas continues to menace California as the nation's future most populous and productive state. Florida some time ago eclipsed New York as the most populous and productive state in the eastern section of the country. New Hampshire dominates the growth statistics of New England. And Tennessee is an island of super-productivity in the Midwest and Upper South.

The experiment could not have been better even if designed in a lab. Add an income tax, get killed in all areas and find yourself boxed into adding still more taxes in a futile effort at remission. Do not adopt an income tax and see your economy soar – and your government revenue accounts get fat.

Data confirmation of consequences that adhere to taxation is overwhelming and virtually without limit. A number of further examples are contained in the main body of this template.

II. GOVERNMENT SPENDING *(SEE CHAPTER 4)*

To give perspective, in the US in 1910 (and earlier), federal government spending was approximately 3 per cent of GDP.[3] Including state and local spending, total government spending was about 8 per cent of GDP (see Figure 3). With government spending at that level, the US economy evolved into being the envy of the modern world. Today, total government spending is nearly 40 per cent of US GDP,[4] and its national debt is some 22 per cent of national wealth.[5] Just how government spending got so far out of hand is far from obvious, but surely it is partially due to the fact that those in government who actually spend the money don't bear the consequences resulting from the excess. Incentives have consequences. With these numbers in mind, spending restraint is highly recommended. Combining the appropriate policies for taxation and spending, the policy framework considers: i) how taxes are collected; ii) how government revenues are spent; and iii) how much government collects and spends. All three matter.

FIGURE 3: US GOVERNMENT CURRENT EXPENDITURES AS A SHARE OF GDP (annually, 1910–2024)

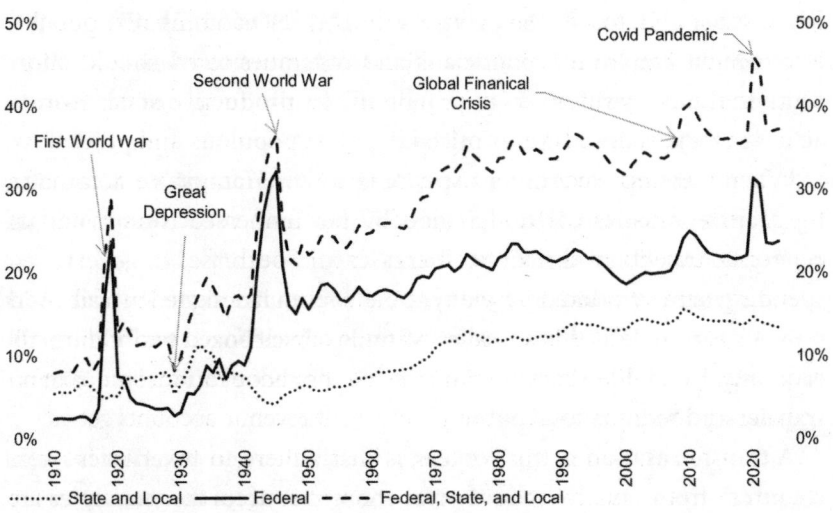

Source: BEA, USgovernementspending.com

Government spending should be limited, as best as is possible, to providing products and services that government alone produces more efficiently than the private sector. These categories frequently include the judiciary, military, police, highways, schools and some other highly specialised activities. The role government plays in how it spends its revenues is central to prosperity. A government that is too small will definitely hold back prosperity, as will a government that is too large. Government, like any other provider of goods and services, has an optimal size: for spending, the correct size of government should occur at that point where the benefits of the next pound spent is just above the damage done by the next pound collected in taxes. And in conjunction with spending restraint, government workers should be incentivised to act in the public interest. In other words, teachers who teach well should be paid more than teachers who don't teach well. This is the key to ensuring government spending is aligned to the North Star of economic growth.

Government should produce as efficiently as possible what it does produce using the least number of resources as is feasible to get the job done. Thus, not only is the level of government spending well defined, but the specific incentives used by government to produce the correct amount of goods and services must also be optimised. This set of criteria should also be a central feature of all projects sponsored by government while subcontracted to the private sector. In as much as it is possible, government employees, politicians and others involved should be incentivised monetarily to do their jobs efficiently. To rely on altruism to achieve efficiency is a serious mistake.

When viewing government spending in conjunction with taxation, the transfer theorem is understood by few and yet it dominates the economic trajectory of nations. Increases and decreases in government spending are considered by many to be a stimulus to the overall economy. Unfortunately, this so-called stimulus spending actually hurts the economy. Everything the government spends above its ideal amount is a transfer and reduces total output.

A transfer, as used in this context, is basically when government takes resources from one group and gives those resources to another group. Most prominently, the transfer theorem applies when government takes from those who have a little bit more and gives to those who have a little bit less.

By taking from those who have a little bit more, their incentives to produce decline and they produce less. By giving to those who have a little bit less, they now have an alternative source of income other than working and they too will produce less. The result: whenever resources are transferred, total production falls, full stop. Intuitively, if the government taxes people who work and pays people who don't work, you shouldn't be surprised if there's less work. This is a theorem, not opinion.

The lemma from this theorem should be obvious: the more that's transferred, the greater the loss in production.

And finally, the limit function of the transfer theorem is the fact that if you were able to transfer resources in such a way that all after-tax, after-transfer incomes were equalised, there will be no income whatsoever. To equalise all net incomes, government would have to tax everyone who earns above the average income 100 per cent of the excess and subsidise everyone below the average income up to the average income. If government actually did this, we can stipulate that everyone will be equal at zero net income. This is economics. Attempts to redistribute income always reduce total income. That doesn't mean we shouldn't have safety nets and payments to those less fortunate. But what it does mean is that one needs to know what all the consequences will be. To be warm-hearted, you also need to be clear-eyed.

This theorem is in perfect sync with the data in I. *Taxation* on income redistribution, where we look at taxation on the rich (the top 1 per cent) in relation to i) economic performance, ii) tax revenues from the rich and iii) the impact of those on the lowest rungs of the economic ladder.

As for independent evidence confirming the role played by government spending as opposed to taxes, I find the following figure convincing. In Figure 4, I plot federal government spending as a share of GDP versus the real detrended (CPI-adjusted) S&P 500 on a quarterly basis. The important feature of stock prices in this figure is that stock prices reflect what people and markets believe will happen. When government spending rises, stock prices fall. When government spending falls, stock prices rise. This plot is about as good as could be imagined using macroeconomic data.

FIGURE 4: FEDERAL CURRENT EXPENDITURES PERCENTAGE OF GDP VS S&P 500 INDEX/CPI DETRENDED

(quarterly, Q1 1960–Q4 2019, CPI: January 2020 = 100)

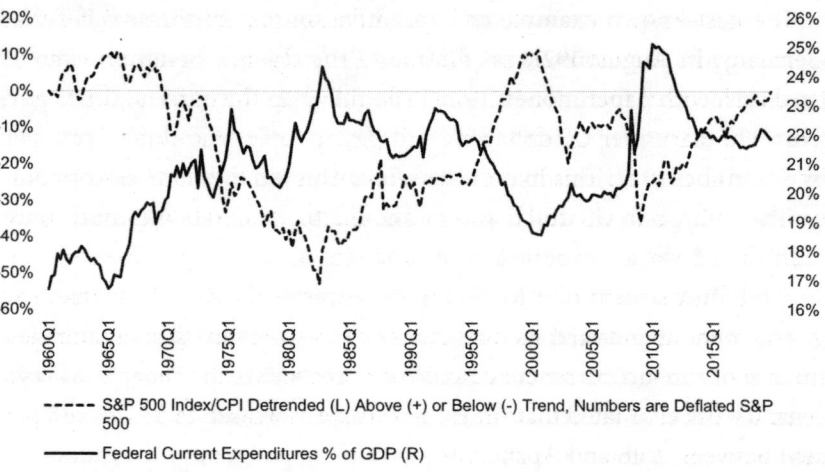

- - - - S&P 500 Index/CPI Detrended (L) Above (+) or Below (-) Trend, Numbers are Deflated S&P 500

——— Federal Current Expenditures % of GDP (R)

Source: BLS, OMB, Multpl

On an intuitive level, an economy cannot be taxed into prosperity, nor can a poor person spend themselves into wealth. On a formal level, the transfer theorem is as clear as a theorem can be: redistribution reduces production. And lastly, the evidence overwhelmingly confirms, demonstrates and corroborates the principle that more government, whether via taxation or spending, seriously damages overall prosperity.

III. MONETARY POLICY (SEE CHAPTER 5)

There is little that can bring an economy to its knees faster than unsound money, unhinged paper currencies and the accompanying inflation and high interest rates that invariably attend bad monetary policy. A key function of a sound numeraire, such as the UK pound or the US dollar, is to provide a stable valued medium of exchange where all participants know what that numeraire's value is and also what its value will be. Secular inflation and excessively high interest rates destroy the information content of the unit of account and damage markets in the present and capital markets where future goods and services are exchanged. Unsound money is a major cause of poverty, despair and economic underachievement, while sound money is the antidote.

The best-known example of hyperinflation is post-First World War Germany. In August 1921, the German central bank began purchasing hard cash with paper money. Prices soared while the currency collapsed from 320 marks per US dollar in mid-1922 to 7,400 marks per US dollar by December 1922. This hyperinflation continued into 1923, and by November 1923, one US dollar was worth 4,210,500,000,000 marks. More recently, Zimbabwe experienced hyperinflation, peaking at an estimated 79.6 billion per cent in a MONTH in November 2008.[6] After that, the government abandoned its own currency as worthless and encouraged the use of foreign currencies. Even more recently still, Venezuela's own central bank estimated that the inflation rate increased to 53,798,500 per cent between 2016 and April 2019.[7]

In the past five years, Argentina has had the highest inflation in the world, peaking at 289.4 per cent in April 2024. Under the policies of the then newly elected President Milei, not only has inflation fallen back to an estimated 30 per cent for 2025[8] but real GDP growth has also recovered to 5.8 per cent for Q1 2025.

It is worth noting, however, that the appropriate objective of monetary policy is to stabilise the value or price of the numeraire, not the number of units of that numeraire. When it comes to money, we have a price objective pure and simple, and therefore the economy needs a price rule.

Prior to the founding of the US Federal Reserve, the federal government played three roles in the monetary system. First, it defined what a dollar was, i.e. 1/20.67th of a Troy ounce of gold or an ounce of silver. Second, the federal government, along with many other private mints, provided minting services where people could bring in gold or silver bullion and have coins minted. The government and private mints competed with each other and charged a commission for these services. Lastly, the government audited and certified the financial statements produced by private banks, which distributed their liabilities in the form of currency or bank notes as well as checking accounts to customers. This system – prior to 1913 – was a private money and banking system overseen by the federal government.

Starting with the Federal Reserve Act of 1913, the monetary system was increasingly nationalised, ostensibly to stabilise the real economy by preventing business cycles and inflation. In March 1933, Congress passed, and the President signed, the Bank Holiday Act, which prohibited Americans from owning gold and limited bank activities dramatically. This Bank Holiday Act of March 1933 was followed by an enormous wealth tax in September 1933. After confiscating all gold from US citizens at $20.67 an ounce, the President by executive order devalued the dollar in terms of gold from $20.67 per ounce to $35 per ounce. As time marched on, there was the Interest Equalization Tax, the Voluntary Foreign Credit Restraint Program, the Smithsonian Accord and on and on to the present. Today, the monetary system of the US is run 100 per cent by the government.

In the 139 years prior to 1913, responding to a series of changing market forces, prices and interest rates experienced fluctuations. There were panics and bank collapses. But the average rate of inflation over that period (1774–1913) was zero. Since 1913, US prices have risen 33-fold, or at an average rate of 3.2 per cent per annum with the value of the dollar now less than 1/3,400 of an ounce of gold, down about 165-fold from its 1913 value of $20.67 per ounce. And just to make it perfectly clear, the worst depression of all time came during the era of government control of money and lasted for more than a decade.

The tools available to re-establish a sound money price rule include, but are not limited to, exchange rates, bank reserves and price rules vis-à-vis commodities or other goods. Setting and changing interest rates and inflation targets, as is now practised in the global central bank community, don't work on their own.

IV. REGULATION (SEE CHAPTER 6)

The subject matter of the fourth grand kingdom of macroeconomics contains a number of highly diverse policies which makes general principles far from clear. Regulations cover an enormous area of economic activities and take on a vast array of forms. But from a 60,000-foot perspective, the principles become a lot clearer. Regulations exist to minimise negative market externalities that would result from unregulated private activity and to maximise positive market externalities also resulting from private activity.

We all know we need government regulations over a wide range of activities. People can't be free, for example, to choose to drive on the left side of the road one day and then change their minds and drive on the right side of the road the next. Transparency rules, traffic rules, judicial rules etc. are all critical to the well-functioning of a prosperous market economy. Also thrown into this vast heterogenous mixture would be all sorts of public–private partnerships, utility regulations, anti-trust regulations, and the list goes on and on. Properly thought-out and well-executed regulatory policies can be an enormously positive stimulus for an economy.

Excessive regulation can also be stifling to economic prosperity and growth, taking up business time, adding to costs and increasing risks. In all, regulations should be directed to the specific externalities at hand and avoid as much as possible unintended deleterious consequences and collateral damage. Given the lack of proper incentives, regulations have spun way out of control. As a general rule, regulations and oversight have been justified by overstating benefits and understating costs. As such, to align to the North Star of economic growth, oversight should be to optimise and simplify the amount, extent and timing of regulations. Enacting regulations should be difficult and require as much political oversight as possible. Independent boards, committees and agencies, unless legislatively authorised, should not be allowed to impose regulations on their own authority. Virtually every regulation should have a sunset provision where its effects can be evaluated before it is renewed, removed or reformed.

The existence of private market failures which cause economic harm is a necessary condition for, but not a sufficient condition to warrant, government oversight and control. If private markets are functioning well, there is no need for government control. In the words of Teddy Roosevelt back in 1905, 'If the cards do not come to any man, or if they do come, and he has not got the power to play them, that is his affair. All I mean is that there shall not be any crookedness in the dealing.'[9]

For government control to make sense, it must also be true that the harm done by government actions in controlling the market are less harmful than existing private market failures. Never should we let the best be the enemy of the good. Regulatory costs should always be estimated before implementation, and regulations should not be imposed where the costs outweigh the benefits.

This is not to say that regulations never make sense. For example, in Los Angeles in the 1960s and 1970s, the air people breathed was often toxic. Today, LA is doing just fine. Also, in my hometown, Cleveland, Ohio, in the 1950s, the Cuyahoga River and Lake Erie were polluted beyond belief. Today, they are clean. Regulations can be an enormous benefit.

On the other side of the ledger, one of the most startling affirmations of the consequences of broad-based regulations that I was personally involved with occurred in January 1981.

On 28 January 1981, eight days into his presidency, Ronald Reagan removed price and allocation controls on the domestic oil industry. These decontrol measures included removing well-head price controls on oil production, retail gasoline price controls and an excess profits tax on oil companies among others. Since the Nixon price control era of the early 1970s, oil producers and distributors had to keep watch on governmental overseers who collected information and kept records and enforced guidelines on prices and distribution of product. When Nixon's price controls were eliminated, they were eliminated everywhere except for oil.

President Reagan's edict ended all of that. 'The president's action will allow oil companies to raise prices at will,' a UPI story reported that day. The *New York Times* held that 'as a result of the President's executive order, the cost of gasoline and heating oil is expected to rise ... Consumer groups put the likely increase at 10 to 12 cents by the end of the summer (of 1981)', on top of the current 'average of $1.22 a gallon nationally'. The report continued, 'Analysts said that the price of heating oil ... would rise by a larger amount than gasoline.'

On a personal note, I was an adviser for Occidental Petroleum president Robert Abboud at the time of President Reagan's decontrol of oil. At a board meeting around that time, I stated to the assembled group that with Reagan's oil decontrol, oil prices would fall sharply. There and then Armand Hammer, chairman of the board, fired me and had me escorted out of the building. Ouch!

In January 1981, the price of oil was at its highest, $38 per barrel, that it would see for the remainder of the millennium. West Texas intermediate crude (one of the industry's bellwethers*) was at that price from January to May 1981 and then fell, to a low of $28 the following May, up again briefly to $36, and then down and down, even below $12 in 1986. There was no increase at all, even in the short term, on Reagan's announcement of decontrol in January 1981. The January 1981 price was the peak oil price for a multi-decade spell. Moreover, the fall in oil prices in the several years after oil decontrol was a true collapse. Peak to trough – January 1981 to July 1986 – oil fell by 68 per cent.

Regulations come in so many different forms, shapes and sizes that general evidence of a limited nature is extremely hard to come by. As an addendum to specific data analysis, I use the following testimonial by the well-known ex-senator and Democratic nominee for President in 1972, George McGovern:

> In retrospect, I wish I had known more about the hazards and difficulties of such a business, especially during a recession of the kind that hit New England just as I was acquiring the inn's 43-year leasehold. I also wish that during the years I was in public office, I had had this first-hand experience about the difficulties businesspeople face every day. That knowledge would have made me a better US senator and a more understanding presidential contender ...

---

* The others are Brent Crude and Dubai Fateh.

Too often, however, public policy does not consider whether we are choking off those opportunities.

While I never have doubted the worthiness of any of these goals, the concept that most often eludes legislators is, 'Can we make consumers pay the higher prices for the increased operating costs that accompany public regulation and government reporting requirements with reams of red tape?'

In short, 'one-size-fits-all' rules for business ignore the reality of the marketplace.

I also include a quote from former President Jimmy Carter exalting his efforts to deregulate the economy:

> When I took office, I inherited a heavy load of serious economic problems besides energy, and we've met them all head-on. We've slashed government regulations and put free enterprise back into the airlines, the trucking and the financial systems of our country, and we're now doing the same thing for the railroads. This is the greatest change in the relationship between government and business since the New Deal.

V. INTERNATIONAL TRADE (SEE CHAPTER 7)

Going back as far as records have been kept, trade has been as important as any factor in creating prosperity and economic growth. Intrinsically, international trade and the benefits derived therefrom are an extension of benefits from specialisation described so eloquently in Adam Smith's *Wealth of Nations*. There are some things that one country produces better and more efficiently than other countries. And likewise, those other countries produce products and services more efficiently than the first country. Each country in its turn would be foolish in the extreme if it didn't realign its production to export those products it makes more efficiently than its trading partners, while importing those products its trading partners produce more efficiently than it does. This is called 'comparative advantage' or 'the Ricardian gains from trade' and is a win-win-win for all participants.

Tariffs, quotas and non-trade barriers are anathema to economic growth, prosperity and the elimination of poverty. And, what seems so intuitively obvious to the trade economist is completely alien to most politicians. Economists should be trained to understand that consumption and investments are the benefits resulting from costs, such as employment and depreciation. Jobs are only as good as the goods they produce, and yet governments the world around prefer jobs (exports) over consumption (imports). It makes no sense. Trade barriers placed on foreign products are mistakenly considered a benefit by many politicians, when in fact they hurt their own citizens and economy and in turn make exports more difficult.

Just as people use their capital and work to earn the wherewithal to buy goods and services, so too nations export products to foreigners to purchase goods and services from foreigners. These exports are the cost a country must pay to import, which is the benefit. The supply of exports is the demand for imports (see Figure 5). Any impediment such as a tariff or quota on imports will have the same effect on trade as a tax on exports. Try that line on a politician.

Figure 5 shows the exceptionally close relationship between a country's exports and its imports and is precisely analogous to what we would expect to see between a family's income and its expenditures. Tax income and there will be less spending. Tax spending and there will be less income. Export taxes do the same damage as tariffs.

Trade also has another wonderful beneficial effect by allocating capital from net saver nations to net investor nations, known as the Alexander gains from trade. A country's trade deficit is not only its imports exceeding its exports; but it also is the country's capital surplus. One country's savers can fund another country's investments, thereby creating jobs output and production. Free trade and world capital allocation is a win-win for all involved. Trade deficits and surpluses mean that capital is being allocated more efficiently on a global scale, therefore rewarding savers with higher returns and lowering the cost of capital to investors everywhere, thus encouraging growth and productivity where it is most needed.

FIGURE 5: GOODS AND SERVICES: IMPORTS AND EXPORTS AS A SHARE OF GDP

(2021, OECD countries, excludes Luxembourg)

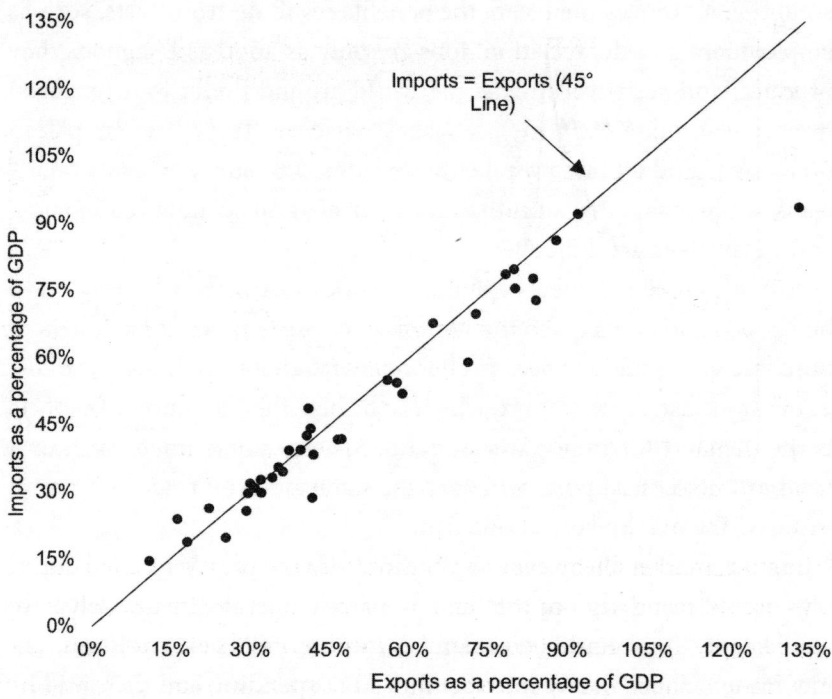

Source: OECD

The most powerful evidence of the importance of the gains from trade comes from evidence following US passage of the Smoot–Hawley tariff in the fourth quarter of 1929 and then President Herbert Hoover's signing of the bill in mid-1930. According to my colleague Robert Mundell, as stated in his Nobel laureate address in Stockholm, it was the Smoot–Hawley tariff that led to the Great Depression, which in turn led to the Second World War. It is hard to imagine anything more consequential. Just look at Figures 6 and 7 below.

Figure 6 shows just what actually happened to total US trade (exports plus imports), the trade balance (exports minus imports) and the stock market before, during and after the passage of the Smoot–Hawley tariff.

FIGURE 6: TARIFFS AND TOTAL TRADE SURROUNDING
THE 1930 SMOOT–HAWLEY TARIFF

(Trade: annual, $ billion, 1925–39. Dow Jones: monthly, January 1925–December 1939,
end of period)

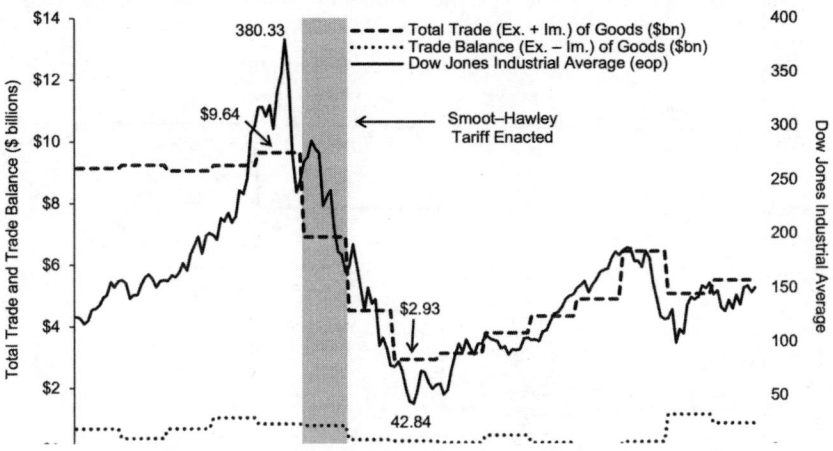

Source: BEA, Historical Statistics of the US, US International Trade Commission

The stock market fell by over 88 per cent from the peak it reached during the period of passage of the Smoot–Hawley tariff to its low following its passage. Total trade (exports plus imports) fell by 70 per cent and the trade balance barely moved. And then there were the employment effects and government's ill-conceived responses (Figure 7).

Figure 7 shows again, with actual data, what happened to the US employment rate before, during and after the Smoot–Hawley tariff and how the government responded with the highest personal income tax (PIT) rate.

In addition to the collapse of both the stock market and total trade, the US unemployment rate rose from about 3 per cent of the labour force in late 1929 to 26 per cent in 1933. The unemployment rate wouldn't fall below 10 per cent until the onset of the Second World War. Facing financial shortfalls, the US government in response to the onset of the Great Depression also raised taxes on everyone and everything it could get its hands on. The highest marginal income tax rate rose from 25 per cent in 1931 to 63 per cent in 1932 to 79 per cent in 1937. Whenever politicians make decisions when they are either panicked or drunk, the consequences are rarely attractive.

FIGURE 7: HIGHEST PIT RATE VS UNEMPLOYMENT RATE

(Personal: annual, 1925–39; Unemployment: monthly, January 1925–December 1939)

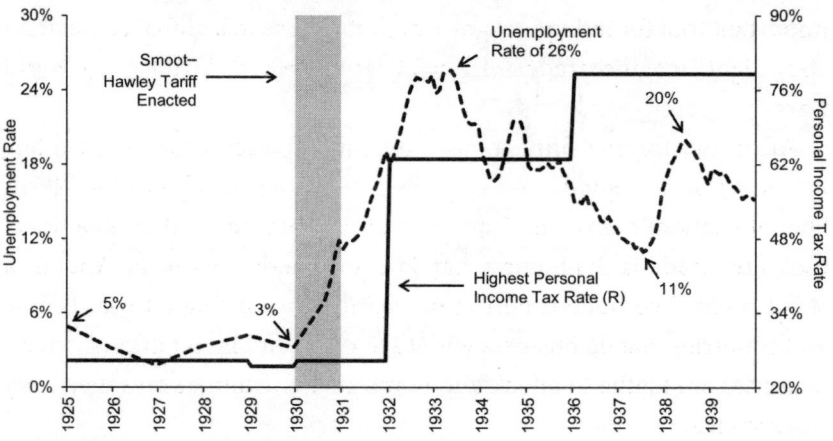

Source: BLS, Historical Statistics of the US, Tax Policy Center

Trade has always had a special place in the history of mankind, dating back to our earliest ancestors. From the early eighteenth century to the present, total US trade (exports plus imports) as a share of GDP has demonstrated the steady expansion of global interconnectedness and the resulting Ricardian gains from trade. Trade played a pivotal role in US economic development – its growth is closely tied to America's rise as a global power. Similarly, the US trade balance (or capital account deficit), viewed as a share of GDP, reflects the Alexander gains from trade, emphasising how foreign capital has long financed American investments. These trends underline the central role of open markets, sound money and capital inflows in fuelling US prosperity.

It was trade in conjunction with low taxes, limited government spending, a sound currency and minimal regulations that created the miracle of all economic miracles: the US in the eighteenth, nineteenth and twentieth centuries.

Trade also has social and political aspects that can be equally, if not far more, important than they are from the four other grand kingdoms of macroeconomics. Imposing and removing trade barriers are important points of global leverage and have been used as such from time immemorial. It is true that everyone loses in a trade war, but it is also true that those losses are not evenly distributed. Threats of trade restrictions is an important tool for individual governments to use in a global context. As you might imagine, trade with belligerents ceased during both world wars.

All in all, for the fifth grand kingdom of macroeconomics, international trade in goods and services is essential to achieve the North Star of economic growth. Trade should seldom be used as a political tool. Free trade is the highest standard for good economics. And, as a side benefit, free trade is best at preventing or warding off war. People and countries that do business with each other and invest in each other's countries are loathe to attack and bomb their customers and their own investments.

There are, of course, circumstances where the need for security of supply or to counter nefarious trade practices means that trade policy actions are required. But otherwise, their roles should be minimised.

In all, the standard of government oversight (i.e. the North Star) should be:

i.   Low-rate, broad-based flat tax;
ii. Spending restraint;
iii. Sound money;
iv. Minimal regulations; and
v.   Free trade.

Countries that achieve these targets enjoy the fruits of prosperity through growth.

CHAPTER 2

A SHORT INTRODUCTION TO SUPPLY-SIDE ECONOMICS

'It is a central axiom of the supply-side people that it is easier to get people to produce more than it is to persuade them to do with less.'
– WILLIAM F. BUCKLEY

Even if you are not a professional economist or you haven't studied economics for the past thirty years, you will probably remember Paul Samuelson's parrot's description of the subject 'supply and demand'. What is funny is if you have continued your study of economics in a professional capacity, you'll probably only know the word 'demand'. In contemporary macroeconomics, supply has been discarded, leaving only demand. And this has occurred to the enormous detriment of both professional economics and economic outcomes for real people.

It's worth just thinking a bit about why the supply curve has gone out of fashion. It is partly because of Keynesian economics with its implicit suggestion that demand creates its own supply. This is true in certain conditions, but actually pure Keynesian economics only applies in very limited sets of circumstances (the key element is prices actually falling) which have not been relevant in recent years. The other reason is the widespread presumption of economies of scale, especially in the modern information economy, which can encourage the illusion that supply is infinitely elastic.

And yet supply always means someone, somewhere, having to make an effort to do something that they don't have to do. Incentives are still important, and our analysis shows how their importance increases in an information economy.

In the following discussion where we delve into a number of the intricacies of demand and supply, always remember there are important symmetries. For example, the reason people work, save and invest is to acquire the wherewithal to buy goods and services. The supply of work effort is, in fact, the demand for goods and services. Countries export goods and services to be able to import other goods and services. People can't demand something without having something else to pay for it. Prices are nothing more or less than the ratio of two goods in exchange.

In any normal market, the demand for a product is usually represented as a relationship, in a written equation or on a graph like Figure 8 between the quantity demanded and the price demanders must pay. In terms of graphs, if the horizontal axis is quantity and the vertical axis is price, then the line relating quantity demanded and price paid – the 'demand curve' – will go from upper left to lower right (see Figure 8). This demand curve shows how, as the price rises, the less the quantity demanders will demand, and the lower the price, the more will be demanded. The higher the price of a product, the less of that product people will demand and vice versa.

Turning our attention now to the supply curve, which relates the quantity of a product supplied and the price suppliers receive for the product, we find the reverse of what we found for the demand curve. In the case of supply, the lower the price, the less supplied, and the higher the price, the more supplied. The supply curve in Figure 8 starts in the lower left and moves to the upper right. Note that the point at which the supply curve and demand curve meet shows the *equilibrium* market-clearing price. When there is no interference or inefficiency in the market, the baker and her customer agree on the fairest price for both actors, at equilibrium.

As depicted in Figure 8, the demand curve, supply curve, prices and quantities are abstract concepts. Demand, quite naturally, must be effective demand – where those who demand (think: consumers) have the wherewithal to exchange what they have (think: money) for what they demand, as determined by the price. Prices, of course, are nothing more than the ratio of two commodities in exchange. We will speak much more on this later. The basic notions are well covered by the description above. What matters is how behaviour (i.e. the shapes of demand and supply curves) respond to changes in incentives (i.e. the price ratio) in determining outcomes (i.e. quantities).

FIGURE 8: DEMAND AND SUPPLY CURVES

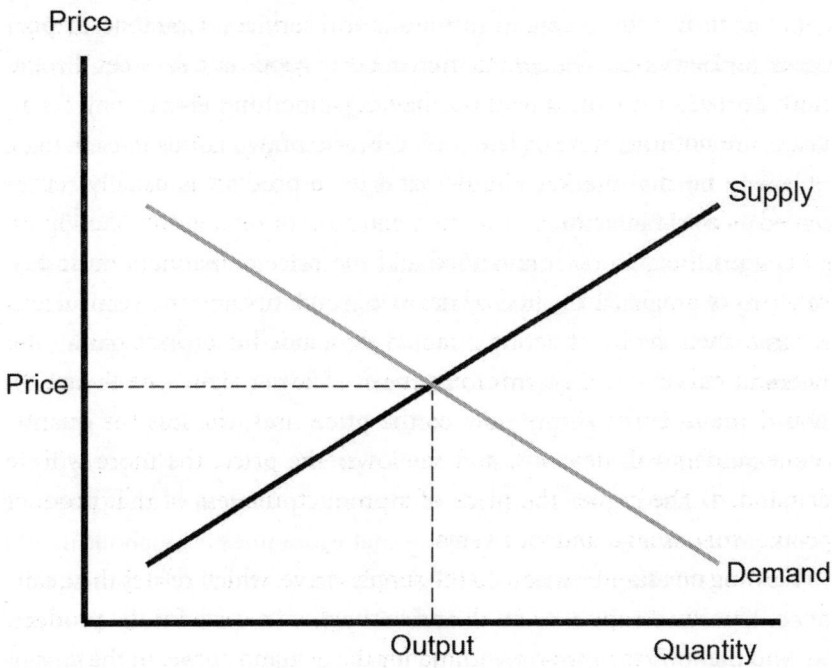

Source: Laffer Associates

In the same market depicted in Figure 8, the relationship between the supply of a product and its price will be the opposite of the demand for a product and its price. In it, we can see how the higher the price, the less will be demanded and the more supplied, and with a lower price, the more demanded and the less supplied. We illustrate conceptual demand and supply curves as they relate to both price and quantity.

In the most basic sense, the elements of Figure 8 – supply, demand, prices and quantities – are the axioms of economics. Supply curves and demand curves describe consumers' preferences, budget constraints, firms' profit motives and technology constraints. The cardinal tenet of classical economic analysis is that consumers and producers alter their behaviour when economic incentives change. If the incentives for doing an activity increase relative to applicable alternatives, such as a price decline for demanders or a price increase for suppliers, the now more attractive activity gets a boost. Likewise, if impediments (disincentives) are imposed upon an activity, the now less attractive activity gets knocked. People face both time and resource constraints in their quest for happiness and profit. Accordingly, time and resource limitations necessitate prudent management as people pursue their objectives. Government, with its full power of enforcement, can alter the structure of constraints imposed by nature and man and, for better or worse, alter the economy's behaviour.

The form of the constraints emanating from government is limited solely by the expansiveness of man's own mind: government can partake in boundless series of actions, including taxes, subsidies, regulations, restrictions and requirements to mention a few of the better-known economic actions. The magnitude, composition and financing of government spending all affect a wide range of private activity. The precepts of classical economics are founded on consumer preferences and producer costs, which is a fancy way of saying that economics is all about incentives! Incentives are malleable and government actions can dramatically affect those incentives, in good and bad ways. In the sections to come, we will demonstrate how government actions have the potential for significant repercussions. Indeed, the very presence of government itself alters market structures and the incentives surrounding everything it touches.

Capitalism is perhaps the finest aspect of modern society. Because of capitalism, we are privileged to live in what may only be described as an anomaly in history, a fluke of monumental proportion. We live in a time where most people have more wealth, better lifestyles and more freedom than has been the case across a vast expanse of history. This is capitalism at play. Our children grow taller, we live longer and we have more peace of mind than ever before. For these reasons, it is not a stretch of the imagination to say that the average person in the Western world at least – as well as many in emerging economies – is better off today than most kings in history ever were. We live like kings! And we have capitalism to thank for it. And in recent years, the wealth that was previously the preserve of a relatively small proportion of the world's economies is now spreading to the majority of countries across the world. All thanks to capitalism.

What makes capitalism work so well for us? To put it simply, capitalism hinges on the *creation* of wealth – where before there was not wealth, and now there is. People, acting rationally and for their own benefit, are enticed to work together – and, magically, do so to each other's benefit. 'It is not from the benevolence of the butcher, the brewer, or baker, that we expect our dinner, but from their regard to their own interest,' says Adam Smith.[1] It is by their incentive to make a profit – and our willingness to give them it – that the butcher, the brewer and the baker give us our dinner. Smith also observes that for this to work, people must act rationally and have a sense of security. Why would they give us our dinner if for no other reason than that a buyer will pay a reasonable price? And why would they accept a reasonable price unless they are secure in the belief they won't be robbed of their earnings? Alas, this is not the focus of this template. We begin in this way to remind us that, in all our thoughts about economics, we must remember it is through the self-interest of others that we find prosperity. Quite literally, it puts the food on our tables. We should avoid, at all costs, undermining it. As we shall see, the biggest threat to this prosperity, as well as the greatest assurance of this prosperity, comes from government policies and their impact on the economy.

Good economics, where the word 'good' has meaning, should be scalable and time-invariant. This template develops a step-by-step, supply-side, or classical, framework for the economy in general and for the UK economy specifically. It focuses exclusively on the role played by government in creating or destroying prosperity, not so much on other factors. Not because these other factors are not important (they are), but because government policies are both important and actionable. This book exposes individual factors that influence output, employment and production and views different periods of UK history in context. No period, once the analysis takes place, is overlooked. The very essence of good economics is that it explains the comings and goings of all periods, not just selected eras.

CHAPTER 3

THE FIRST KINGDOM: TAXATION

*'I think tax rates matter. You can go too far, and you've got to look
at the tax system as a whole and ideally have low rates [across]
as broad a base as possible.'*
– LORD MACPHERSON OF EARL'S COURT

*'Tax reduction thus sets off a process that can bring gains for everyone,
gains won by marshalling resources that would otherwise stand idle –
workers without jobs and farm and factory capacity without markets.
Yet many taxpayers seemed prepared to deny the nation the fruits of tax
reduction because they question the financial soundness of reducing taxes
when the federal budget is already in deficit. Let me make clear why, in
today's economy, fiscal prudence and responsibility call for tax reduction
even if it temporarily enlarged the federal deficit – why reducing taxes is
the best way open to us to increase revenues.'*
PRESIDENT JOHN F. KENNEDY, 'ECONOMIC REPORT
OF THE PRESIDENT', JANUARY 1963

The first of our five kingdoms is taxation. Taxation is critical to economic activity.

In the realm of macroeconomics, government tax policies make the
taxed activities less attractive; likewise, subsidies make certain activities,
those subsidised, more attractive. Sometimes, they can affect things not
directly targeted by levy or loan. Unintended consequences from time to
time can be most consequential. Government, when it taxes and spends,
causes markets to shift away from the now less attractive activities, thereby reducing both the supply and the demand of all productive factors
(labour and capital) and products now being taxed. Depending upon
how the government spends the proceeds, the increase in aggregate

supply and demand created by government taxing and spending is offset 100 per cent by the loss in both supply and demand from the products and producers of those taxed products. Government redistributes resources; it does not create resources. In the end, as we shall see, government spending amounts to nothing more than taxation.

This chapter looks at the theory underlying taxation; at the evidence in the US, particularly that of different levels of taxation at state and local level; at the international evidence, including new previously unpublished research on the economies transitioning from communism; at the Scully curve, which is an extended Laffer curve taking into account government spending and the optimal level of government spending and concludes that a low-tax, low-government-spending state is far more likely to deliver economic growth than a high-tax, high-spending state.

ON THE MARGIN

In this and the next section, we describe through a series of stylised examples how tax and spending leads to lower work, output and employment. In demonstrating just how impactful government taxation and spending can be, it is crucial to recognise the effect of government spending and taxation on an individual level. When people choose careers, many factors and choices are weighed for their benefit, one of which is whether to earn income at all. Once ensconced in a chosen profession, however, people base their work and leisure decisions on marginal considerations. For example, if offered the opportunity to work overtime, a rational person will balance the loss of leisure that results from working overtime against the added income and thus the net gain from working overtime. Not only is the overtime pay offered important but so too is the marginal tax rate that will apply to that overtime pay. In the case of overtime pay – or even a higher-paying job or which country the rational person should move to for that matter – a key tax rate is the highest marginal tax rate facing those specific income earners.

The choice of working overtime pits the lost pleasure of the leisure time sacrificed against the after-tax benefit of the compensation earned. Obviously, the higher the marginal tax rate and all else held the same, the less attractive working overtime is and the less the worker will work overtime. It really is as simple as that.

Imagine an income earner, facing a flat 25 per cent tax rate on any and all income, who has some choice as to how much income they can earn. If that income earner chooses to earn £10,000 per annum pre-tax, they will pay £2,500 in taxes and will keep £7,500 after tax. Given that the income earner chooses to earn exactly £10,000, it is at this chosen threshold we find that the value of the leisure lost exceeds the after-tax benefit of earning more than £10,000, and, symmetrically, that the benefit of earning less than £10,000 in leisure gained is not as great as is the after-tax benefit of the income forgone. This is the point where the marginal rate of substitution between labour and leisure is exactly equal to the after-tax wage of the worker.

TABLE 3: COMPARISON OF FLAT, PROGRESSIVE AND REGRESSIVE TAX SYSTEMS

Tax System	How It Works	Tax Paid	After-Tax Income	Work Incentive Near £10,000
Flat Tax	25 per cent on all income	£2,500	£7,500	Neutral: earner stops at £10,000 – next £10 only gives £7.50
Progressive Tax	0 per cent on first £5,000, 50 per cent above £5,000	£2,500	£7,500	Less Work: next £10 only gives £5 – not worth the leisure loss
Regressive Tax	50 per cent on first £5,000, 0 per cent above £5,000	£2,500	£7,500	More Work: next £10 gives full £10 – extra work is more rewarding

So far, we have concerned ourselves with a single tax rate on all income. In practice, however, tax systems have deductions, exemptions, exclusions and a myriad of different tax rates. Our challenge is how to choose and select the correct parameters and how those parameters affect individual incentives based on the foundations of classical or supply-side economics. This challenge is far less difficult and not nearly as confusing as is the whole array of tax law. (The exact length of the US tax code is hotly debated, but the code itself is generally estimated to be over 6,000 pages long, and with the relevant accompanying regulations, the total length is often believed to build up to over 20,000 pages.[1] For the UK, the Chartered Institute of Taxation estimates the length of the code as 'over 21,000 pages'.[2])

The economics itself is actually fairly simple: people operate 'on the margin'. Another way of saying this is that the value of the leisure gained by earning less than £10,000 is less than the value of the after-tax income forgone by earning less than £10,000.

To see practically what 'on the margin' means, let us move from a flat tax of 25 per cent on income to a progressive tax, where tax rates increase at higher levels of income (illustrated in Table 3). Going back to our example above, in order to isolate the effect a progressive tax system has on behaviour, we need to keep our tax revenues the same at the £10,000 level of income. Let us imagine a two-tier tax system where the first £5,000 of income is tax-free but all income above £5,000 is taxed at 50 per cent. Our question is what will be the consequences on total work effort and tax revenues under this progressive tax system versus the flat 25 per cent tax rate on all income?

If the income earner were to choose to earn the same £10,000 pre-tax as they had earned when all income was taxed at 25 per cent, taxes collected would still be £2,500 and after-tax income would still be £7,500. In other words, under these new circumstances, the income earner could have been in the same circumstances as they had been in the previous example by choosing the exact same pre-tax income, after-tax income and total leisure if they were so inclined. Alas, this is not what will happen.

With a flat tax rate of 25 per cent on all income, the income earner in the vicinity of £10,000 income chooses to stop exactly at £10,000 because at that point, the leisure sacrificed by earning an additional £10 and keeping £7.50 after tax was no longer worth the trade-off. That is why the worker chose not to earn more than £10,000. However, the worker also chose not to earn less than £10,000, i.e. they chose to earn the final £10, keeping £7.50, versus the additional leisure they could have had by earning £10 less, or £9,990. The marginal rate of substitution between earning more income and having more leisure at the £10,000 income level was exactly £7.50 kept after tax per £10 earned (i.e. leisure sacrificed).

Now, with the new two-tier progressive tax system, if the person earned more than £10,000, their after-tax income per £10 earned would drop from £7.50 to £5. If £7.50 of after-tax income is not worth the lost leisure time, then neither will £5 of after-tax income be worth the lost leisure time. The income earner would still choose not to earn more than £10,000. But if the income earner chose to earn less than £10,000, then for every unit of leisure gained, they would sacrifice only £5 in after-tax income, not £7.50, because the loss of after-tax income is less per unit of leisure gained. The income earner will then choose to earn less income than £10,000 because the value they place on the leisure gained by earning less after tax exceeds the after-tax income lost. Total income, thus, will fall, as will total tax revenues.

As an aside, it is interesting to note that in this example, where we move from a flat tax of 25 per cent to a progressive, static, revenue-neutral tax, the highest income earner is actually better off by earning less than £10,000, while government tax revenues, jobs and employment all fall. This effect is the central core of supply-side economics.

To round out the full example properly, let us imagine that we take our original income earner at a 25 per cent flat tax rate where they earn £10,000 and pay £2,500 in taxes. Now let us impose a regressive tax system where the income earner pays a 50 per cent tax on the first £5,000 of income and no tax on any income over £5,000. The income earner will choose to earn more than £10,000 pre-tax income and will have less leisure, more after-tax income and pay the same amount in taxes. By assuming that we have not changed the total after-tax income at a pre-tax income of £10,000, only the substitution effect has been altered: the circle is closed. Lower tax rates on income, especially lower marginal tax rates, will increase income, output and employment (again shown in Table 3).

People operate on the margin especially when it comes to income taxes. While holding overall income constant, the effect of changing tax rates on the behaviour of an income earner is called the 'substitution effect'. However, there is more.

INCOME AND SUBSTITUTION EFFECTS
– THE SLUTSKY EQUATION[3]

In the previous examples, we had a person who chose to earn £10,000 pre-tax and thus kept £7,500 after tax in a market with a flat 25 per cent tax rate on all income. Then, our income earner reduced their total number of hours worked when the tax system taxed income at a 0 per cent tax rate up to £5,000 and at a 50 per cent tax rate over £5,000 income, even though they could have had exactly the same leisure, after-tax and pre-tax income as they had at the 25 per cent tax rate. The income earner's change in behaviour is due exclusively to the change in the marginal tax rate, or as economists would call it, the marginal rate of substitution between income and leisure. In that example, the change in behaviour is a demonstration of the substitution effects of changes in tax rates. One immensely powerful implication of the substitution effect is that holding total taxes constant, there will be more work, output and employment with lower marginal tax rates than there would be with higher marginal tax rates. This means that taxing higher income earners at higher rates hurts the economy and growth. To justify taxing high-income earners at higher tax rates, the bar needs to be set very high indeed. All this is illustrated in Table 4.

TABLE 4: WORK INCENTIVES AND ECONOMIC EFFECTS OF DIFFERENT TAX SYSTEMS

Tax Scenario	Income Effect	Substitution Effect	Net Work Incentive	Economic Outcome
Flat Tax: 25 per cent	Neutral baseline	Neutral baseline	Neutral: worker chooses balance of leisure and income	Baseline: optimal, stable choice
Progressive: 0 per cent up to £5,000, 50 per cent above	Negative: feels poorer for every extra £ earned	Strongly negative: extra work yields less reward	↓ Work (earns less, chooses more leisure)	↓ Output, ↓ Tax Revenue
Regressive: 50 per cent on first £5,000, 0 per cent after	Positive: must work more to get same take-home pay	Strongly positive after £5,000: more reward for added effort	↑ Work (earns more, takes less leisure)	↑ Output, ↑ Tax Revenue
Modified Flat: 0 per cent up to £5,000, 25 per cent after	Positive: more after-tax income for same work → more leisure	Neutral: same marginal rate as flat tax	↓ Work (due to feeling richer)	↓ Output, ↑ Leisure

However, unlike the specific example cited above, where we only looked at the substitution effects, tax rate changes will usually have both income and substitution effects on an income earner's behaviour.

In order to demonstrate the income effects of a tax rate change, imagine once again our example of the income earner who chooses to earn £10,000 pre-tax at a flat tax rate of 25 per cent, leaving them with £7,500 net income after paying their tax bill of £2,500. Now, imagine what would happen to our income earner's behaviour if taxes on the first £5,000 of income were eliminated while keeping the same 25 per cent tax rate on all incomes in excess of £5,000.

Quite obviously, if the income earner chose to continue to earn £10,000 pre-tax, they would have £1,250 in extra after-tax income. Their after-tax income would be greater, their leisure time would not change and their marginal rate of substitution between income and leisure would also be the same. But all of this is true only if the income earner chooses to continue to earn £10,000 pre-tax.

With having more after-tax income, however, for the same amount of work and facing the same marginal tax rates, it is only reasonable that the income earner prefers to give up some of their additional income in exchange for added leisure. In other words, this income earner will choose to consume more goods and more leisure with their additional after-tax income. With the same marginal rate of substitution between income and leisure as represented by the 25 per cent marginal tax rate, this income earner will choose to earn less pre-tax income to a point where they have both more after-tax income and more leisure. The amount of pre-tax income they choose to forego is what we economists call the 'income effect' of a tax change.

Holding marginal tax rates the same, a tax cut will engender an income effect, lowering work, output and pre-tax income. Holding income constant, a marginal tax-rate cut will engender a substitution effect, increasing work output and income. There we have it: a tax rate reduction will have substitution effects leading to more hours worked and income effects leading to fewer hours worked. Voila! These opposing income and substitution effects, however, are relevant only for a single income earner.

Of course, if tax rates on all levels of income are raised, the income earner will have less incentive on the margin to earn pre-tax income (the substitution effect), leading them to work fewer hours, but they will also have less after-tax income for the time they work (the income effect), leading them to work more hours. The net effect on hours worked, from a tax rate increase, most economists believe, is indeterminate.

In general, for an individual with any specific tax rate increase, we cannot be sure which effect will dominate. Yet we do know that, in the extreme, over the whole range of tax rates from zero to 100 per cent, the income earner will work less at a 100 per cent tax rate than they will work at a 0 per cent tax rate – that is to say, over the whole range of tax rates, the substitution effect must dominate for any one single income earner.

In an economy, however, where we have all manner of income earners and government spending beneficiaries, we are not so focused on any one individual's behaviour as we are on the behaviour of the economy as a whole. Now, in order to look at these effects over all income earners, we rely on what is called the Slutsky equation. The Slutsky equation breaks down the effects of a price or tax rate change into two components: an income effect and a substitution effect. When a price or tax rate change occurs, the income effects for all people combined in the whole economy sum to zero, but the substitution effects always aggregate.

On an individual basis, for high-income earners, the substitution effect of a tax-rate cut in lower – i.e. not marginal – income brackets is zero, while the income effect induces higher income earners to work, produce, earn and hire less, *not* more. For lower income earners, a tax-rate cut in lower income brackets may have a positive substitution effect not experienced by high-income earners, but it will also have a negative income effect, just as it does on higher income earners. The different impact of a tax-rate cut in lower income brackets on high- and low-income earners is truly important. Many politicians fail to understand economics and think that a lower tax rate on low-wage workers' income is equally stimulative as a tax-rate cut on the highest income earners. Well, it isn't.

So far, we have discussed, separately, the income and substitution effects of various tax rate changes of single income earners. In this section, we will combine the income and substitution effects for the whole economy, including net taxpayers and net beneficiaries of government spending. What the government collects in taxation, it redistributes to others in terms of government spending.

As you can easily see, if a tax rate increase has no effect on the hours income earners work, then the aggregate after-tax income of all income earners will fall by the increase in total tax collections or the increase in the tax rates times the total income earned. This is the direct income effect on all income earners. With less after-tax income for all income earners, the value of additional after-tax income will rise, leading to an income effect increasing work effort.

If all taxes collected are paid out to net beneficiaries, then net beneficiaries will have an increase in the funds they receive by the increase in the total taxes collected. This increase in net benefits to the beneficiaries of government largesse is the negative income effect on all net beneficiaries. For net income earners who pay taxes, the aggregate positive income effect exactly equals the aggregate negative income effect for all net beneficiaries of government spending. For an economy in aggregate, the income effects of a tax rate change always sum to zero.

To restate and simplify this process and make an incentive example, we will use a change in the price of apples, rather than a change in the tax rates, to illustrate both the aggregate income and substitution effects.

Imagine first an increase in the price of apples and, second, how that price change affects the behaviour of two groups in the economy: apple growers and apple consumers. If the price of apples increases, it is true that apple growers will be wealthier and have higher incomes. As a result of these positive income effects, taken alone, apple growers will spend more and will choose more leisure (i.e. less work).

But with an increase in the price of apples, it is equally true that apple consumers will now be poorer and will have lower incomes. They, too, will have income effects and, as a result of their negative income effects, will spend less and choose less leisure (i.e. more work).

When combined, an increase in the price of apples will have positive income effects for apple growers and precisely the same sized negative income effects for apple consumers. In fact, these two income effects – both positive and negative – will offset each other by the hour, day, week, month and year to the very last decimal place. The crucial point is that in an aggregate economy considering all participants, all income effects of a price change, tax rate change or a welfare payment change will offset each other totally. As long as (all) the proceeds of taxes are distributed back to the people, there are no aggregate income effects from a tax rate change in an economy. Full stop! This is important when discussing Keynesian stimulus spending or tax rebates etc.

While the income effects of a price or tax rate change always sum to zero, the substitution effects aggregate in the same direction over all participants. In the case of apple growers and apple consumers, the substitution effect from higher priced apples will both reduce the demand for and increase the supply of apples. Therefore, both groups, whether producers or consumers, find the same incentive to conserve on apple consumption and expand on apple production. All of these incentive or substitution effects for every participant work in the same direction and, therefore, aggregate for the economy as a whole. This reasoning can be seen in examples where we have higher tax rates and more generous transfers, in which the substitution effects incentivise both net taxpayers and net transfer recipients to work less and demand more leisure. Again, the substitution effects are all that remain from a tax rate increase/transfer increase, which unambiguously leads to lower work, output and employment.

THE HIGHER THE MARGINAL TAX RATE, THE LESS THE INCENTIVE TO EARN INCOME PER POUND OF TAX PAID

Remember that it is the after-tax rate of return on work, the marginal rate of transformation between labour and leisure, that is the incentive that propels output and employment growth. People don't work to pay taxes. People work to obtain an after-tax wage. In the same vein, investors and savers don't invest and save to go bankrupt; they save and invest to earn an after-tax return on their savings. There are many factors that have an effect on employment and investment incentives, including tax rates. Tax rates, however, have an indirect effect on employment incentives. In truth, because people work to obtain an after-tax wage, it is one minus the tax rate, or the incentive rate, that is the direct effect on incentives. Therefore, the relationship between tax rates and incentives to earn additional after-tax income is not all that obvious.

Suppose for a moment, two people each earning the same pre-tax income. The first person, however, faces a tax rate of 99 per cent and the second a tax rate of 1 per cent. Therefore, the first person earns £1 after tax for every £100 earned pre-tax, while the second person earns £99 after tax for every £100 pre-tax. In terms of output, employment and production, it is the £100 earned pre-tax that is the relevant economic metric, such as in the calculation of GDP. The question we ask is this: What happens to tax revenues and after-tax incentives if we cut both people's tax rates by 1 percentage point on their pre-tax income? Obviously, in static terms, a 1 percentage point tax cut of pre-tax income on each will imply a £1 loss in tax receipts per £100 earned pre-tax.

The first income earner who faces the 99 per cent tax rate will, after the 1 percentage point reduction in their tax rate, now earn £2 after tax instead of £1 after tax and pay £98 in taxes, rather than £99 in taxes for every £100 earned pre-tax. Moving from a £1 after-tax return per £100 earned pre-tax to a £2 after-tax return per £100 earned pre-tax is a 100 per cent increase in that person's incentives to earn income for a 1 per cent reduction in static tax revenues.

If we cut the second income earner's tax rate by 1 per cent of their pre-tax income, they will earn £100 after tax instead of £99 for every £100 earned pre-tax, which is an increase of a smidgeon over 1 per cent in that person's incentives to earn income, and that person will pay no taxes whatsoever. And so it goes.

The principle here is that those earners facing the highest tax rates will have the greatest increase in incentives to produce income and create jobs for any given static revenue loss tax cut. And those earners with the lowest tax rates will have the least increase in incentives per pound of static revenue loss tax cut. We will demonstrate this concept a bit more in depth in an example where tax rates were actually cut during the 1960s in the US. An analogous situation occurred in the UK in the 1980s, when the highest rate of tax on earned income was cut from 83 per cent to 40 per cent.

We will also show that income earners often respond to tax rates and tax rate changes by changing their use of tax shelters, the location of earning income, the composition of their income, the timing of their receipt of income, as well as the volume of their income. When it comes to money, income and finances, it is amazing how ingenious people can be in pursuit of their self-interest.

Cutting the highest tax rates has a magnified effect over cutting the lowest tax rates on economic incentives per dollar of static tax revenue loss, which in turn creates robust growth and sometimes even higher tax revenues. We will demonstrate in the next section, on changes in incentives, why this 'magnification effect' is based on the marginal tax rate that a taxpayer faces.

NOT ALL TAX RATES ARE ON THE MARGIN

Very few income earners face the lowest brackets' tax rates as their marginal tax rates and yet all taxpayers pay the lowest tax brackets' tax rates on part of their taxable income. The highest income earners pay taxes in each and every tax bracket up to, and including, the bracket where they pay their marginal tax rate. For those people in the higher tax brackets, the tax rates applicable to the lower income tax categories are what we economists call inframarginal tax rates. Inframarginal tax rates have no incentive or substitution effects inducing people to earn more or less income. The lower the tax bracket, the smaller the per-centage of total taxpayers who pay that bracket's tax rate on the margin and, conversely, the more taxpayers there are for whom that tax rate is inframarginal.

Now consider the following: 100 per cent of those earners in the high-est income tax rate bracket face the highest tax rate as their marginal tax rate and therefore directly benefit in incentive terms from a tax-rate cut for the top tax bracket. In 2005, only about 1 per cent of US taxpayers who paid taxes in the lowest bracket actually faced the lowest tax rate as their marginal tax rate and thus benefited in incentive terms from a tax-rate cut to the lowest tax bracket. Stated differently, 99 per cent of income taxpayers who pay taxes in the lowest bracket do *not* face the lowest tax rate as their *marginal* tax rate and are therefore unaffected in incentive terms from cuts in the lowest tax rate.

Out of every pound in taxes collected in the lowest tax bracket, at least ninety-nine pence comes from higher income earners, not those who are actually on the margin in that bracket. Rhetoric aside, cutting the lowest tax rate reduces the tax bills of higher income earners far more than it reduces the tax bill of the lowest income earners. And yet it does nothing to stimulate higher income earners to earn more.

This means that, for high-income earners, changes in the tax rates applicable to lower income tax brackets will have anti-growth individual income effects and virtually no pro-growth incentive effects. As a result, cutting tax rates in ever lower income tax brackets will progressively create greater and greater deadweight revenue losses for government tax revenues and yet will influence only fewer and fewer people's decisions to increase their taxable income through output responses. Tax-rate cuts in the lowest brackets reduced output (i.e. GDP) and tax revenues. This fact is a powerful force for adopting a truly flat tax.

In Table 5 below, we have listed for calendar year 2005 the marginal tax rate for each tax bracket, the number of tax returns where that tax bracket is the marginal tax rate, the percentage of all returns that pay taxes in that tax bracket at that tax rate and lastly, the percentage of all returns in that tax bracket that pay that tax rate as their marginal tax rate.

TABLE 5: 2005 US TAX FILERS BY TAX BRACKET[4]

Highest Tax Rate	Tax Returns on the Margin	Percentage of All Filers Paying This Rate*	Percentage of Filers Paying This Rate for Whom it Is the Marginal Rate[†]
5 per cent	1,186,478	100 per cent	1.1 per cent
8 per cent	651	98.9 per cent	0.0 per cent
10 per cent	25,508,822	98.9 per cent	24.7 per cent
15 per cent	49,321,395	74.4 per cent	63.5 per cent
20 per cent	2,960	27.1 per cent	0.0 per cent
25 per cent	21,996,816	27.1 per cent	77.7 per cent
28 per cent	3,730,002	6.0 per cent	59.2 per cent
33 per cent	1,479,592	2.5 per cent	57.5 per cent
35 per cent[‡]	1,094,617	1.0 per cent	100 per cent

Source: IRS, Statistics of Income

---

* Total tax returns paying this rate marginally or inframarginally.

† Percentage of all taxpayers paying this tax rate on the margin.

‡ This category also includes 141,612 tax returns of people who use Form 8615 which includes the Alternative Minimum Tax and the associated tax returns of people eighteen and under who pay tax rates in their parents' bracket.

The table is central to the argument because it clearly demonstrates that very few taxpayers actually face the lowest tax brackets as their marginal tax rates. For example, only 1.14 per cent of tax filers paying the 5 per cent rate face that rate on the margin. The overwhelming majority of those paying taxes in the lowest brackets are higher income earners for whom those rates are inframarginal. Since inframarginal tax rates do not affect behaviour – they carry no incentive or substitution effects – cuts to the lowest tax brackets provide no stimulus to increased output. Yet these same cuts significantly reduce the tax liability of higher income earners who pay those lower rates on portions of their income. In this way, the table quantifies how rate reductions in the lowest brackets disproportionately benefit those at the top without encouraging them to earn more, resulting in revenue losses without offsetting growth – a compelling rationale for moving towards a flat tax.

FIRMS' INCENTIVES

Applying the framework we have created up until this point, let us now look at how firms' decisions are affected by tax rates. Firms base their decisions to employ workers or to acquire capital assets, in part, on the total cost to the firm of employing workers or acquiring capital, always in an effort to enhance the value of the firm for its owners. Holding all else equal, the greater the cost to the firm of employing each worker, the fewer workers the firm will employ. Conversely, the lower the cost per worker, the more workers the firm hires. Incorporated in the decision-making process are all costs associated with each worker's employment, including filing requirements, payroll taxes, rest facilities and fringe benefits, among others. For the firm, the decision to employ is based upon gross wages paid, a concept which encompasses all costs borne by the firm. This is the price component of a firm's demand curve for labour. Symmetrical sets of criteria apply equally when contemplating the decision to acquire capital. Again, from the perspective of the firm, the explicit objective is to garner surplus value from each decision and thereby enhance the value of the firm.

The worker who supplies the labour and the saver who supplies the capital, on the other hand, care little about the cost to the firm of employing each worker or acquiring each unit of capital. Of concern from the workers' standpoint is how much they receive for providing work effort, net of all deductions and taxes. Savers, also, do not save as a matter of social conscience. Savers choose saving over consumption, enticed by the prospect of earning an after-tax return on those savings to be enjoyed at a future point in time. Within the classical framework, workers concentrate on net wages received while savers are preoccupied with their yields on savings after tax. The greater net wages received, the more willing the worker is to work; the higher the net yield on savings, the greater total savings will be. Conversely, if net wages received fall, workers would find work effort less attractive, and they will provide less of it. Savers will also save less if the net yield to savings declines. This, then, when combined with the ability of the firm to create output from labour and capital, is the firm's supply curve.

For an economy as a whole, the supply of work effort and the contributions of capital to total output are, in fact, also the demands for all goods and services. People work and invest to get paid after tax so they can buy goods and services, including investment capital. Therefore, demand will always equal supply. When focusing on specific goods, there is no reason whatsoever why the suppliers of those specific goods should or have to be the demanders of those same goods. Markets trade labour and capital. Factors (capital and labour) may effectively trade some of the goods they produce for goods other factors produce. The possibilities are endless, with the single constraint that the demand for all goods and services in the aggregate and in the specific market must equal their respective supplies. With the introduction of other countries, these constraints apply to the world as a whole. In the words of Bob Mundell, 'The world is the only closed economic system.' We await with bated breath extraterrestrial settlements.

The difference between what it costs a firm to employ a worker or acquire a unit of capital and what that worker or saver receives net (of tax) is the tax wedge (see Figure 9). From the standpoint of a single worker or a single unit of capital, an increase in the tax wedge has two types of effects: an increase in the wedge raises the cost to the employer in the form of higher wages paid or higher yields paid for capital. Clearly, as a result, firms will employ fewer workers and acquire less capital. On the supply side, an increase in the wedge also reduces net wages received and the net yields savers receive. Again, less work effort will be supplied and there will be less savings. In sum, an increase in the tax wedge reduces the demand for, and the supply of, productive factors. An increase in the tax wedge, therefore, is associated with less employment, less investment and lower output. In dynamic formulations, as the tax wedge grows, output growth falls and vice versa. Within the context of classical economics, regulations, restrictions, requirements and government spending, along with explicit taxes, are all parts of the so-called tax wedge.

FIGURE 9: THE TAX 'WEDGE'

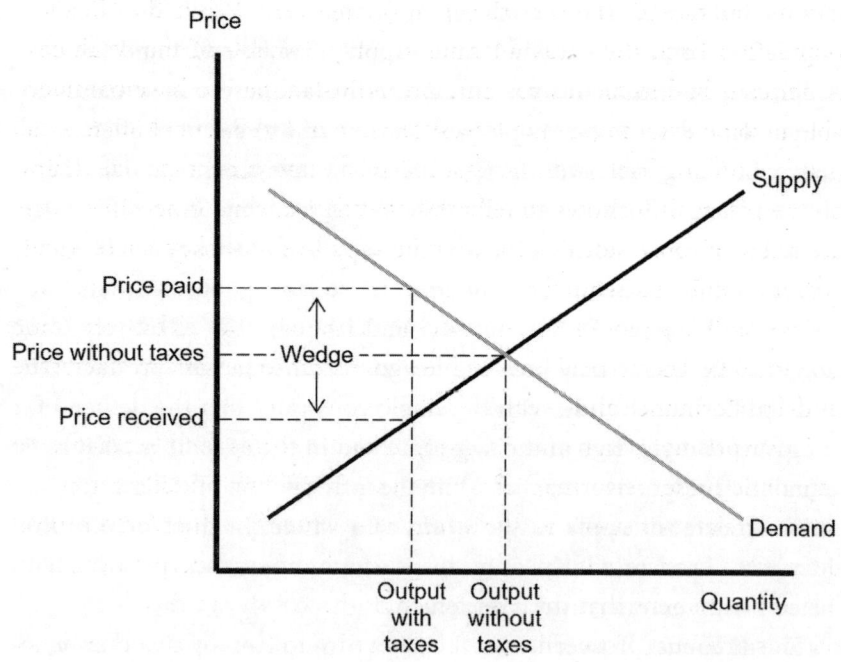

Source: Laffer Associates

The take-away here is simply that as the tax wedge increases, factor prices paid by a firm also increase and the firm's demand for those factors declines. Likewise, as the tax wedge decreases, the prices received by factors decline and, as a consequence of declining returns to factors, the supply of factors also declines.

While we've tried to keep these concepts uncomplicated by looking at one firm, one product, one tax and two prices (price paid and price received), we will expand this framework later in as many meaningful ways as we can. There are many lessons to be learned, and those lessons are quite consequential.

IN SCIENTIA VERITAS/WHAT HAPPENS WHEN YOU TAX THE RICH[5]

In October 1913, eight months after the ratification of the 16th Amendment to the US Constitution, the federal graduated income tax was legislated and subsequently signed into law. The decades-long quest for the tax of all taxes had finally paid off. At its inception in 1913, the highest income tax rate for the very richest was 7 per cent. While the US adult population back then was 64 million, only 358,000 of the wealthiest Americans had to file tax returns. An individual had to have considerable income even to pay the lowest tax rate of 1 per cent. And so it all began. Looking back over the past 100-plus years, it becomes clear how all the pieces fit together to tell a fascinating but gruesome story. Here are a few of those stories, along with analysis of how they relate to the current political discourse.

Figure 10 is a plot of the top income tax rate in the US by year from 1913 to 2023. The vertical lines in the figure refer to periods of economic underperformance and overperformance.

Unsurprisingly, high and rising top tax rates correspond to periods of economic underperformance, while periods of low and falling top tax rates correlate with periods of exceptional prosperity. Other factors most definitely correlate with periods of prosperity and underperformance, but any argument that the tax history of the US shows that prolonged periods of robust prosperity can be achieved with high top tax rates finds no support.* However, while prosperity requires low top tax rates, low top tax rates alone cannot guarantee a prosperous economy.

---

* Obviously, there are exceptions to this rule in wartime, though even then, non-defence GDP growth underperformed.

FIGURE 10: TOP INCOME TAX RATE (US)
(annual, 1913–2025)

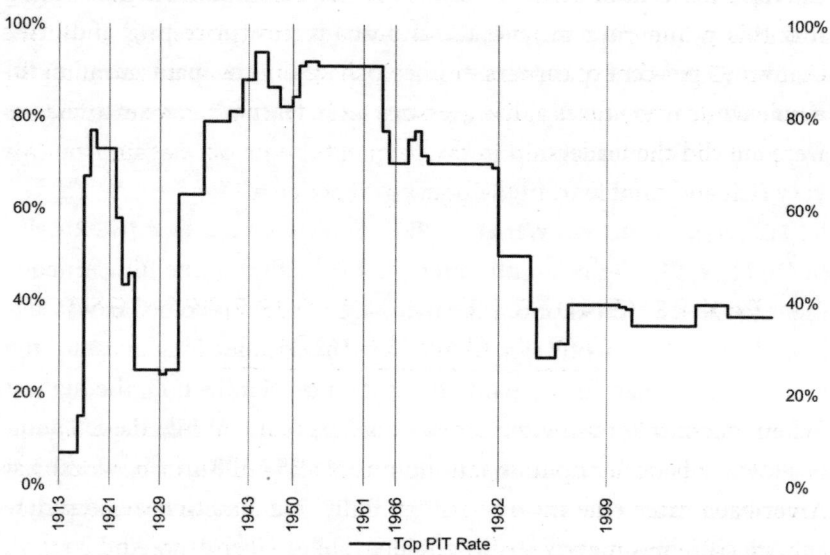

Source: Tax Policy Center

If you know that higher tax rates go hand in hand with both underperformance of the economy as well as greater income equality, then you can infer that when tax rates are high, the drop in reported income of the rich is greater than the drop in incomes of the rest of the economy. Far from higher top tax rates benefiting the non-rich, under high top tax rates, lower income earners get poorer but the rich get poorer faster – thus less income inequality. Taxing the rich at ever-higher rates does not improve the lot of those in lower income categories, but it does reduce income inequality.

The history of the income tax has lessons alternatively obvious and shocking. High tax rates can bring the economy to heel, while low and/or lowered tax rates can yield phenomenal bursts of economic productivity and prosperity – these findings comport with common sense. Then come the shockers. Income inequality tracks the top tax rate inversely – but with the fatal caveat that high tax rates cause reductions in the income of the highest earners and compel the rich to shelter their income from tax reporting. High tax rates gain small assessments from the top 1 per cent of earners – while low tax rates redouble the amount that this group pays in taxes. And perhaps most arresting of all: the bottom 95 per cent of earners saw their share of taxes paid zoom up the whole while when taxes at the top were high. Only when taxes at the top were cut did the leadership in tax payments come once again from the very rich and tumble from the bottom 95 per cent.

TAX REVENUES FROM THE TOP 1 PER CENT OF INCOME REPORTERS

When it comes to raising top tax rates on the rich, the old adage 'anyone is allowed his or her opinion, but no one is allowed his or her facts' has never been more relevant. For well over 100 years, the Internal Revenue Service (IRS) has meticulously compiled, collected and stored tax return data on every single tax filer. This monumental effort on behalf of the IRS has resulted in an enormous trove of data attesting to how actual tax reporters and filers respond to tax law and changes in tax law. This isn't a hypothetical 'what if' scenario or even a sample of a much larger universe.

It is widely believed that taxation on the top 1 per cent of income earners can materially, by its impact on income inequality, improve the economic well-being of those income earners in the bottom echelons of the economic ladder. Using data from the MIT Institute for Income Inequality, we show exactly what happens when tax rates on the rich (the top 1 per cent of income earners) rise and fall. Using as a measure of income inequality the income share of the top 1 per cent of income earners, we follow the measures as well as use the data from Thomas Piketty, Emmanuel Saez and Gabriel Zucman's article 'Distributional National Accounts'.[6] The actual data show that i) whenever tax rates on the rich increase, the economy underperforms, tax revenues from the rich decline and the poor get hammered; and ii) almost every time when tax rates on the rich are lowered, the economy outperforms, tax revenues from the rich rise and those earners on the lowest echelons of the economic ladder greatly benefit. See the three charts below:

FIGURE 11: TOP INCOME TAX RATE AND ECONOMIC PERFORMANCE
(annual, 1913–2025)

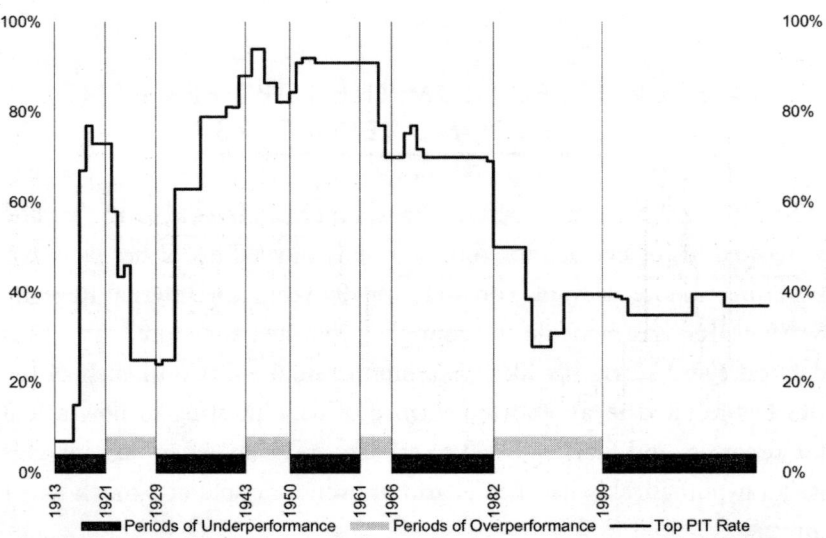

Source: Tax Policy Center, PSZ

In Figure 11, from 1913, the very beginning of the income tax in the US, raising the top tax rate on the rich is exceptionally closely and contemporaneously correlated with economic underperformance of the US economy and cutting the top tax rate on the 'rich' is also in lockstep with economic overperformance.

In Figure 12, the relationship between higher and lower retention rates (i.e. the money you have left after tax) on the rich are plotted along with lessened (increased) tax revenues from the rich. The relationship is as good as it gets. The fit is like a hand in a glove made to perfection. Whenever the rates on the rich go up, tax revenues from the rich go down and whenever tax rates on the rich go down, tax revenues from the rich go up. More in-depth research, not shown here, shows that much of the effects on tax revenues from the rich is a result of tax sheltering.

FIGURE 12: AVERAGE REAL TAX REVENUES PER TOP 1 PER CENT EARNER DETRENDED VS RETENTION RATE OF TOP PIT (1 MINUS THE TOP TAX RATE)

(annual, 1913–2023, detrended using a 1.5 per cent trend)

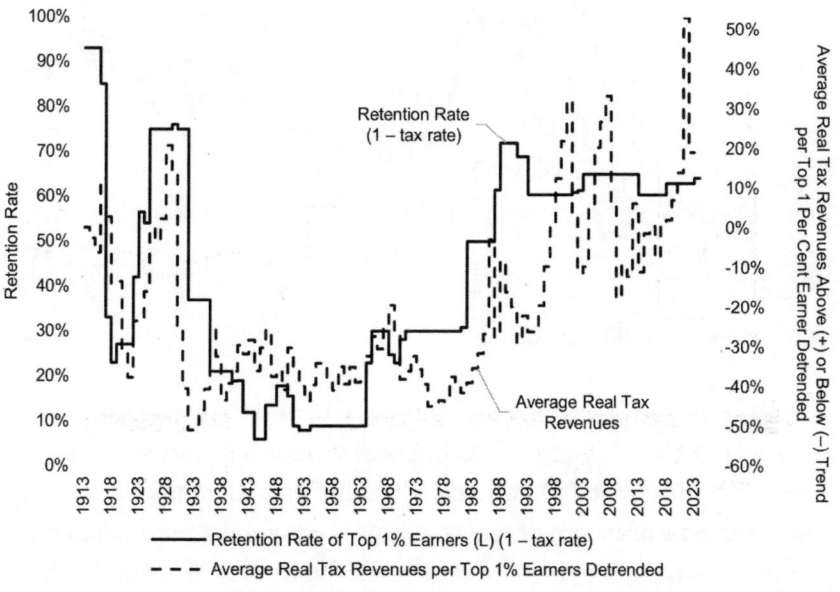

Source: *Tax Policy Center, PSZ, IRS Statistics of Income*

Lastly, in Figure 13, we show what happens to the income cohort shares of GDP of total taxes paid when tax rates on the 'rich' are higher or lower. The simple facts are: when tax rates on the rich are high, the share (as a percentage of GDP) of total taxes paid by the rich is low and stagnates, while taxes paid by the bottom 95 per cent is high and soars. When tax rates on the rich are lower, the share of taxes paid by the rich is high and rises and the share paid by the bottom 95 per cent is low and falls – as we predicted!

FIGURE 13: TOP 1 PER CENT AND BOTTOM 95 PER CENT TAX REVENUES
AS A SHARE OF GDP

(annual, 1916–2023)

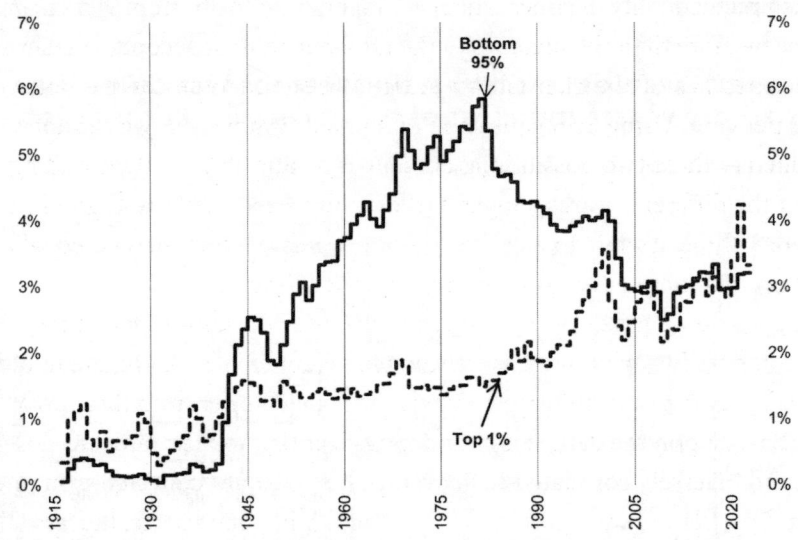

Source: IRS Statistics of Income, Laffer Associates

As shown by the preceding three figures, whenever tax rates on the rich
were raised, the economic consequences were less attractive for everyone. In addition, the facts also clearly show that when tax rates on the
top 1 per cent of income earners are lowered, good things happen for
the entire spectrum of income earners. In the words of President John F.
Kennedy, 'A rising tide raises all boats.'

Because Piketty, Saez and the other inequality experts use the income
share of the top 1 per cent of income earners as their measure of inequality, an enormous ambiguity envelops their findings. An increase in
income inequality can be caused by one or other of two factors. First,
an increase in income inequality can result because incomes earned by
the top 1 per cent rise faster than the incomes of the bottom 99 per cent.
Second, an increase in income inequality can result from a fall in the incomes of the bottom 99 per cent by more than the fall in the incomes of
the top 1 per cent. From their measures of income inequality, we simply

can't tell in which of the two ways inequality increases. From our use of their data, however, we can easily see how these changes occur.

Likewise, there are two ways income inequality can decline. First, income inequality declines whenever incomes of the bottom 99 per cent rise by more than the incomes of the top 1 per cent, or second, whenever the incomes of the rich fall by more than the incomes of the bottom 99 per cent. Using Saez's measure of inequality, however, we cannot tell which of these two possibilities actually is responsible for their findings. But the differences are as night and day, black and white, and good and bad. I think it's fair to say that no one wants greater income equality when that means everyone is worse off, including the poor.

Because we have every single tax return over the entire span of the US income tax history, our measures can tell the difference. And these results totally reverse everything these inequality experts infer from their work.

Based upon the data, it is abundantly clear that top tax rates are closely and inversely correlated with average tax revenues collected from the top 1 per cent of income earners. The higher the top tax rate, the less tax revenue collected from the top 1 per cent of income earners. With the obvious exception of the first year of the income tax, if you raise top tax rates, then the average tax revenues from the top 1 per cent of income earners go down. Lower those top tax rates, and average real tax revenues from the top 1 per cent of income earners go up. The correlation could scarcely be clearer or stronger. And the intuitive logic could not be more straightforward. Please note that we are *only* looking at own tax revenues which do *not* include secondary, tertiary or additional tax revenue gains or losses from other sources. If these other revenues were included, the results would be reinforced.

The top 1 per cent of income earners are laser-focused on top tax rates. As top tax rates rise, the top 1 per cent turn their attention to tax lawyers, tax accountants, deferred income specialists, fixers and lobbyists just to name a few. Their calculations are simple. If the tax savings from hiring these tax advisers is high enough to cover their costs, these advisers will be hired and reported taxable incomes will fall. If the tax savings are not worth the cost, these advisers won't be hired, and tax payments will increase. With high and rising top tax rates, the likelihood of the affluent hiring tax advisers rises, and as a result government tax revenues fall.

IMPACT OF FISCAL INTERVENTION: THE ELLIPSE[7]

In earlier sections, we were previously only concerned with, and therefore only considered, the demand for and the supply of one factor with respect to a single tax. A more comprehensive classical perspective on the impact of fiscal policy on economic activity can be achieved by including two factors of production as well as two taxes in the analysis. For discussion purposes, these two factors will be characterised as capital and labour.[*] The results derived with only one factor, of course, are still fully valid: an increase in the tax wedge increases the price paid for and reduces the price received by a factor of production, reducing both the demand for and supply of that factor. A depressed level of economic activity ensues. For example, an increase in the tax wedge on labour will raise wages paid, lower wages received and reduce the amount of labour employed and thus reduce output. But this is not the end of the story.

In a two-factor model, though, the process accompanying a tax increase on labour does not stop here: the presence of fewer employed workers causes the value of each unit of capital, from the employer's perspective, to decline. There is a point, or mixture, of capital and labour that optimises the price of each: in this case, it could be that, say, a trucking company needs one truck per driver but has ten trucks and only eight drivers. Therefore, the demand for capital falls, the yield declines to clear the market and less capital will be employed. In this example, two trucks are not driven, and the owner has two spares, so no reason to invest in upkeep or buy new ones. Taking the tax increase on labour to its final state, an increase in the tax wedge on labour will lower:[†]

---

[*]   To clarify, other than the effects of factor substitution, this stylised model does not allow for changes in productivity.

[†]   For the purposes of this exposition, all proceeds from taxation are presumed to be returned in the form of neutral transfer payments.

- output
- the quantities of both capital and labour employed
- wages received
- yields to capital, both paid and received

In addition, an increase in the tax wedge on labour will raise wages paid due to the higher cost of drivers due to the tax on labour.

Similarly, an increase in the tax wedge on the returns to capital will lower:

- output
- the amount of both capital and labour employed
- wages received and paid
- yields received by the owners of capital

The cost of capital paid by employers for capital will rise.

Within this two-factor model, which contains capital and labour as well as one market output, the effect on total tax receipts of an increase in the tax on either factor of production has conflicting influences. For example, an increase in the tax wedge on labour will elicit the following tax revenue responses:

- More revenue will be collected per worker employed, thus tending to increase revenues.
- Fewer workers will be employed, thus lowering tax revenues.
- Less capital will be employed, thus lowering tax revenues.
- And, of course, there will be less output, which, if it were taxed, would also lower tax revenues.

Under certain circumstances, the additional revenue collected per worker will dominate and an increase in the tax wedge on labour will raise revenues. When total tax revenues rise from a specific tax increase, we refer to the tax as being in its normal range (Figure 14). Sometimes, however, the second, third and fourth effects dominate, and less revenue will be forthcoming. When tax revenues fall from a specific tax increase, we refer to the tax as being in the prohibitive range (Figure 14). The same set of conditions pertains to changes in the tax wedge on capital. In actual practice, of course, a number of additional influences are felt.

What are not included in this specific analysis are the sheltering, reporting and after-tax avoidance schemes that will be implemented following a tax rate increase. All of these sheltering schemes will work to lower tax revenues from the initial tax rate increase.

With higher tax rates, there will be more tax avoidance and evasion and this would aggravate the offsetting revenue impact accompanying tax rate increases. Where possible, factor substitution will reduce the economy's reliance on the now higher taxed factor. The longer the time lapse, the greater the offsets, and the higher the initial level of tax rates, again, the greater the offsets will be. Overall, the relationship between tax rates and tax revenues is far from obvious. Higher tax rates could well yield less revenue. Higher tax rates always yield less output. When a tax rate increase yields higher revenues, the tax is in the normal range. When a tax rate increase leads to lower total tax revenues, the tax is in the prohibitive range.

An important point often missed by economists, and especially journalists, is that it is not just what happens to the specific tax revenues of a particular factor that is taxed more or less, but what happens to total tax revenues from all sources when a particular factor is taxed more or less. Tax changes on labour affect tax revenues on capital and output, and everywhere else, too.[8] And, as we'll see later on, tax changes also affect employment, incomes and consequently transfer payments, subsidies and bailouts.

One way to analyse the effects of tax rate changes is to specify the combinations of tax rate changes on capital and labour where total revenues are left unchanged. This framework is useful because it separates the issues of government spending from those of tax policies. Thus, if the taxes on labour and capital are both in the normal range, then a tax rate reduction on labour will have to be accompanied by a tax rate increase on capital to maintain tax revenues, or vice versa. On the other hand, if the tax rate on labour was in the prohibitive range while the tax rate on capital was in the normal range, then a tax rate reduction on labour, which by definition would lead to higher tax revenues, would require a tax rate reduction on capital as well to maintain tax revenues.

A representative pairing of such tax rates on labour and capital can be depicted on a two-axis graph, as shown in Figure 14.

The horizontal axis is the tax on capital, t_k, and the vertical axis is the tax on labour, t_l. The locus of points describing the different pairings of tax rates that yield the same amount of tax revenue is named the iso-revenue line. One such line is drawn in Figure 14 in the form of an ellipse. In the illustration, the location and angle of the ellipse are purely arbitrary, depending as they do on many factors. The diagram is drawn as it is for illustrative purposes only.

Four distinct regions can be identified on the iso-revenue line. In the region from locus P to locus S, both tax rates are in their 'normal' range: an increase in the tax rate on capital alone, or the tax rate on labour alone, will raise net revenues. Therefore, if revenues are to stay the same in the PS region of the iso-revenue line, an increase in either tax rate must be accompanied by a reduction in the other tax rate.

FIGURE 14: THE ELLIPSE

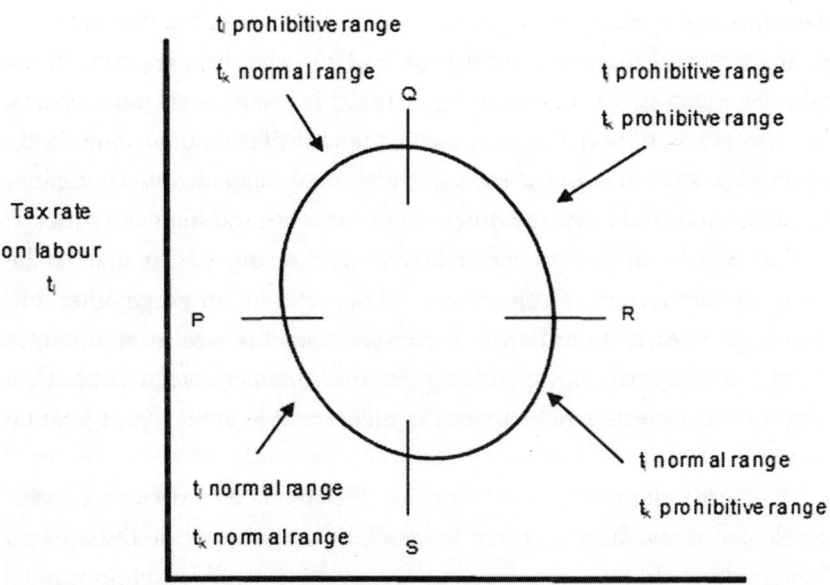

Source: Laffer Associates

In the PQ region, the tax on labour is in its prohibitive range, while the tax on capital is in its normal range: an increase in the tax rate on labour loses net revenues, while an increase in the tax on capital increases net revenues. Thus, an increase in the tax rate on labour (moving up the vertical axis) must be accompanied by an increase in the tax rate on capital (moving to the right on the horizontal axis) to maintain the same level of revenues. Hence, the iso-revenue line in this region is upward sloping to the right. Holding revenues constant, the higher the tax rate on labour, the higher the tax on capital must be.

QR is the region where both tax rates are in the prohibitive range. In this region, an increase in either tax rate lowers revenues. Thus, if the tax on capital is increased (movement to the right), the tax rate on labour must be reduced (movement down) to keep total revenues constant. The iso-revenue line here is downward sloping to the right and concave to the origin.

Finally, in the region RS, the tax on labour is in the normal range and the tax on capital is in the prohibitive range. Here a rise in the tax rate on labour, which increases revenues, must be accompanied by an increase in the tax rate on capital, which lowers revenues, in order to keep total revenues constant.

In each of the three regions, PQ, QR and RS, at least one tax rate is in the prohibitive range. That is, an increase in the tax rate lowers net revenues. In the range QR, both tax rates are in the prohibitive range. Only in the one range, PS, are both tax rates in the normal range, where an increase in either one tax rate or the other raises net revenues. Returning back to our discussion of how to correctly analyse the issue of any tax change, there should never be a constellation of tax rates in any range other than PS. Why on earth would anyone ever want any tax rate so high that its height loses tax revenues? Moving on from one iso-revenue ellipse, we can now investigate what happens at higher and lower levels of total tax revenues.

A new tax ellipse inside the one just described can represent a higher level of tax revenues: a lower level of revenues being described by a larger ellipse. In all cases, four regions would exist. A maximum point of revenue exists beyond which revenues cannot be increased. Whether tax rates are raised or lowered, less revenue will be forthcoming. In sum, a whole family of iso-revenue lines or ellipses exists, one for each level of revenue and spending. The existence of these ellipses allows for a separation of the effects of tax rates per se and total tax revenues and spending.

THE LAFFER CURVE AND SOME OF ITS CRITICS

The original Laffer curve was drawn on a napkin (see Figure 15 for the original and Figure 16 for the proper chart). It is based on the proposition that there are two rates of tax where the yield is zero – a 0 per cent tax and a 100 per cent tax. In between, the yield for any given tax rate will rise to a maximum and then subside. This is, in a sense, obvious, though some people pretend otherwise.

What is obviously the interesting thing is the actual shape of the curve and the rate of tax that maximises revenue (although the rate that maximises welfare will be below this).

We have set out some of the quotes and comments on this below.

Tax Rates and Income Tax Avoidance

Senator Russell Long (D-LA), chairman of the Senate Finance Committee, said in 1977:

Revenue estimates have a way of being very, very far off base because of the failure to anticipate everything that happens … Now, when we put the investment tax credit on, we estimated that we were going to lose about $5 billion … Instead of losing money, revenues went up in corporate income tax collections. Then we thought it was overheating the economy. We repealed it. We thought that the government would take in more money. But instead of making $5 billion, we lost $5 billion. Then, after a while, we thought we made a mistake, so we put it back on again. Instead of losing us money, it made us money. Then, after a while, we repealed it again and it did just exactly the opposite from what it was estimated to do again by about the same amount. It seems to me, if we take all factors into account, we wind up with the conclusion that taking the investment tax credit alone and looking at it by itself, it is not costing us any money. Because the impression I gain from it is that it stimulated the economy to the extent, and brings about additional investment to the extent, that it makes us money rather than loses us money.[9]

John F. Kennedy, in his address to the Economic Club of New York on 14 December 1962, said, 'In short, it is a paradoxical truth that tax rates are too high today and tax revenues are too low and the soundest way to raise the revenues in the long run is to cut the rates now.'

FIGURE 15: THE ORIGINAL LAFFER CURVE

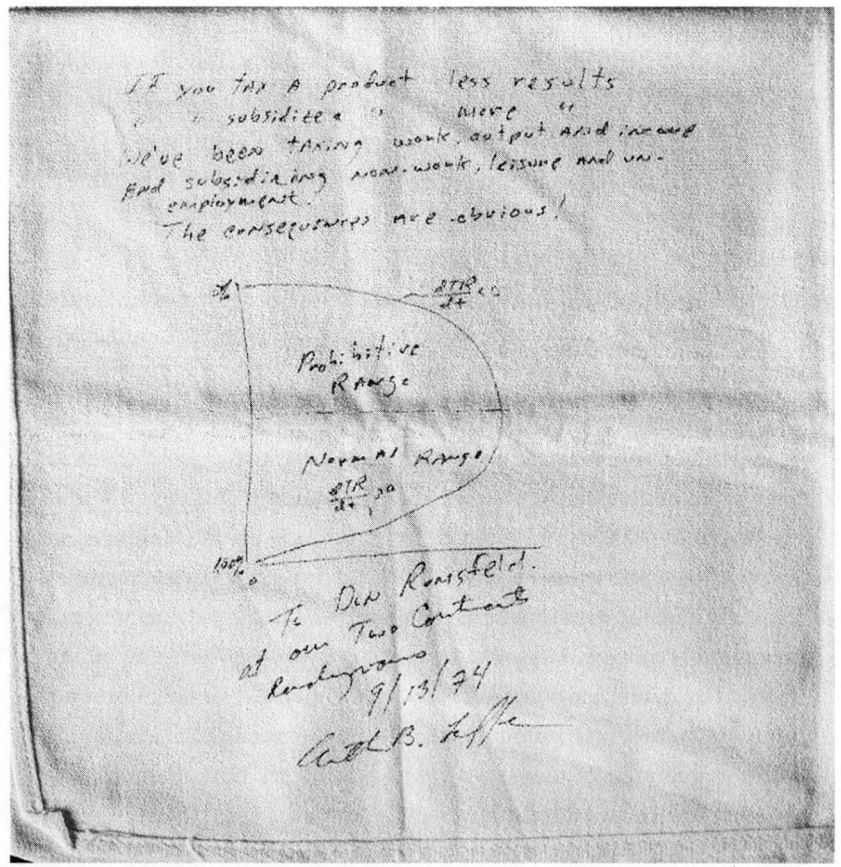

Source: Dr Arthur B. Laffer, Smithsonian National Museum of American History

FIGURE 16: THE LAFFER CURVE

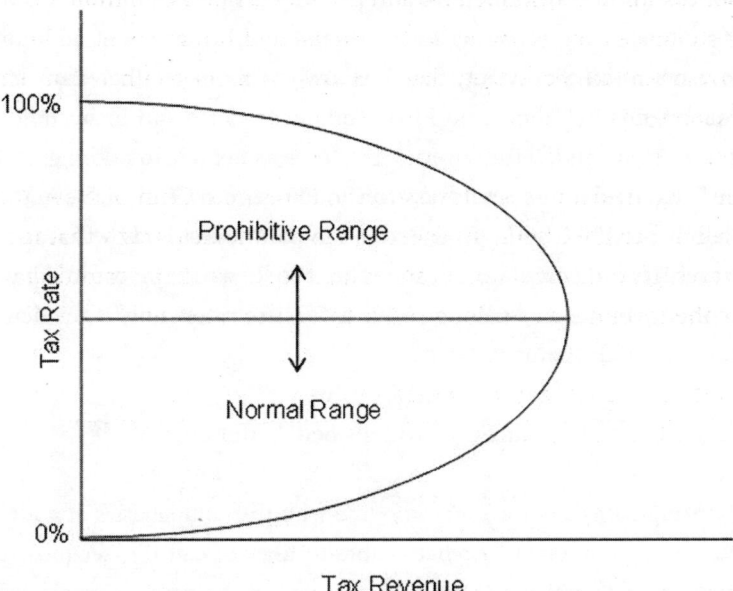

Source: Laffer Associates

In 1979, economist John Kenneth Galbraith wrote to Professor Laffer:

Dear Professor Laffer:

It is obvious that you read your press notices with some care; I am delighted not only by the way you accept my designation as an alternative source of essential public services but also by your good humour. I thank you very much for the fire engine; in due course I am sure my grandchildren will be no less grateful. As to my response, I am promptly initiating a search for a silver or gold-plated wishbone which is the nearest known approximation to the Laffer Curve. This I will hope to have in the mail to you in due course. Whether you get it or not will, of course, depend on whether the postal service survives your policies.

My thanks and cordial good wishes once again.

Yours faithfully,

John Kenneth Galbraith

March 1979[10]

In the early 1980s, the Laffer curve became a widely understood and misunderstood economic tool and pop culture phenomenon:

> Is it not a thing of beauty bare? As any child can see [true, any child can see this but almost no PhD economists can] from inspecting the curve's lower end, if the government drops its tax rate to nothing, it gets nothing. And if it raises its tax rates to 100 per cent, it also gets nothing [tell that to the CBO]. Why? Because in that case nobody will work for wages. If all income went to the state, people would revert to a barter economy in which a painter paints a dentist's house only if the dentist caps one of the painter's teeth.[11]

On mathematician Martin Gardner's neo-Laffer curve:[12]

> To bring Laffer's curve more into line with the complexities of a mixed economy dominated by what Galbraith likes to call the 'technostructure', and also with other variables that distort the curve, I have devised what I call the neo-Laffer (NL) curve. (See my 'Changing Perspectives on the Laffer Curve', in *The British Journal of Econometrics*, Vol. 34, No. 8, pages 7316–7349; August 1980 – [this is his joke not mine]) ... Near its end points this lovely curve closely resembles the old Laffer curve, proving that it was not a totally worthless first approximation. As the curve moves into the complexities of the real world, however, it enters what I call the 'technosnarl'.

And there you have it, ladies and gentlemen, a scientific refutation of the Laffer curve. Aren't scientists silly?

Few concepts in modern economics have sparked as much debate, or been as frequently misunderstood, as the Laffer curve. Some view it as a powerful insight into how tax rates affect economic behaviour; others dismiss it as ideological oversimplification. But what's undeniable is how many serious thinkers, across centuries and ideologies, have engaged with its central idea: that beyond a certain point, higher tax rates can discourage work, investment and innovation, ultimately reducing the very revenue they seek to increase. The following voices, from Nobel laureates and textbook authors to statesmen, philosophers and magazine editors, reveal the remarkable breadth of opinion and historical depth surrounding the Laffer curve. Whether sceptical or supportive, academic or political, their comments reflect just how far-reaching this deceptively simple curve has become in shaping economic thought.

Greg Mankiw, professor of economics at Harvard, retitled his 'Charlatans and Cranks' section after complaints from an editor and some readers that the title was 'too inflammatory for a textbook description of a policy debate'.[13] Starting with the second edition of his textbook published in 2000, the section was retitled 'The Laffer Curve and Supply-side Economics'. He had this to say about the Laffer curve in 2010:

> My guess is that the short-run answer and the long-run answer are quite different. For example, if you raised the top rate from 35 to, say, 60 per cent, you might raise revenue in the short run. Over time, however, you would get lower economic growth, so the additional revenues would fall off and eventually decline below what they would have been at the lower rate ... I will pass on offering a specific number, as it would require more time and thought than I can offer just now, but I will opine that I think the long-run answer is actually more important for policy purposes than the short-run answer.[14]

Another Harvard economics professor, Martin Feldstein, said the following when asked by the *Washington Post*, 'Where does the Laffer curve bend?':

> Why look for the rate that maximizes revenue? As the tax rate rises, the 'deadweight loss' (real loss to the economy) rises so as the rate gets close to maximizing revenue the loss to the economy exceeds the gain in revenue ... I dislike budget deficits as much as anyone else. But would I really want to give up say $1 billion of GDP in order to reduce the deficit by $100 million? No. National income is a goal in itself. That is what drives consumption and our standard of living.[15]

In 1967, Paul Samuelson, Nobel laureate in economics, wrote:

To the extent that a tax cut succeeds in stimulating business, our progressive tax system will collect extra revenues out of the higher income levels. Hence a tax cut may in the long run imply little (or even no) loss in federal revenues, and hence no substantial increase in the long run public debt.[16]

When questioned in 1970 on the Kennedy tax cuts, Walter Heller, economic adviser to President Kennedy, said, 'The upsurge of tax revenues flowing from economic expansion would finance higher levels of local, state, and Federal spending than we would have had without the tax cuts stimulus.'[17]

In 1774, when arguing against over-taxation of the American colonists before Parliament, the philosopher Edmund Burke said, 'Your scheme yields no revenue; it yields nothing but discontent, disorder, disobedience; and such is the state of America, that after wading up to your eyes in blood, you could only end just where you began; that is, to tax where no revenue is found.'[18]

William F. Buckley, founder of the *National Review*, responded in 1980 as follows to the Carter administration's claims that supply economics was 'stupid':

> Professor Arthur Laffer, with whose rigidities one can legitimately quarrel, is nonetheless onto something when he says that sluggish performance by workers using creaky industrial equipment and paying high taxes results in low output and, derivatively, smaller returns to the government through the existing tax setup. We have, these days, suffocating tax rates. These give rise to a reduced incentive to work.[19]

In his 1933 work *The Means to Prosperity*, John Maynard Keynes stated:

> Nor should the argument seem strange that taxation may be so high as to defeat its object, and that, given sufficient time to gather the fruits, a reduction of taxation will run a better chance than an increase of balancing the budget. For to take the opposite view today is to resemble a manufacturer who, running at a loss, decides to raise his price, and

when his declining sales increase the loss, wrapping himself in the rectitude of plain arithmetic, decides that prudence requires him to raise the price still more – and who, when at last his account is balanced with nought on both sides, is still found righteously declaring that it would have been the act of a gambler to reduce the price when you were already making a loss.[20]

In Adam Smith's 1776 *Wealth of Nations*, he wrote, 'High taxes, sometimes by diminishing the consumption of the taxed commodities, and sometimes by encouraging smuggling, frequently afford a smaller revenue to the government than what might be drawn from more moderate taxes.'[21]

In a 1982 article, James M. Buchanan, Nobel laureate, and Dwight R. Lee wrote:

Those who argue that government would never operate on the down slope of the Laffer curve [i.e. what we would call the normal range], and who adduce evidence in support, are implicitly adopting a short-run perspective. Those who argue that rate reductions will stimulate supply-side responses sufficient to generate increases in revenues [i.e. in what we would call the prohibitive range], are implicitly adopting a long-run perspective.[22]

In its 1999 issue on 'The Century's Greatest Minds', *Time* magazine said that the Laffer curve was one of 'a few of the advances that powered this extraordinary century'.[23]

In 1989, the *Wall Street Journal* stated that 'supply-side thinking was at the heart of Ronald Reagan's economic policies during his eight-year Administration'.[24]

Bloomberg Businessweek described the Laffer curve as 'one of the most disruptive ideas of the past 85 years' in 2014.[25]

The *Los Angeles Times* named Professor Laffer as one of 'a Dozen Who Shaped the '80s'.[26]

In 1992, *Institutional Investor* noted that 'the creation of the Laffer Curve is a "memorable event"'.[27]

As Ronald Reagan said in 1983, 'I know my economic policies are working because they don't call them Reaganomics anymore.'[28]

And nearly 200 years ago, one British economist, David Ricardo, summed up Laffer curve effects like this:

> Every new tax becomes a new charge on production... A portion of the labour of the country which was before at the disposal of the contributor to the tax, is placed at the disposal of the State, and cannot therefore be employed productively. This portion may become so large, that sufficient surplus may not be left to stimulate the exertions of those who usually augment by their savings the capital of the State. Taxation has happily never yet in any free country been carried so far as instantly from year to year to diminish its capital. Such a state of taxation could not be long endured; or if endured, it would be constantly absorbing so much of the annual produce of the country as to occasion the most extensive scene of misery, famine, and depopulation.[29]

Cardinal de Richelieu, chief minister to King Louis XIII, noted:

> The increase in taxes is capable of reducing many of the King's subjects to idleness, being certain that the majority of the poor people and craftsmen employed in the factories would rather remain idle and do nothing than consume their whole life in ungrateful and useless work, if the size of the [taxes] prevents them from receiving [the salary] of the sweat of their body.[30]

LOCATIONAL EFFECTS OF TAXATION WITHIN THE US

One of the important factors in the twenty-first century is the growth of mobility of both business and people. It is because of this that it is highly valuable to analyse the impact of state and local taxation on location in the US since there are few barriers to mobility within the US. While geographical mobility within the US is generally considered to be declining,[31] it is still considered to be much higher than in other countries.[32]

For this reason, it is important to understand the impact of tax incentives on locational mobility within the US. This section looks at five different case studies that demonstrate this: 1) the decline in the economies of Michigan and Detroit as car making within the US shifted elsewhere; 2) the impact of regulation and tax on California; 3) the impact of property taxes in California and Tennessee; 4) the impact of local death taxes; and 5) the impact of local income taxes.

The states of the United States are really the laboratory for experimentation, because it has a federal government. There are two clauses in the Constitution where: i) you cannot prohibit anyone from moving from one state to another, and ii) you can't have any impediment to moving goods and services across state lines. So those two are there. Looking at different types of taxation in different states and localities helps compare economic approaches.

IMPACT OF LOCAL TAXES ON DETROIT AND MICHIGAN

Imagine for a moment that a person builds a factory based upon the presumption that the highest marginal corporate profits tax is 10 per cent and will remain at 10 per cent well into the foreseeable future. The size and the extent of this factory will reflect its owner's perceptions of the discounted present value of all future after-tax profits versus the cost of the factory itself. The size of the factory will supposedly be determined by the juxtaposition of the last dollar spent on the factory and that dollar's net contribution to the discounted present value of all future profits. Investors today regularly use this concept of a discounted cash flow (DCF) analysis; our factory owner determines he needs, say, 50 per cent of the revenue in order to operate the factory without losing money (capital expenditures, wages, mortgage payments etc.): above 50 per cent are tax liability, profits and the unknown.

Now imagine that the moment the investor finishes construction of his factory, the government raises the highest marginal corporate tax rate from 10 per cent to 90 per cent. What's the owner to do?

Obviously, he will not tear his factory down. If he is able, he will likely choose to operate at a loss (recouping one-fifth of losses), but over time he will reduce his commitment to this investment by not replacing worn-out equipment or adding new advances in technologies. As time goes on, the value of the factory will shrink until its size corresponds to the appropriate size for a 90 per cent corporate tax rate. The basic principle here: it takes a long time for an economy to destroy its capital stock. As a warning to those who expect overnight miracles from the adoption of supply-side policies, it also takes a long time to create a world-class capital stock. In technical terms, the longer the time period under consideration, the more elastic the tax revenue and output responses to tax rates are. Few examples can compete with the stories of the city of Detroit, Michigan, and the state as a whole.

Michigan and, to an even greater extent, Detroit suffered mightily from the same economic downturn from which the rest of the US ached during what has come to be known as the global financial crisis. Michigan and Detroit, however, were particularly hard-hit by this downturn as a result of poor economic policies that the state and city have had in place for years. The damage done by the global financial crisis was only a continuation of the relative damage done *by* Detroit and Michigan *to* Detroit and Michigan since the early 1960s. If the seeds of damage were the long-standing policies, the global financial crisis was the harvest season.

The problems of Michigan and Detroit are often associated with the US motor vehicle industry and in some minds with the rise in the number of imported vehicles. Yet US production of motor vehicles rose from 7.89 million in 1960 to a peak of 13.02 million in 1999, though the level has fallen back since.[33] The decline in state and city relative performance substantially preceded the peak and then gradual fall in US vehicle production.

In 1967, under Governor Romney's leadership, Michigan initiated a state personal income tax, initially setting the highest tax rate at 2.6 per cent using the federal adjusted gross income (AGI) as Michigan's tax base. The state's income tax rate peaked in 1983 at 6.35 per cent and is now down to 4.25 per cent, but the long-term damage had already been done for this forced-union, high-tax state (see Figure 17).

FIGURE 17: MICHIGAN GROSS STATE PRODUCT AS A SHARE OF US GROSS DOMESTIC PRODUCT

(annual, 1962–2024)

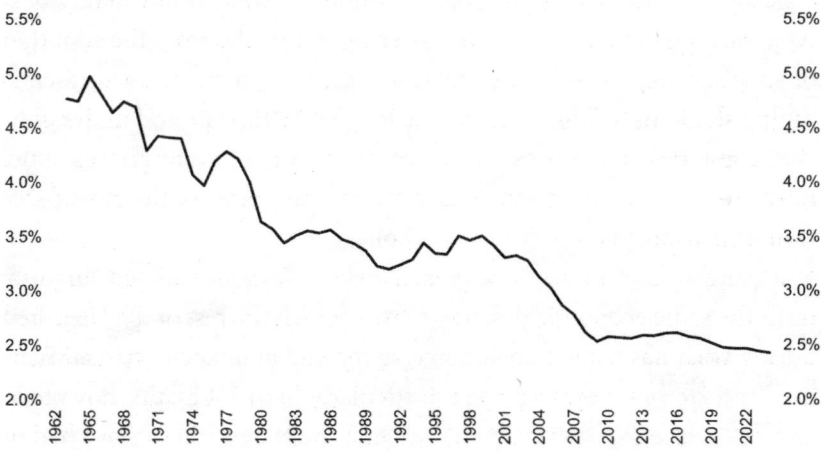

Source: Bureau of Economics Analysis

Even though a 4.25 per cent maximum tax rate is a lot better than 6.35 per cent, those high historical tax rates have damaged Michigan's economy today. The state's corporate tax rate stands at 6 per cent. If all of this weren't enough to doom Detroit, add to it that Michigan and Detroit are highly unionised and have minimum wages above the federal minimum wage. These unwarranted burdensome taxes and regulations on business have surely added to Detroit and Michigan's decline. Sadly, there's no real solution for Detroit that doesn't include tax reform in Michigan.

Then we come to the ills of Detroit itself. In 1962, the City of Detroit adopted a 1 per cent net income tax for residents and 0.5 per cent for non-resident income earners. In 1964, Detroit initiated a 1 per cent corporate tax as well. The city's income tax stands at 2.4 per cent today, and the corporate tax is 2 per cent. Businesses that *can* locate outside Detroit *do*. In 1950, there were approximately 1.85 million residents of Detroit.

Today, the population of Detroit would be lucky to top 700,000. You just can't balance a budget levying taxes on people who either have left or are unemployed (see Figure 18).

FIGURE 18: TOTAL US POPULATION VS DETROIT POPULATION

(Detroit: 1950–2010: decadal, 2014: annual; US: 1950–2023: annual; thousands)

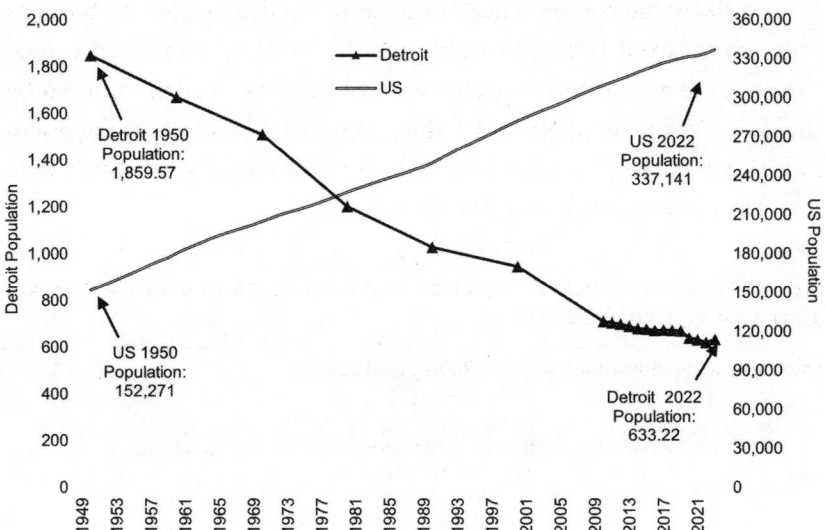

Source: US Census Bureau

Indeed, the story of Michigan and Detroit and their exile from prosperity is sad but is, nevertheless, a good object lesson: capital stocks, while slow to deplete, can indeed disappear over time with sufficiently bad economic policies in place. The state of Michigan has, since hitting rock bottom, started making some positive policy changes. Passing laws to restrict trade union powers was a good attempt to staunch the bleeding and to begin rebuilding the state's capital stock. However, economic health, once lost, is very slow to return. The most recent catastrophic story of the city of Flint and its switch from the Detroit water system to sourcing water from the Flint River is a tragic case in point. Momentum goes in all directions.

IMPACT OF REGULATORY AND TAX POLICIES IN CALIFORNIA
Another clear demonstration of the captive or inelastic taxpayer effect

can be found in housing prices. Houses can't move (out of state) when times are bad; instead, their prices drop. In Figure 19, the Case–Shiller San Diego, San Francisco and Los Angeles housing market price indices are plotted alongside the Case–Shiller US national composite price index of twenty cities (which also includes San Diego, San Francisco and Los Angeles). The far sharper decline in the three California indices is most likely the consequence of excessive regulatory and tax burdens imposed on fixed factors in California. In the short run, fixed capital cannot leave a state and as a captive must bear the burden imposed by the state. Of course, when, and if, the economy rebounds, housing prices in highly regulated environments will rise exceptionally rapidly as well. Regulations render supply curves less elastic.

FIGURE 19: CASE–SHILLER CALIFORNIA HOUSING PRICES VS NATIONAL AVERAGE HOUSING PRICES

(monthly, seasonally adjusted, April 2006–April 2024)

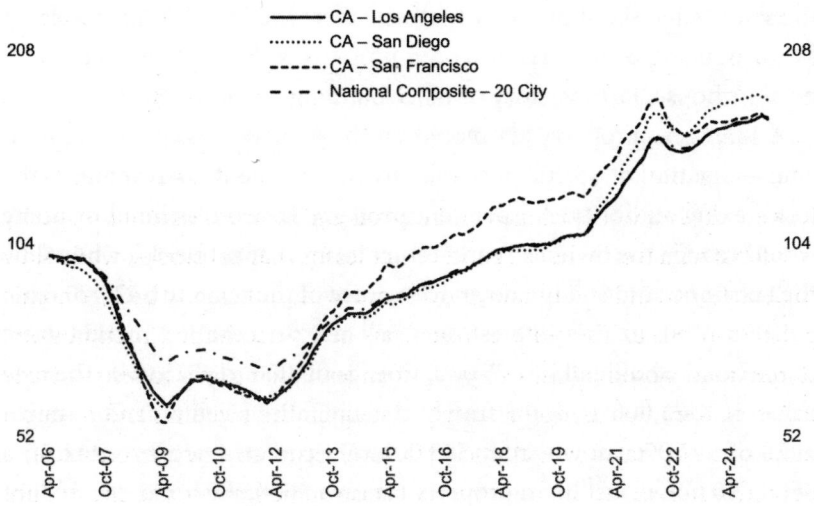

Source: S&P Case–Shiller, Laffer Associates

Finally, the longer the time horizon, the greater the revenues lost from tax rate increases. In technical terms, the longer the time horizon, the more elastic both factors' supplies and demands will be. With time, the mobility of most factors of production is increased. Machinery is not repaired or replaced. New job opportunities lure labour out of the taxing district, or a lack of opportunities leads to a below-average growth in employment. Thus, over time, any economy becomes more sensitive to the imposition of the tax wedge. The elasticity of both the supply and demand for factor services increases. Revenue increases realised in the very short horizon may be more than undone over distant horizons.

PROPERTY TAXES ARE, IN REALITY, A WEALTH TAX

Bonds and real property are similar in that they both are investments that provide returns to their owners and are significant components of their owner's wealth.

A $600,000 bond with an 8 per cent coupon yield would pay its owner $48,000 per year and, if the appropriate market rate of interest were also 8 per cent, that bond would be worth twelve and a half times $(1 \div 0.08)$ the annual yield of $48,000. It's pretty straightforward.

Placing an annual tax on the face value of that bond or property of the same value (i.e. a property tax) will affect the value of the bond just as introducing a property tax on a property will affect the value of a person's house, farm, factory or office building.

A 1 per cent property tax placed on the $600,000 asset will result in a tax obligation of $6,000 per year and an equivalent tax revenue to the local taxing authority. A 1 per cent property tax on this bond or home would reduce the owner's yearly return from that property or home by the tax amount of $6,000, down in the case of the bond to $42,000 from $48,000. With market interest rates still at 8 per cent, the market value of the bond would fall by $75,000, from $600,000 to $525,000. The new value of $525,000 is again simply the capitalised value of the annual yield of $42,000, down from $48,000. A 1 per cent property tax on a $600,000 home, just like a property tax on a $600,000 bond, will reduce that home's value by $75,000, down to $525,000. And for all it's worth, the government that imposed the tax would only collect $6,000 per year in property taxes. This is a ridiculous trade-off: a $6,000 property tax bill resulting in a $75,000 net loss in wealth for everyone.

As damaging as a 1 per cent tax is, there are any number of states where effective property tax rates are well over 1 per cent. Some are as high as 4 or 5 per cent. Based upon the above example, a zero tax $600,000 home would be worth only $450,000 at a 2 per cent property tax rate, $375,000 at a 3 per cent tax rate and crushed to $300,000 when the effective property tax rate is 4 per cent. The highest property tax rate we have heard of is 28 per cent somewhere in Detroit. There are numerous examples of really high property tax rates, all in extremely depressed neighbourhoods.

If the effects of the property tax rate spilled over completely into rents, then a 1 per cent property tax rate would require increases in rents of $500 per month ($6,000 per annum). At property tax rates of 2 per cent, 3 per cent and 4 per cent, a $600,000 property would have to charge annual rents of $60,000, $66,000 and $72,000, respectively. Whether the tax burden falls on property values or higher rents, the consequences are extreme. Home builders will shun higher property tax jurisdictions, as will renters. Businesses and factories will do all they can to exit the area. For those renters, property owners and banks holding mortgages in those now higher taxed areas, the loss of wealth and solvency would be immediate.

Most likely, the initial effects of property tax increases will fall on property values and rents, but sooner or later the exodus will kick into high gear and the desolation of many of our nation's formerly great cities will emerge just as they have actually done in the past. An ounce of prevention is worth a pound of cure.

IMPACT OF PROPERTY TAXES IN TENNESSEE
Population movements responded quickly to the pattern of property tax rates, particularly within the United States where there are few constraints on movement. Figure 20 shows how, as a result, property tax payments in Nashville have responded dramatically to reductions in the statutory rate.

Consider Davidson County in Tennessee compared with nearby counties. It had had positive population growth every year and averaged

0.57 per cent yearly growth in population from 2016 to 2020. From 2020 to 2021, Davidson County lost 1.6 per cent of its population, a swing of -2.17 percentage points away from recent growth trends. This shrinkage was exceptional with respect to its peers in the Metro areas of Tennessee. Shelby County, which because of long-standing high property taxes has for years had low population growth, lost at a rate of 0.45 per cent, and Knox County gained at a rate of 1.36 per cent and Hamilton gained at 0.58 per cent.

FIGURE 20: NASHVILLE: TOTAL PROPERTY TAX PAYMENTS VS STATUTORY PROPERTY TAX RATES

(annual, 2010–24, property tax payments in millions of dollars)

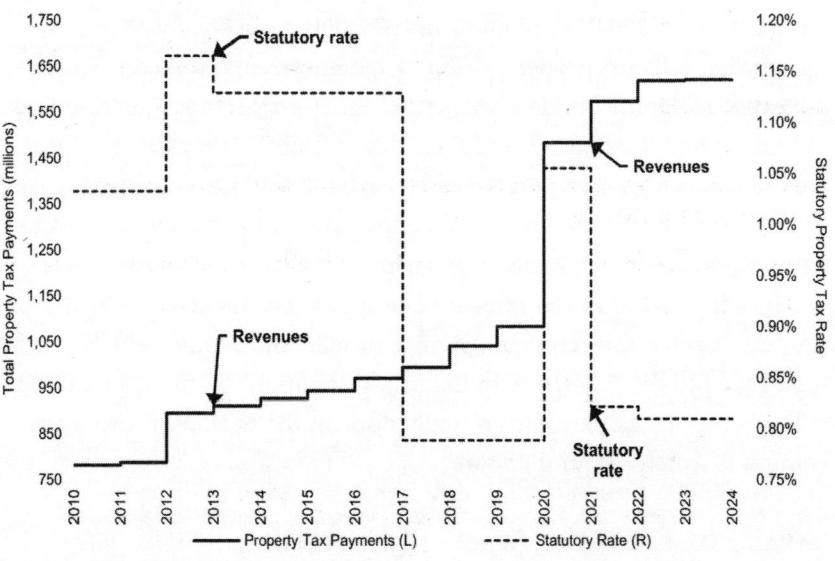

Source: Davidson County CAFRs, Tennessee Comptroller

To visualise just how devastating Nashville's Metro Council/Mayor Cooper's tax rate hike of 34 per cent was, Figure 21 shows Tennessee County population growth over the period 2010 to 2020 and Figure 22 from 2020 to 2021. No other county had anything like Davidson County's tax increase, and you can see how people voted with their feet.

FIGURE 21: TENNESSEE COUNTY POPULATION GROWTH: 2020–21 AVERAGE ANNUAL PERCENTAGE CHANGE

(2010–20, counties include Nashville, Memphis, Chattanooga and Knoxville regions)

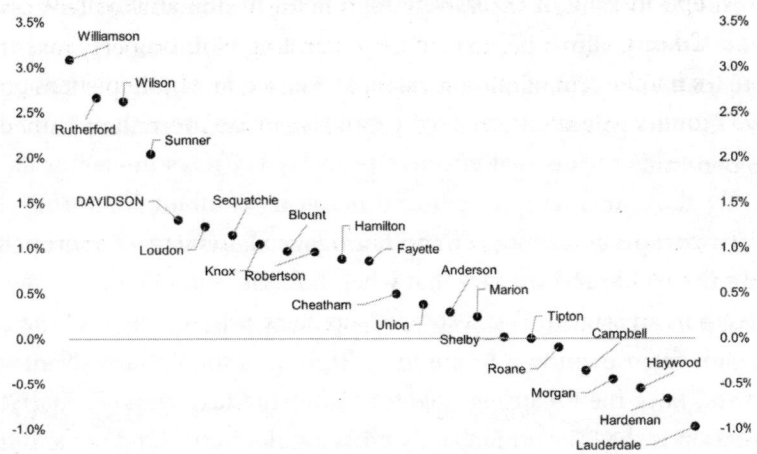

Source: Census Bureau

FIGURE 22: TENNESSEE COUNTY POPULATION GROWTH: 2020–21 PERCENTAGE CHANGE

(2020–21, counties include Nashville, Memphis, Chattanooga and Knoxville regions)

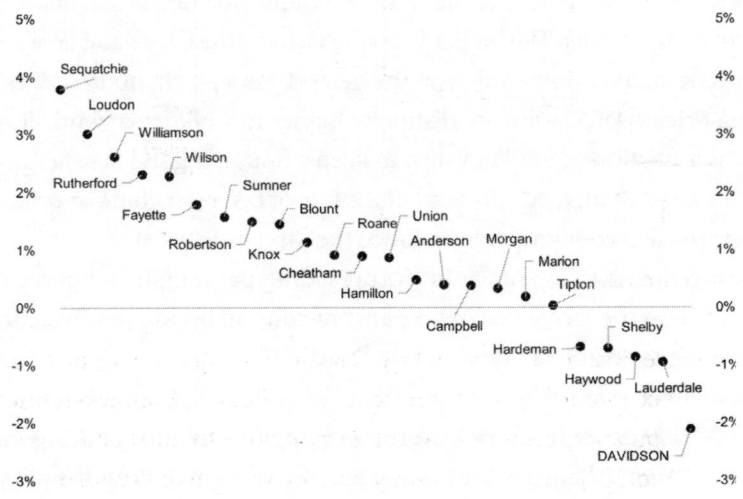

Source: Census Bureau

LOW PROPERTY TAXES MAKE – AND HIGH PROPERTY TAXES BREAK – THE HOMEOWNER FROM CALIFORNIA TO CLEVELAND

The basics of property value calculations explain why California remains so resilient in spite of excessively high taxes in domains outside of the property tax. California's property tax rate is constitutionally fixed at no more than 1 per cent of market value. Moreover, any homeowner's property tax bill, again constitutionally, can rise by no more than 2 per cent per year. This means that effective property tax rates in California are slightly above one-half of 1 per cent per year. Combine California's low effective property tax rate with both unrealised home price appreciation being untaxable and the fact that when the house is sold or transferred at death to an estate it is at a stepped-up basis without any tax. The capital gain from owning a home in California is highly tax-advantaged, and you have the breathing hole for California taxpayers. Property tax limitation is the Californian's holy cross amulet in the land of vampires.

Common bond price formulas reveal the degree to which high property tax rates can drag down the value of a house. A thirty-year coupon bond yielding $50 dollars per year, or 5 per cent of a $1,000 face value bond, would sell for $600 if the after-tax coupon payment were reduced because of a $20, or 2 per cent, tax on the bond's face value. The difference between the Cleveland area tax rates and California tax rates is about that, 2 percentage points. The higher carrying costs in the Cleveland area spell a distinctly smaller home value on the market. As a result, house prices and home price appreciation are distinctly higher in California, while it takes less, as a fraction of market value, to keep a house in good tax standing. It is the way of all finance. The level of the rate of tax, on income or principal, is a prime determinant of the value of the asset.

Just remember, as shown in the preceding paragraph, a 2 percentage point tax on the face value of a 5 per cent coupon bond is equivalent to a 40 per cent income tax on that bond's yield.

Moreover, even when a house is sold, a capital gains tax exclusion of $500,000 at all levels of government applies for most homeowners. The top federal long-term capital gains tax rate (including the applicable Obamacare surtax) is 23.8 per cent, and most states also tax capital gains. If the home becomes the asset of an estate due to the death of the homeowner, the value of that asset is transferred to the inheritors without a capital gains tax (this is known as the 'stepped-up basis'). Home price appreciation is a tax-advantaged form of appreciation.

Consider, for example, when a California couple buys a house for $500,000, lives in it for ten years and sells it for $1 million. There is no capital gains tax. Without the tax law provision, the $500,000 capital gain would have resulted in additional taxes of upwards of $119,000 at the federal level and $65,000 to the state. Initially, when this California house was purchased, the property tax on it was $5,000 per year and at most was about $6,090 per year when sold. In addition to restricting property taxes not ever to exceed 1 per cent of the home's value, Proposition 13 permits the taxable portion of home prices to rise no more than 2 per cent per year if the home does not change owners.

In Cleveland, by contrast, the $350,000 house sold ten years later probably did not appreciate (because of the high property tax obligation), negating the capital gains tax advantage, and the homeowner shelled out a total of over $100,000 in property taxes. Sadly, there is no legal protection for the Cleveland homeowner from annual increases in property taxes. In other words, in Cleveland, the house costs the owner more and yields the owner less. Is it any wonder why that home sells for less?

A wealth gap develops between homeowners in low and high property tax jurisdictions. For retirees, this can be devastating. Retirees in California can continue to live in their home and pay low property taxes, if they so choose. Or they can sell, realise the appreciation in the value of their home and then move elsewhere with far lower living costs, perhaps to Arizona or Florida on the proceeds, all or mostly tax-free. To take this option in Cleveland is another matter entirely. The home price never appreciated, the capital gains exclusion was worthless and annual property taxes dispensed with fat amounts of the homeowner's money (in tax payments that are less federally tax deductible because of the state and local tax 'SALT' deduction cap) that the homeowner otherwise could have saved and invested over the years.

High property tax rates dog those regions of the country whose glory is fading. Or perhaps we should write that high and rising property tax rates infect those regions of the country causing economic senescence and ultimately necrosis. Chicago has property tax rates that are cruising towards 2 per cent. New Jersey's rates are comfortably over 2 per cent. Western Pennsylvania's average is 3.5 per cent, and several cities in Connecticut are over 5 per cent. The national average is just under 1 per cent. In Detroit, the property tax rate is near 3 per cent. Detroit has recently installed an affordable housing programme, even though inexpensive houses priced under $100,000 (about one quarter of the national average) abound in the city. This is a clue indicating that home affordability is not merely about price. Carrying costs, in the form of the property tax, as well as the potential for home value appreciation are decisive in making a home affordable or out of reach.

The higher the property tax rate, the more likely the house will struggle to maintain its market value. The high property tax rate also applies to any and all home improvements. High property taxes incentivise the homeowner not to make improvements, because they too will be taxed at the high rate. The lower the property tax rate, the more houses will attract buyers and bids, and the more they will encourage improvements by their current owners. Home affordability is about far more than home prices. A major factor that can keep home prices low – and, paradoxically, unaffordable as well – is a high property tax rate.

Property taxes on real estate function in just the same way as a general property tax – a wealth tax – would. If wealth faces an annual tax, the extent of that wealth necessarily goes down. As in the above example, if $600,000 in wealth faces a 1 per cent per annum tax, the value of that wealth will fall to $525,000. Property taxes on real estate provide invaluable insight into the temptation *du jour* on the part of governments in many parts of the world today – to address inequality and revenue needs through a wealth tax. Taxes on property in any form reduce the value of that property. The numbers from the markets are clear. Each percentage point of tax on property – or wealth – significantly reduces the real value of that property or wealth.

Wealth taxes reduce prosperity.

The examples of the impact of property taxes within a country with a high degree of mobility show how wealth taxes, if imposed, would be likely to operate. They discourage wealth accumulation, entrepreneurship and economic activity; they encourage capital flight; they rarely generate anywhere near the revenues that had been predicted; and most states that impose them initially remove them eventually. In 1995, twelve OECD economies imposed wealth taxes, but by 2022 only five of them still imposed such a tax.

STATES WITH A DEATH TAX

Here's one reality check as it relates to one form of a wealth tax, i.e. the death tax. In 1976, there was only one state, Nevada, which did not have a state death tax and forty-nine states that did.* Today, the tables have flipped. There are now only seventeen states with a death tax and thirty-three states that don't have death taxes, one of which, California, is listed above as a tax-the-rich state. California had its death tax removed in 1980 by a ballot initiative, not by its legislature. The simple fact is that back in the old days, rich people, in anticipation of meeting their maker, moved lock, stock and barrel to states without a death tax. Unfortunately for the states these rich people abandoned, the rich took their incomes, businesses, employees, investments and purchasing power with them to the no-death-tax states, thus hollowing out those states that clung on to their death taxes. For all of the states except the dumbest, it was a lesson learned.

It is important to understand the impact of death taxes because the UK's inheritance tax is one of the highest in the world and applies at one of the lowest levels of wealth in the world.

The death tax is about as illogical a tax as ever existed. Today in America, you can earn your income and pay your taxes fair and square and as far as the federal government is concerned, it's your money and you can spend those proceeds on gambling, carousing, smoking and drinking as

---

* There were five states that had only a 'pick-up' death tax, which was a credit against the federal death tax.

you will. But if you take those same after-tax savings and bequeath the money to your children or to others, the government will tax you up to 40 per cent. What's with that? It makes no sense. In addition to the lack of logic, the government collects next to nothing from the death tax. Tax revenues from the federal death tax are almost exactly one half of 1 per cent of total tax revenues. Go figure! And that's at the federal level.

The ratio in Figure 23 is the average annual adjusted gross income (AGI) flowing into each state divided by the average AGI leaving the state for both today's seventeen death-tax and thirty-three no-death-tax states. States with no death taxes are attracting higher income earners, while states with death taxes are losing higher income earners. The point here is simply that among all states, death taxes appear to be closely correlated with net out-migration. Surprise, surprise.

FIGURE 23: RATIO OF AVERAGE AGI INTO AND OUT OF DEATH-TAX AND NO-DEATH-TAX STATES

(annual, 1993–2021)

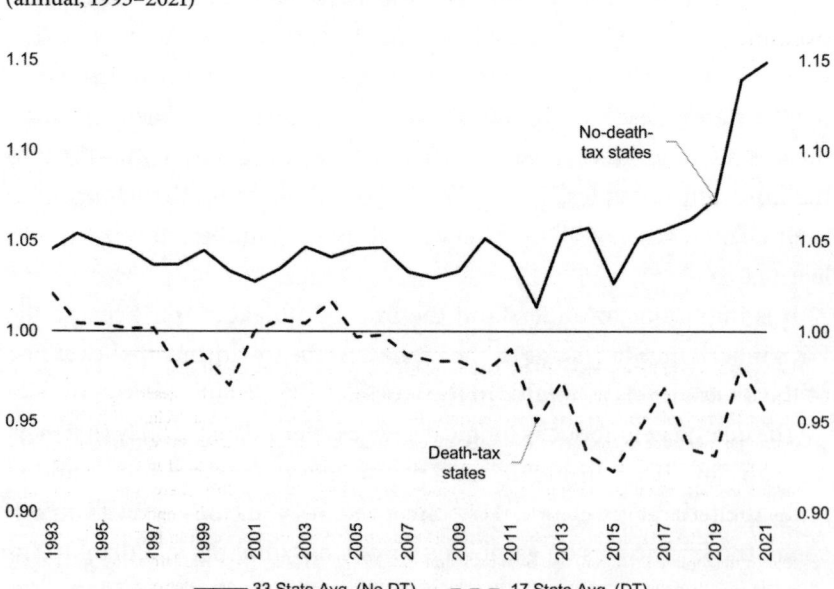

Source: IRS Statistics of Income

FIGURE 24: SIZE OF AVERAGE FEDERAL ESTATE FILED IN TENNESSEE AND FLORIDA[*][†]

(annual 1995–2015)

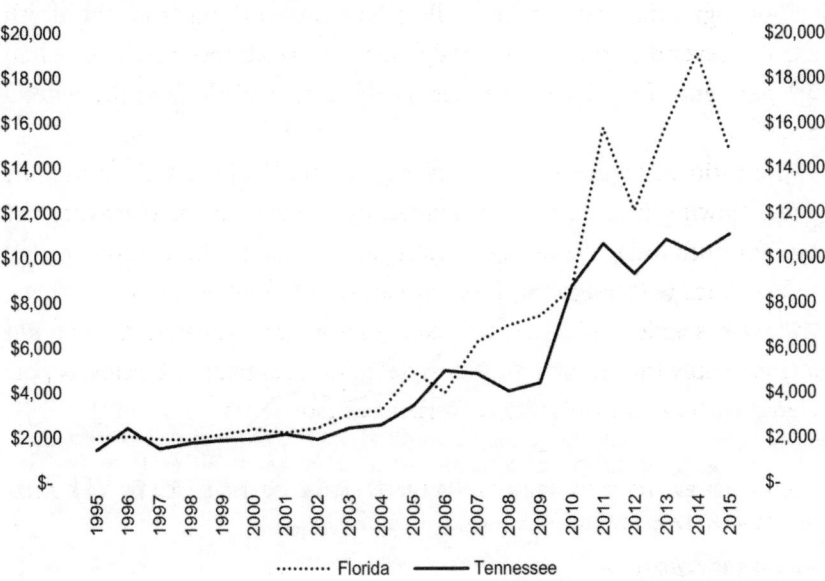

Source: IRS

FIGURE 25: NUMBER OF FEDERAL ESTATES TAX RETURNS FILED PER 100,000 PEOPLE IN TENNESSEE AND FLORIDA*

(annual 1995–2015)

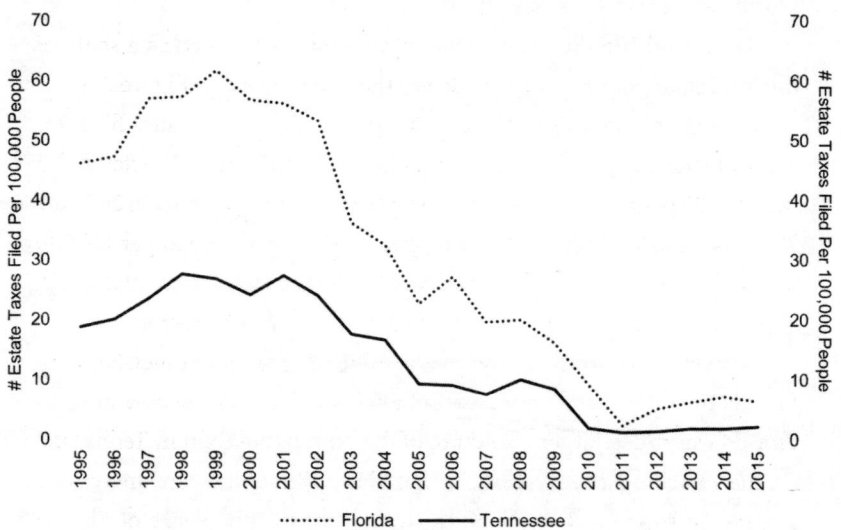

Source: IRS, US Census

TENNESSEE'S EXPERIENCE WITH ITS DEATH TAX

Tennessee is one of the most recent states to abolish its death tax (passed in 2012). But even in Tennessee, the state phased its death tax out over four years. The following passage is a section of our 2011 analysis comparing Tennessee, at the time a death-tax state, with Florida, a no-death-tax state:[34]

> In 1997 the average size of an estate in Tennessee was $1,514,000 and in Florida it was $1,922,000. Florida's average estate was a full 25 per cent higher than Tennessee's. In 2009 Florida's average estate was $7,403,000

---

* The above data are based on federal estate tax data reported to the IRS. Due to changes in the federal estate tax law, the federal estate tax data vary over time. The number of estates reported declines significantly for certain tax years due to changes in the dollar exemption level. The federal estate tax exemption level was $600,000 in 1997, rose in $25,000 increments to $650,000 by 2000, increased to $1 million in 2002, $1.5 million in 2004, $2 million in 2006, $3.5 million in 2009 and $5 million in 2011. There is also a temporary elimination of the estate tax completely in 2010 for those estates that chose this option. The applicable tax rate on federal estates also declined over this entire period from 55 per cent in 1997 to 0 per cent in 2010 (if that option is chosen) and then back up to 35 per cent in 2011. These legislative changes alter the number of estates filed, the total aggregate value of estates filed and the average value of estates filed. These discontinuities are strongest in 2010 when the estate tax was temporarily eliminated, which is why we do not include 2010 data in the analysis.

and in Tennessee it was $4,442,000. In 2009 Florida's average estate was almost 75 per cent larger than Tennessee's [Figure 24]. The wealthiest most productive people in anticipation of an estate tax event move to Florida and leave Tennessee.

The second IRS data series, the number of estates filed as a share of the total state population, only drives the nail in deeper [Figure 25].

In 1997 in Tennessee there were on average 24 estates filed for every 100,000 people. In that same year in Florida there were 57 estates filed per 100,000 people – well more than double the Tennessee rate. In 2009 the Tennessee estate filing rate had dropped to eight estates filed per 100,000 of population (federal tax laws had changed on filing requirements) and in Florida there were sixteen estates filed per 100,000 of population.

To reiterate, not only was the average federal estate size much larger in Florida than it was in Tennessee, but also the number of people filing in Florida was much larger as a share of the population than in Tennessee.

The shocking observation is that these differences are increasing sharply. In the two charts [above], we have the average size of Florida and Tennessee's estates from 1997 through 2009 and the number of filers per 100,000 of population in each state.

People really did move as a result of Tennessee's gift and estate tax.

ADOPTING VS NOT ADOPTING STATE INCOME TAXES: THE EVIDENCE IS OVERWHELMING

Previously pointed out in Chapter 1, the United States has, whether intentionally or not, conducted a remarkably clean economic experiment on the effects of state income taxation. In 1960, nearly 40 per cent of states, nineteen in total, did not levy a personal income tax, while the remaining thirty-one did. Over the following decades, eleven of the original no-income-tax states introduced one, while eight held firm and continue to operate without one. Alaska, uniquely, eliminated its income tax in 1980 after previously having one. This staggered pattern of adoption created an unusually well-controlled opportunity to observe how income tax policy shapes long-term economic outcomes across diverse regions and populations.

The results of this real-world trial have been nothing short of striking.

Over time, the states that resisted implementing an income tax have dramatically outperformed those that adopted one, across nearly every key economic indicator such as GDP growth, population gains, income levels and overall fiscal health. In contrast, the adopting states, particularly those that implemented income taxes between the 1960s and early 1990s, have seen their share of national economic output and influence decline markedly. What began as a difference in tax structure has become a difference in trajectory.

In stark contrast, the nine states that maintained their zero-income-tax status, later joined by Alaska in 1980, have captured a growing share of the national economy across all major metrics. States that have avoided implementing a personal income tax have emerged as clear leaders in the key drivers of economic growth. Their population, employment, personal income and gross state product have all grown at impressive rates, reinforcing their consistent resistance to adding an income tax.

One of the most striking data points from the available comparisons concerns tax revenue at the state and local levels. States that expanded their tax systems to include an income tax have experienced disappointing results in terms of revenue growth. Meanwhile, the states that refrained from adding this additional tax layer have seen strong gains in tax collections. The pattern is clear: those that stayed out of the income tax game have generated revenue far more effectively than those that joined it.

The stories of the states that adopted an income tax run the gamut from the disappointing to the truly pathetic. The first state to move was West Virginia. Long among the poorest states in the union, it cemented this status by adopting an income tax in 1961. Every state within the fabled 'Rust Belt' – the string of states from the brownfields of New Jersey to the shores of Lake Michigan – adopted an income tax from 1963–76. Industrial and other businesses that had been ploughing capital investment into this previously dominant industrial era exited en masse. The state of Ohio, for example, regularly complains that its industrial glory was in the past. Indeed, it was. In 1970, Ohio had a zero income tax. In 1983, its top rate was 9 per cent. Businesses withdrew investment from the state like they were pitching valuables out of a house engulfed in flames.

Another losing element of this story is that when it rains it pours.

Basically all of the states that adopted an income tax after 1960 ended up adopting additional forms of taxation – because the adoption of the income tax proved an abject failure. Sales and particularly property tax rates have soared in the states that adopted an income tax after 1960. New Jersey is a particularly backward example. Lacking both a sales and income tax as of 1965, and at that point about the fastest growing state in the nation, it adopted a sales tax in 1966. Revenues came in so much lower than expected, it took on an income tax in 1976. Now the place is about the highest tax state in the nation, haemorrhaging population and business to low-tax (and zero-income-tax) climes such as Florida.

There was, without question, a better path. Washington State, which never implemented an income tax, became a magnet for the entrepreneurial energy that defined the modern economy, giving rise to companies like Microsoft, Amazon and Starbucks. Nevada drew in people and wealth from neighbouring California. Texas continues to rival California as the likely future leader in both population and productivity. Florida surpassed New York some time ago as the most populous and economically productive state on the East Coast. New Hampshire consistently leads New England in economic growth, and Tennessee stands out as a hub of high productivity in the Midwest and Upper South.

This natural experiment could hardly have been more well constructed. States that adopted income taxes struggled across nearly every economic measure and often resorted to adding even more taxes in response. States that avoided income taxes saw their economies thrive and their public revenues rise without the added burden on income.

INTERNATIONAL EVIDENCE ABOUT TAX, SPENDING AND GROWTH

This section looks at the international evidence about different levels of taxation or government spending on growth.

It starts with an examination of all the transition economies[*] that

---

[*] The transition economies are all those economies that had previously been communist and moved towards forms of democracy (not always fully) after the late 1980s.

moved from communism to democracy after the fall of the Berlin Wall in 1989. It then looks at the impact of past major tax changes in the UK. Finally, it considers the international evidence on tax and growth.

THE TRANSITION ECONOMIES

It is rarely possible in the real world to disentangle economic influences as one might in a laboratory to perform real-life experiments. But the end of communism in many Central and Eastern European and some Asian economies around 1990 is about as close as economics gets to a laboratory test of the impact of different economic policies.

It is surprising that so few economists have interrogated the data of the transition economies to learn what it shows about the performance of comparative economic systems. Most of the highly cited papers on transition are from 1990–2000 with just a few a little later. None easily available examine the longer period to see what the data shows. Yet this data is a treasure trove for the real-life experience of comparative economic systems emerging from a fairly similar starting point.

There is little reliable data on the size of government spending in relation to the economy in pre-transition times. But most evidence suggests that it was at least 50 per cent even just accounting for the prices paid for resources consumed – e.g. nuclear scientists were accounted for at their wages which were typically below most market valuations of their value.

According to defence analyst Julian Cooper,[35] military spending in the USSR was equal to 16.6 per cent of the gross national product (GNP) in 1987. This gives an indication of the misallocation of resources and would be consistent with very high levels of government expenditure as a share of GDP. In a state-controlled system, formal taxes are not the only way in which government spending is paid for, since prices for goods can be set at levels generating surpluses over cost which count as government revenues.

Post-communism, approaches have varied between low-tax states like Turkmenistan, Armenia, Tajikistan, Georgia and Kazakhstan and much higher tax states like Hungary, Slovenia, Croatia and Bosnia. In between are the Baltic states, many of which have reformed their tax structures but still have relatively high overall tax rates.

The evidence is especially relevant because many of the transition economies tried different approaches to taxation, including flat taxes.

The comparison of growth and tax policy for all the transition economies is shown in Table 6. Those with the tax share below 30 per cent of GDP in 2000–2025 have grown GDP per capita at an annual rate of 5 per cent from 2000–2025; those with the tax share between 30 per cent and 40 per cent have grown by 4 per cent, while those with a tax share above 40 per cent have grown by 3 per cent.

TABLE 6: ECONOMIC GROWTH VS TAX SHARE, ALL TRANSITION ECONOMIES

Country	Average Tax Rate 2000–2025	Real GDP Per Capita Growth 2000–2025
Turkmenistan	11.6%	5.2%
Kazakhstan	19.2	4.2
Armenia	24.9	6.3
Uzbekistan	25.2	4.6
Georgia	26.5	6.4
Albania	27.1	4.5
Tajikistan	27.4	5.4
Kosovo	28.5	3.6
Romania	30.7	4.2
North Macedonia	30.9	2.9
Kyrgyz Republic	32.9	2.9
Moldova	33.2	4.4
Mongolia	34.4	4.5
Russia	35.2	3.0
Bulgaria	35.2	4.2
Lithuania	36.4	4.6
Latvia	40.1	4.1
Czech Republic	40.4	2.0
Serbia	40.4	3.8
Estonia	40.4	2.8
Slovak Republic	41.1	3.2
Poland	41.9	3.7
Hungary	42.3	2.5
Slovenia	44.8	2.0
Ukraine	45.7	2.3
Croatia	45.9	2.9

Source: Data from IMF World Economic Outlook Database April 2025

Average tax rate 2000–25 (tax receipts as a percentage of GDP); real GDP growth 2000–25 (annual percentage)

We have deliberately excluded the period from 1990–2000 where growth was highly variable and the data questionable; by 2000, most economies had 'settled down' to something approximating to steady state performance.

These economies eventually broke into twenty-eight transition economies. For Montenegro, we have excluded the economy from the sample because of lack of data.

Regression analysis shows a powerful influence – a 10 per cent reduction in the tax burden boosts annual GDP growth by close to 1 per cent.

The conclusion is backed by a very detailed econometric study of the impact of tax policy on inward investment in transition economies. This study concludes:[36]

> We show that, although tax policy seems an important determinant of FDI [foreign direct investment], its effects seem to be conditional on the level of technological development. Given these findings, reducing corporate income tax may be considered an effective tool in promoting FDI, which seems to be of particular importance for less developed transition economies.

The performance of the former East Germany[37] post-unification also provides potent evidence of how high taxes and Western-style regulation can hold back an economy. German unification gave the former East Germany a Western European level of tax and regulation, though the transition was cushioned by massive fiscal transfers. The scale of these was measured at 6.5 per cent of the GDP of West Germany.[38]

At the time of unification, it is conventionally estimated that the East German GDP was 16.9 per cent of West German GDP,[39] so this implies fiscal transfers of about 39 per cent of East German GDP.

Although initially the transfers boosted East German growth and productivity, the effect appears to have worn off since 2000, after which point, according to one of the more thorough studies of the impact of unification, both GDP per capita and the share of population in the East have stagnated relative to the West[40] and GDP growth has stayed down around 1 per cent[41] over the period 2000–25 compared with the much faster growth in the other transition economies.

The experience of the transition economies is very powerful evidence about the scale by which high taxes and high government spending suppress growth.

The experience is also relevant because so many of the transition economies moved to a flat tax or at least low rates of tax.

THE UK'S EXPERIENCE

By far the most thorough investigation of the UK evidence on the relationship between tax changes and growth is a paper by James Cloyne.[42] He uses the framework set out by Christina and David Romer,[43] whose approach identifies 'exogenous' tax charges and separates them out from 'endogenous' tax changes forced on governments by external circumstances. In this way, Cloyne is able to estimate the full impact of tax changes on the economy after removing the 'noise' from external events.

He analyses 2,500 tax changes in the UK to identify tax rises and cuts that are not endogenous 'actions to manage demand, to stimulate production, to offset a debt crisis and those to fund spending decisions'. This gives him a series of 'exogenous' tax changes – 'actions to improve long-run economic performance, ideological changes related to party political or social causes, rulings from external bodies such as courts, and fiscal consolidation measures based on long-run considerations'.

He covers all the exogenous fiscal actions of the Thatcher, Major, Blair and Brown governments in his series.

He concludes:

I find that a 1 per cent cut in taxes stimulates GDP by 0.6 per cent on impact and by 2.5 per cent over three years. These findings are remarkably similar to the corresponding estimates for the United States. The results reinforce the view that tax changes do indeed have powerful, persistent and significant effects on the economy.

The tax changes that are largely not covered in the Cloyne analysis are the introduction of the additional rate of tax at 50 per cent in 2009–10 and the reduction in this rate from 50 per cent to 45 per cent in 2013.

His Majesty's Revenue and Customs (HMRC) and the Office for Budget Responsibility (OBR) have analysed the former tax increase and concluded that 'the estimated underlying yield for 2012–13 from the introduction of the 50p tax rate was also reduced from £2.6 billion to £0.6 billion'.[44] So, in fact, the underlying (this is important, because the rise was announced some time in advance, creating the option to shift income forward to avoid it) yield turns out to have been negligible at only 23 per cent of the initial estimate. Analysis by the consultancy Cebr[45] shows that the revenue from high rates of tax tends to drop over time, so if even the initial revenue from the tax is negligible, it seems likely that this tax will over time have led to a reduction in revenue.

The Cebr report concluded:

Higher rates of Value Added Tax and National Insurance Contributions mean that the revenue maximising rate of Income Tax for the very rich has fallen over the past year. Combined with increased labour and capital mobility, this means the revenue maximising top rate of Income Tax is likely to be less than 40 per cent.

The cut in the additional rate of tax from 50 per cent to 45 per cent has been claimed to have brought in £8 billion in additional revenues. The data supports this but should be treated cautiously since announcement effects meant that incomes were deferred from being taxable at 50 per cent to being taxable at 45 per cent. But even Paul Johnson of the Institute for Fiscal Studies (IFS) admitted that the underlying cost in revenues from cutting the rate would be negligible if it existed at all,[46] while the Cebr analysis quoted above suggests an increase in underlying revenues from the tax reduction.

The UK experience provides powerful evidence not only that the Laffer curve works in the UK but that the UK has roughly the same elasticities as in the US.

EVIDENCE FROM AROUND THE WORLD

The seminal work suggesting that high levels of government (current) spending hinder economic growth was by Robert Barro in 1991.[47]

His study showed that 'for 98 countries in the period 1960–1985, the growth rate of real per capita GDP is positively related to initial human capital (proxied by 1960 school-enrolment rates) and negatively related to the initial (1960) level of real per capita GDP'. Barro concluded:

> Countries with higher human capital also have lower fertility rates and higher ratios of physical investment to GDP. Growth is inversely related to the share of government consumption in GDP, but insignificantly related to the share of public investment. Growth rates are positively related to measures of political stability and inversely related to a proxy for market distortions.

There is also an interesting concept called the Scully curve.[48] This is like the Laffer curve but relates directly to public spending.

What it says is that there is a quadratic relationship between economic growth and public spending as a share of the economy. Economic growth varies positively with the share of public spending and negatively with the square of public spending. This gives a curve where initially growth rises with higher public spending but as the quadratic term starts to dominate, the relationship between growth and public spending first levels out and then shows lower growth for higher public spending.

When public spending is too low, the economy lacks the infrastructural support to grow strongly. When it is too high, public spending crowds out the entrepreneurial sector and causes taxes to be so high that they destroy incentives.

The latest estimates of the Scully curve from the Fraser Institute in Canada show that the difference between public spending at 25 per cent of GDP as in much of Asia and 45 per cent as in the UK can be the difference between GDP growth at 1.5 per cent per capita per annum and growth at 3 per cent.[49]

The analysis of public spending and growth has developed more dimensions since the initial work. In general, the latest research suggests that educational spending can boost growth and that infrastructural spending at least does not hinder growth but that other areas of public spending remain generally negative for growth. Spending on welfare in particular appears to reduce growth both through the public spending mechanism and more directly through affecting the labour supply.

And research confirms that the damage to growth from public spending rising as a share of GDP grows substantially as the share rises from 40 per cent. We have put together Table 7 showing the results of various relevant studies.[50]

TABLE 7: STUDIES OF TAXES, SPENDING AND GROWTH[51]

Author	Data coverage	Main explanatory variables	Comment
Barro (1991)[52]	Ninety-eight countries in the period 1960–85	Human capital, government consumption, political instability indicator, price distortion	1 percentage point increase in tax-to-GDP ratio lowers output per worker by 0.12 per cent
Koester and Kormendi (1989)[53]	Sixty-three countries for which at least five years of continuous data exists for the 1970s	Marginal tax rates, average tax rate, mean growth in labour force and population	10 per cent decrease in marginal tax rates would increase per capita income in an average industrial country by more than 7 per cent
Hansson and Henrekson (1994)[54]	Industry-level data for fourteen OECD countries	Government transfers, consumption, total outlays, education expenditure and government investment	Government transfers, consumption and total outlays have a negative impact on growth while government investment is not significant
Cashin (1995)[55]	Twenty-three OECD countries over the 1971–88 period	Ratio of public investment to GDP, ratio of current taxation revenue to GDP, ratio of expenditure on transfers to GDP	1 percentage point in tax-to-GDP ratio reduces output per worker by 2 per cent
Engen and Skinner (1996)[56]	US modelling together with a sample of OECD countries	Marginal tax rates, human capital, investment	2.5 per cent rise in tax-to-GDP ratio reduces GDP *growth* by 0.2–0.3 per cent
OECD (Leibfritz et al.) 1997[57]	OECD countries over the 1965–95 period	Tax-to-GDP ratio, physical and human capital formation, labour supply	Ten-point increase in tax-to-GDP ratio reduces GDP *growth* by 0.5–1 per cent

Alesina et al. (2002)[58]	Eighteen OECD countries over the 1960–94 period	Primary spending, labour taxes, transfers, government wage consumption, indirect taxes (all as shares of GDP)	1 per cent increase in government spending relative to GDP lowers the investment-to-GDP ratio by 0.15 per cent and a cumulative fall of 0.74 per cent after five years
Bleaney et al. (2000)[59]	Seventeen OECD countries over the 1970–94 period	Distortionary tax, productive expenditure, net lending labour force growth, investment ratio	1 per cent increase in distortionary tax revenue reduces GDP *growth* by 0.4 percentage points
Folster and Henrekson (2000)[60]	Sample of rich OECD/ non-OECD countries over 1970–95 period	Tax to GDP, government expenditure to GDP, investment to GDP, labour force growth, investment ratio	Ten-point increase in tax-to-GDP ratio reduces GDP *growth* by 1 per cent
Bassanini and Scarpetta (2001)[61]	Twenty-one OECD countries over the 1971–98 period	Indicators of government size and financing, physical capital, human capital, population growth	1 percentage point increase in tax-to-GDP ratio reduces per capita output levels by 0.3–0.6 per cent
Karel Mertens and José Luis Montiel Olea (2018)[62]	Individual income tax changes from 1946–2012	Positive	1 percentage point decrease in the tax rate increases real GDP by 0.78 per cent
Owen Zidar (2019)[63]	Federal income tax changes across different states and income groups from 1950–2011	Positive, but no effect for tax cuts on top 10 per cent earners	A 1 per cent of state GDP tax cut for bottom 90 per cent of earners increases real GDP by 6.6 per cent
Alexander Ljungqvist and Michael Smolyansky (2018)[64]	State corporate tax changes from 1970–2010	Positive, strongest effect during recessions	1 percentage point cut in the corporate tax rate increases employment by 0.2 per cent and wages by 0.3 per cent
Gunter et al. (2019)[65]	Value added tax changes in fifty-one countries from 1970–2014	Positive, stronger effects when initial tax rate is very high	Estimates a tax multiplier of -3.6 for European industrialised countries
Nguyen et al. (2021)[66]	Income and consumption tax changes in the UK from 1973–2009	Positive, strongest for income tax cuts	1 percentage point cut in the average income tax rate raises GDP by 0.78 per cent
Cloyne et al. (2018)[67]	Variety of tax changes in the UK from 1918–1939	Positive	1 percentage point tax cut increases GDP by 2 per cent
Nazila Alinaghi and W. Robert Reed (2021)[68]	Meta-analysis of forty-nine studies of OECD countries on tax changes and economic growth	Positive, but depends on combination of taxes and spending, and which taxes are cut	A 10 per cent decrease in distortionary taxes or taxes that fund unproductive investments increases GDP *growth* by 0.2 per cent

In this section, we incorporate information from Jon Moynihan's impressive and recently published two-volume analysis *Return to Growth*.[69]

Chart 2.46 of *Return to Growth Volume One*[70] shows the correlation between lower tax and higher growth. It provides evidence from a wide sample about how lower taxes are associated with higher growth.

An important set of work that became known as the 'Barro growth regressions' has been widely used to investigate policy effects since Barro's 1991 work.[71] These take the form of a regression of either GDP growth or productivity growth on initial income (to control for convergence or 'catch-up'), some factors to account for other influences and a variable measuring the policy factor under investigation. Models of this type are often estimated in a panel of cross-country and time-series data with observations averaged over five-year periods to smooth out the impact of the business cycle. Barro used data for ninety-eight countries between 1960 and 1985.

G. Leach[72] and the Organisation for Economic Co-operation and Development (OECD)[73] document the empirical literature on the effects of taxation on growth and output levels. Table 7 sets out a selection of the major studies, noting their data set, the explanatory variables used and the main effects of tax on growth that are found. All control for various factors other than taxation (usually different variables across different studies). Some of these studies use tax as the explanatory variable and others use government spending.

In theory, the latter is preferable because government spending measures the total claim on the economic resources of government. Barro did, in fact, consider that some government spending might have a positive impact on growth.

He believed that there may be a positive effect of education spending on human capital formation and therefore on growth and takes that into account. As such, he examined the impact of real government consumption net of spending on both education and defence as a percentage of real GDP over the period 1970–85 on both real economic growth (averaged over the period 1960–85) and on private investment. He found a negative correlation between net government spending (so defined) and growth.

Reinhard Koester and Roger Kormendi[74] examined the effect of measures of the marginal and average tax rates, as well as population and labour force growth on economic growth. In a cross-country analysis for the 1970s, they found a significant negative effect of marginal tax rates on the level of real GDP per capita but not on the rate of growth when this was controlled for the initial level of income. They suggested that, holding average tax rates constant, a 10 percentage point decrease in marginal tax rates would increase per capita income in an average in-dustrial country by more than 7 per cent (and in an average developing country by more than 15 per cent). Thus, a revenue-neutral tax reform which reduced tax progressivity would raise incomes.

Alberto Alesina et al.[75] focused on the extent of government spending of various sorts on the investment-to-GDP ratio (and hence by impli-cation on growth). They concluded that, via the effect of raising private sector labour costs, a 1 percentage point increase in government spend-ing relative to GDP resulted in a decrease in the investment-to-GDP ratio of 0.15 percentage points and a cumulative fall of 0.74 percentage points after five years. In general, these studies, with their varying meth-odologies, find that there are measurable negative effects of higher tax rates on growth.

The order of magnitude of this effect was estimated to be around 0.5–1 per cent for a 10 per cent rise in the ratio of taxation (or government spending) to GDP.

The OECD's own conclusion[76] from its survey was as follows:

A number of studies, influenced by the new growth theories, have taken a top-down approach to assess the impact of taxes on per capita income and growth at the macro level. Several of them purport to demonstrate a significant negative relationship between the level of the tax/GDP ratio (or the government expenditure ratio) and the growth rate of GDP per capita, implying that high tax rates reduce economic growth …

Our estimates [using a top-down cross-country regression] suggest that the increase in the average (weighted) tax rate of about 10 per-centage points over the past 35 years, may have reduced OECD annual growth rates by about 0.5 percentage points.

The OECD study suggested that a 10 percentage point cut in the tax-to-GDP ratio could increase economic growth by 0.5 to 1 percentage points. Thus they also argued that 'up to one third of the growth deceleration in the OECD [over the 1965–95 period] would be explained by higher taxes. In some European countries, tax burdens increased much more dramatically than the OECD average, which would imply correspondingly larger effects on their growth rates.'

Taken together, all these studies seem to show that subsidies and government current expenditure other than on education have the worst negative effects on growth on the spending side. Overall, the tax (or government spending) and growth studies indicate a strong association between the two variables.

As a rule of thumb, the conclusion of the studies is that it would appear that a 10 percentage point fall in the share of national income taken in tax would lead to around a 1 percentage point increase in the growth rate – results of this order of magnitude occur over and over again. It's worth remembering that an additional 1 percentage point per annum of GDP growth leaves GDP 10.4 per cent higher after ten years and 28.2 per cent higher after twenty-five years.

The analysis of the Scully curve suggests that the growth-maximising average spending ratio is 17.5–22.5 per cent of national income and the welfare-maximising point is 27.5–32.5 per cent of national income. Broadly, the model suggests that a cut in government spending to the welfare-maximising point from current levels might imply a rise in the economic growth rate by around 1 percentage point; and a cut to the growth-maximising point would imply a rise in the economic growth rate by a further 0.8 percentage points. These are clearly orders of magnitude and the effects of cutting government spending are unlikely to be a simple linear function of the extent of the cut. However, there is a lot of evidence from different sources that points towards figures of this order.

Nazila Alinaghi and W. Robert Reed[77] have conducted a meta-analysis on the effects of taxes on growth for OECD countries. Their sample includes 979 estimates from forty-nine studies. Unlike other papers discussed in this review, this paper considers both the effects of taxes and spending on growth. The authors disaggregate policy changes into three categories: tax-negative fiscal policies, tax-positive fiscal policies and tax-ambiguous fiscal policies. Tax-negative fiscal policies include increases to fund unproductive investments or increases in distortionary taxes combined with a decrease in non-distortionary taxes. Tax-positive fiscal policies include tax increases to fund productive investment, decreases in distortionary taxation combined with increases in non-distortionary taxation, or tax increases to reduce the deficit. Tax-ambiguous fiscal policies are those where the overall economic effect is unclear. Using these classifications, the authors find a 10 per cent decrease in taxes of a tax-negative fiscal package increases GDP growth by 0.2 per cent. The same-sized tax increase for tax-positive fiscal policies reduces GDP growth by 0.2 per cent.

CONCLUSION

The evidence about tax, spending and growth around the world, in the US and in different states and localities in the US is substantial – it shows that incentives work.

Moreover, this evidence is historic. The data from within the US, which shows an even stronger impact of incentives, gives an indication of the likely increase in the effect of this relationship in an increasingly mobile world.

Looking forward, incentives are likely to become an even more relevant part of economics.

CHAPTER 4

THE SECOND KINGDOM: GOVERNMENT SPENDING

'In effect, government expenditure is the expenditure that we are forced to make on our own behalf, rather than choose to make on our own behalf. The less we choose, the less value that's created, because the harder it is for the money to go to where it's actually needed.'
– LORD WOLFSON OF ASPLEY GUISE

As we pointed out above, the microeconomics of government spending is simple:

Government spending should be limited, as best as is possible, to providing products and services that government alone produces more efficiently than the private sector. These categories frequently include the judiciary, military, police, highways, schools and some other highly specialised activities. The role government plays in how it spends its revenues is central to prosperity. A government that is too small will definitely hold back prosperity, as will a government that is too large.

The correct size of government should occur at that point where the benefits of the next pound spent is just above the damage done by the next pound collected in taxes.

The Keynesian economic arithmetic where the components of spending add up to GDP might make it appear intuitively probable that government spending boosts GDP: $Y = C + I + G + X - M$ (Y = GDP; C, I,

G, X and M are consumption, investment, government non-investment spending, exports and imports).

The macroeconomics is less simple. Sometimes government spending boosts GDP but surprisingly often it does not. To understand why, consider the example of post-Second World War spending below.

DOES GOVERNMENT SPENDING BOOST GDP?

There are examples of government spending being associated with boosting growth – for example, during the First World War and the Second World War and cuts in spending being associated with depressed growth (e.g. the end of the First World War). But it is not always the case.

Specifically, was the massive increase in defence spending at the outset of the Second World War and the subsequent expansion of the US economy proof positive of the validity of the Keynesian stimulus framework, or was the massive decline in defence spending immediately after the Second World War and the absence of a depression proof positive of the failure of Keynesian economics?

In other words, if defence spending stimulated the wartime boom from 1941 on, then why didn't the end of defence spending in 1946 cause an equivalent post-war depression? It is not a stimulus when it replaces resources from transfer payers to transfer recipients, as transfers do. Many economists thought the withdrawal of defence spending at the end of the Second World War would cause a depression, though the fact that consumption had been held back during the war might have caused some to be cautious about such a prediction.

The answer to the stimulus question – based on supply-side economics – rests quite simply on how government spends what it spends and the meaning of boom and bust. The secret to finding the answer lies in aggregate 'income effects' of government policies and not on some magic multiplier.

Keynesian economics doesn't fare well during the Second World

War and after. And equally as important, monetary theory has not a clue when it comes to describing the changes in output, income and employment surrounding the Second World War. As reported in his blog, Chicago economist John Cochrane described a 1946 episode when Keynesian economists were caught flat-footed because the US economy hadn't collapsed, as they thought it would, in the wake of post-war budget cuts and the removal of so much 'stimulus'.[1] The lesson that many Keynesian economists took away from the first several years of the Second World War era was that government spending was 'stimulative'. Therefore, when that spending was withdrawn at war's end, the Keynesian economists quite naturally thought the economy would collapse. It didn't, although measured GDP did fall by 11 per cent in 1946 as defence spending fell, private sector GDP rose by 7 per cent in that year and the unemployment rate stayed well below 5 per cent throughout the second half of the 1940s.[2]

In 1946, writing in the *Journal of Political Economy*, Professor Larry Klein discussed the failed forecasts from the year before:

> We all recall clearly the headlines in last autumn's press, declaring that 'Government economists predict 8 million unemployed by 1946' ... We now find ourselves in the first half of 1946 with about three million unemployed and facing one of the greatest inflationary pressures that we have ever experienced. The economists who were warning us of a deflationary danger during the early months of the postwar transition period should have been stressing precisely opposite economic policy.[3]

With the benefit of our supply-side fiscal framework, we can explain why government economists in 1945 went awry when they warned of a renewed depression.[4] As the war ended, American workers saw productivity jump in terms of real consumption per man-hour and, hence, their incomes rose. This is the (positive) 'income effect' referred to in Chapter 3. Because the government financed wartime defence spending primarily by government debt and not taxes, Second World War workers had a lot of net assets with which to purchase goods and services after the war without having to work. In other words, those with lots of wartime-issued debt were able to acquire goods and services without working or working less.

For the same amount of effort, the workers also could enjoy a much larger flow of private sector output – increased rewards accruing to a given input of labour hours than they could enjoy during the war – even though total GDP fell. Workers, in 1946, spent their incomes and assets enjoying a larger flow of conventional goods and services (e.g. higher private sector output or non-defence GDP), as well as partaking in more leisure (this was a true peacetime dividend). It was a win-win for one and all. The real take-home wage of the average American worker soared. This is consistent with the official measurements, which show that total GDP dropped while private GDP took off like a rocket. Interestingly, UK GDP didn't even fall in 1946, though the scale of the cutbacks in public spending in that year was less than that for the US.

An example is by French economist Léon Walras. His point is that if the price of apples rises, apple growers will be wealthier, they will have higher incomes and they will spend more on goods and services. But if the price of apples rises, apple consumers will be poorer, their incomes will be lower and they will spend less. The income effects for apple growers and apple consumers literally offset each other to the 5,676th decimal place, by the hour, by the day, by the week, by the month and by the year. It's basic maths and accounting. There are no lag effects where one group happens to respond faster than another. It just doesn't happen that way.

In fact, in 1946, workers took the opportunity to renegotiate their employment contracts with employers. As a result, 1946 was the all-time record year in the US for work stoppages as a share of man-hours worked (see Figure 26).* Again, this was a direct consequence of the reduction in overall taxation via the reduction in defence spending: increased consumption and more leisure. Remember, government spending is taxation!

---

* The numbers plotted in this chart are the square of days idle as a percentage of estimated working days because our statistical scoring model described later uses ordinary least squares to estimate coefficients.

FIGURE 26: WORK STOPPAGES: DAYS IDLE AS A PER CENT OF ESTIMATED
WORKING DAYS IN THE UNITED STATES

(annual, percentage points, work stoppages from 1927 to 1948 include any number of
workers, 1948 onwards it includes only stoppages involving 1,000 or more workers)

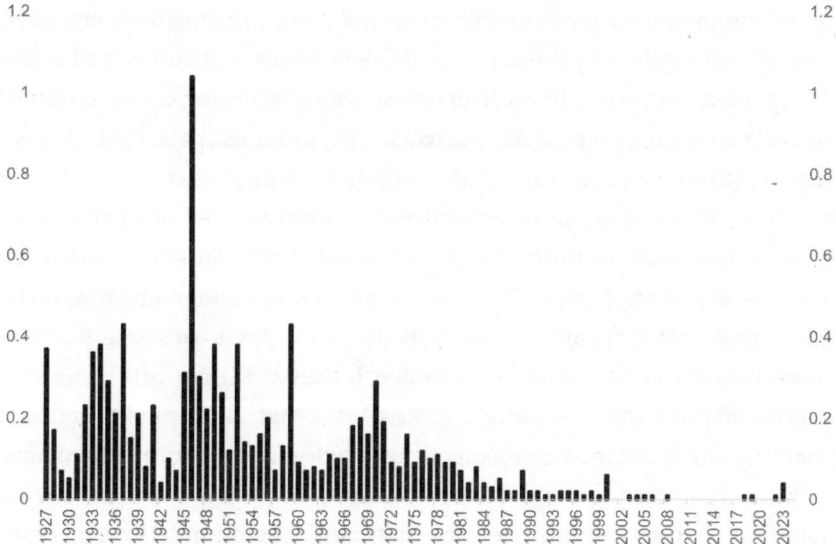

Source: Historical Statistics of the United States, US Bureau of Labor Statistics

FRAMEWORK FOR EXPENDITURE POLICY

In outlining our framework for understanding fiscal policy, as it applied
in and around the Second World War, we focus on five broad conceptual
categories. The first four relate to spending. They include discussions
and the effects of: i) nationalised government enterprises; ii) transfer
payments; iii) public goods; and iv) stimulus goods. We will review the
income and substitution effects associated with each. Lastly, we will discuss v) the role of deficit financing and taxes and their impact on both
the value of output and its timing. We will show that higher spending
will tend to lead to higher taxes and reduced prosperity.

Shall we begin?[5]

THE FIRST CATEGORY OF GOVERNMENT SPENDING: NATIONALISED ENTERPRISES

The first category of government spending, which we will soon set aside for the reasons set forth herein, consists of nationalised enterprises, where the government is the explicit owner of the means of production. In this capacity, the government, as would any other business, employs labour and capital to produce conventional goods and services that the government in turn sells to consumers. Familiar examples in Western democracies include post offices, toll roads, water utilities, rubbish collection, sewage, railways and state-operated liquor stores.

After the war, communist countries had virtually all of their industries nationalised. In the first half of the twentieth century, economists such as Friedrich Hayek, Paul Baran and Oskar Lange engaged in a great debate over the *efficiency* of private versus public ownership of the means of production. From our vantage, however, the important macroeconomic point for nationalised industries is that, conceptually at least, there are no direct income or substitution effects when government acts as a business owner, employer and vendor. Spending and revenues at state-run business enterprises are methodologically no different than spending and revenues at private companies. As important as this category may be to both microeconomic theory and world history, it will play no further role in our discussion of the cyclical and secular nature of government spending in the economy. This topic is far more important when we discuss privatisation.

Save for ordinary business 'spending' at state-run enterprises, all other government spending is always taxation.

The entity being taxed does not receive an equivalent *quid* for its *quo*, and the recipients of the spending get paid with other people's money. Every bit of government spending is taken from someone without compensation. Government reallocates income; it doesn't create income. Whenever government spends, it redirects real resources (i.e. as opposed to nominal) away from the people who produced those resources to people who did not produce those resources. Whether the spending is financed by taxation, the hidden taxes of regulation and inflation or through government borrowing, workers and producers foot the bill. In the case of government spending financed by debt, there is an explicit intertemporal* component of who foots the bill.

If an economy produces 100 apples and the government takes ten of those apples for whatever purpose other than to pay the workers who produced those ten apples, the workers and producers who produced the 100 apples receive only ninety apples. It's as simple as that. Government does not create resources.

THE SECOND CATEGORY OF GOVERNMENT SPENDING: TRANSFER PAYMENTS

The second category of government spending includes all transfer payments, where the government redirects resources to people based on some criteria *other* than their work efforts. Standard examples of transfer payments are government unemployment benefits, subsidised healthcare, corporate bailouts, regulations, interest on the national debt, food stamps and welfare payments.

In addition to significant bureaucratic barriers to economic growth, redistribution causes severe distortions in a person's incentives to contribute to output, employment and production. Of the government's many spending categories, transfer payments are perhaps the least complex, and yet few factors are as important in determining the path of an economy as transfer payments and dependency criteria. In order to evaluate redistribution's impact on an economy, we need only look at redistribution's impact on real wages.

A transfer payment per se means that a worker is able to receive income through some channel other than their own work effort. The transfer recipient has found an alternative source of income other than working. On the margin, both workers (transfer payers) and transfer recipients will now have less incentive to work. We, therefore, should expect to find that in the aggregate, workers choose to work fewer hours.

For any individual, government transfers have an income effect that is positive for the transfer recipient and negative for the implied transfer

---

* More on this later in this chapter. Specifically, in 'Deficit Financing and Taxes'.

payer and, in the aggregate, these income effects sum to zero. The substitution effects, on the other hand, aggregate. That is why, in today's society, if government taxes people who work and pays people for not working, we shouldn't be surprised to see less work, and the more government taxes work and pays for non-work, the less work there will be.[6]

A decrease in taxes will raise after-tax real wages for income earners, while a reduction in transfers will lower the income of transfer recipients. A tax cut fully compensated by a cut in transfers will raise the real wages of taxpayers and lower the incomes of transfer recipients.

In anticipation of future sections of this book which focus on explicit measurement and estimation of these effects, we should be conscious of the fact that those measures must logically include a zero output point when transfers and taxes equal 100 per cent. Those who argue that the output effects on the overall economy are small in one range or another must, in turn, acknowledge that these effects are large in other ranges – this is how it balances (and thereby remaining grounded in reality) to end up with the same end point: zero output at 100 per cent taxes/transfers.

The Welfare/Dole Trap

The economic effects of the dole are at once staggering and generally misunderstood. Giving money to those who are in difficult circumstances or down on their luck – even when such benevolence is necessary to get at the truly needy – creates an incentive structure that is at odds with economic flourishing. Terms such as the 'welfare trap' and more recently the 'welfare cliff' have arisen to get at the nub of the problem.

Means-testing and income-testing has been a mainstay of dole/welfare programmes for decades. Council housing, aid to families, unemployment compensation, food assistance etc. require the recipient to earn less than a given income threshold. The incentive effects from such a system are perverse. The poor and the struggling – the very persons we should hope can improve themselves – stand to lose their housing, their food ration, their family payments, if they do in fact improve themselves.

The actual figures give rise to the term 'welfare cliff'. If you are receiving a full complement of benefits, once you start to earn money again, your real compensation 'falls off a cliff' – on account of losing benefits that in some cases are worth more than the pay cheques that replaced them. A notorious but all too true and representative example came from the city of Philadelphia in 2012. A single woman making $30,000 per year and collecting benefits would lose money, net including benefits lost, at every point past where her wage compensation doubled. It would take this Philadelphian woman making fully $70,000 to break even against welfare benefits lost and to be in a position in which making more money would actually yield more take-home income to her.

An economy facing a sluggish labour market has to have a system of the dole that clears out perverse incentives to work and helps people improve themselves.

THE THIRD CATEGORY OF GOVERNMENT SPENDING: PUBLIC GOODS

There are, on occasion, situations where government is far more efficient in producing some products than the private sector is. These goods are generally called public goods and are distributed to the public for 'free' or way below cost. Public goods are seen more often than not to include large positive externalities that would be overlooked by private producers. Some argue that these public goods include schools, national defence, highways, libraries, police protection, judicial structures, regulatory frameworks and public utilities, to mention only a few. If true, the taxes to pay for the government production of these products will have universal negative substitution effects across all factors of production. Because government production of these public goods is so much greater than private production would be per pound of resources used, the negative income effects on factors of production resulting from taxes will be more than offset by the positive income effects of the 'free' goods themselves on the economy as a whole. For all of the pounds that are taxed, much more is returned to the economy. From a measurement standpoint, irrespective of government's enormous efficiency in producing public goods, GDP will still only be equal to the monies government spends and not the value the private sector receives.

For this category of increased government spending and taxes, there will be an unambiguous decline in measured work, output and employment resulting from both substitution and aggregate income effects. But, in truth, the benefits of government spending often far outweigh the losses in measured output. In terms of aggregate measures, it is similar to a universal increase in productivity. In this instance, the aggregate positive income effects include both taxpayers and product beneficiaries.[*]

THE FOURTH CATEGORY OF GOVERNMENT SPENDING: STIMULUS GOODS (GARBAGE GOODS)

The fourth and final category of government spending is on so-called 'stimulus' goods. Stimulus goods are goods that the private sector cannot or would not produce on its own. They are also goods the private household sector does not directly consume. They can be either welfare-enhancing, such as defence spending during a war, or welfare-diminishing, such as Cash for Clunkers or digging ditches and filling them up again, but they all have the same effect on the economy.

Government spending on stimulus goods has an aggregate negative 'income effect' on the economy, along with the universal negative substitution effects resulting from taxation. For any given level of work effort, stimulus spending reduces the amount of income that workers and producers have to consume ordinary or regular goods and services. As is the case of any tax, those who are taxed to pay for the stimulus goods will have a negative income effect that will lead to more work. This form of spending is equivalent to a reduction in overall economic productivity. In the case of the Second World War, real hourly consumable wages were reduced back to where they had been a century earlier.

However, as opposed to the transfer payment, where a separate segment of the population then receives the benefits from taxation, stimulus goods fail to provide a positive income effect for any segment of the population. In the case of defence spending, which is the single most important stimulus good presently and historically, those goods and services are blown up, hopefully, in faraway lands. With regard to income effects, there will be an aggregate negative income effect leading to more

---

[*] For those of you old enough and savvy enough to remember Al Capp's cartoon *Li'l Abner*, public goods are perfectly represented by Shmoos, capable of producing the necessities of life at no cost.

labour and less leisure. The negative income effect on taxpayers is not offset because there are no spending beneficiaries.

In extreme cases, as we will see, these aggregate economic income effects can press to the very frontiers of the human condition. In the case of wartime spending or digging ditches and filling them up again, aggregate output including government stimulus spending rises while the output of ordinary goods and services as well as leisure decline. Employment goes up and private consumption and leisure go down. To think of the effect that an increase in stimulus goods has on the economy, think of government confiscation of a fixed amount of output, which is never returned to the economy. In the case of an increase in government spending on stimulus goods, people have to work more even though they consume less and, as a result, the demand for leisure declines. The marginal rate of substitution (i.e. the real wage) between leisure and private goods declines.

Putting on your economics hat, what would you expect to happen to income, output and employment in an entire economy if the real wage rate for all workers suddenly falls to half its former level? While this autonomous, shocking decline in real wages may be hard to imagine, it is almost exactly what happened in post-earthquake San Francisco and post-Second World War Japan. With capital stocks greatly depleted, both economies effectively had huge drops in their real wages. Even more to the point, a sharp drop in real wages is basically what happened in the US during the Second World War. While total production increased, the goods available for consumption fell sharply, requiring people to work harder and longer to survive.

The effect to an economy when there is a fall in real wages should be the mirror opposite of what happens to an economy when there is an equivalent increase in real wages. The same laws of economics that 'explain' the consequences of higher real wages should work just as well when real wages fall. Fortunately, economies with increases in real wages are quite commonplace, and economies with decreases in real wages are few. In these higher wage economies, the income effect of higher real wages leads to increased consumption of leisure on the part of workers and, thus, less man-hours spent working. If symmetry holds, the income effect of lower real wages should then lead to more hours worked and less leisure. It is our contention that it is precisely these income effects, lower and higher real wages, which explain the behaviour of the US economy during and after the Second World War. And by the way, for the record, an increase in real GDP resulting from defence spending does not increase prosperity or welfare.

Thus, it was the destruction of goods and services brought about by military spending that caused the hugely reduced real consumption potential per man-hour worked during the Second World War period and, therefore, the increase in total output (i.e. the income effect engaged). Had the wartime spending been on either transfer payments or public goods, there would have been no aggregate income effect or increase in total output.

In *Return to Prosperity*, an example of Charles Manson was used where he hypothetically burns almost all of the homes in the US to the ground and then is caught and executed. After removing the risk of a recurrence, we asked the question, with almost no homes left standing and no further threat, what happens to new housing starts, employment etc. and what happens to private consumption (especially of housing services)? The obvious answer is that we will have full employment and we will be living in poverty. Charles Manson's activities are stimulus spending. A real-world example was the post-war full employment and rapid economic growth in Japan right after the total destruction of Japan's economy.

DEFICIT FINANCING AND TAXES

In addition to the different categories of government spending, our fiscal framework must also consider the role of taxation versus deficit finance. For example, in 1944, circumstances were such that massive social harm would have occurred without enough production of defence goods but that, if successful, the need for defence spending would disappear in the near future. Therefore, *without* the possibility of deficit finance in 1944, higher than normal defence spending would have necessitated *pari passu* an equivalent amount of higher than normal taxation. Higher explicit taxation would have meant even greater negative 'substitution' effects on work and output going almost to the point of 100 per cent marginal tax rates. Government defence spending would have been constrained, in part, by the disincentive effects of these much higher explicit tax rates on the incomes of workers and producers.

By choosing deficit finance over taxation, the government has the option of 'intertemporal transfers', i.e. borrowing from prospective future workers to pay current workers, guaranteed by perpetual power to tax.* These intertemporal transfers can affect how workers perceive the benefits of working in one period or the next. Consequently, the option of running budget deficits can change the optimal amount of government spending in a given year by being able to affect the timing of aggregate output. People can change not only how much they work but also when they work. Isn't economics wonderful?

With the possibility of deficit finance, the government could acquire far greater amounts of defence products in 1944 than it otherwise could have acquired. By raising additional funds to pay for government spending from the capital markets (through issuing government debt), the government in effect levied taxes on producers in *future* years in order to compensate producers in 1944. This is the essence of today's oft-repeated phrase that deficit spending is burdening our grandchildren with having to pay for today's consumption. Germany paid off their First World War debt in October 2010.[7] The UK paid off the last of its 1917 'War Loans' in 2015.[8]

Deficit finance isn't a mere shell game, nor does it involve alchemy with time machines. Deficit financing incentivises more physical (real) inputs available – for example, workers in 1944 will rationally decide to enjoy less leisure when faced with lower explicit tax rates but more leisure in the future when future workers are faced with higher explicit taxes needed to service the government debt that was issued in 1944.

---

* This sounds more confusing than it is: it just employs a stricter notion of identity. Intertemporal transfers are transfers across time between different people, where people are understood with a time-sensitive identity. So, by this logic, I am a different person in five years than I am now. This relates to our conversation because the government can borrow from me in five years and can enforce the loan via the power to tax – that's an intertemporal transfer: spend now, collect the taxes over time or at a later time.

This deficit financing will have a huge effect on output for the peak war years and in the years immediately following the cessation of hostilities.

Financing government spending to change the timing of production by means of higher deficits is completely different than using deficit spending as standard practice. When used as standard practice, deficit-financed government spending results in increased and increasing government debt over time, which is simply a promise of future taxes. Prospects of future taxes will materially reduce economic growth today. In the limit, deficit-financed government spending can increase the national debt sufficiently to result in a death spiral: lower growth→more spending→more debt→even slower growth. In such instances, the only way out for an economy is to default on its debt.

THE TRANSFER THEOREM

Tax rates and welfare generosity change in concert, guided by a consistent budgetary context: you can't have one person's tax rate change without something else changing as well. Tax-rate cuts, for example, would be matched with government spending cuts and/or other tax increases. This is analogous to accounting, where debits require credits, and credits require debits. Nothing the government does transpires in a vacuum.

There have been a number of articles and treatises in favour of and opposed to the type of redistribution theses proposed by Thomas Piketty in his book *Capital in the Twenty-First Century*. While each of these articles makes its points carefully and clearly, they all unwittingly adopt the single tragic flaw in logic. Piketty writes as if he believes governmental efforts to redistribute income will not affect other variables, including the total amount of income available. The incentives to earn income drop with the implementation of higher taxes and drop even further when the transfer recipients of the transfer's incentives not to work increase.

A transfer occurs whenever government takes resources implicitly or explicitly from one group and gives those resources to another group. Pay-as-you-go Social Security is a clear example of taking from younger workers and giving to older non-workers. Whatever the worthiness is of the recipient group is versus the less worthy nature of the mandated 'donating' group, taking resources from one and giving them to the other is a transfer, pure and simple. It's easiest to think of the transfer payers as taxpayers and the other group as the transfer recipients or tax beneficiaries. But, in truth, each and every transfer, whether financed by taxes or not, constitutes a transfer all the same. Governments don't create resources; they only redistribute resources.

To see and understand this powerful concept and its meaning in political economy, the example of redistributing income from those who have a little bit more (the rich) to those who have a little bit less (the poor) is a perfect illustration of both the theorem and the fact that incentives matter. The transfer theorem truly is a theorem. It's all about maths and has nothing to do with feelings, hopes or aspirations. And most of all, the validity of the transfer theorem is not political.

The reasoning behind the transfer theorem lies in what economists call the Slutsky equation, which breaks down the effects of a price change, tax rate change or transfer into two components: an income effect and a substitution effect. The substitution effect describes the change in consumption patterns that arise from a change in the relative price of goods – when the price of a good increases, consumers will choose to substitute less costly alternatives for these more expensive goods. The substitution effect also operates on the incentives to produce goods and employ people: the higher the price, the more suppliers will supply the product. In technical terms, the substitution effects of a redistributive tax/subsidy always work in the same direction for both taxpayers and subsidy recipients, i.e. any and all redistributions reduce everyone's incentive to work and thus reduce total income.

The income effect describes the change in demand for a good as a result of a change in income or, alternatively, it is the amount of work hours/pre-tax income a consumer chooses to forego given a tax change. In an aggregate economy considering all participants, all income effects of a price change, tax rate change or transfer payment change will offset each other 100 per cent as long as the proceeds of the taxes are distributed back to the people. In other words, the negative income effect of the taxpayer is offset by the positive income effect of the transfer recipient.

This reasoning can be seen in examples where we have higher tax rates and more generous transfers, in which the substitution effects incentivise both net taxpayers and net transfer recipients to work less and demand more leisure. Here, again, the substitution effects are all that remain from a tax rate increase/transfer increase, which unambiguously leads to lower work, output and employment.

When government takes a sum from those who have a little bit more, the incentives to produce for those who have a little bit more is reduced, and they will produce a little bit less. In tax terms, if you tax high earners more, those high earners will earn less: the substitution effect.

In the same vein, if the sum taken from those who have a little bit more is then given to those who have a little bit less, those who have a little bit less will now have an alternative source of income other than working or producing and they too will produce a little bit less: both as an income effect and a substitution effect. In terms of subsidies, if the government taxes production and subsidises non-production, production will be reduced.

Taken altogether, a transfer will reduce the transfer payer's incentive to produce. No matter who you are, where you work, your age, ethnicity or what have you, whenever the government transfers resources from one group to another group, total production and income decline. Taxing the rich and giving that money to the poor unambiguously reduces total income and production. Transfers always and everywhere reduce production and income. QED!

This template is a voluminous documentation of this theorem, which is central to any and all government actions. Transfer payments reduce income and production. For an extreme form of this tax/subsidy style of redistribution applied not only to income but also to physical and mental abilities, give Kurt Vonnegut's short story 'Harrison Bergeron' a read – you will find it both horrifying and enlightening. While the human qualities being redistributed are different in Vonnegut's world than the income being redistributed in our world, the ideas and the end result are exactly the same. Government stimulus spending does not stimulate the economy. Quite the opposite. Government stimulus spending retards growth.

The lemma from this theorem should be obvious to everyone, but we'll state it here frankly without proof. The more government transfers resources, the greater the reductions in both production and income will be.

What is most important and at the centre of any number of income inequality political/economic debates is the limit function of the transfer theorem: the desire, hope and goal to have everyone have the same income after taxes and transfers. The limit function of this theorem is simply that if government were able to transfer income in such a way where everyone came out exactly equal (they all had the same after-tax/after-transfer income), there would be no income whatsoever. Income inequality is only achieved where everyone is equally poor.

To show this result, it's first necessary to illustrate just what government would have to do to assure equality of income for everyone. What government would have to do is tax everyone who earns above the average income 100 per cent of the excess. They would also have to subsidise everyone below the average income 100 per cent of the deficiency. Only in this way could it be guaranteed that everyone would have exactly the same amount of after-tax, after-subsidy income.

Now if government actually did tax everyone earning income above the average income 100 per cent of the excess, and if they actually did subsidise everyone earning below the average income 100 per cent of the difference, we will stipulate today, counsellor, everyone will be equal only at zero income. At 100 per cent prohibitive tax rates, no one would be willing to produce or work and at 100 per cent subsidy to non-workers and to non-producers, everyone would be incentivised not to work. There would be no work, no production and no output.

The limit function of the transfer theorem should be a warning to one and all. Whatever the hoped-for or perceived benefits of income redistribution are, any and all transfers reduce income, output and production. The more income the government transfers and redistributes, the greater the reductions in income, output and production will be. And finally, if government were successful in redistributing income through transfers to the point where all after-tax and after-transfer incomes were the exact same, there would be no income whatsoever.

If everyone who worked, no matter how hard, was only able to receive the average income and everyone who didn't work or worked very little also received the average income, in short order, all income would fall to zero. Who would work for nothing and who wouldn't choose not to work if everything were free? Thus, 100 per cent redistribution equates to zero income/output.

As a matter of principle, we should do all we can to raise everyone's income irrespective of that person's status. Even more to the point, it is self-evident that the poorer a person or family is, the more we need to secure for that family all possible opportunities for economic advancement. In other words, reducing poverty and economic deprivation by elevating the poor is the right thing to do, while reducing inequality by inhibiting the wealthy is the Devil's mission. The dream never has been to make the rich poorer. The dream always has been to make the poor richer.

ADDITIONAL ECONOMIC BURDENS FROM REDISTRIBUTION/FISCAL LEAKAGES

It is worth pointing out:

i. The tax collected from someone who earns more income is far less than the total tax that person actually pays. That person who earns more has all sorts of expenses, inefficiencies and costs associated with 'the tax'. In the study 'The Economic Burden Caused by Tax Code Complexity', John Childs and Arthur Laffer estimate that for every dollar of income taxes actually paid in the US to the Internal Revenue Service (IRS), taxpayers pay an additional thirty cents in out-of-pocket expenses to lawyers, accountants and other tax service providers to comply with the tax codes. Therefore, income taxes cost the taxpayer a lot more than just the tax they remit to the government. These additional costs create further disincentives to the high-income earner from an act of redistribution than the tax itself and cause the high-income earner to work/produce and report even less than they would from the tax payment alone. This thirty cents does not include the inefficiencies of tax shelters, exemptions, exclusions, transformations, deductions, credits and other manipulations of the tax codes. The thirty cents is strictly an out-of-pocket cost.

ii. Likewise, the process of collecting taxes is not costless either. The IRS and its state and local counterparts are huge government bureaucracies employing hundreds of thousands of people and costing billions upon billions of dollars to run. In fact, in fiscal year 2023, the IRS alone – not including any state or local revenue agencies – had about 83,000 full-time equivalent employees and a budget of more than $16.1 billion.[9] What the government, therefore, gets to spend 'net' on those who earn less is significantly smaller than the amount of taxes actually collected, and this sum, in turn, as Arthur Laffer pointed out in *The Wealth of States*, is less than what the taxpayer pays 'gross', all expenses included. If the government targets the amount paid to those who earn less, then the government would have to tax high-income earners even more to make up for government costs; an additional drop in income ensues. These discrepancies, too, are huge. Further, to point out the obvious, these additional costs including the IRS, tax lawyers, accountants etc., even though they are included as part of GDP, are most definitely not additions to the country's well-being or happiness. Even despite the fact that the IRS is one of the most cost-efficient organs of the executive, with tiny amounts of spending per dollar, the point is that for all of the (supposed) good provided by tax dollars spent, they will not exceed, nay even equal, that which they took from the economy. Imagine what happens to efficiency once the money leaves the IRS and goes to the inefficient governmental departments?

iii. Also, for the government, the total cost of subsidies to those who earn less is far greater than the actual subsidies to the recipients because of the bureaucratic costs the government incurs by actually giving recipients the money. It costs the government a lot of money in bureaucratic infrastructure to transform tax dollars received into subsidy dollars spent. Just think of all the government apparatuses and expenses associated with, say, one hour of a teacher's classroom attendance. In 2012, for example, there were 6.7 million full-time equivalent state and local employees involved in elementary and secondary education, while there were only 3.7 million full-time equivalent elementary and secondary school teachers. The ratio in the UK is similar – there were 979,085 full-time equivalent staff in state education in 2023 and 468,693 full-time equivalent teachers, although there were also 282,925 teaching assistants whose role was partly frontline and partly doing teaching work.[10] The additional costs are not small and consequently reduce incomes and output even more.

iv. Similarly, the subsidies paid by the government directly to those who earn less is greater than the 'net' subsidies received by those who earn less because the recipients of the subsidies paid by the government have to expend resources in order to get the subsidies. It's not inexpensive to qualify for welfare subsidies. Any system of subsidies requires time and effort on the part of the potential recipients in addition to documentation and proof – not inexpensive items. Therefore, the total cost of a subsidy incurred by the government is considerably greater than the 'cash' subsidy paid by the government to the recipients (point iii), which, in turn, is greater than the 'net' subsidy received by the recipients. There are further declines in income/output. It would seem that every step of the way from payer to the beneficiary of government largesse, there is someone waiting for their cut of the money: the toll for the troll.

v. The taxes on those who earn more and the subsidies to the recipients who earn less are usually highly skewed against work, output and employment in both the taxpayers' progressive income taxes and subsidy recipients' means tests, needs tests and incomes tests. In practical terms, attempts to redistribute income have a hyper-accentuated effect to reduce total income. This is the actual transfer theorem writ large.

vi. Finally, as everyone who has read George Orwell's classic book *Animal Farm* knows, government employees and politicians are money-motivated like the rest of us, only they, unlike the rest of us, deal with other people's money, not their own money. Orwell's way of putting it was, 'All animals are equal, but some animals are more equal than others.' Corruption and thievery are always better practised when the prospective thieves are surrounded by other people's money and also where the prospective thieves make and enforce the rules regarding corruption and thievery. Whenever money is transferred through a lengthy governmental process, expect lots and lots of shrinkage, if you know what we mean.

If you still don't believe us, that the redistribution of income always reduces total income, you need only to open your eyes. To quote President Ronald Reagan, 'The government that is big enough to provide you with everything you'll ever want is also big enough to take everything you'll ever have.'

Instead of focusing on the redistribution of results, we should focus on making sure our government policies do not show preference, or favouritism, towards one individual over another. This view perfectly matches President Theodore Roosevelt's description of his 'Square Deal', favouring neither capital nor labour, neither rich nor poor. 'If the cards do not come to any man, or if they do come, and he has not got the power to play them, that is his affair. All we mean is that there shall not be any crookedness in the dealing.'

YOU DON'T GET ALL THE GOVERNMENT YOU PAY FOR (THANK GOODNESS!)

'The whole business thing is predicated a lot on the tax laws ... It's why we rehearse in Canada and not in the US. A lot of our astute moves have been basically keeping up with tax laws, where to go, where not to put it. Whether to sit on it or not. We left England because we'd be paying 98 cents on the dollar. We left, and they lost out. No taxes at all.'
– KEITH RICHARDS, 'INSIDE THE ROLLING STONES', 2002

To pay taxes, the costs taxpayers actually incur are far greater than the net sums the government collects. Individuals and businesses as taxpayers must pay substantially more than one dollar in order for government beneficiaries to receive one dollar of federal government services. Before individuals and businesses pay their tax liability, they must first spend time collecting records, organising files and wading through the tax code to determine exactly what their tax liability is. In addition, individuals purchase products and services, such as tax software or an accountant, to assist them in determining their tax liability. These are tax compliance outlays. Thirdly, in effect, taxpayers must also pay the administrative costs needed to run the IRS etc., solely for tax collection purposes. Still there is more.

Businesses, large and small, hire teams of accountants, lawyers and tax professionals to track, measure and pay their taxes. This tax infrastructure is also used to optimise the tax liability of the business. Individuals and businesses change their behaviour in response to tax policies, hiring tax experts to discover ways to minimise their tax liabilities. The efficiency costs from both legal tax avoidance and illegal tax evasion are difficult to quantify but could be the highest costs of all.

One can only imagine what the full burden of government on the well-being of society might be. In our analysis, we estimate that US taxpayers pay $431.1 billion annually, or 30 per cent of total income taxes collected, just to comply with and administer the US income tax system.* This cost estimate includes:

- Approximately $31.5 billion in direct outlays (e.g. paying a professional tax preparer such as H&R Block or purchasing tax software) (2010 data).
- Total IRS administrative costs of $12.4 billion (2010 data).
- The Taxpayer Advocacy Service of the IRS estimates that individuals and businesses also spent 6.1 billion hours complying with the filing requirements of the US income tax code. We estimate the dollar value or cost of these hours to be $377.9 billion as of 2008. The 6.1 billion

---

* According to the IRS, total gross individual income tax collections in 2008 were $1.4 trillion: https://www. irs.gov/downloads/irs-soi?page=0. Although, as of the time of writing, total tax collections from 2010 are available, the detailed breakdown of income taxes paid by adjusted gross income are only available through 2008. For consistency, data on tax collections from 2008 are used throughout this study.

hours number was estimated by multiplying the number of copies of each form filed in tax year 2008 by the average amount of time the IRS estimated it took to complete the form.

- Individuals spent 3.16 billion hours complying with the income tax code, which, weighted by time spent by income group, costs the US economy $216.2 billion annually.
- Businesses spent $2.94 billion complying with the business income tax code, which cost the US economy $161.7 billion.
- Comprehensive audits also impose an additional taxpayer burden of at least $9.3 billion annually.

One of the major advantages of a flat tax is that it makes tax a lot more simple.

CONCLUSION

If the government wants to fund a transfer payment to Paul, then taking money from Peter through a lump-sum head tax will reduce output less than if the government takes the money from Peter through a proportional income tax, which will in turn reduce output less than taking money from Peter through a progressive income tax. The hierarchy of taxes moves from least damage to most damage: from a head tax,[*] to a flat tax, to a progressive tax.

All three types of taxes reduce Peter's *total* after-tax income for a given amount of total work effort, but only the income taxes reduce the *marginal* increment in after-tax income from an *additional unit* of work effort. A progressive tax, of course, increases the marginal tax more than a proportional tax does. The tax lesson here is that the less marginal and the more inframarginal the tax code is, the more output per dollar of tax revenue.

In the times since the Second World War, the political realisation of the damage done by progressive marginal tax rates per se is best expressed

---

[*] A tax based not on income but simply on citizenship: the idea being that everyone pays the same amount and then is off the hook. It's like the ultimate realisation of equal rights.

in the 1986 Tax Act. The Act flattened the whole structure of personal income taxes as the highest marginal income tax rate was lowered from 50 per cent to 28 per cent, and reduced fourteen tax brackets to two brackets, 15 per cent and 28 per cent. The highest corporate tax rate was lowered from 46 per cent to 34 per cent, while enough loopholes, deductions, exemptions and exclusions were eliminated to make the 1986 Tax Act static revenue-neutral. This bill passed in the US Senate ninety-seven to three.

To reiterate some of a major theme of this book, we cut tax rates on the highest income earners for both output and revenue reasons. The higher statutory tax rates are – those on the 'rich' – the greater the increase in incentives per dollar of static revenue loss. In the highest tax brackets, the percentage of filers facing those tax rates 'on the margin' is the greatest. Given the revenues of the wealthy and the ways to avoid taxes, the elasticity of supply of taxable income (Adjusted Gross Income (AGI)) to changes in tax rates is the greatest in the top tax brackets.

When evaluating fiscal policy, it is important to consider both the levels of and the changes in the volume of taxation/spending, i.e. how spending is carried out and how taxes are collected. For example, if the income tax rate rests at 10 per cent for a decade and suddenly trebles to 30 per cent, that would have a negative impact on growth. On the other hand, if the income tax rate had been 50 per cent for a decade and then suddenly were cut to 30 per cent, that would have a positive impact on growth. Of course, the reason why changes in the level of taxes affect income growth is because the level of taxation affects the level of output, employment and production. This distinction will prove important in our analysis of the top marginal income tax rate in the post-war era.

Of course, if the income tax rate had been 10 per cent for decades, not 50 per cent, the levels of output would be very different. The reason a move from 10 per cent to 30 per cent will result in lower growth than one from 50 per cent to 30 per cent is because output will have been higher at 10 per cent than it would at 50 per cent. Sometimes this process of convergence takes a long time.

Our analysis in this section implies a few principles of sound fiscal policy:

i. For a desired revenue objective, the government should raise those funds in the least damaging manner. For example, given a government is going to raise $1 trillion in tax receipts, it is much more efficient to do so through a broad-based low-rate flat tax than a highly progressive tax schedule from a voluminous and arcane tax code on incomes, output and employment.

ii. Whatever the level of resources at its disposal, the government should direct those resources to their most beneficial uses. In fact, the government should only spend when it is most beneficial for government alone to do so. Paying people not to work or, worse yet, requiring people not to work to receive government funds will hurt the economy far more than government funds spent on infrastructure and certain types of research will.

iii. The government should set its level of resource usage such that the marginal benefit of the last pound it spends is slightly higher than the marginal cost of extracting that last pound from the private sector.

If the government follows these general principles, its fiscal policy will universally contribute to economic efficiency.

CHAPTER 5

THE THIRD KINGDOM: MONETARY POLICY

A SUPPLY-SIDE FRAMEWORK FOR UNDERSTANDING MONETARY POLICY

'By a continuing process of inflation, government can confiscate, secretly and unobserved, an important part of the wealth of their citizens.'
– JOHN MAYNARD KEYNES

It may seem obvious to a lay observer, but inflation is bad for growth. Economists have studied the subject empirically to check this intuitive conclusion and discovered that the facts support the theory.* A substantial survey article by the National Bureau of Economic Research[1] reached three important conclusions:

i.   Higher inflation NEVER boosts growth in the longer term.
ii. Lower inflation generally leads to higher growth.
iii. The boost to growth from reducing inflation generally increases, the lower the starting rate of inflation.

As the examples of post-First World War Germany, Zimbabwe, Venezuela and Argentina show, high inflation is associated with value destruction and ultimately lower GDP.

---

* Unfortunately, this does not always happen! Economics is more like biology than traditional physics, where what 'ought' to happen occasionally does not. Although we should always look carefully at the evidence, we should not be put off by occasional instances where the evidence does not back up the theory provided that the bulk of the evidence points in the right direction. There are so many moving parts that it is statistically inevitable that there will be occasional examples where some evidence is not fully supportive of an essentially sound theory.

The third kingdom of macroeconomics is therefore sound money and low inflation. The objective is stable prices.

Economies the world over, and for expanded passages of time, have been plagued by unsound money and out-of-control inflation. As a blast from the past, the economic historian Earl Hamilton of the University of Chicago attributed widespread and broad-based European inflation of the sixteenth and seventeenth centuries to the vast increases in gold acquired by the maritime nations from the New World.[2]

And, of course, large price increases have been documented time and time again, resulting from major shortages of specific and general goods during and following wars, earthquakes and natural disasters. Derogatory words such as 'price gouging' and 'profiteering' have become regulars in the economic vernacular all because shortages create profit opportunities for producers. And only if those producers take advantage of the high prices will the shortages vanish. Words notwithstanding, it is the 'greed' of the producer, rather than any 'benevolence', as Adam Smith observed, that supplies the goods to eliminate shortages.

And then, there are the 'one-off' episodes of inflation from post-Second World War military scrip in such countries as Germany and Japan. In post-war occupied countries as well as in prisons, prices are often defined in terms of products such as cigarettes or what have you. Often periods of hyperinflation are the stuff of legend in some African countries such as Zimbabwe, as well as South American economies in the 1970s. We could continue this discussion ad infinitum with examples of hyperbolic inflation, but we think we've made our point. These episodes are the grist of economic histories of virtually every economy.

As far as modern countries go, the UK has a long information-rich economic history including prices, inflation and monetary policy. In the following chart, the retail price index or its equivalent is plotted from 1700 to the present, using a semi-log scale. It is all here. Please keep this chart primarily in mind. It is this chart and its extension into the future that is the entirety of what we are focusing on in this section.

FIGURE 27: UK RETAIL PRICE INDEX

(annual, 1700–2024, 2010 = 100, semi-log scale)

Source: *measuringworth.com*

And then naturally we have further stories of inflation in the industrial world of the past seventy-five years. Under the Bretton Woods era, it was the US's exclusive obligation to fix the dollar price of gold even though US citizens were not themselves allowed to own gold. Other countries under the Bretton Woods umbrella were mandated to fix the value of their currencies to the US dollar. And as might be imagined, some of those countries were more successful than others, which led to devaluations (relatively frequently) and revaluations (occasionally) and differential rates of inflation. The post-Bretton Woods era, 1970 to 1990, was that in which gold convertibility was abrogated as the base value of world money.

EXCHANGE RATE STABILISATION, OUTSIDE MONEY AND INFLATION RATES: THE CLASSIC HISTORICAL EXAMPLE

When a country considers adopting a plan for low inflation and preserving the internal value of money, it is imperative that the plan be based upon facts and only facts. Opinions, theories and hopes are totally inappropriate as a foundation for a serious plan. One place to start is to examine the history of just how countries actually eliminated chronic inflation or hyperinflation.

The most successful strategy countries have ever adopted to end serious inflationary episodes is to fix their currencies' exchange rate to 'outside money' – gold or high-quality foreign exchange. There are fewer cases of countries ending inflationary episodes via domestic money-supply management. This is only partly a point about the relationship between money and inflation; it also reflects the fact that when a country's monetary authorities have lost credibility, it takes a long time to regain it. As we discuss below, outsourcing monetary policy in its entirety to a currency board can work wonders.*

The lessons of these historical experiences extend far beyond countries enduring a crisis. Any country interested in keeping prices stable, real growth high and useful money ample and constant in value should take note. (Stable prices in this context means stable price levels. Relative prices – the price of one good in terms of another – can change frequently, for all sorts of reasons ranging from the weather to technological innovation. Over the decades, television sets have plummeted in relative price to food, for example.) In any event, for many countries, their top monetary policy priority should be the stabilisation of their currencies against outside money. Even non-monetary policies such as wage and price controls never cut the mustard. Inflation is monetary in nature. The great nineteenth-century banker Walter Bagehot's dictum to the Bank of England is worth recalling in this regard. In a crisis, lend freely at penalty rates – and let people who really want money, and who are ready to pay for it, determine how much of it is supplied.

---

* A principal theoretician and designer of currency boards is Steve Hanke. A primer on his currency board position is Steve H. Hanke, 'Currency Boards', *Annals of the American Academy of Political and Social Science*, Vol. 579, January 2002.

The major periods of inflation in the late eighteenth and nineteenth centuries ended with currency 'resumption' into gold or gold or silver convertible currency. The French Revolutionary 'assignat' inflation,* the British inflation of the Napoleonic era, and the inflation at the time of the American War of 1812 and the US Civil War all ended with recommitments to convertibility. Furthermore, in each case, real economic growth soared under the conditions of resumption of currency convertibility for the long term. In the twentieth century, when commitments to specie weakened, the standard rule still applied: the more countries committed to fixing their currencies to outside money, the more they stopped inflationary episodes cold and restored booming real growth.

The first highly illustrative case of the 1920s concerned the newly formed country of Austria, which experienced an exceptional 10,000-fold inflation over 1920–22. The problem was that the fledgling government ran large budget deficits, and the fledgling central bank bought the debt while issuing currency and bank loans on the basis of this debt. The two institutions kept at it for two years, enabling the issuing of ever more notes and loans as inflation burst past all records. A reform insisted upon by the League of Nations and the Bank of International Settlements required the Austrian authorities to issue the new currency, the krone, only on the presentation of gold or foreign exchange (and in some exceptional cases bills of exchange). In the summer of 1922, as the reform took hold, the currency stabilised immediately and permanently against foreign exchange. Against the dollar, for example, the krone, having devalued by 4,500-fold, stayed stable for the duration beginning in mid-1922. It is important to note that domestic krone circulation in the same period went up – that's right, *up* sixfold from 1922–24 as the exchange rate stayed stable and inflation (which had been gigantic) all but vanished. Consumer price increases from 1922–24 totalled 20 per cent, compared to an inflation rate of 1,000 per cent in 1921 and 2,000 per cent over the first half of 1922. The great increase in monetary

---

* The assignat was the currency issued after the French Revolution. Unfortunately, the continued printing of this currency to fund spending and the regular revolutionary wars meant that it became a textbook case of high inflation. Napoleon first established himself as France's leader by cutting spending and bringing order to France's finances.

circulation after the stabilisation of the currency corresponded to an increased commitment to real economic projects in the country, to real (non-government) employment, production and economic growth. In this era of extremes, the basic truth shone forth: economic growth and increased quantities of money because of that growth were the results of establishing sound money.

In the 1980s, Arthur Laffer and Milton Friedman, both members of President Reagan's economic advisory board, disagreed over whether jointly to endorse a recommitment to gold while letting the money supply rise with tax-rate cuts. Up the money supply went – without any quantity controls, as tax-rate cuts and plummeting interest rates increased the demand for money, to the tune of inflation decelerating and a growth boom. Gold prices fell sharply because the dollar was not just as good as gold – it was better than gold. In this case, the appropriate policy was not to fix the exchange rate but to allow it to appreciate to reflect the supply-side improvements and to prevent them spilling over into inflation. The huge rise in the money supply did not lead to an acceleration of inflation.

The important point here in the Austrian and US examples is that by stabilising the value of the currency to specie and sound currencies, the quantity of money increased sixfold and the economy boomed, while inflation collapsed. The demand for money is as important as supply when looking at monetary aggregates. Anyone who tells you that all you need to do is control the supply of money, and inflation is done for, does not understand monetary dynamics.

The more famous German case of approximately the same period held all the same lessons. After the First World War, especially from 1921 to late 1923, the Weimar government allowed the backing of its currency to collapse and printed money with abandon, which caused prices to rise ludicrously, beyond almost the realm of calculation. A reform of 1923–24 began, via the new currency of the Rentenmark, a transition to convertibility achieved with a reform of 1924–25 that made its successor currency, the Reichsmark, convertible into the gold-backed dollar. Over late 1923 and 1924, the inflation ceased, the holding of real money balances soared, government employment dropped and private sector growth took off.

In his classic 1982 study of the end of the central European inflations, economist Thomas Sargent (the 2011 economics Nobelist) made this reflection on the Austrian experience, and its general applicability across time and place is apparent:

> From August 1922, when the exchange rate suddenly stabilized, to December 1924, the circulating notes of the Austrian central bank increased by a factor of over 6. The phenomenon of the achievement of price stability in the face of a sixfold increase in the stock of 'high-powered' money was widely regarded by contemporaries as violating the quantity theory of money, and so it seems to do. However, these observations are not at all paradoxical when interpreted in the light of a view which distinguishes sharply between unbacked, or 'outside', money, on the one hand, and backed, or 'inside', money, on the other hand ... Before the protocols, the liabilities of the central bank were backed mainly by government treasury bills; that is ... after the execution of the protocols, the liabilities of the central bank became backed by gold, foreign assets, and commercial paper ... The willingness of Austrians to convert hoards of foreign exchange into crowns ... is not surprising.[3]

THE UNITED KINGDOM'S OPTIONS IN MODERN HISTORICAL PERSPECTIVE: OTHER POLICIES MATTER AS WELL

Those who might object that the United Kingdom's resumption of the gold standard in the 1920s ultimately led to the abandonment of gold in 1931, a destructive deflation and the Great Depression should be aware that, throughout the 1920s, the UK kept its marginal income tax rate exceptionally high – always at 50 per cent or higher. A half generation before, this tax had not existed – and in the 1920s, major trading partners such as the United States were reducing their top tax rates to 25 per cent. Tax-rate cuts, especially in progressive tax structures, attract foreign capital and enhance investment interest from all sources foreign and domestic, increasing the demand for the home currency. Britain's unprecedented high tax rates in the 1920s compelled holders of pound sterling, once resumption was underway, to have a greater preference for gold redemption than they would have, had Britain seriously cut progressive tax rates down from near-confiscatory levels. Very conceivably, a commitment to a tax-rate reduction to pre-First World War levels could have staved off the Great Depression, let alone pound sterling convertibility. Both the United States and Britain resumed a gold standard after the First World War. Only one nation did so successfully – the United States. It cut tax rates as it returned to gold, supporting the real demand for money and suppressing redemption interest in gold. Only after the United States mimicked 1920s-style British tax policy in the early 1930s and raised tax rates prodigiously (the top income tax rate taken from 25 to 63 per cent in 1932, for example) was the gold standard broken in the United States.[4]

More contemporary examples convey similar lessons. In the early 1970s, after final abrogation of the gold standard, all countries experienced inflation. Even the transaction areas of the strongest of major currencies – the Swiss franc, the West German mark,[5] the Japanese yen – saw inflation of 5 or 10 per cent per annum, well past the nil standards of the gold-standard era. The currencies that depreciated against these strong currencies (of which the German mark was strongest), such as the dollar, the lira and the pound sterling, correspondingly saw even greater increases in inflation in their domestic economies. In the United States in 1974–75, for example, inflation ran at 10 per cent per year; in Great Britian, it peaked past 20 per cent. When currencies en masse abandon gold and fixity against foreign exchange, a general inflation develops as economic actors globally develop dubiousness about currency in any form. On the forsaking of a monetary standard, the domestic inflation that results is most modest among those countries whose currencies depreciate the least and most severe among those countries whose currencies depreciate the most.

The United States at last vanquished its inflation when it embarked upon an era of tax-rate cuts that began in 1978 with a capital gains tax-rate cut and culminated in the Tax Reform Act of 1986 that dropped the top income tax rate to 28 per cent, far below the 1978 level of 70 per cent. The dollar's appreciation over this period was massive. As tax-rate cuts made the American economy attractive, the chronic domestic inflation of the 1970s *largely diminished* in the 1980s, *as the dollar's exchange rate appreciated* – a lesson sharply relevant to any would-be fiscal and monetary reformer today. As we explore in the following section, Reagan's tax-rate cuts, coming in tandem with an exchange rate that appreciated, ruined the atmosphere for inflation and brought on a trade deficit/capital surplus, as well as enormous growth in output and employment.

FIGURE 28: ARGENTINA'S CONSUMER PRICE INDEX

(annual, 1980–2011, index 2011 = 100, semi-log scale)

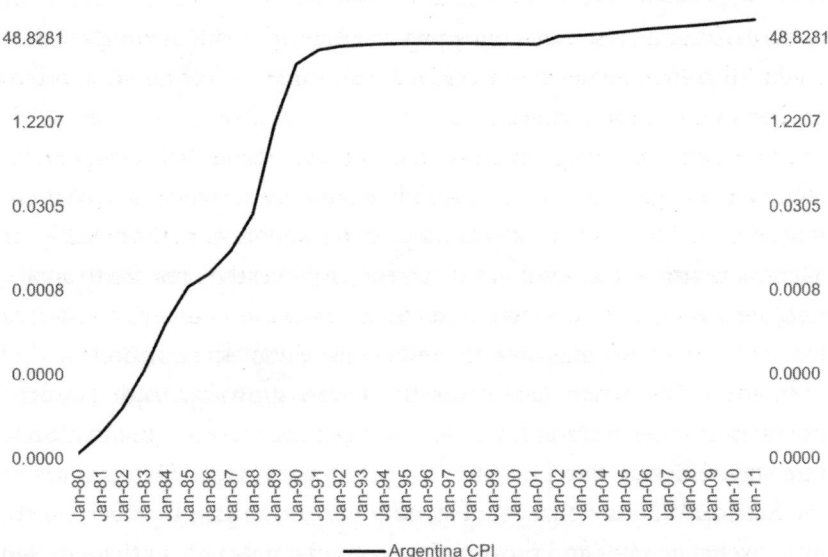

Source: World Bank

HONG KONG AND ARGENTINA IN THE 1980S AND 1990S

In 1983, perceiving the newly robust demand for the American dollar, Hong Kong re-established a currency board in that medium of foreign exchange. The monetary authority would issue a Hong Kong dollar only upon presentation of a US dollar. Over the following fifteen years, inflation, while moderate at 7 per cent per annum, was less than in the inflation-cursed 1970s and early 1980s. Real economic growth was nearly 6 per cent per annum. Argentina's currency stabilisation was a scene so awesome it could have come out of the early 1920s (see Figure 28 of the Argentine consumer price index above). This country's adoption of a currency board in 1991 brought the inflation rate down from the 2,000–3,000 per cent range of 1989–90 to seven years of nil inflation – totally stable prices – from 1994–2001. The temptation of the dollar stash within the currency board became too appealing for the authorities. The country scrapped the currency board in 2002, the board's dollar holdings quickly dissipated and inflation sharply accelerated for the long term.[6]

A CAUTIONARY TALE OF EXCHANGE RATES, THE TERMS OF TRADE AND INFLATION

A word of caution is in order regarding countries that truly are ready to proceed with growth-enhancing domestic fiscal reforms. A country that makes its domestic economy attractive to capital, investment and entrepreneurialism, through measures such as tax-rate cuts and regulatory and spending reduction, is likely to increase the demand for its currency as a result of foreigners and domestic residents wanting to invest more in the now higher after-tax returns on assets. Such a currency will feel the pressure to appreciate against foreign exchange. If the newly attractive country's authorities maintain a fixed exchange rate, the result will be domestic inflation.

In the 1960s, when Japan was the fastest growing major country, its inflation rates were at times 8–9 per cent per year, as the exchange rate stayed tightly fixed (at 362 yen per dollar) under the auspices of the Bretton Woods dollar–gold standard arrangement. In other words, fixed exchange rates and pro-growth economic polices lead to increased inflation, because the country's terms of trade need to rise to adjust to the changed economic situation. Later on in its history, Japan became a big-spending, high-taxing, slow-growth country, and its domestic inflation fell sharply, even though its exchange rate remained sound.

The UK shadowed the Deutsche Mark between early 1987 and late 1988 shortly after lowering the top income tax rate by a third. The booming economy and the failure to let the currency appreciate led to a sharp rise in prices totalling 30 per cent between 1988 and 1992. This more than anything else led to Margaret Thatcher's political demise. This British experience contrasted with the American willingness, after 1978, to permit the dollar's exchange rate to soar, and domestic prices to disinflate, as the United States enacted tax-rate cuts. The general point is that if a country wishes to attract capital, enhance its growth and minimise the risk of inflation, the proper strategy is to proceed with growth-en-hancing reforms – above all tax-rate cuts – while pursuing an exchange rate management strategy that permits the currency to appreciate as the domestic boom, complete with stable prices, comes.

After this, the UK then again got trapped by fixing its currency by joining the European Exchange Rate Mechanism (ERM) in 1990, just at the time when German interest rates were rising because of unification. The timing was unfortunate and the foreign exchange market's belief that the UK could not sustain a high interest rate policy led to the sterling's ejection from the ERM in 1992. The evidence both of shadowing the Deutsche Mark and ERM membership doesn't totally prove that fixing the sterling exchange rate will not work, but it does show that for it to work in the UK, the timing has to be propitious. It is for this reason that although we argue for the UK Monetary Policy Committee to pay close attention to the exchange rate, we do not at this stage recommend a fixed currency policy.

The magic touch was exhibited in the monetary/trade policy mix of the United States in the Reagan era: no mistakes, no fumbles and no whiffs – well, at least not as far as monetary policy was concerned (see Figure 29).

In 1978, the huge California constitutional property tax rate limitation called Proposition 13 passed overwhelmingly against the wishes of almost all members of the political class. The Steiger–Hansen capital gains tax-rate cut was also put into law that same year, much to the consternation of the Carter administration. And lastly, 1978–79 saw the appointment of hard money champion Paul Volcker as chairman of the Federal Reserve. What a year. America had begun its 180° turnaround from anti-growth to pro-growth policies.

President Reagan took office on 20 January 1981, with tax cuts, spend-ing restraint, sound money, regulatory reform and free trade as his promised goals. Save for some serious but ultimately inconsequential glitches, he was amazingly successful. Looking only at taxes, the high-est marginal individual income tax rate was cut from 70 per cent to 28 per cent, the corporate income tax rate from 46 per cent to 34 per cent, eleven tax brackets were replaced with only two and heretofore tax loop-holes were closed. The capital gains tax base excluded 60 per cent of all gains and only the remaining 40 per cent were taxed at the highest tax rate. America was back. But President Reagan and Chairman Volcker were careful not to make the inflation mistake.

FIGURE 29: US DOLLAR STRENGTH INDEX VS US INFLATION RATE
(monthly, July 1978–June 1985, left axis (Dollar index) semi-log scale)

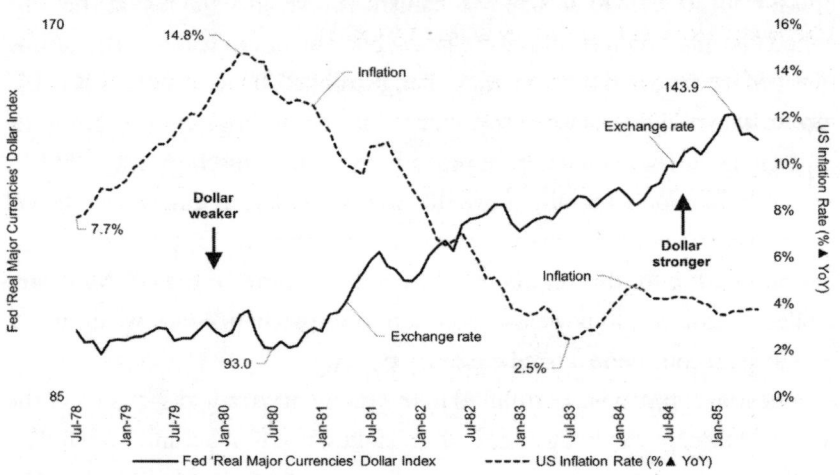

Source: Fed Board of Governors, BLS

From midway through 1980 to January 1985, the US dollar was allowed to appreciate by a little less than 50 per cent in the foreign exchanges, thus avoiding the inflation trap that supply-side economics often creates.

By having such large increases in pro-growth incentives, foreigners and domestic residents wanted to increase their investments in the US economy. Thus, there were sizeable increases in the amount of productive assets as well as asset prices, all as a consequence of the radical shift in US policy. The trade deficit/capital surplus increased enormously, forcing a huge increase in the US terms of trade. Without exchange rate appreciation, the increase in the terms of trade would have led to markedly higher inflation in the US. But the insightful policies of Chairman Volcker in conjunction with President Reagan provided an expansive economy like no other and continued declines in inflation (see Figure 29), a very strong dollar and a huge capital surplus. What's not to love?

In the late 1980s, the United Kingdom managed badly the transition that Reagan had mastered in the United States. In 1988, the top income tax rate in the UK fell abruptly from 60 to 40 per cent. After the dramatic cut, a large flood of capital into the country appeared – as the exchange rate stayed fixed.

FIGURE 30: UK INFLATION, MARK PER POUND EXCHANGE RATE AND UK TOP MARGINAL PERSONAL INCOME TAX RATE

(inflation is year-over-year percentage change in monthly RPI, exchange rate is end of month, January 1983 to January 1993)

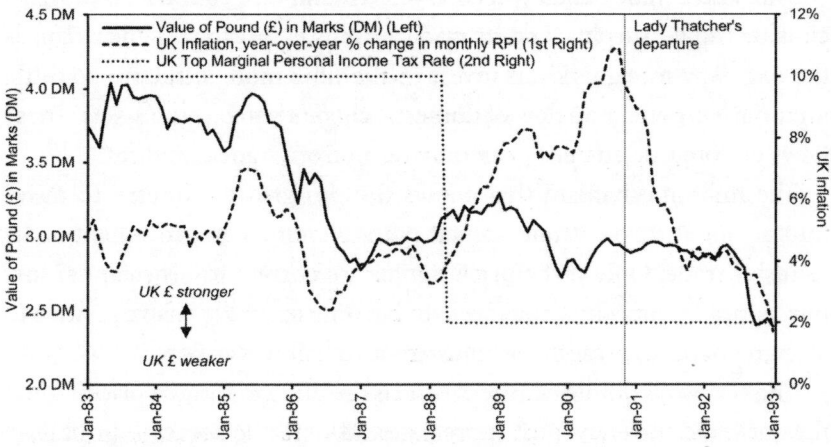

Source: UK Office of National Statistics, Bloomberg

Instead of allowing the British pound to revalue to accommodate an increase in the UK's terms of trade as the UK should have done, the UK government took it upon itself to fix the British pound to the German mark. The logic was simple and wrong. The UK government thought that preventing pound appreciation would maintain British goods' competitiveness. Unfortunately, nothing could have been further from the truth. British goods had to become non-competitive by hook or by crook to allow capital to enter the country.

As shown in Figure 30, from early 1988, British inflation rose from a little below 4 per cent per annum to well over 10 per cent in late 1990. The high inflation never would have happened if the pound had been allowed to appreciate. International economics does matter.

The logic underlying the link between the adoption of pro-growth policies – most notably tax-rate cuts and spending restraint – goes something like this. By cutting tax rates and reducing government spending, the after-tax rate of return on assets increases. Both foreign and domestic investors will want to invest more in the pro-growth country. This will lead to an increase in prices of domestic assets. But for foreigners, their increase in demand for the now higher return assets means that they will have to sell more goods to the now more attractive country and buy fewer goods from the now more attractive country. Imports will rise, exports will fall and a trade deficit will emerge. Remember, a country's trade deficit is its capital surplus, and its trade surplus is its capital deficit. This is the *only* way foreigners can invest in the now more attractive country. They have to generate a flow of domestic currency to buy the assets. These flows of domestic currency can only result from trade surpluses.

The micromechanism that allows the pro-growth country to move into a capital surplus/trade deficit is the *necessary* improvement in its terms of trade. Only if the price signals are correct will the capital surplus appear. Domestic goods have to become more expensive relative to foreign goods for a capital surplus/trade deficit to develop.

The two ways domestic prices can rise relative to foreign prices are: i) the domestic currency must appreciate and/or ii) the domestic price level must rise. If the tax-cutting, pro-growth country fixes its exchange rate and does not allow its currency to appreciate, it will experience domestic inflation, which at times can be very high and politically disabling. If the tax-cutting, pro-growth country allows its currency to appreciate, it can avoid higher inflation and yet still accommodate unbridled growth.

A country that does not bestride the world as a colossus needs to pay huge attention to its exchange rate policy. The world votes on the value of money despite any actions by such a country. Therefore, a country that is not a bona fide superpower should permit the exchange rate to rise as the fruits of proper domestic economic reforms set in. Example upon example has shown that putting priority on appropriate exchange rate management in no way hinders the domestic money supply, is a cure for inflation and when paired with the slimming of the fiscal profile of the state corresponds to excellent levels of economic growth.

A PRICE, NOT A QUANTITY, RULE FOR MONETARY POLICY

Price and quantity – the two grand measurements of macroeconomics. Businesses generally 'take' prices from the market in which they operate and seek to produce the maximum quantity of their wares that they can sell at a profit at a given price. Money is no different. Suppliers of money properly wish to get it on the market as much as possible at the given price.

The 'quantity theory' of money would have it differently. The proponents of this theory postulate that the authorities should target an amount of money as the goal to be achieved. No business aspires to produce a specific amount of product and wait to see how the price shakes out. Price rules are better than quantity rules for monetary policy.

A classic illustration of this maxim came at the great juncture, the great transition in the world economy in 1982. In that difficult recession year, Ronald Reagan committed to not repealing the tax-rate cuts he had signed into law the previous year. While the tax-rate cuts were in jeopardy, the demand for money was low. Once those tax rates were secured, demand for money was set to soar. Managing monetary quantities in such a volatile environment was a fool's errand. The Federal Reserve came to this conclusion, targeted prices and the great real-sector boom of the 1980s found its complement in expansive monetary policy that coincided with price stability.

Here is how Arthur Laffer and Charles Kadlec put it in the *Wall Street Journal* in October 1982:

A price rule for monetary policy – the final precondition for the roaring '80s – is being put into place … [The Fed has had] to choose between stabilizing commodity prices and keeping within its target range for money supply growth. Under a price rule, commodity prices are stabilized within a narrow range. Under a quantity rule for monetary policy, the emphasis has been to stabilize the growth rate in the money supply.

For the past three years, the Fed has attempted to control the quantity of money, and the volatility in interest and inflation rates was the inevitable consequence. If the Fed is now on a price rule, interest rates and the price level can be stabilized. But growth rates in money will become volatile.

[Over] the previous two weeks, spot commodity prices had been falling ... The choice was to lower the Fed funds rate. The fall in commodity prices was stopped.

In conclusion, Laffer and Kadlec noted that a price rule for monetary policy 'would imply continued growth in the monetary aggregates above the target range, a secular decline in interest rates, an acceleration of economic growth, and gains in equity prices'. The accompanying chart showed the relationship between the commodity index and the federal funds rate:

FIGURE 31: SPOT COMMODITY INDEX VS. FEDERAL FUNDS RATE
(Daily, 1 June 1982–15 October 1982; 31 Dec 1974 = 100)

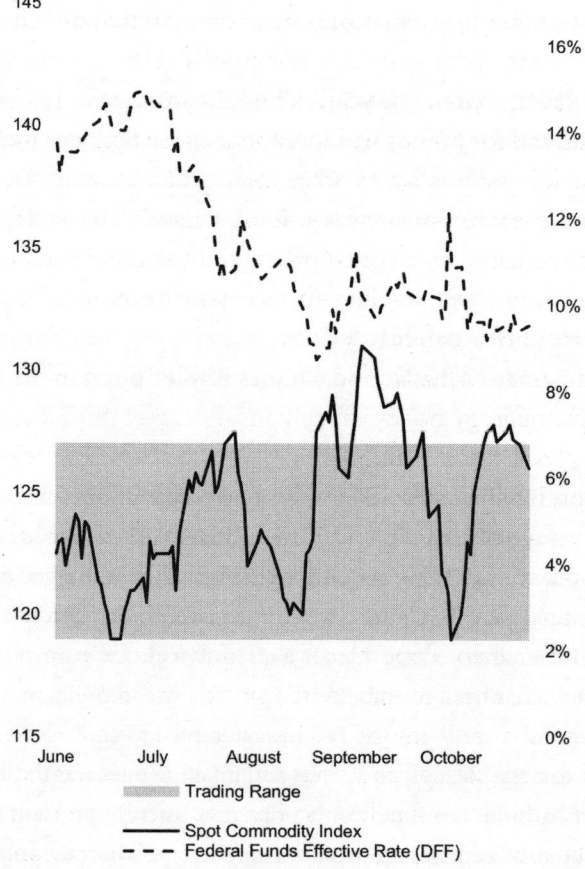

Source: Dr Arthur B. Laffer, Wall Street Journal

If the United Kingdom commits to real growth-oriented tax, regulatory, spending and trade policies, it will court the same transition that the United States experienced in 1982. The demand for the pound sterling will soar if the UK makes free market commitments that break with its recent past and that its neighbours are not willing to make to the same degree. Monetary policy quantity targeting will be wholly inappropriate to these circumstances. Monetary demand will surge as the after-tax return to investment and enterprise goes up, as the displacement of the economy by the fiscal sector goes down and as barriers to trade lessen. Expansionary monetary supply in such a circumstance will not be inflationary, given that monetary demand will be increasing for real purposes. All one has to do to ensure that the boom is financed, while prices remain stable, is for the monetary authority to target low inflation.

ENERGY PRICES AND MONETARY EXPANSION

The recent inflationary bouts have been associated with the monetary expansion that accompanied the start of the Covid pandemic and the boost to energy prices after Russia invaded Ukraine in 2022. Hard-line monetarists would claim that a boost to energy prices need not be associated with higher prices generally if monetary policy is not accommodating.

This is probably a correct analysis in the very long term, but in the shorter term, demand for money is not stable and also part of the adjustment to higher energy prices is likely to be weaker output and a higher overall price level. Since a supply shock of a sharp rise in energy prices is likely to be both deflationary and inflationary, managing the inflationary consequences is genuinely complicated. Modern economies are highly dependent on energy (a dependence that is likely to grow in a world of big data) and there are risks in taking too aggressive a monetary response at a time when economies are already weakening.

The consensus now appears to be that it is critical that macro policy prevents second-round knock-on inflationary effects; that ideally the cost effects for businesses and households of the rise in energy prices are NOT cushioned by subsidies, however politically difficult this might be, and that any remaining inflationary consequences are gradually squeezed out over a period of a small number of years. It is paradoxical, but the solution to high prices is high prices, since the initially high prices stimulate increased supply and reduced demand that ultimately lead to lower prices.

The effects of the energy price rises in 2022 were exacerbated by the authorities' response to Covid. In April 2020, when Covid first started to have an economic effect in the West, the US money supply was expanded sharply. The M1 money supply roughly tripled from $4.79 trillion to $16.24 trillion in May 2020, while M2 rose from $15.994 trillion in March 2020 to $21.750 trillion in April 2021, an unprecedented 36 per cent rise, which took place over a handful of months.[7] The main means by which this happened was so-called quantitative easing. The rise in the US money supply led to monetary expansion elsewhere, including in the UK.

As the economy started to recover post-Covid, supply shortages emerged. The combination of these and the impact of the Ukraine War energy shock, with commodity prices generally boosted by the rise in the world's money supply that followed the US's jump in its own money supply, meant that inflation[*] spiked worldwide, peaking at 9 per cent in the US in June 2022 and 11.1 per cent in the UK in October 2022. However, restrictive monetary policies and a turnaround in the energy markets caused inflation to fall back, though at the time of writing it remains at 2.7 per cent in the US and 3.6 per cent in the UK.[†]

GLOBAL MONEY GROWTH AND INFLATION

The inflation and recession of recent years are clearly a world phenomenon, affecting all developed nations with only minor differences. Talk of economic 'interdependence' is widespread. Yet economic policy is usually thought of on a national basis, as if the economies of different nations were only loosely connected, and it is to an extent. Although world finance ministers and central banks do coordinate policies to some degree, most central banks' mandates are to do with their domestic economy.

This is particularly relevant when attempting to control inflation. Experience ought to be teaching us that economists can no longer focus exclusively on domestic factors to explain domestic inflation. While

---

[*] Measured as the increase in consumer prices over the past twelve months.
[†] As of 29 July 2025.

such a narrow view may have been appropriate at some time in the past, it clearly no longer is. What is even more important about the worldwide view of inflation, as opposed to the closed economy view, is that the policy implications are very different.

One can imagine that somehow the monetary authorities can control a closed economy's money supply – say demand deposits plus currency. In the world economy, control, as a practical matter, borders on inconceivable and, most assuredly, has not been practised in recent years. The role of any one country's monetary authority – such as the US Federal Reserve Board – wanes dramatically in the perspective of the world.

Money is, after all, one of the easiest commodities to move across national borders. Individual banks and other financial institutions operate in numerous US and foreign locations. Even when the foreign operations are not direct subsidiaries, correspondent relationships and other close associations have been developed. The money markets not only within the United States but also in the world economy are closely interrelated by this vast financial network. Even the recent advent of floating exchange rates has not led to the dissolution of integrated money markets. With spot and forward foreign exchange markets, floating rates, at most, have only added somewhat to the costs of operating in those markets.

In light of the case with which money can be moved across borders and translated from one currency to another, it would seem that any anti-inflation policy will have to concentrate on world monetary factors. However, in numerical terms, no such figure is regularly available, and in trying to construct it, there are numerous problems with data. But we can construct a statistical series measuring the world money supply in terms of US dollars.

Our series defines world money as the domestic money supplies of fifteen major countries plus net eurodollar deposits. Domestic money supplies (demand deposits plus currency) were converted into dollar amounts using appropriate exchange rates.

We have also constructed similar series for world GNP and world inflation, also defined in dollars, covering the same fifteen countries. World GNP was simply the sum of every country's GNP converted into dollars. Worldwide inflation was merely the average of changes in foreign consumer price indices, after conversion to dollars and weighting the size of each country's GNP.

These three series are closely associated. See, for example, Figure 32 on world money growth measured in dollars and world inflation also measured in dollars. The close correspondence of the data tells nothing about whether money expansion causes worldwide income growth and inflation or whether the reverse is true. There can be little doubt, however, that these series do follow each other closely.

FIGURE 32: WORLD MONEY GROWTH AND WORLD INFLATION*
(annually, 1958–74)

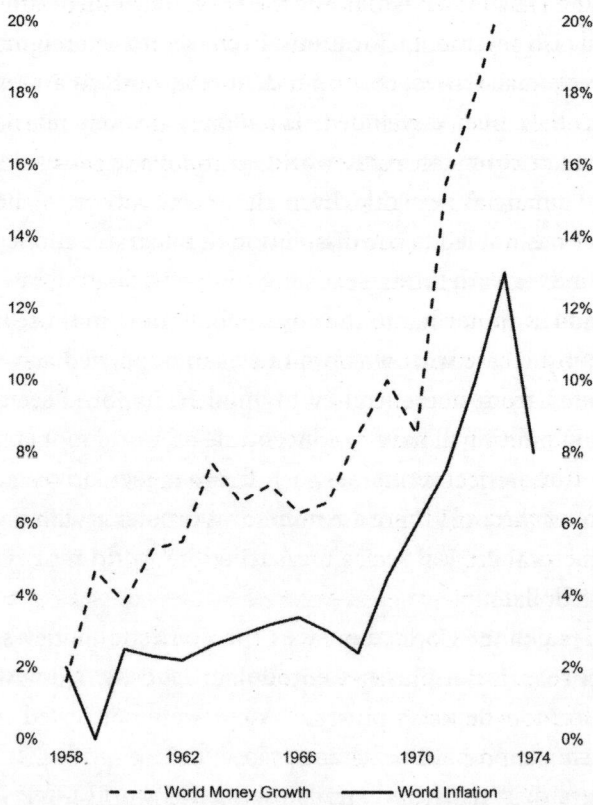

- - - World Money Growth　——— World Inflation

Source: Dr Arthur B. Laffer, Wall Street Journal

---

*　The growth of the world money supply – the domestic money supplies of fifteen nations converted into dollars plus eurodollar deposits – compared with the world inflation rate, also measured in dollars.

Indeed, the worldwide series are more closely associated than comparable series for the United States alone. Therefore, based on data, as well as theory, the worldwide view of inflation appears more relevant to real events than its closed economy counterpart. And no one familiar with these facts would even be comfortable asserting that the Fed controls the lot.

Any strategy to control world money growth will have to be based on an understanding of the various sources of growth. Four different sources come to mind: the US money supply, the domestic money supplies of other nations, the eurodollar market and the effect of exchange rate changes.

The effects of domestic money supplies are no doubt familiar to most readers. When the money supply of the US or any other nation increases, this will also represent an increase in the world money supply, other things being equal. Others might prefer to use some measure of domestic money other than demand deposits and currency, particularly for the purposes of strict comparison with eurodollar deposits. This would somewhat increase the weight of domestic money supplies in the world's money supply but would change no basic conclusions.

Since eurodollar deposits are not included in the domestic money supply of any nation, they have to be included separately in the world money supply. The inclusion of eurodollars is particularly important because they have systematically moved in the opposite direction from the effect of domestic money supplies.

That is, if the effect of domestic money supplies is to increase the growth rate of the world money supply, then the eurodollar effect is to decrease the total growth rate, and vice versa. In thirteen of the last fifteen years, for example, the growth rate of eurodollars has risen when the growth rate of the US money supply slowed and slowed when the US growth rate rose. It is as though eurodollars were deliberately offsetting the efforts of monetary authorities.

Ideally, we would have preferred to include not only eurodollars but eurocurrency deposits everywhere in the world. Unfortunately, the lack of readily available historical data precludes this. Given the lack of precision of the existing data, even this major exclusion should not alter the qualitative implications of our results. If anything, the inclusion of non-dollar eurocurrencies plus dollar liabilities outside Western Europe should greatly strengthen the implications of the following analysis.

The final source of growth in the world money supply results solely from our choice of using the US dollar as the unit of measurement for the world money supply. Even if eurodollars and each country's money supply remains unchanged, a devaluation of the dollar relative to other currencies will imply an increase in the dollar value of the world's money supply.

To illustrate, let us imagine that there are 100 Swiss Francs, and the exchange rate is four francs to the dollar. Thus, the dollar value of these 100 francs is twenty-five dollars. If the dollar devalues to the point where there are two francs to the dollar, then the dollar value of the 100 francs now equals fifty dollars. Thus, even if the supply of francs is stable, they would contribute twice as much to the world money supply measured in dollars.

The exchange rate effect depends solely on the specific currency that is used to measure the world money supply. If measured in a generally appreciating currency, say the franc, world money growth would be slower. Correspondingly, world inflation *as measured in francs* would also be lower. The sole reason for using dollars is that we felt more people were concerned with dollar inflation than inflation in any other single currency.

In Figure 33, all four of these sources are plotted over the time interval. Series one represents the effect on world money supply growth of the US money supply alone. Series two adds in the effect of the other countries' domestic money supplies. Series three adds in the additional effect of eurodollars. Finally, series four adds in the final effect – that of exchange rate changes – to get the overall rate of growth of the world money supply.

In recent years, the most striking feature of these four sources is the insignificance of US money supply growth to the growth rate of the world's total. In the past five years, US money supply growth has never accounted for as much as 25 per cent of the total money supply growth. In each and every year for the past five years, money supply growth rates of countries other than the US were well over twice as important as US money supply growth. Save one year, eurodollars were more important than US domestic dollars. In three out of the five years, the effect of exchange rate changes was more important than US money supply changes.

FIGURE 33: SOURCES OF WORLD MONEY GROWTH*

(annually, 1958–74)

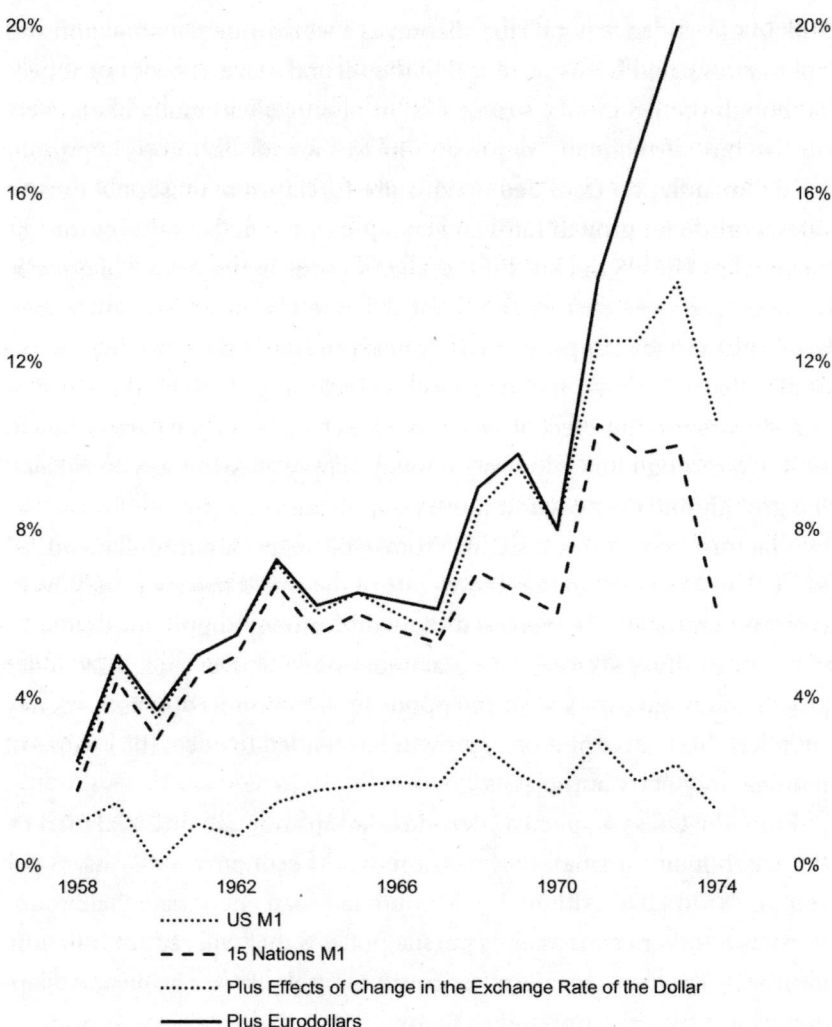

.... US M1

– – – 15 Nations M1

.... Plus Effects of Change in the Exchange Rate of the Dollar

———— Plus Eurodollars

Source: Dr Arthur B. Laffer, Wall Street Journal

---

*   Series one is US domestic money supply (demand deposits plus currency). Series two adds the domestic money
supplies of fourteen other developed nations, translated into dollar amounts at appropriate exchange rates. Series
three adds eurodollar deposits. Series four includes the effect of movement in the exchange rates of the dollar.

Without making any excuses for particular policies of the Federal Reserve System, it would seem hard to justify single-minded attention to the US money supply on the basis of this evidence. In the first place, the bulk of the evidence points to inflation as a worldwide phenomenon and not as an isolated US occurrence. In the second place, it does not appear as though the US money supply has, in practice, had much of an effect on the rate of monetary expansion in the world. Far more important for dollar inflation than Fed actions are foreign money supply growth rates, eurodollar growth rates and changes in the dollar value of foreign currencies. The US has little, if any, control over these sources of growth.

To extend even further the point that the US has little control over the world money supply growth, we can compare the combined effect of all fifteen domestic money supplies (including the US), the effect of eurodollars and the effect of exchange rate changes for the period 1958 to 1974. Up through 1968, domestic money supply growth rates dominated the growth rate of the world money supply and the effects of the other two factors were, at best, slight. From 1968 to 1974, eurodollars added more than 2 per cent to the growth rate of the world money supply every year and cumulatively increased the world money supply by almost 20 per cent in those six years. And as mentioned above, since eurodollar growth rates have moved in the opposite direction to domestic money supplies, this source of money growth has tended to offset the actions of national monetary authorities.

From the UK's perspective, despite London's role as a financial market, the UK remains a small player in the world economy with only 3 per cent of world GDP. Although UK politicians can encourage their counterparts in other economies to pursue policies that will reduce inflation, ultimately they have to take other countries' policies as a given and adapt domestic policies to respond to them.

Even on a worldwide basis, one is hard pressed to be sanguine about the ability of the world to control inflation. Without major institutional changes, much of the world's monetary expansion is outside of the control of monetary authorities. With the freeing of exchange rates on the ratification of eurodollars, the monetary authorities' roles have diminished sharply.

Within the framework described here, inflation is a worldwide phenomenon. Individual countries' policies appear far less potent for combatting inflation than is currently believed. As far as we can tell, the best hope for controlling inflation is to re-establish control over the world's monetary growth. In order to do this, it is obvious that domestic restraint has to be exercised. In addition to domestic monetary restraint, monetary authorities must also control the effects of exchange rate changes in eurodollars. This means that movement towards more fixing of exchange rates and action to control the expansion of the eurocurrency liabilities must be part of a viable strategy to combat world inflation.

CONCLUSION

The key insight of this chapter is that although controlling money is important, exchange rate policy is especially so for small economies. It is for these reasons that we recommend, in the context of targeting nominal GDP, that attention is paid to both the currency and the money supply. It is likely that if the UK changes to a growth-orientated supply-side policy, the exchange rate will probably have to be allowed to rise for a period to offset the inflationary effects of faster growth. Failure to do this led to the policy problems of the late 1980s and early 1990s in the UK.

CHAPTER 6

THE FOURTH KINGDOM: REGULATION

'There's no doubt that the animal spirits of Britain's
entrepreneurs are being choked and restrained.'
– BORIS JOHNSON

One of the best ways of making an economy grind itself to a halt is by overregulation. As we pointed out earlier:

The subject matter of the fourth grand kingdom of macroeconomics contains a number of highly diverse policies which makes general principles far from clear. Regulations cover an enormous area of economic activities and take on a vast array of forms. But from a 60,000-foot perspective, the principles become a lot clearer.

We all know we need government regulations over a wide range of activities. People can't be free, for example, to choose to drive on the left side of the road one day and then change their minds and drive on the right side of the road the next. Transparency rules, traffic rules, judicial rules etc. are all critical to the well-functioning of a prosperous market economy.

Excessive regulation can also be stifling to economic prosperity and growth. In all, regulations should be directed to the specific externalities at hand and avoid as much as possible unintended deleterious consequences and collateral damage.

The key point about regulation is that the impact and side effects of any proposed regulation are studied in advance – that the regulation is proportional to the scale of the problem that is intended to be rectified and that regulations incorporate sunset clauses that require the case for their continuation to have to be remade after a suitable period.

This chapter looks at various areas of regulation where regulation damages incentives. We look at the labour market, energy (and environmental regulations), competition and land-use planning. But we also show areas where regulation has been essential to achieve laudable government objectives. We conclude with the principles for good regulation.

THE LABOUR MARKET

There are reasons why employees want to be protected from decisions by their employer that affect them adversely. But equally, employers want the flexibility to make business decisions about their labour force. In an ideal world, regulations affecting employment should not be pursued beyond the point where the costs of such regulations in lost flexibility and potentially higher costs outweigh the benefits to employees of such regulations. And it should be noted that most policies that in theory 'help' employees also discourage employers from hiring employees, especially those in more marginal groups. The assessed benefits to employees need to be offset against the non-hires when employers are put off hiring by the regulations, which can have devastating effects on those condemned to a life outside the employment system.

DECONTROL OF ENERGY PRICES

Energy prices become a grinding issue in an economy only when governments intervene to make it so. Countries with strong currencies and minimal taxation and regulation of energy supply, transport and sale generally have lower energy prices. The common view that things such as energy price instability, energy producer cartels and supply stocks are inescapable, that they leave a nation helpless before energy volatility, is often invalid. A country with a strong currency and a good fiscal and regulatory regime will have lower energy prices and an economy that thrives on account of the availability and low cost of energy.

A strong and stable currency is the first foundation of a proper energy policy. Energy sources can serve as a store of value, a classical feature of money itself. If a currency is declining, energy suppliers the world over, in particular suppliers of energy commodities that do not degrade quickly, will find a market for their products among not only energy consumers but also currency hedgers. The Organization of the Petroleum Exporting Countries (OPEC) oil shock of the 1970s was in great part a grandiose effort to hedge the decline of the major currencies – led by the pound sterling and the dollar – after the final abrogation of the gold standard in 1971. The scramble was on to find something that held its value, and petroleum (along with gold itself) sufficed.

FIGURE 34: REAL VS NOMINAL CRUDE OIL PRICES

(annually, 1970–82)

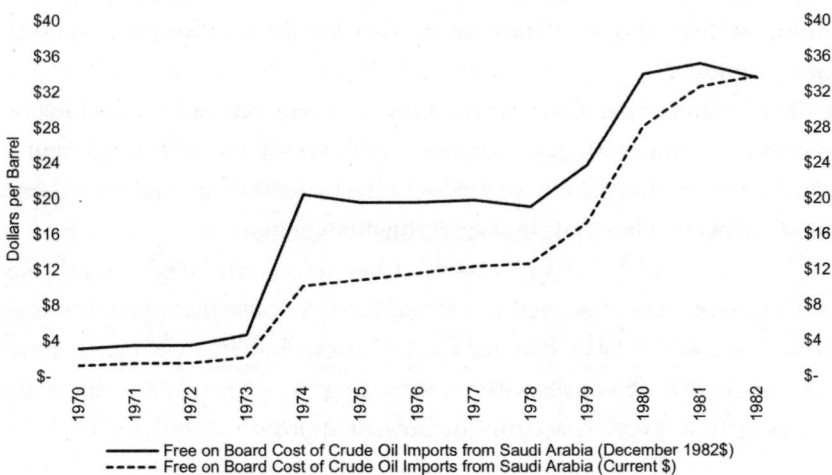

— Free on Board Cost of Crude Oil Imports from Saudi Arabia (December 1982$)
---- Free on Board Cost of Crude Oil Imports from Saudi Arabia (Current $)

Source: US EIA, BLS, Georgetown

When the dollar strengthened in the 1980s and US energy policy was deregulated, the price of energy did fall back, when oil tumbled in dollar terms from a 1980 peak of $39 per barrel to a 1986 low of $12. The dollar appreciated in value tremendously over the first half of the 1980s, as large tax-rate cuts made the dollar-denominated investment environment attractive, and the monetary authorities pursued price as opposed to quantity targets in monetary policy. The hedging of the dollar came to an end. The exclusive buyers of energy at last became energy users themselves, as prices fell appropriate to energy's actual role in the economy. The lesson: having a strong currency can eliminate a primary cause of energy price inflation.

Taxes and controls on energy are further tickets to energy price volatility and inflation and energy shortages. Energy sources, such as petroleum, can be highly tradable goods globally. There is a world price for these sources, established in deep markets across many economies. A tax in one country on energy will chase supply away to other ready outlets. A tax on one energy source will increase uses and prices of substitutes for that energy source. Just as clearly, elimination of a tax on energy opens a country to the ample supply of energy from global sources and lowers the prices of substitutes.

Energy policy should confine itself to having a strong currency and minimal taxes and regulation upon the production, transport and sale of the product.

The pursuit of net zero has complicated energy policies in many major economies. This book does not specifically take sides on environmental policy, and in this chapter, we highlight the benefits of environmental improvements that have taken place through regulation.

But it is critical that any pursuit of net zero is managed carefully so that the benefits outweigh the costs and to maximise the role of innovation. Our 24/7 Growth Plan for the UK shows how the UK can achieve environmental objectives without imposing the damage to its domestic industry that is resulting from the present approach.

COMPETITION

Classical microeconomics puts great emphasis on the need for competitive markets to yield the benefits of a healthy economy. As a result, governments around the world pursue anti-trust policies with greater or lesser enthusiasm. But in practice, anti-trust policy has to be pursued with circumspection: first, there is a risk that it can become a tax on success and that firms that capture market share by being more competitive get punished because of this; and second, many governments (especially from small economies) want to build up national 'champions' to compete with businesses from abroad.

Ensuring that regulations do not act as a barrier to market entry is an especially important way of ensuring competition. Incumbents are often surprisingly enthusiastic about their industries being regulated because most government regulations make it much more difficult for new entrants to enter the market.

Getting competition policy right is one of the most difficult areas in economics to optimise and, in practice, especially in a world where economies of scale are increasingly pervasive, getting it completely right is well-nigh impossible even looking on a case-by-case basis. But it is absolutely critical that when regulations are imposed, their anti-competitive effects are closely studied and taken into account. This is an area where the law of unintended consequences often applies and well-intended rules end up doing considerable damage by protecting uncompetitive oligopolies or monopolies.

LAND-USE PLANNING

There is good experience in the US of the impact of different regulatory restrictions on land-use planning. A fascinating study about hotels in Texas shows how different zonal restrictions within the same state affect the performance of the hotel sector in different localities.[1] In less restricted localities, set-up costs can be up to a third less and the empirical evidence from micro data shows that this can double the amount of competition in the sector, keeping prices down and increasing consumer choice.

The tendency for governments to impose ever-growing land-use requirements was cited by McKinsey's study of the UK, commissioned by Gordon Brown, as the single biggest explanator of low productivity in the UK service sector.[2]

The principle of good land-use planning is to ensure that every new regulation can be justified when its potentially negative effects on the economy can be properly evaluated against the potential environmental and social benefits (which are often less well evidenced and can prove illusory, whereas the economic costs are genuinely real). It is best to incorporate sunset clauses so that regulation has to be continually justified to prevent outmoded regulations.

GOVERNMENT CAN AND HAS GOT IT RIGHT MANY TIMES

EXAMPLE #1: THE INTERSTATE HIGHWAY PROGRAMME

The Problem: The abundance of unsafe roads, inefficient routes and traffic jams that were limiting the nation's economic growth potential and its ability to respond to national security threats.

The Solution: Though plans for a national highway system had been discussed by President Franklin Roosevelt as far back as 1936, it wasn't until Congress passed President Eisenhower's Federal-Aid Highway Act of 1956 that words became action. The federal government agreed to pay 90 per cent of the cost of the Interstate System but left much decision-making in the hands of the states. The Interstate System ended up costing $425 billion in 2006 dollars and was completed in 1992 – covering 200,733 miles.[3]

EXAMPLE #2: CLEARING THE SMOG IN LOS ANGELES

The Problem: In 1943, Los Angeles documented its first cases of smog.[4] The smog, which scientists tied to automobile use, made irritated eyes, irritated respiratory tracts, chest pains, coughs, nausea and headaches a regular occurrence and led to long-term lung damage.

The Solution: In 1947, LA started the Air Quality Management District (AQMD) and began monitoring smog levels. The AQMD passed rules limiting emissions from cars, factories and farms (tyres were often burned to keep crops warm). The guidelines were enormously successful in reducing smog levels. A 2016 study found smog reduction was critical to improving the health of children in Southern California.[5]

And the example that made all of these other great achievements possible:

EXAMPLE #3: US ENTRY INTO THE FIRST AND SECOND WORLD WARS

We'll leave it to historians to explain the causes and consequences of the First and Second World Wars. But it is an incontestable fact that the decision by the United States to enter into both wars was crucial to the victory of the Allied powers and to the preservation of democracy and Western values. Furthermore, even under wartime controls, the US economy demonstrated the productive superiority of the market system to the centrally planned economies of its enemies.

EXAMPLE #4: PREVENTING SPECIES FROM EXTINCTION

> 'We do not know the true nature of the entity we are destroying.'
> – ARTHUR C. CLARKE, CITING THE LARGE BRAIN SIZE
> OF THE BLUE WHALE IN 1962

In 1963, there were only 478 breeding pairs of bald eagles in the US. The species was on the verge of extinction due to deforestation, overhunting of prey and the widespread use of the insecticide DDT, which caused eagles to lay eggs with thin shells that cracked before hatchlings were ready.

Banning DDT, prohibiting the killing of bald eagles, improving water quality and protecting nest sites all served to boost the number of breeding pairs to just under 10,000 by 2006. The bald eagle was taken off the endangered species list in 2007. There were an estimated 10,000 breeding pairs of bald eagles in the contiguous US as of 2006.

The blue whale is considered to be the largest animal on earth (ever!), measuring between 82 and 105 feet and weighing up to 200 tons. The blue whale typically lives eighty to ninety years, but some live much longer. Prior to the 1860s, blue whales were too swift and powerful for hunters to kill, but the advent of harpoon cannons enabled hunters to capture them in large numbers. Between 1900 and 1965, some 360,000 blue whales were slaughtered, leaving them on the brink of extinction with a population of 1,000. In 1966, the blue whale fell under the global protection of the International Whaling Commission. The blue whale remains an endangered species. There are an estimated 10,000–25,000 blue whales alive today.

In the sixteenth century, 30–60 million bison roamed throughout North America. The westward expansion of European settlers and Native Americans put pressure on bison populations over the next 300 years. Bison were hunted for their pelts and killed in large numbers to clear land for railways. In the 1870s, one railway company shipped 500,000 bison hides back to the east. By 1889, a mere 1,000 were living in the US and Canada and the trade in bison hides ended. In the 1890s, states and the federal government took action to preserve the bison. Markets also played a role: the high market value of the remaining bison (695 sold for $170,000 in 1912) incentivised private preservation and breeding. While still on the endangered species list, the bison population is estimated at 500,000.

OTHER SPECIES PRESERVED THROUGH GOVERNMENT ACTION

After forty-two years on the endangered species list, the Yellowstone grizzly bear – whose population has grown from 150 to 700 – was taken off the list in 2017.

In the 1970s, between twelve and twenty Florida panthers lived in the wild; that population grew to between 100 and 160 by 2015. 'Indeed, there are so many big cats in the Everglades that they are venturing out in search of new territory,' said the *New Yorker*.

After dwindling to 324 nesting pairs in 1975, there are now between 2,000 and 3,000 nesting pairs of peregrine falcons in the United States.

EXAMPLE #5: CUYAHOGA RIVER AND LAKE ERIE

'Anyone who falls in the Cuyahoga does not drown. He decays.'
– CLEVELAND CITIZEN QUOTED IN *TIME MAGAZINE*,
1 AUGUST 1969

The Problem: The growth of the nineteenth and twentieth centuries was borne by the waterways which transported goods, people and, unfortunately, waste. The Cuyahoga River became so polluted with industrial waste that it caught fire thirteen times![6]

The Solution: Due in part to the 1969 Cuyahoga fire, Congress passed the National Environmental Policy Act (NEPA) in 1970, which led to the creation of the Environmental Protection Agency (EPA) and the Clean Water Act, the latter of which mandated that water be clean enough for humans and fish to safely swim in and devoted funds to clean-up efforts. By the 2000s, the Cuyahoga River and Lake Erie met or exceeded most EPA benchmarks.

EXAMPLE #6: ACID RAIN
The Problem: Acid rain is a broad term that includes any form of precipitation with acidic components, such as sulphuric or nitric acid, which falls to the ground from the atmosphere in wet or dry forms. This can include rain, snow, fog, hail or even dust that is acidic.[7]

The Solution: Enable economic principles and property rights to work their magic. The Acid Rain Program (ARP) of the 1990 Clean Air Act used a market-based system to achieve emission reductions, meet environmental goals and improve human health. The improvement has been so great that acid rain is no longer a topic of conversation.

EXAMPLE #7: REDUCED PREVALENCE OF SMOKING
The Problem: The dramatic increase in deaths due to cancer among adults in the 1940s and beyond.

The Solution: In 1964, the US Surgeon General released a landmark first-of-its kind report on the harmful health effects associated with tobacco smoking. Drawing upon over 7,000 scientific studies, the report tied smoking to lung and laryngeal cancer.[8]

The Surgeon General's report dominated the headlines and at the time was one of the biggest stories of 1964. The Federal Cigarette Labeling and

Advertising Act of 1965 and the Public Health Cigarette Smoking Act of 1969 limited how cigarette companies could promote tobacco products. Since then, smoking rates among adults and teens have been reduced by half.

CONCLUSION

This chapter describes inefficient areas of regulation and some areas where regulation has proved a success. The key to good regulation is to ensure that all regulation is cost-justified before implementation and that (often but not always) optimistic assessments of social and environmental benefits are rigorously scrutinised. Potential environmental benefits are especially likely to be overstated – as a general rule (though there are of course well-known exceptions), the most economic solutions often turn out to be the most environmentally friendly solutions because economic efficiency reduces waste. It is no coincidence that the least environmentally friendly factories have been found in the former communist states where free market economics has not been applied. And to ensure that regulations that have served their purpose are taken off the statute book, it is necessary to have sunset clauses so that regulations are time-limited and need regular assessment to ensure that they have not outlived their purpose.

CHAPTER 7

THE FIFTH KINGDOM: INTERNATIONAL TRADE

'I'm a believer in free trade. That's a minority opinion these days.'
– Rishi Sunak

We point out in Chapter 1, 'Going back as far as records have been kept, trade has been as important as any factor in creating prosperity and economic growth.'

In this section, we explain the simple Ricardian theory of comparative advantage from trade, extend it to incorporate the Alexander gains from trade and look at why we should not be automatically scared of trade deficits (some of the strongest economies have run them) and why devaluations are often not a panacea.

The theories we develop here are especially important in the context of reforms to move the UK from being an economy that is roughly flat-lining to a growth economy. The experience of the 1980s shows that such a transition tends to encourage inflows of capital and that unless the exchange rate is allowed to adjust to take some of the strain, such inflows can prove inflationary.

THE RICARDIAN COMPARATIVE ADVANTAGE GAINS FROM TRADE*

To set the stage for international trade and the benefits derived therefrom, we focus first on the individual countries that will be involved once

---

* Named after the renowned British economist David Ricardo. The theory of comparative advantage was set out in his seminal book *On the Principles of Political Economy and Taxation*, John Murray, 1817.

trade begins. Once trade among the countries is fully developed, there are two broad categories of associated benefits between the pre-trade period and the full-trade period to wit: Ricardian comparative advantage and the Alexander global reallocation of capital (and also when tariffs are appropriate). Prior to trade, each country involved has its own autarkic economy composed of a large set of products, each with its own unique set of producers, consumers and local currency prices. In this pre-trade circumstance, there are no exports, no imports, no capital flows and no terms of trade or exchange rates, which is literally the meaning of autarkic.

Taking each country in turn, prior to international trade, we can list each product the country consumes and produces and its local currency price where supply equals demand. Using the same categories of products for each country, we can compare each of the country's local currency prices with those same prices for each of the other countries. To keep matters simple and easy to understand without loss of content, we'll use a two-country example – the US and the UK – with dollars and pounds as local currencies, respectively.

Table 8's rows represent each product, and the columns represent each country's local price for each product: US in dollars and UK in pounds. In the final column we can take the ratio of the two prices for each product, i.e. the price in dollars for each product divided by the price in pounds for that same product (see below). This final column can be thought of as the exchange rate, or better yet, the terms of trade, for the price of each specific product in each country.

TABLE 8: TERMS OF TRADE

	Products	Price in Dollars	Price in Pounds	Ratio of $/£
1				
2				
3				
...				
n				

Once the table is filled out – remembering that all of this takes place prior to international trade – we can then re-arrange all of the products, their respective local currency price ratios (terms of trade) and rank them from the highest ratio (i.e. largest dollar price/pound price) to the lowest ratio. Now the fun begins.

If we open up trade, the product with the highest US dollar price to UK pound price ratio (i.e. terms of trade) represents the best opportunity for UK exporters to profit by selling to the US and the best opportunity for US consumers to benefit from importing the product from the UK. The next highest dollar/pound price ratio product in the hierarchy represents the second-best product for UK exporters and US importers and on down the line.

By the time we get to the last product in this column, we have the product with the lowest terms of trade (US dollar/pound price ratio). Here the relative attractiveness to suppliers and demanders by country are reversed. This lowest ratio represents the best opportunity for US exporters to profit by selling goods to the UK and UK consumers to benefit by buying those goods from the US. Without burying ourselves in transportation costs – cost, insurance and freight (CIF) and free on board (FOB) – and complicated demand and supply curves, it's easy to see how trade will occur. In general, one would expect UK exports and US imports where dollar/pound prices are high and US exports and UK imports where dollar/pound price ratios – i.e. the individual products' terms of trade – are low. And for this we need only to imagine our exchange rate between the dollar and the pound – e.g. how many dollars it takes to buy a pound in the foreign exchange market (which, by the way, is the inverse of how many pounds it takes to buy a dollar).

The fewer dollars it takes to buy a pound (i.e. the more pounds it takes to buy a dollar), the greater the gains from trade to British exporters and US consumers will be for all products. The more dollars it takes to buy a pound, the greater the gains from trade for US exporters and British consumers will be for all products. Take note here that higher and lower terms of trade/exchange rates not only determine which goods are exported and which goods are imported but also how much of each good is either exported or imported.

Hypothetically, with an exchange rate (US dollar price of a pound) equal to or greater than the product with the highest dollar/pound price ratio, everyone will want to export all UK goods to the US, and no one will want to import any US goods into the UK. With only two countries, there will be no trade if the UK has an absolute advantage in all products because neither country will have any foreign exchange earnings to buy imports in return for their exports. Thus, the exchange rate/terms of trade will migrate downward.

Likewise, at a dollar/pound price ratio lower than the lowest autarkic cost ratio, the US will have an absolute advantage in all products and there will also be no trade. In order to have trade, exporters need to be able to use foreign exchange proceeds from selling their products in order to buy imports. Without any incentives to import, exporters will have no incentive to export. It makes no sense to sell your products if you can't use the proceeds to buy things. For trade to make sense, the dollar/pound exchange rate therefore has to be lower than the autarkic highest dollar/pound price ratio and higher than the lowest dollar/pound price ratio.

If we conceptually lower the dollar price of the pound – the exchange rate – from its highest point or raise the dollar price of the pound from its lowest point, trade will emerge. The more we lower the exchange rate (i.e. the dollar price of the pound) from its highest point or raise the exchange rate from its lowest point, the more products will be traded – exported or imported. Moving these two separate hypothetical exchange rates (one high and one low) towards each other, trade will continue to increase until the two exchange rates converge. At that point, there will be only one exchange rate where both the pound value of exports equals the pound value of imports, as well as the dollar value of exports equalling the dollar value of imports.

This exchange rate is the Ricardian comparative advantage exchange rate/terms of trade. Consumers in the US and consumers in the UK benefit greatly by importing less expensive UK or US products, respectively. In the same vein, the more efficient producers in the UK expand their production as a result of trade, as do the most efficient producers in the US. This is a win-win gains-of-trade for both consumers and producers.[*]

---

[*] You may note that non-trade prices of export goods for each country were lower than their prices with trade – thus, disadvantaging some consumers in each country. Likewise, inefficient producers in each country that are replaced by imports will also earn less after trade. The total benefits, however, to the consumers and producers in each country are greater than total losses.

Obviously, costs, frictions, variations in tastes and other natural impediments will affect the size of the gains from trade. But because our focus is going to be on government-imposed policies such as tariffs, quotas and non-tariff barriers, this above description will be just fine to explore the Ricardian system of the gains from trade.

A final point, which we will turn to in the next few pages, is the relationship between what we referred to as hypothetical exchange rates, i.e. terms of trade and each country's exports and imports. While we use the words exchange rate or real exchange rate, in this circumstance economists refer usually to the 'exchange rate' as the terms of trade (the ratio of the value of one country's goods relative to other countries' goods). The distinction between exchange rates, which are purely monetary in nature, and terms of trade, which are the ratio of the value of goods in exchange, is crucial. This distinction is especially important when countries devalue their currencies or run separate monetary policies. As you will see, countries get into all sorts of problems when they confuse devaluation (a monetary phenomenon) and changes in the terms of trade (a real phenomenon). In modern times, governments can directly control exchange rates but only indirectly affect the terms of trade.

With this as our segue, we can now use an intellectual experiment within the Ricardian comparative advantage framework that will serve as a bridge between the Ricardian gains from trade and the Alexander gains from trade.

Imagine we start with the Ricardian exchange rate (terms of trade) where trade is balanced. If we allow ourselves the luxury of not being concerned with a balanced trade position (the value of exports must equal the value of imports), we can imagine what would happen to a country's trade balance if its terms of trade or real exchange rate appreciated. To do this we need to move from product to product to assess what would happen to exports and imports were there to be a change in the terms of trade. For example, using our US/UK example, if the dollar appreciated above the Ricardian real exchange rate (the US terms of trade went higher), then more and more products would be profitable for the UK to export to the US and more of each product would be profitable to export as well. US exports would decline, US imports would increase and, as a result, the US trade balance would move into a deficit position (trade balance being equal to a country's exports minus its imports). The increase in the US trade deficit would be identical to the increase in the UK's trade surplus.

Likewise, if the dollar terms of trade were to fall, all else the same, US exports to the UK would increase in every category and imports would decline. The further down the US terms of trade fall, the greater the US trade surplus/UK trade deficit will be. Table 9 illustrates this point.

TABLE 9: RICARDIAN TRADE BALANCE SHIFTS: US VS UK UNDER CHANGING $/£ RATIOS

Highest $/£ cost ratio	US Trade Balance	UK Trade Balance		
...	-	+	↑	Increasing US terms of trade (opposite for UK terms of trade)
...	-	+		
...	0	0	**Ricardian Rate**	
...	+	-	↓	Declining US terms of trade (opposite for UK terms of trade)
...	+	-		
Lowest $/£ Cost Ratio				

This hypothetical relationship between a country's terms of trade and its trade balance is absolutely crucial to the next section as we investigate the next category of the gains from trade in the capital balance or Alexander gains from trade.

THE ALEXANDER GAINS FROM TRADE WITH CAPITAL FLOWS[*]

The second – quite separate – class of benefits from trade arises from the net transfer of goods and services from one country to another. These gains are referred to as the capital flows or Alexander gains from trade. Within an economy, these net flows occur between savers – people whose incomes exceed their consumption – and investors. But

---

[*] Named after the renowned American economist Sidney Alexander, on the basis of his article 'Effects of a Devaluation on a Trade Balance', *IMF Staff Papers* 2, No. 2, 1952.

international capital flows also take place and are important in the international balancing of payments to match trade flows. Prior to describing the generic case of the capital flows or the Alexander gains from trade, a short example may help.

Imagine a machine sitting in a factory in Hokkaido, Japan, that is not performing well. In fact, imagine this machine is losing money and has a negative rate of return. Also, imagine this machine, if located in Denver, Colorado, would have an attractive positive rate of return. The owner of the machine, based on the profitability differential in the rates of return, decides to move the machine from Japan to Colorado.

First, the machine is loaded on a lorry in Hokkaido and driven to Tokyo Harbour. Once there, it is loaded onto a cargo vessel headed to San Francisco. When the vessel arrives in San Francisco, the machine is offloaded, put on a truck and sent to the factory in Denver, where it begins its new profitable existence. Everyone is better off. The losses in Japan accruing to this machine are replaced by profits accruing to the machine once located in Denver.

Loading the machine onto a ship in Tokyo Harbour constitutes a Japanese export and an increase in Japan's trade surplus. Offloading the machine in San Francisco is a US import and a reduction in the US trade surplus. Transportation costs make the export (Japan) / import (US) difference and thus are the difference between CIF and FOB. But these technical differences in how exports and imports are valued in various locations is not a material consideration at this point. And as far as international accounts go, it's clear: the shipment of the machine to the US from Japan is a US trade deficit and a Japanese trade surplus.

But what is also clear is that the US now has one additional machine than it had before the trade and Japan now has one less machine. Having one more machine in the US is a capital surplus for the US while having one less machine in Japan is a Japanese capital deficit. In other words, the US trade deficit is one and the same as the US capital surplus, while the Japanese trade surplus is also Japan's capital deficit. Trade deficits and surpluses are one and the same as capital surpluses and deficits, respectively. You can't have one without the other.

Given the policies of each country and the circumstances at hand, these capital account surpluses and deficits greatly benefit the world economy and each country involved. Japan is better off, the US is better off and the world economy is better off. The owners of the machine are better off. This Alexander trade balance effect is also a win-win gain from trade, just as is the Ricardian comparative advantage gain from trade. This international net flow of goods and services among countries, via trade surpluses and trade deficits, is a global benefit for all countries because it matches net savings by country with net investment. Net savings countries earn higher returns and net investing countries are provided with more capital.

Of course, there are losses due to an increase in the rate of return on capital in Japan and a fall on the return on capital in the US, as well as effects on wages in both countries. But these losses are more than offset by the gains from trade.

FIGURE 35: US CURRENT ACCOUNT DEFICIT MIRRORED BY THE ANNUAL NET INFLOW OF FOREIGN INVESTMENT

(annually, 1980–2021)

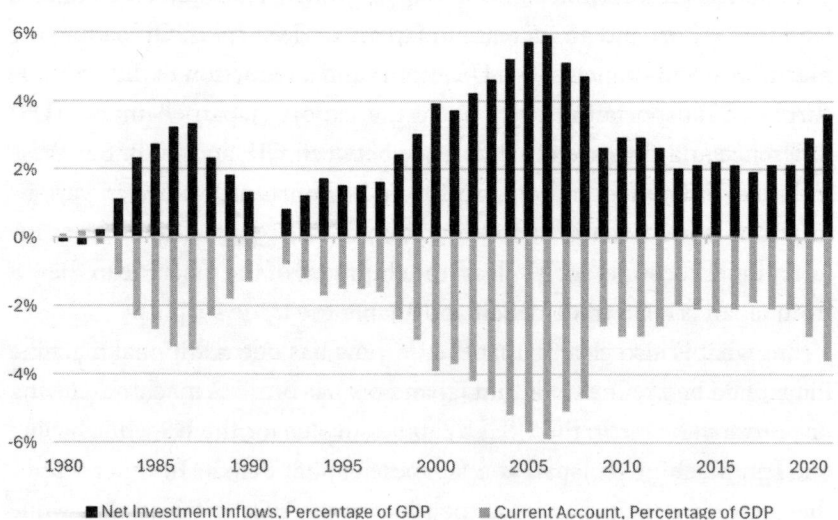

Net Investment Inflows, Percentage of GDP   Current Account, Percentage of GDP

Source: BEA

It is important to note that capital surpluses arise not only from the imports of capital goods but from any merchandise trade deficit of any sort.

If a country imports more than it exports, it means the world wishes to acquire that country's assets net to an even greater extent than it wishes to acquire that country's goods and services. The only thing to do with a country's money left over after buying to one's satisfaction that country's exports is to buy that country's financial or real assets. Countries that run trade deficits necessarily see demand, from foreigners, for their stocks, bonds, bank accounts or physical assets – everything in their investment universe. Correspondingly, countries that run trade surpluses invest in those countries which have the trade deficits. Countries that create a high level of foreign interest in their investment prospects are in an enviable position – the world thinks this is where the growth and opportunity will be. Likewise, countries that seek high returns on their savings are also in an enviable position to benefit from their trade surpluses and earn higher returns.

The scary word 'deficit', especially when juxtaposed with the comforting word 'surplus', should not obscure the fact that trade deficits mean capital surpluses – and countries running capital surpluses are often global investment magnets. One question that often puts deficit phobia to rest is which would you prefer: investors lined up on your country's border trying to get into your country or trying to get out of your country? It isn't all that bad when foreigners want to invest in your country. That's a capital surplus or a trade deficit, whichever phrase you prefer. Either way, investors (trade deficit countries) benefit from the capital flows, as do the savers (trade surplus countries).

As a matter of accounting and economics, a country's trade surplus is equal to its exports minus its imports, as well as its capital deficit, its savings minus its investment and its expenditures minus its income. Each of these phrases is just another way of saying the same thing.

Now comes the real fun. We're going to combine the Ricardian gains from trade with the Alexander gains from trade into a comprehensive international trading system. But do remember as comforting and tidy as this information is, there's still a lot more to trade, such as immigration, non-economic issues etc. But we are off to a good start.

On a worldwide scale, it should be obvious that each and every export from one country will also be an import for some other country. Not only is each export also an import, but all exports equal all imports. Therefore, if one country has a trade surplus/capital deficit, the sum of all the remaining countries will have a trade deficit/capital surplus of the same size. The world as a whole is a closed or autarkic economy with no trade or capital flows, while each country in the world will have exports, imports, capital surpluses and deficits, all of which provide the gains from trade.

Imagine now a totally free-trade world with any number of countries similar in nature to our previous discussion. Also imagine that each country in the world is in perfect balance, where all Ricardian gains from trade are fully optimised – each country produces and exports goods and services where it has a comparative advantage and consumes and imports goods and services where it is comparatively disadvantaged. All after-tax returns on assets and all after-tax wages for the same work are the same everywhere. Each country will also have its own price level, exchange rate and unique set of terms of trade. Now imagine that one of these countries' governments makes a mistake and raises tax rates on capital. This example would also include other mistakes such as monetary mistakes, spending mistakes, regulatory mistakes etc.

With now higher tax rates, the after-tax return on capital in this country will fall and some capital owners will try to move their capital to other countries where the tax rates have not been raised.* The now higher tax country will lose capital and experience a trade surplus/capital deficit reflecting the capital that has left the country, while the rest of the world has a trade deficit/capital surplus up to the point where after-tax returns are equilibrated everywhere once again.

In fact, in a more realistic description, each and every country's government will be doing all manner of things that affect the after-tax returns to capital and labour everywhere. One country's trade surplus/ capital deficit signals that that country, on balance, will be doing things that repel capital relative to the trade deficit/capital surplus countries'

---

* There will also be real effects from this. The country with higher taxes is likely to have lower production as some production becomes uneconomic; this will reduce exports and boost imports. The lower production and resulting lower incomes are likely to reduce spending and hence imports. In real life, it is generally remarkably hard to observe all the effects that emerge, so without theory it can be hard to understand what is happening.

governments. And don't just think that all of these effects only apply to goods and services. People move as well, sometimes because they are attracted to other countries and sometimes because they are being forced out of their countries. Economics is complicated.

Referring back to our hypothetical trade balance/terms of trade discussion in the Ricardian section without stretching your imagination too far, assuming it's costly to change exports, imports and capital flows, the terms of trade will have to change in such a way as to accommodate these net capital flows among countries. Now here's the rub and the full integration of Ricardian comparative advantage with Alexander comparative advantage.

Remembering our table of the pre-trade dollar/pound cost ratios for specific goods in the US/UK example where we ended up with a Ricardian trade balance, terms of trade and an exchange rate – now we have to imagine what would happen to the actual terms of trade/exchange rate relative to the Ricardian exchange rate if one of the countries feels the need to export capital (run a trade surplus) with other countries which also want to import capital (run a trade deficit). In order to export more and import less, the country courting the trade surplus/capital deficit would need to increase its comparative advantage by having its prices fall relative to all other countries. With a falling terms of trade/exchange rate/low price ratios, the country will be inclined to export more and import less of every single product that is traded. If the real exchange rate change or, if you will, terms of trade change is large enough, prior imports may even become exports.

The more capital that tries to leave this country as a result of the tax rate increase, the greater the decline in the terms of trade (i.e. the real exchange rate) should be. And the more capital flees the country, the more future production and future growth in that country must be imperilled. Because capital leaves and wants to leave, job prospects and wages will diminish and people will also want to leave. Trade theory has a great deal to say about all of these effects, but even so, there's always a lot more. For further reference, the economic changes from the movements of capital among countries and the changes in the terms of trade are the force of the Stolper and Rybczynski theorems. But for this book, we've gone far enough.

On the other side of the ledger, countries whose governments' policies have made their country more attractive to capital will experience an increase in their terms of trade (i.e. exchange values) in order to import more/export less and run larger trade deficits/capital surpluses. They will also see people wanting to immigrate, along with the capital inflows. Voila, we have just integrated Ricardian and Alexander gains from trade. Here goes. At this point in our discussion, it's important to note that a country's terms of trade, i.e. the relative prices of its goods rising vis-à-vis other countries' prices, can improve in two ways. Its exchange rate can appreciate or if the exchange rate doesn't appreciate, it will experience higher inflation relative to its trading partners. Often both will occur, i.e. higher inflation and a stronger economy.

If, for example, the US, under President Ronald Reagan, or the UK, under Prime Minister Margaret Thatcher, enacts a whole series of supply-side pro-growth policies, the country in question will become far more attractive for capital from the rest of the world. In these two examples, each country's relative prices (i.e. their terms of trade) have to rise sharply in order for each country to reduce its Ricardian comparative advantage and thereby import more goods and services and export less. Only in this way will market forces lead to each country – the US under Reagan and the UK under Thatcher – running trade deficits/capital surpluses. It's as simple as that.

Comparative advantage and the terms of trade must change in order to accommodate capital flows. When we distinguish nominal (exchange rates) and real (terms of trade), a country's terms of trade can rise if its currency appreciates or, if its currency doesn't appreciate, that country's price level has to rise relative to other countries' price levels in order to have the terms of trade rise. Sometimes it's a combination of both. We show in further sections several examples of each of these responses and their consequences. The economics is tricky and often ignorance leads to bad outcomes.

Just as certainly, one can see in the long sunseting of the pound in the

2010s and 2020s one of the consequences of first the UK coalition government of 2010–15 and then the Conservative governments thereafter keeping many of the policies of the previous Labour government. What foreigner would direct capital towards the UK on the understanding that Conservative after Conservative will maintain, as opposed to turn back, the left-wing opposition's policies? The top rate had been raised by the Labour government in 2009 from 40 per cent to 50 per cent. Although the coalition reduced the top rate, it was only reduced to 45 per cent and the Conservative governments after 2015 did not reduce it further.* The top rate of tax applies especially to people most successful running businesses in the UK, and raising it forces them into a work–leisure/tax shelter/out-migration trade-off. This necessarily repels foreign capital, making the owning of enterprises in the UK less remunerative. In turn, this means that such enterprises will attract less foreign investment inclusive of the depreciation of sterling.

To reiterate, capital flows worldwide move in such a way as to arbitrage changes in differences in rates of return – primarily due to government policy changes. The ensuing trade deficits/capital surpluses and trade surpluses/capital deficits need to change the terms of trade, i.e. the real exchange rates, in such a way as to incentivise greater imports and fewer exports in capital-attractive countries and to incentivise fewer imports and more exports in capital-repelling countries. If countries move to pro-growth supply-side policies, they will generally have strengthening currencies, trade deficits and capital surpluses. And, if they aren't very careful, they also experience higher inflation. If a country adopts anti-business, larger government policies, its currencies will weaken, growth will be slower and it might have trade surpluses. It could even have lower inflation, though a weakening currency isn't a good recipe for low inflation.

What also should happen is once the capital and other flows reach a

---

* The short-lived Truss government in 2022 did in fact announce a reduction back to 40 per cent, but this was never implemented. One should also note that National Insurance contributions for the higher paid had been raised to an additional 2 per cent, so in reality the top income tax rate was 47 per cent.

new equilibrium, the terms of trade/exchange rate effects should revert back to their previous levels.

In the chart below, we have plotted the US trade balance as a share of GDP. From 1790 until about 1880, the US ran trade deficits almost each and every year. It was these trade deficits, i.e. capital surpluses, that, in conjunction with abundant labour and capital, thrust the US economy into the forefront of developed nations. In fact, even prior to 1790, perhaps as far back as 1640, the US also had significant trade deficits accompanying extraordinary economic growth. However, what Figure 36 also shows is that after 1880, the US ran a trade surplus on average for almost a century. This was the century when the US led the world as by far its largest, most successful and strongest economy. Singapore, which we have mentioned before as one of the world's most successful economies, also, after running huge trade deficits in its early years of development, has run a surplus since 1980. The important thing is that trade balances need to be seen in context. A deficit isn't axiomatically 'bad' or a surplus 'good' or vice versa.

FIGURE 36: US TRADE BALANCE AS A SHARE OF GDP
(1790–2024)

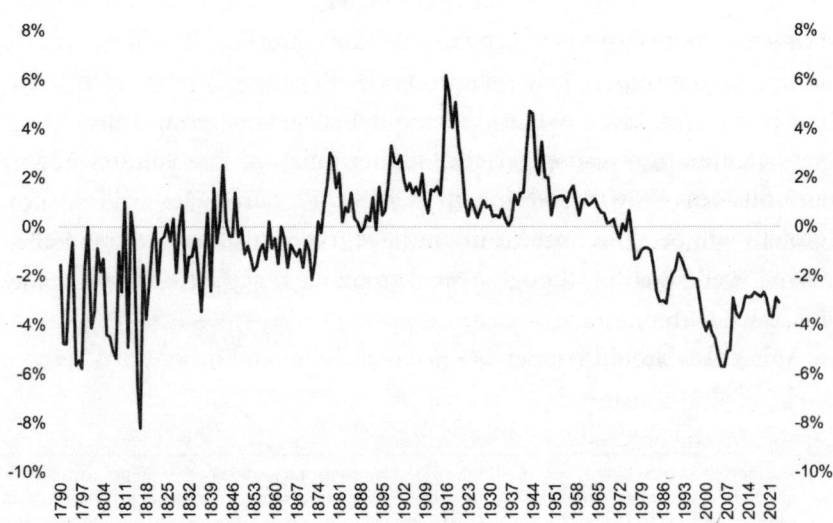

Source: MeasuringWorth, Historical Statistics of the United States

GOVERNMENT POLICY ACTIONS/THE BENEFITS FROM TRADE

In the previous two sections, we laid out the traditional economic framework for trade through the laws of government policies of tariffs, quotas and non-tariff barriers. It is this idealised state that economists evaluate. This section looks at the classic arguments why international trade is so important to the well-being of all countries. From this discussion and analysis, you can understand why academics are such firm advocates of free trade. Their arguments are sound and important but as is so often the case, there is a lot more to the subject of trade.

I) AUTARKY: A WORLD WITHOUT TRADE

Imagine there were only five people in the whole world, each of whom produces a given product, say, apples in Ohio, coffee in Brazil, kiwis in New Zealand, bananas in Costa Rica and silk in China. If there were no trade, each producer would consume only what that producer produces. The same consumption day in and day out would soon get pretty tiresome. Without trade, you'd have five unexcited but fully employed producers who have to consume what they alone produce.

II) THE CONSUMPTION GAINS FROM TRADE

Now, imagine trade. The apple producer trades some of his apples for bananas, coffee, kiwis and silk, as do the producers of silk, coffee, kiwis and bananas. Just how far this trade would go depends upon the preferences of each of the five producers. But everyone would be better off, not because of more jobs but because trade enhances the quality of income. No one could possibly be worse off, because each of the five people trade voluntarily. The monotony of consuming only one product is replaced by novel, new and more exciting products acquired through trade. This is called the 'consumption gains from trade'. Exchange rates and the terms of trade will reflect the world's preferences for these five products.

III) THE PRODUCTION GAINS FROM TRADE

We now can imagine autarkic producers in each of these countries who produce each of these products with widely varying degrees of efficiency. When the producers in various countries engage in trade, each country will produce and export products they produce relatively more efficiently and import products they produce relatively less efficiently. Total production everywhere will be higher, with the exact same amount of employment. Again, no one could possibly be worse off because each trades voluntarily. These gains from relative differences in efficiency are called the 'production gains from trade'. This diversification of consumption and production is what trade is all about. It's called a win-win, the gains from trade, comparative advantage. It's the economics made famous by the English economist David Ricardo. This is why economists to this very day espouse free trade and are highly critical of tariffs, quotas, non-tariff barriers and other mercantilist schema.

IV) PROTECTIONISM HURTS EVERYONE EVERYWHERE

Any country's protectionism hurts each country's economy by reducing the quality of each country's consumption and production via total trade (exports plus imports). Retaliatory protectionist measures, often called trade wars, do not offset the damage done by the original protectionist policies, but instead, these retaliatory measures cause even greater overall damage to both economies. But let's add here something that should be obvious but very often isn't. The gains from trade may be highly skewed in favour or less in favour of one country or another. Threats of tariffs are often used as a negotiating tool to realign the relative positions of trading nations. Those large countries with strong economies have enormous leverage to extract maximal benefits.

To see just how actual protectionist retaliation makes no sense, imagine the US develops a cure for colon cancer and Japan develops a cure for Alzheimer's. Also, imagine Japan, as a ruse to protect domestic healthcare services, disallows the import of the US cure for colon cancer to Japan. Should the US retaliate against Japan's protectionism and prohibit Japan from selling its cure for Alzheimer's in the US? NO! Japan's protectionism hurts Japanese consumers (they die from more colon cancer). Any retaliation with additional US protectionist measures would devastate Americans with Alzheimer's.

V) EXPORT EARNINGS PAY FOR IMPORTS

To acquire the gains from trade, each country uses the products it produces (exports) to trade for the products other countries produce (imports). Exports earn the wherewithal to pay for imports. The relationship between exports and imports among countries is in principle no different to the domestic relationship between income and spending among individuals. High-income earners generally spend more than low-income earners. If they didn't spend more, then why do they earn more? Each country earns income by producing and exporting goods, the proceeds from which are used to buy goods other countries produce. There is a unique one-to-one correspondence between what a country earns in the global marketplace (its exports) and what it buys in the global marketplace (its imports).

Boiling it all down, countries sell products to foreigners (exports) in order to buy products from foreigners (imports). And as such, any attempt to reduce imports such as tariffs, quotas or non-tariff barriers is precisely equivalent to a measure to reduce exports – Lerner's symmetry theorem. This is a point that virtually no politician finds intuitive.

VI) A COUNTRY'S INTERNATIONAL CAPITAL ACCOUNT IS THE CONVERSE OF THAT COUNTRY'S TRADE ACCOUNT

Another important point to realise is that a country's trade surplus or deficit is one and the same as its capital deficit or surplus.

Foreigners generate a dollar cash flow by selling more goods to the US and by buying fewer goods from the US, which allows those foreigners to buy US-located assets. The trade balance of a country in balance of payments accounting terms is the counter account to a country's capital balance. Thus, a country's trade surplus is also its capital deficit, and its trade deficit is also its capital surplus. In order for the US to have a net capital inflow, foreigners have to have a trade surplus with the US. Think of this in terms of attracting capital from abroad. The more attractive your country, the greater will be your net capital inflow and your trade deficit will be. You'll also have greater pressure pushing your terms of trade higher (i.e. domestic inflation and/or currency appreciation).

DO DEVALUATIONS REALLY HELP TRADE?

In policy as well as academic circles, it is widely believed that changes in exchange rates cause changes in trade balance. Devaluations are believed to lead to improved trade balances, while revaluations are supposed to lead to worsened trade balances. Yet faced with evidence to the contrary, according to many people, just a little more time is needed for the devaluation to have its effects.

While obviously not definitive, the evidence presented here places doubt on the notion that devaluations bring about improvements in trade balances; the trade balance being one of the major components of the amount of payments, that component thought to be most responsive to exchange rate changes. In addition, the evidence points very strongly to a close and lasting relationship between changes in trade balances and changes in relative rates of growth. The theory of this trade balance/ growth differential relationship is firmly placed on the well-accepted notion that a country's net demand for foreign goods depends on its level of income.

The popular theory behind the relationship between exchange rates and trade balances is straightforward. A representative statement of that theory as it pertains to the UK might proceed as follows: by raising the pound price of foreign exchange (devaluation of the pound), the pound cost of foreign goods will naturally rise. In a like manner – because the foreign exchange price of the pound has fallen as a consequence of devaluation – the foreign currency price of British export goods will now be lower. The British will buy less of the now higher priced foreign goods, while at the same time, British export goods should sell better abroad because of the decline in the price foreigners have to pay for them. The end result of a pound devaluation should be an improvement in the overall trade balance (UK exports minus UK imports), though perhaps only after a lag of as much as two years.

During the Bretton Woods period, sterling was devalued in 1949 and 1967. Although there were temporary reductions in the trade deficit on each occasion, they did not persist. The general story of the era and rather more importantly the post-Bretton Woods period, when sterling fell further, was of a gradual deterioration in the UK trade balance which only started to change towards the end of the 1970s when North Sea oil came on stream.

Although some argue that the failure of the UK to improve its trade balance was due to offsetting special circumstances, it should not come as a total surprise to those who have observed other countries' experiences with devaluations.

An important study has considered whether trade balances actually did improve after devaluations,[1] investigating sixteen different examples. It concluded that the evidence did not support the theory. The revaluation picture is not very different, but there are very few examples, and German mark valuations account for nearly all of them. The effective number of revaluations Germany has carried out depends on how one treats changes in border tax adjustments. But, irrespective of precisely how many times the German mark has been revalued, it would be no mean task to discern a substantial deterioration in the German trade balance. Thus, given at least a casual look at the historical experience of foreign countries, it should not come as a complete surprise that the US trade balance has not turned around since the foreign currency value of the dollar started to decline.

While trade balances may not respond predictably to exchange rate changes, they do appear to be quite closely related to differential growth rates. When a country increases its economic growth rate relative to its trading partners, we often find deterioration in that country's trade balance. Perhaps the closest of these relationships is to be found between the US and other advanced economies.

In the most recent of times perhaps more policy measures than ever have been pushed through in the hope of improving the US trade position. The dollar has been devalued, capital controls and trade restrictions have continued to sprout everywhere, export–import bank outlays have grown, voluntary quotas have been placed on a number of commodities, anti-dumping and countervailing duty measures have been threatened and so on.

In the face of it all, the trade balance has proceeded much as usual.

When we consider how rapidly the US has grown recently, it seems reasonable that the growth rate will taper off in the future. The rest of the world, on the other hand, has recently been growing slowly relative to historical norms and should show some resurgence. If foreign growth does rise and US growth slackens, we should expect a noticeable improvement in the US trade balance. This improvement should, in our opinion, be attributed to US growth relative to foreign growth and not (as it probably will be) to the delayed effects of devaluation.

INCOME AND IMPORTS

From a theoretical standpoint, the relationship between a country's trade balance and its relative rate of growth is based entirely upon the well-accepted notion that the higher a country's income is, the more that country will import. Thus, as is well documented in virtually all elementary textbooks, net imports depend on income. Changes in net imports depend, therefore, on changes in income. And, as displayed in Figure 37, changes in net imports, as a share of GDP, depend on a country's growth rate.

Any one country's imports are necessarily the exports of the rest of the world, and its exports are the rest of the world's imports. Therefore, a country's trade balance surplus is the rest of the world's deficit. Because one country's trade balance surplus is all other countries' deficit, that country's trade balance must likewise depend upon the growth of the rest of the world, as well as its own growth rate. Therefore, based solely on the notion that the level of a country's imports depends on its income, we find that changes in its trade balance (or current account) should depend upon changes in its growth rate relative to the rest of the world.

From a policy standpoint, there are several observations that can be made concerning the balance of trade. (Readers must again be careful to distinguish between the balance of trade and overall balance of payments.)

First, while no one can say for sure that exchange rate changes do not matter, it appears fair to say that many of the claimed effects on the trade balance and thereby domestic employment have been greatly exaggerated in policy discussions.

Second, the use of the trade balance as a policy indicator distinct from domestic growth has probably been overdone and should be played down.

Third, both official and private pessimism as to the future American trade position also appear to us to have been substantially overstated. While we may not soon again see the surpluses of the late 1940s, the very recent trade deficits also appear to be somewhat abnormal.

Finally, although no one can ever deny it with certainty that trade measures other than exchange rate changes help the trade balance, there is a widely held presumption in policy discussions that these trade measures do matter and matter a lot. This point of view has clearly been given too much weight in trade policy. The trade balance, like many other economic indicators, responds both predictably and in a logical way to the overall economic environment. Using gimmicks to alter the trade balance is to a large extent futile and perhaps even mischievous.

FIGURE 37: TRADE IN OECD COUNTRIES*: IMPORTS AND EXPORTS AS A SHARE OF GDP

(annual, 2014)

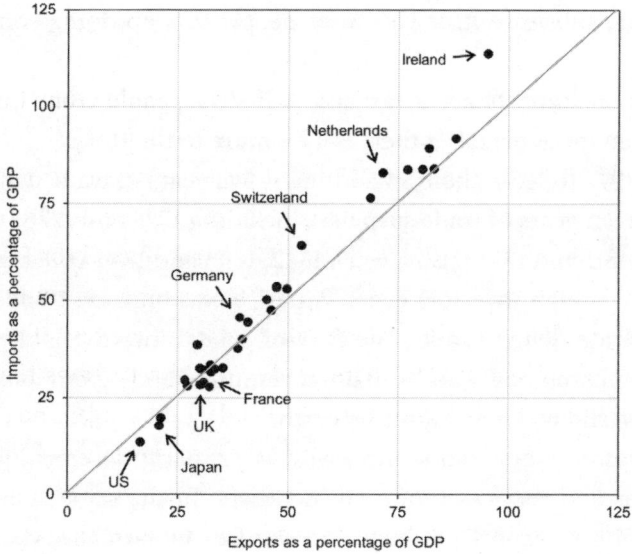

Source: OECD

---

*   Countries other than those named in the above chart are: Australia, Austria, Belgium, Canada, Czech Republic, Denmark, Finland, Greece, Hungary, Iceland, Italy, South Korea, Mexico, New Zealand, Norway, Poland, Portugal, Slovakia, Spain, Sweden, Turkey, Chile, Estonia, Israel and Slovenia.

Each country exports some of the products it produces to earn the wherewithal to pay for imports from other countries. This relationship between exports and imports among countries is no different to the relationship between income and spending among individuals. Income is earned by producing goods, which are sold in order to buy goods others produce. A country's imports equal its exports without capital flows.

'Even though economics is a very old subject, it has not truly come to grips with the main difficulty, which is the inordinate practical importance of a few extreme events.'
– BENOIT B. MANDELBROT, 1983

THE TRUTH ABOUT TARIFFS AND TRADE

The reality of incentives is straightforward. If you want more done of something, subsidise it. If you want people to stop doing something, tax it.

Tariffs on imports are a tax and will stop people from importing goods from foreigners. But there is a lot more to the story.

From 1747 to 1854, the US had ninety-five years of trade deficits and only thirteen years of trade surpluses including 1775 and 1776 (the Revolution), 1811 and 1813 (also a war), 1842, 1843 and 1844 (the biggest US default to foreign investors ever). America was built on trade deficits. The US trade deficit funded the flow of capital into the United States and, when combined with US natural resources and labour, created the most powerful economic force on earth.

The reason people work and invest is primarily to earn income to buy goods and services produced by others. In the same vein, people in one country export products and services to earn the wherewithal to buy imports from other countries. If you tariff imports, you reduce the demand for imports which, in turn, reduces the need for the proceeds from the sale of exports and thus reduces exports. Tariffs, therefore, reduce both imports and exports and, in static terms, create jobs in inefficient domestic industries to replace the loss of efficiently made foreign imports and then lose jobs in efficient domestic industries that formerly were exported.

Not only are tariffs a tax but they are far worse than income taxes because they are a gross receipts tax. And here we have to be careful to distinguish among various types of items on which the government imposes taxes. First, we have income or value added taxes which correspond to taxes on the returns to factors of production such as capital and labour. Second, we have turnover or gross receipts taxes which correspond to the volume of total revenues a business has irrespective of that business's purchases or pass-through expenses. In general, gross receipts can be thought of as about four times larger than incomes.

Finally, we have wealth taxes, which year after year tax the same item irrespective of the volume of business that item generates or its income. Wealth in general can be thought of as six or seven times larger than income and two or three times larger than gross receipts. In our experience, wealth taxes, percentage for percentage, are about three times more damaging than turnover or gross receipts taxes are, which in turn are percentage for percentage four times more damaging than taxes on incomes. And goodness knows income taxes can do a helluva lot of damage.

Moving on from words to facts, it's not clear that tariffs actually raise prices as much as theory would suggest. After the Smoot–Hawley tariff, the US price level actually fell, and fell by a lot. Under the Kennedy Round tariff reductions, there appears to have been little effect on inflation. Nor did the Reagan/Clinton North American Free Trade Agreement (NAFTA) trade liberalisation appear to have had any noticeable effect on inflation. Nixon's 10 per cent import surcharge was in response to higher inflation numbers and again inflation did not appear to increase. We could look all across the world but suffice it to write – inflation most likely isn't the issue either way.

Tariffs also do not per se change a country's net exports or what is called its trade balance, as is also evident from the exports and imports chart. If imports and exports move in lockstep, their difference (i.e. the trade balance) won't change. Looking back in time at the period surrounding the Smoot–Hawley tariff, there was an enormous drop in the volume of trade, the stock market and total employment, but the objective of the tariffs – the trade balance – barely wiggled. Figure 38 shows total trade, the stock market and the trade balance in and around the Smoot–Hawley tariff. The stock market fell from top to bottom by 88.7 per cent. Total trade fell by 69.6 per cent. But the trade balance? Nada.

FIGURE 38: TARIFFS AND TRADE SURROUNDING THE 1930 SMOOT–HAWLEY TARIFF

(Trade: annual, $ billion, 1925–39, Dow Jones: monthly, January 1925–December 1939, end of period)

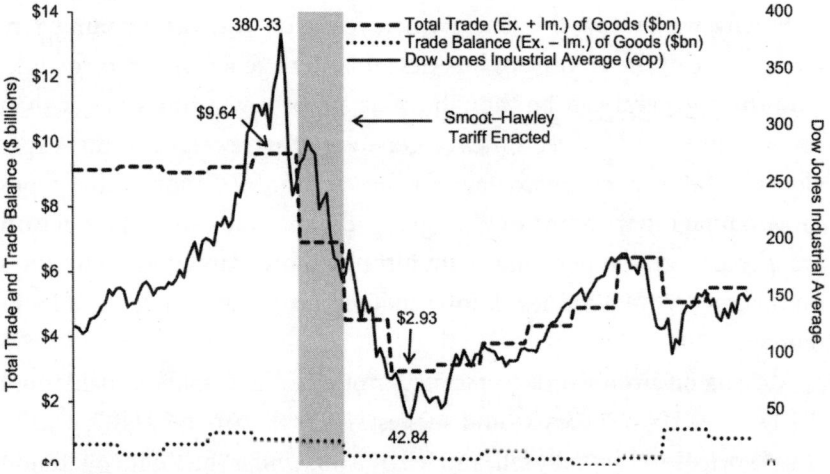

Source: Bureau of Economic Analysis, Historical Statistics of the US, US International Trade Commission

Tariffs do cost jobs and do reduce productivity as a result of a loss of the comparative advantage gains from trade. Also, the collapse in total commerce as a result of tariffs leads to domestic tax revenue shortfalls and prompts domestic governments to raise tax rates everywhere. This perverse government response is a sure-fire way of causing an economic bust. Figure 39 shows the time sequence of a) the adoption of the Smoot–Hawley tariff, b) subsequent increases in unemployment, c) government response of raising tax rates and d) further increases in unemployment.

It's all a vicious cycle spiralling the economy further and further into the Great Depression. This truly is a race to the bottom.

FIGURE 39: HIGHEST PERSONAL INCOME TAX RATE VS UNEMPLOYMENT
(Personal: annual, 1925–39; Unemployment: monthly, January 1925–December 1939)

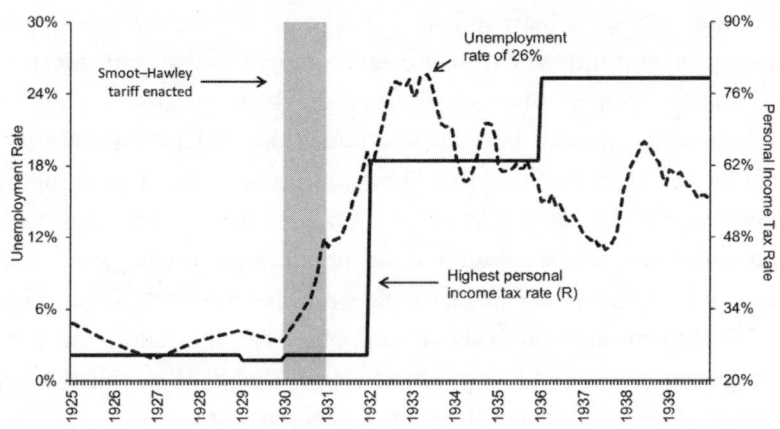

Source: Tax Policy Center

Tariffs also lead to further job losses because of atavistic urges of foreign governments to enter a trade war.

Matching tariff increase for tariff increase is precisely the wrong thing to do yet governments everywhere at all times do just that. The end result of the trade war in addition to a stock market collapse is a magnified decline in trade for both imports and exports and very little if any change in the trade balance.

Tariffs in addition to everything else will not raise much, if any, net revenues for government. As an add on, increased tariffs will reduce the overall take from taxes. This point was a central tenet of Adam Smith in his book *The Wealth of Nations*. After 1929 and the large hike in tariffs, the economy collapsed and government tax revenues disappeared. The same occurred with the Nixon tariffs of 1972. Overall tax revenues increased and the US budget went into surplus when Kennedy in the 1960s and Clinton in the 1990s lowered tariffs.

The idea that low-priced foreign-made goods constitute dumping and cost jobs is generally not correct. It is also incorrect to measure damage to the US economy by specific industry job losses. Even during the greatest periods of boom, there are a few industries that suffer. And, conversely, during periods of bust, there are a few industries that do well. People work and invest to buy goods and the higher the quality of those goods and the lower their price, the better off workers and investors are. Protecting this industry or that industry from foreign competition by imposing tariffs comes at the expense of everyone. As individual consumers, we all like bargains – high-quality products sold to us at low prices. It should be no different for countries. Would we like countries to over-charge us for their products, or worse yet, would we hate it if foreigners sold us high-quality products at low prices? Imagine if Japan, out of gratitude, gave us all of their cars as a gift free of charge, should we declare war? I think not. When the US buys products globally at retail-plus, we call it fair trade. When we negotiate prices and buy products below wholesale, it's called foreign dumping. Go figure! Remember, consumers matter too.

When it comes to government policies, foreigners and Americans alike like low taxes, spending restraint, sound money, minimal regulations and free trade. Bringing manufacturing and jobs back to America requires the same set of policies that expanding manufacturing and jobs in America does. For Americans, the choices are simple – save more, invest more and watch your wealth grow.

Foreigners, on the other hand, can on balance only invest in the US if they sell more goods to Americans (an increase in US imports) and buy fewer goods from Americans (a reduction in US exports). Only in this way can foreigners generate the dollar cash flow to buy US-located assets. In other words, the US trade deficit is the US capital surplus. If you want manufacturing to relocate to the US, the US must run a trade deficit, which is a US capital surplus. Think about it.

A US trade deficit with China can only occur when the Chinese economy invests more in the US than the US economy invests in China. A US trade deficit with China means we win! We get more investments. China's trade surplus with the US (the US trade deficit with China) provided 1.5 million net new jobs in the US in 2017.

FIGURE 40: THE DOLLAR, THE REAGAN YEARS, GDP GROWTH AND THE US TRADE DEFICIT

(monthly, January 1981–March 1985)

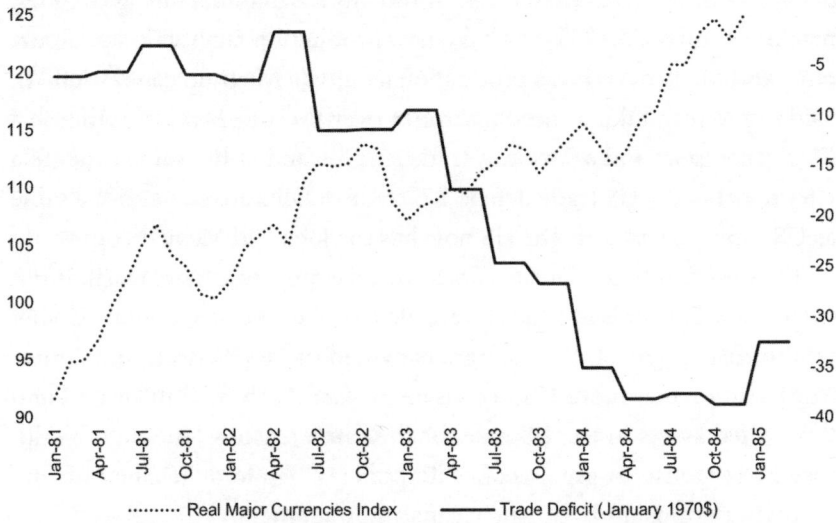

········· Real Major Currencies Index ———— Trade Deficit (January 1970$)

Source: BEA, FRB

Would you rather have investors eager to bring their money into the US or desperate to take it out? Ouch! A US trade deficit is a measure of just how much foreigners are investing in the US.

In Figure 40, the chart of the Reagan years, the 1981 Economic Recovery Tax Act (ERTA) tax bill took effect on 1 January 1983. For the full two-year period of 1983 and 1984, US real GDP grew by 14 per cent or 6.5 per cent per annum. Also starting in the first half of 1983, there was an enormous increase in the inflow of foreign capital into the US as shown by the dramatic increase in the US trade deficit and a sharp rise in the value of the US dollar in the foreign exchanges.

The second part of the consequences of good economic policies in America – in addition to our trade deficit/capital surplus – is a strong dollar. Increased demand for US-located assets, like the increase in demand for any product, will have a quantity effect (trade deficit) and a price effect (a strong dollar). (See Figure 40.)

If a businessman in Mexico as a consequence of President Trump's

189

pro-growth policies decides to move his business to the US, how would he do it and what would it mean? Let's say he loads up all of his capital equipment on a truck in Mexico and drives that truck over the US–Mexico border to its new home in the US. By moving his manufacturing facilities, machines and all, the US now has a new production facility (a capital surplus) and Mexico has lost a production facility (a Mexican capital deficit). Said differently, taking these machines over the US–Mexico border is a Mexican export and a Mexican trade surplus and at the same time it's a US import and a US trade deficit. US trade deficits are one and the same as US capital surpluses. The US now has the jobs and Mexico doesn't.

The idea that trade deficits constitute an export of US net worth is not correct. Our periods of biggest trade deficits have occurred when US net wealth rose the most. Yes, foreigners owned more US assets, but Americans also owned more US net assets. In fact, both foreign-owned and US-owned assets in the US rose for the same reasons. The total wealth rose in response to great economic policies. Trade deficit periods are win-win periods for both Americans and foreigners.

US wealth went up an amazing $75 trillion from 2008 to 2023 – from $60 trillion to $135 trillion – while the cumulative trade deficit from all countries (i.e. the increase in assets owned by foreigners) was $14 trillion over that period. The US is not selling out to foreigners.

Without wanting to carry the arguments to the absurd extreme, the idea, as one tariff advocate said, that 'with tariffs, those empty factories in Detroit can rapidly be filled with American car production' is silly. Detroit is a basket case not because of China, Germany, Japan and Italy. It's a basket case because of Michigan and specifically Detroit: taxes, regulations, minimum wages, death taxes and forced union laws. In Detroit, there are areas where property taxes exceed 15 per cent. Yikes! Whoever would want to move anything to Detroit? No one. Tennessee, Texas and Florida have no problem with manufacturing job losses. In fact, these states almost have too many manufacturing jobs moving in. But then again, these states are pro-growth states without state income taxes. The problem of manufacturing in the US is US federal, state and local policies. If the Rust Belt were to adopt the fiscal structures of Utah,

Nevada, Florida, Texas and Tennessee, the problem would be solved. We've met the enemy and, to quote Pogo, 'They is us.'

TABLE 10: NO PERSONAL INCOME STATES VS INDUSTRIAL STATES

(2020–21 Adjusted Gross Income (AGI) migration, in thousands of dollars)

	0 PIT States*	Industrial States†
Total AGI Inflow	$121,793,619	$85,038,041
Total AGI Outflow	60,527,142	164,092,138
Net AGI Inflow	61,266,477	79,054,097
Average AGI In-Migrant	$113	$84
Average AGI Out-Migrant	74	115

Source: United States Census Bureau, Laffer Associates

SUMMARY

When viewing tariffs in the grand scheme of things, they represent government intervention in the marketplace. Tariffs are the antithesis of free market economics. Many of the arguments used to further the adoption of tariffs are perceptions of market failures. The one overriding theme is that whatever the perceived problem may be, government is the solution. And even when perceptions of the problems are demonstrably wrong, tariff supporters still want a government solution.

In total frustration, one such tariff advocate in response to Elon Musk's paper advocating free trade referred to Musk as 'a car salesman who doesn't understand and only wants to protect his own interests'. Has he never heard of Musk's rewriting of the book of entrepreneurship, namely Musk's business accomplishments? To name a few: the Zip2 disruption of the Yellow Pages; PayPal; Tesla, once an unheard-of car company start-up and the electric-vehicle pioneer; SpaceX, getting NASA out of its

---

* No PIT states include: Alaska, Florida, Nevada, New Hampshire, South Dakota, Tennessee, Texas, Washington, Wyoming

† Industrial states include: California, Illinois, Massachusetts, Michigan, Minnesota, New Jersey, New York, Ohio, Pennsylvania

decades-long funk (even to the degree of rescuing its pair of nine-month-stranded-in-space astronauts); Starlink, globally busting the 'cable-guy' monopoly in internet service; Twitter/X, which has put legacy media to pasture; the Boring Company; Hyperloops; the Nueralinks that give new functionality to victims of paralysis; XAI; and the now totally reasonable prospect of planting civilisation on Mars. Howard Hughes, Jacob Astor, John D. Rockefeller, George Westinghouse and the whole honour roll of top entrepreneurs of the past salute you from the beyond, Mr Musk.

THE DRAGON RETURNS: THE STORY OF CHINA/SUPPLY-SIDE ECONOMICS WORKS

'It takes a PhD in economics not to be able to understand the obvious.'
– Irving Kristol

FIGURE 41: SPENDING CUTS: STATE-OWNED ENTERPRISES AS A SHARE OF GROSS INDUSTRIAL OUTPUT VALUE

(every five years, 1970–2011)

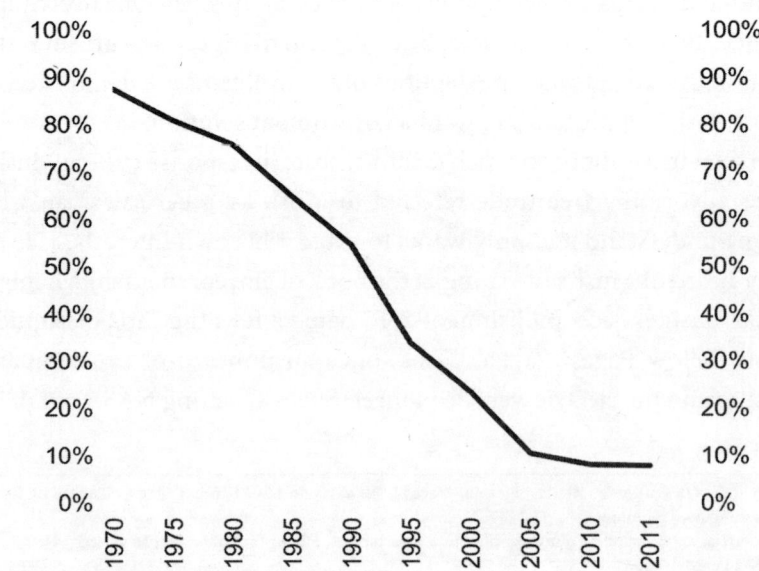

Source: China Statistical Yearbook

FIGURE 42: SOUND MONEY: DOLLAR–YUAN SPOT EXCHANGE RATE
(monthly, January 1994–December 2024, USD per CNY)

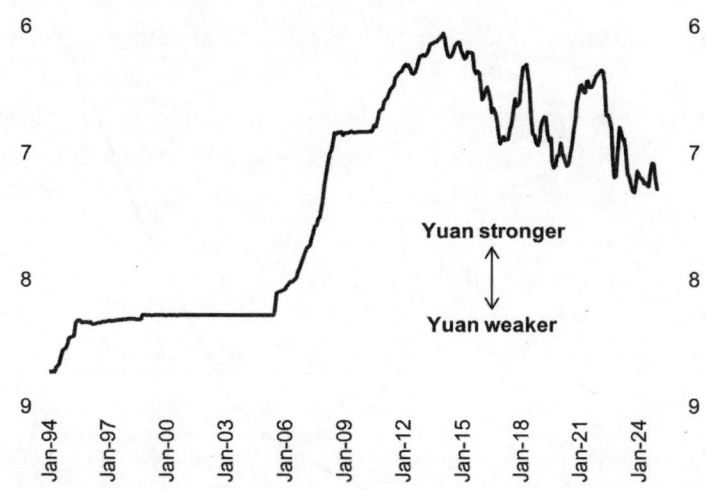

Source: Fed Board of Governors

FIGURE 43: FREE TRADE: CHINA VS US: TOTAL TRADE AS A SHARE OF GDP
(every five years, 1970–2020)

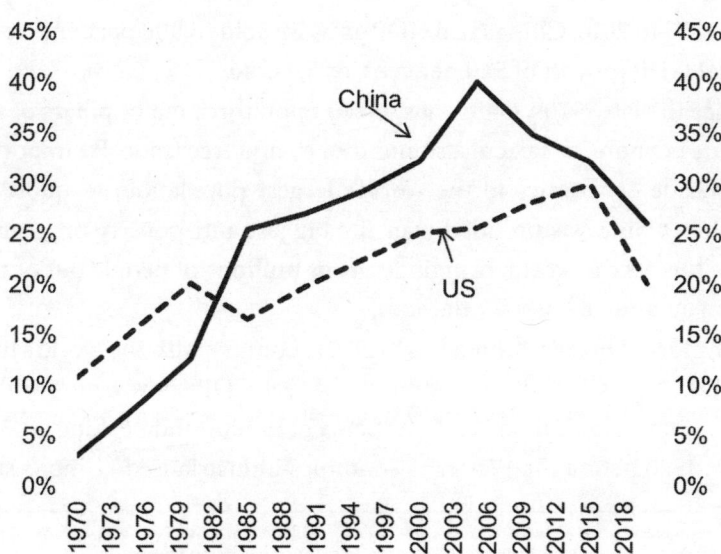

Source: BEA, China Statistical Yearbook, World Bank

FIGURE 44: PROSPERITY: REAL GDP: CHINA VS US
(annual, 1959–2023, indexed 1959 = 100)

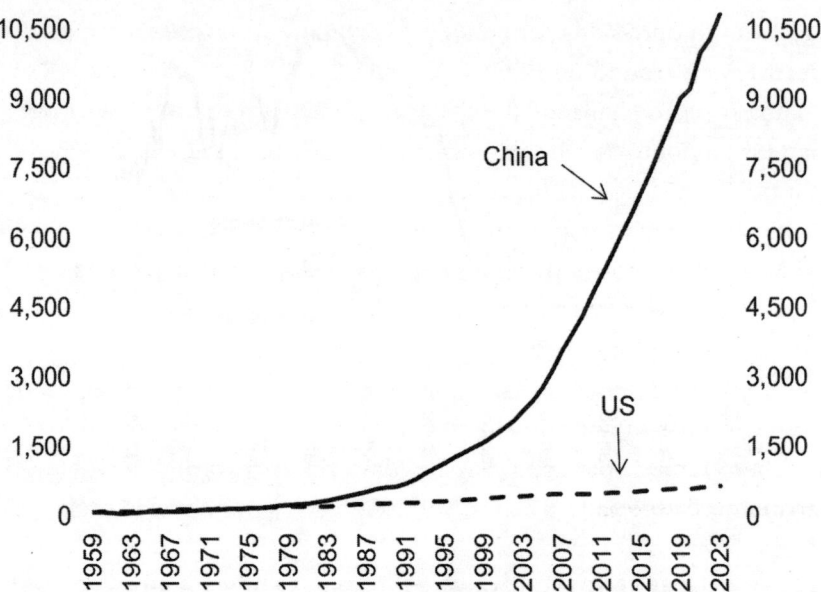

Source: BEA, World Bank

From 1959 to 2016, China's real GDP grew 69-fold (6,900 per cent) versus US real GDP growth of 540 per cent, or 5.4-fold.

Since the late 1970s, China has seized upon three major pillars of supply-side economics: tax cuts, sound money and free trade. By importing supply-side economics to the world's largest population, to quote Bill Shiebler, 'China has presided over the biggest anti-poverty program in the history of the world, bringing tens of millions of people out of poverty on an annual basis for decades.'

For most of history, China has been the country with the world's highest GDP. Angus Maddison's estimates of real GDP show China with 25 per cent of world GDP in Year 1, 22 per cent in 1000 and peaking at 33 per cent in 1820 before the Western economies industrialised.* China's share

---

* Maddison Historical Statistics is the most widely used long-term historical economics database. It is now held by the Groningen Growth and Development Centre (https://www.rug.nl/ggdc/)

then fell to 11 per cent in 1900 and to 5 per cent in 1950 after the Communists had taken over. Its share remained around 5 per cent until 1980 when Deng Xiaoping started to revive the economy.* Since then, after adopting supply-side economics, China's share has staged a remarkable recovery to around 20 per cent depending on which measure is used. China is set to challenge the US and eventually India to be the world's largest economy on all measures (it already is the largest after adjusting for purchasing power) for the rest of the twenty-first century, despite a likely decline in its population in the second half of the century.

Meanwhile, not only has the economy grown but poverty has collapsed. The World Bank claimed in 2022[2] that China has lifted 800 million people out of poverty in four decades and despite this being based on Chinese government data, the claim is supported by other evidence from food consumption to life expectancy.

These remarkable achievements illustrate the power of supply-side economics, especially when introduced to a country previously adopting the communist model.

However, although China has been a free market success story and its growth has contributed to world prosperity, its rivalry with the US and with the West in general has created difficulties.

Some of these difficulties relate to its trade practices – alleged theft of intellectual property (though it isn't the only guilty party); the integration of its trade policy with its foreign policy, for example in the Belt and Road Initiative; and the impact of its rivalry with the West on its role as a secure supplier. It has been argued that China has used trade to subvert existing markets.

It should be noted that remedies already exist for dealing with most such practices and indeed they have been dealt with in relation to other countries in the past. Obviously, the particular problem with China is not just the specific practice but their scale reflecting the huge scale of the Chinese economy.

---

* This is based on the original Maddison (https://www.rug.nl/ggdc/ historicaldevelopment/maddison/ releases/maddison-database-2010). We have cross-checked the more recent data with the latest version of the database and the numbers still look right.

GOVERNMENT POLICY ACTIONS: TARIFFS, QUOTAS, CAPITAL CONTROLS AND OTHER TRADE BARRIERS

The benefits of trade accrue to everyone – importers, exporters, consumers and producers of all trading nations. The consumption of foreign-made, more economically produced products makes the country on balance – consumers and producers – better off. The losses experienced by some domestic consumers of export goods and some domestic producers of export goods will be more than offset by the gains from consumers of import goods and the gains from producers of export goods. And each and every impediment to trade irrespective of which country imposes the impediment hurts both the exporting country and the importing country. The benefits of trade are best measured as total trade – exports plus imports.

Some politicians believe trade to be a 'zero-sum game'. By 'zero-sum', we mean exports create jobs and imports displace jobs. Using jobs as our measure of good and bad, what's good for us (exports) is bad for foreigners and vice versa. In other words, if we're better off, they're worse off. This idea of zero-sum was famously (by Ross Perot) called the 'giant sucking sound coming out of Mexico'. In point of fact, higher quality lower cost Mexican imports are a plus for the US and Mexico, as are US exports to Mexico.

Trade is not about jobs at all or even about total employment. Instead, trade is about the value of income and consumption.

Ignorance of the benefits of trade is probably the only product that is freely traded without borders. Governments far and wide believe that imposing unanswered protectionist measures advantages their economy at the expense of their trading partners' economies (the concept of a zero-sum game). For politicians who insist that trade and trade protectionist measures are all about jobs, their measure of success would be the trade balance – exports minus imports.

Advocates of protectionist measures make at least two serious mistakes. First, they ignore the benefits to the importing country from the consumption of imports. And second, they fabricate illusionary increases in employment by assuming reduced imports are not offset by reduced exports.

Every country exports a proportion of what it produces in order to earn the means to pay for goods it imports from other nations. This exchange mirrors how individuals earn income and spend it – people produce and sell goods or services to earn money, which they then use to buy what others produce. In the absence of capital flows, a country's imports must equal its exports.

Lerner's symmetry theorem – which is maths, not ideology – simply states that there is a precise correspondence between taxes on imports (tariffs) and taxes on exports. Both taxes on imports (tariffs) or exports have the same effect on jobs (none) and on the gains from trade – hugely negative.

Politicians universally frame their country's trade deficit as costing jobs. But, in the same breath, they love businesses moving into their country which is literally net capital inflows on trade deficits. Politicians argue that capital inflows create jobs. Capital inflows provide the wherewithal to employ domestic workers. You can't love capital inflows and hate trade deficits.

In truth, the only way a country can have capital inflows is if it buys more goods from foreigners and sells fewer goods to foreigners, i.e. it has a trade deficit. The trade deficit is one and the same as the capital surplus. That's accounting (and economics). Any and all trade barriers hurt capital flows, exports and imports. Everyone is worse off. And any attempt to retaliate against foreign protectionism only makes all matters worse.

And when considering trade over longer periods of time, a pro-growth country can end up with substantial foreign ownership of assets within the country. There are those who consider this a problem, when in truth it's far more of a solution. Foreigners take a country far more seriously and respectfully if those foreigners have significant assets in those countries. A little bit tongue in cheek, but adversaries are loathe to bomb countries where they have invested a lot or with whom they trade a lot. Likewise, they are far more prone to discuss issues with people they do business with, rather than immediately going for guns or confrontation.

The benefits from trade are multifaceted and extensive way beyond the straightforward Ricardian gains from trade and the Alexander gains from trade.

SUBSTITUTION EFFECTS AND BRITISH WARTIME SHORTAGES

Energy is a key input for economic growth, as is food. Professor Mancur Olson reviewed the economic impact from food shortages in Great Britain during three major wars: the Napoleonic Wars, the First World War and the Second World War.[3] Traditionally, Great Britain has imported a large portion of its food supply. As a direct consequence, in all three wars Great Britain's enemies believed that the island nation could be starved into submission.

As it turns out, the presumption that Great Britain could be starved into submission was the epitome of static thinking in a world that is in fact dynamic. The embargoes and blockades used against Great Britain did not lead to mass starvation or endemic malnutrition as its enemies had wished. Instead, the British people responded to the changed prices of food by changing their food production methods and consumption habits. The British government also changed its policies, furthering the goal of working around the shortages created by Britain's enemies. As Olson documents, the world is dynamic, and free market economies are especially good at overcoming shortages:

> Because of the possibilities for substitution, advanced industrial economies are not as inflexible in the face of shortages as might be supposed. They have a considerable capacity to substitute for anything in short supply ... This substitution is not only – not even mainly – of the obvious kind, where something ersatz, something that is obviously a 'substitute', takes the place of what is in short supply. People may often readjust their patterns of production and consumption in ways such that no one thing, but rather many different things, take the place of what is scarce.[4]

Napoleon's military campaigns met with great success in the early 1800s, and by 1805 France occupied many of the countries that supplied Great Britain with its food. France prohibited any country within its 'sphere of influence' from trading with Great Britain, thereby cutting off a large portion of Great Britain's food supplies. Making matters worse for the British, the Americans were reticent to trade with either France or Great Britain due to each combatant's attempts to disrupt American trade with the enemy; and the British agricultural sector suffered several bad harvests between 1795 and 1814. Despite these hardships,

> the most significant fact about the British food situation in the Napoleonic War, then, is that, while difficult, it was never disastrous, and that by preventing wasteful consumption, encouraging agriculture and subsidizing importation, the British adjusted fairly successfully to the challenge of an abnormally large number of years with bad weather, coinciding with diplomatic and military predicaments that drastically limited food imports.[5]

The Germans took a more proactive approach towards starving the British during the First World War. Their strategy was predicated on statistical logic and static thinking. In light of the volume of shipping Britain was receiving as of 1917, the estimated consumption levels necessary to sustain the military and the poor harvests Great Britain and the United States were experiencing, the German navy calculated that if they destroyed 600,000 tons of shipping a month, the British would be forced into surrendering within six months. The German navy was successful at achieving that goal. Between February 1917 and July 1917, the German navy sunk an average of 642,833 tons of shipping per month. And yet, the British never surrendered. Why?

The answer, briefly, is that the British, sometimes in conjunction with their American allies and sometimes alone, undertook a series of economic countermeasures that enabled them to get along very well without the merchant tonnage lost to the German submarines. By making a series of substitutions or adjustments in shipping and import policies, in food consumption patterns and in agricultural production, it was possible to compensate for the destructiveness of the submarines. The shipping shortage could be overcome only at very great expense, but there was no question, because of the economic countermeasures, that it could be overcome.[6]

The German strategy for starving Great Britain did not change much between the First World War and the Second World War – sink enough shipping tonnage to starve Great Britain into submission. The strategy, not surprisingly at this point, did not lead to starvation in Great Britain.

The essence of the British food situation in the Second World War, then, is that, though before the war British agriculture had declined to the point where the nation imported most of its food, and though the German submarine blockade during the war was to a considerable extent effective, Britain still was able to completely maintain the health and efficiency of its people while at the same time releasing a large amount of shipping for military purposes. This was due partly to a number of adjustments and substitutions in agricultural production, which led to a greatly increased output of food nutrients, and to a series of limitations and substitutions in import and consumption patterns, which led to important additional economies in cargo space and brought complete success in counteracting the submarine campaign to blockade Britain into starvation and submission.[7]

Whether it was the Napoleonic Wars, the First World War or the Second World War, economising behaviour on the part of the British citizens, coupled with sound policies on the part of the British government, were successful in counteracting a significant food supply shock.

The British experience with wartime food shortages has important lessons for our current debates on trade in general. If handled expeditiously and with careful forethought, market forces can be employed to overcome – perhaps not with ease but certainly without undue consequences – a major disruption in trade patterns.

PROTECTIONISM DOESN'T BRING JOBS BACK

'As tragic as the marginal farmer's plight might be, no GOP argument, political or economic, could justify higher tariffs. By restricting foreigners' ability to sell their goods in the US, the Republicans were making it more

difficult for foreigners to pay off their debts to the US and import goods from us. Over time, tariffs would, in essence, have the same inhibiting impact on investment and commerce as an increase in taxes. Herbert Hoover signed the Smoot–Hawley Bill on June 16, 1930, but the stock market started anticipating the act as early as December 1928.'
– JUDE WANNISKI, *WALL STREET JOURNAL*, 1977

A major piece of protectionist US legislation was passed by the full House and Senate in 1929. It was signed into law by President Herbert Hoover in June 1930. Those tariffs had a devastating effect on total trade (exports plus imports), the stock market and unemployment, as well as GDP. This is the story of the catastrophic Smoot–Hawley tariff legislation that led to the demise of President Hoover's administration and the US economy. Thus began the Great Depression.

The lesson is that trade protection measures destroy the gains from trade by lowering total trade (exports plus imports) but create no jobs, as shown by the trade balance (exports minus imports), as well as the large surge in unemployment. As it was in the past, so will it be in the future.

As Peter the Great said:

It is true that the tariff was reduced, so that the articles that were imported paid only about half as much in proportion after the change as before. But then the new laws increased the importations so much, that the loss was very much more than made up to the treasury, and the emperor found in a very short time that the state of his finances was greatly improved.[8]

TWO TO THE POWER OF TWO SQUARED (2^{2^2} 2^{2^2}) FACTS ON TRADE

When it comes to the topic of international trade, there is seemingly no end to the amount of nonsense and misinformation that politicians will believe and say. These points, explained primarily in a US context, should help you understand:

- The US budget deficit and the US national debt are the legal liabilities of all Americans. The trade deficit is not a US liability; it is solely the liability of the individuals who borrowed the money, *not* US taxpayers.
- A US trade deficit with China can only occur when the Chinese economy invests more in the US than the US economy invests in China. A US trade deficit with China means we get more investments. China's trade surplus with the US (the US trade deficit with China) has provided 1.5 million net new jobs in the US.
- The US trade deficit is the US capital surplus, and the US trade deficit creates US jobs just like any other investment in the US. If, because of tax bills (i.e. lowering of corporate and income tax rates), a factory in Mexico, which employs hundreds of Mexicans, moves to the US, where it will employ hundreds of Americans, that move is recorded as a Mexican trade surplus or a US trade deficit. In this instance, the US wins.
- By the numbers, the US trade deficit gets larger during US booms (Reagan, Kennedy) and smaller during US recessions (Nixon, Carter). The reason is simple: during booms, investments in the US are more attractive, and during contractions, US investments are less attractive. Let's make America more attractive again and have larger trade deficits.
- On 1 January 1983, the 1981 Economic Recovery Tax Act took full effect. Over the next several years, the US cut the highest marginal income tax rate from 70 per cent to 28 per cent, the corporate income tax rate went from 46 per cent to 34 per cent and the number of personal income tax brackets went from fourteen to two. All sorts of tax deductions, exemptions, exclusions and credits were eliminated. Individual foreigners desperately tried to invest in the US by moving their capital from abroad to the US. In Figure 45, you can see how the US dollar soared, and the trade deficit grew enormously, all while the Reagan economy boomed as never before. The US built its economic boon, once again, in part on foreign capital. What's not to love?
- If two borrowers walk out of a bank, one having got a loan and the other having been denied a loan, which would you rather invest in? The US is the one that got the loan and is an investor magnet. Growth countries, like growth companies, borrow money – they don't lend it.

- If the US owes too much to foreigners, all it needs to do is relax immigration standards for foreign investors in the country and then it won't owe it to foreigners anymore. This is the essence of the EB-5 visa programme, which grants immigration visas to wealthy foreigners who invest in the US.

- In 2017, it was calculated that the Chinese government owned $1.2 trillion of the United States' national debt, where it earns virtually zero interest and cannot be sold. The old adage is 'If you owe the bank $100, that's your problem. If you owe the bank $100 million, that's the bank's problem.' With all those assets at stake, China cannot afford a US problem. Because of huge Chinese investments in the US, the US has enormous leverage over China.

- China owns an enormous amount of assets in the US. For China, as an investor in the US, remember there's nothing better than seeing a stock you own appreciate in value. China is America's biggest cheerleader.

- Can you imagine how obnoxious and hostile it would be for Japan to say, 'America, we love you so much we want to give you all of our cars gratis' – don't you just hate it when people give you gifts? (Just kidding!)

- When the US purchases goods from around the world at prices above wholesale, we label it fair trade. But when it bargains for lower-than-wholesale prices, it's suddenly considered foreign dumping. Funny how that works. Those who value saving money tend to support free trade.

- In the early post-war period, Japan was the fastest-growing country in the world and ran trade deficits! Since 1990, Japan has been one of the slowest-growing countries in the world and has trade surpluses. Doesn't this just say it all?

- Between 2007 and 2017, US wealth surged by an incredible $40 trillion – rising from $60 trillion to $100 trillion. In comparison, the total trade deficit with all countries over that period was just $2.8 trillion. So, no – the US is not being sold out to foreign interests.

- Growth countries, like growth companies, borrow money (run trade deficits) to create more wealth. The US is a growth country.

- From 1747 to 1854, the US ran trade deficits for ninety-five out of those 108 years, with only thirteen years showing trade surpluses – many of which coincided with major events like the Revolutionary War (1775–76), the War of 1812 (1811 and 1813) and the massive default to foreign investors in the early 1840s (1842–44). In short, trade deficits were foundational to America's economic growth.

FIGURE 45: US WEALTH AND THE TRADE DEFICIT FROM Q3 1982 TO Q1 1989
(quarterly, Q3 1982–Q1 1989)

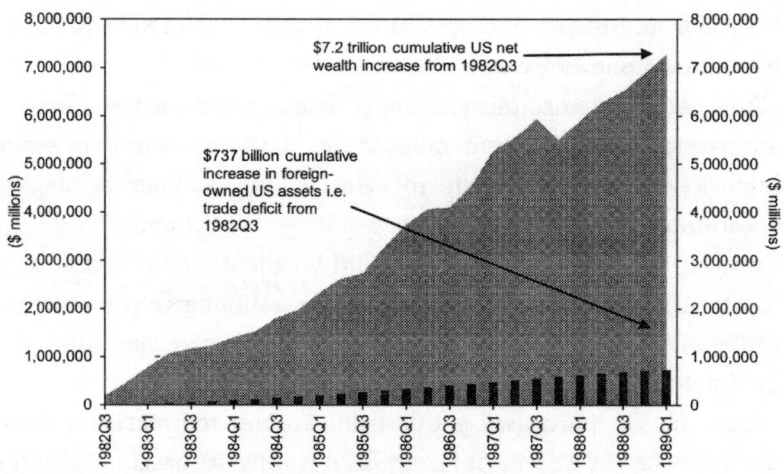

Source: *The Federal Reserve, BEA*

WHEN ARE TARIFFS, THE THREAT OF TARIFFS OR THE PROSPECT OF THE REMOVAL OF TARIFFS APPROPRIATE?

International trade, as the subject is known in academic circles, misses a great deal of extra-economic substance when seen through a political/ economic lens. While the gains from trade are still the same as described in the preceding pages, the roles played by respective governments are very different and span a very wide gamut of action. Government policies, motives and actions burst onto centre stage often obliterating the rigid formalistic framework of academic gains from trade.

To see how one country may want to deviate from 'free trade', imagine a two-country world where one of the two countries is much, much smaller than the other country – say Puerto Rico and the United States. For argument's sake, say that the United States makes up 99 per cent of the world, while Puerto Rico is only 1 per cent of the world. Under totally free trade conditions, highly specialised Puerto Rican manufacturers and product producers could easily have a marketplace where exports are 99 per cent of their sales juxtaposed to equally as specialised US exporters where only 1 per cent of their sales goes to Puerto Rico. Under these circumstances, Puerto Rican exports would still be the same as US imports, and Puerto Rican imports would be the same as US exports, in value terms, and if trade were balanced, US imports from Puerto Rico would, again in value terms, be roughly the same as Puerto Rican imports from the US. This latter point would be true if and only if there were no Alexander capital transfers. So far so good.

Even when we look at the gains from trade, whether Ricardian or Alexander, there's no reason not to believe that, in aggregate, both countries benefit equally. Why shouldn't they? But here's the rub. In Puerto Rico, the gains from trade on a per capita basis are ninety-nine times larger than the US gains from trade on a per capita basis. Ouch. With this highly skewed knowledge in hand, the US government has enormous leverage over Puerto Rico. The mere threat of tariffs, quotas and non-tariff barriers has a vastly different impact on the two countries. The US has a significant advantage over Puerto Rico in negotiating the terms of trade and manipulating the terms of trade via tariffs, quotas and non-trade barriers. Puerto Rico desperately needs access to the US marketplace, while the US has a much smaller need for Puerto Rico's market. In the world economy of today, there is no leader more aware of this asymmetric power than the current President of the United States. Trump sees trade through an entirely different lens than academic economists do. And his lens is not flawed, it's just different. The strict adherence to classic trade theory is far less obvious when power and economics are highly concentrated in only a few countries. This is part of the reason why some countries join trade blocs.

The United Kingdom is not without influence on the world stage but must be keenly focused on the countries with which it trades and engages in trade agreements. Enough said. Facing hostile foreign governments is not a new phenomenon for the UK.

But to reiterate, when it comes to the Ricardian and Alexander gains from trade, there are no winners in trade wars, that's true, but the losers in a trade war are not equally damaged. In any number of cases, some parties are hurt far more than others, and some are barely hurt at all. And these comments only pertain to the economic effects of trade conflict. Once you get into the geo-political arena, there may well be huge winners and big losers. But the first theorem of Game Theory always applies: 'In a two-party game, if the first party has the power to destroy the second party and the second party does not have the power to destroy the first party, then any solution other than a one-party solution is unstable.'

There is no reason why it would be illogical or irrational for a country with considerable leverage to not use that leverage by threatening tariffs or promising tariff relief. Without carrying out the threats, the dominant country with considerable leverage suffers no loss. There is only upside for the highly leveraged country in capturing the entire gains from trade. This is a serious area of gains (or losses) that is simply not covered by academic economists. To these extra-economic arguments, the academic economists inappropriately shout about the dangers of a trade war and protectionist retaliation.

The existence of these extra-economic gains from trade, tariffs and tariff relief in no way obviate the Ricardian and Alexander gains from trade. They simply are benefits or costs in addition to the academic gains or losses from trade. And in many cases, they may well be far larger than are the academic gains from trade. But if history is our guide, governments rarely handle trade issues well: whether they be the Hoover administration's Smoot–Hawley tariff, Nixon's Camp David 10 per cent import tax surcharge or virtually every government's use of sanctions. The US has sanctioned Cuba since 1959. Sixty-five-plus years of sanctions have only intensified Cuba's disdain for America and provided a lifeline to Cuba's terrible authoritarian government.

The costs of trade impedimenta can be astronomical. In his Nobel laureate address in 1999, Professor Robert A. Mundell linked the Smoot–Hawley tariff to the Great Depression followed on by the Second World War. He was correct.

CONCLUSION

Free trade is one of the five kingdoms of macroeconomics and, especially for a relatively small economy like the UK (less than 1 per cent of the world's population and about 3 per cent of world GDP), it is impossible to generate a strong economy without it.

Since an economic recovery programme of the kind that we are proposing is likely at least in its early stages to generate capital inflows that will be associated with balance of payments current account deficits, we should not get too worried about such deficits. But we should be aware that we are proposing a break in the trend of past policies, which is likely to create capital flows that could well be on an unstable scale. Policy will have to be aware of this possibility and allow for it.

Equally, we need to be prepared to allow the currency to appreciate at the same time, since the experience of the 1980s is that such recovery programmes are ultimately likely to become inflationary. We have devised a monetary policy plan for the UK (set out in Part II) that is specifically designed to take this into account.

THE POLICIES FOR ECONOMIC GROWTH: THE 24/7 GROWTH PLAN

'We are in a crisis. The platform is burning. You could disagree or argue about how much time we have left, but the answer is, not a lot. I don't know whether it's three weeks, three months, three years, but in the grand scheme of things, it's very short and very finite.'

– DAVID GIAMPAOLO

In Part I, we described the optimal policies for the five kingdoms of macroeconomic policy: low taxation, restrained government spending, sound money, sensible regulation and free trade. These together form the North Star for setting the sextant to navigate the UK's economic progress.

Part II of this book sets out the specific polices that we believe need to be implemented to set the UK economy on the path towards prosperity within these kingdoms. Please note that in many cases, these policies are just early steps and implementing the guidance from the five kingdoms will require taking these steps much further forward.

We call it the 24/7 Growth Plan because we have put forward twenty-four different policies that fit together and we believe that their implementation would add an additional 7 per cent to GDP by the fifth year after implementation. This means that instead of 9.3 per cent real growth to 2029 as forecast by the OBR, growth is forecast to be 16.8 per cent cumulative over that period.

The chapters mirror those in Part I and show how the five kingdoms of policy can be implemented by real-life changes to the current official plans.

Chapter 8 explains our plans for a flat tax system and other tax improvements.

Chapter 9 explains our ideas for making the public sector more efficient, to freeze welfare payments at their current real levels and to adjust the state pension system to limit its increases in cost, so that the UK public sector can focus on what it needs to do in building nuclear power stations, roads and spending on defence.

Chapter 10 looks at the importance of sound money to restoring confidence and growth.

Chapter 11 shows how better regulation could both save much waste and duplication and enable increased growth.

Chapter 12 shows the importance of an open economy and how that can support an economy like the UK which has traditionally been very much part of an open trading system.

Annex 1 shows how these plans add up by costing them cautiously, working out the impact on growth and revenues and showing how they are affordable while reducing borrowing. For the arithmetic, we have planned to phase the tax changes in. But in reality, assuming that the markets react favourably to the plan, it is likely that sufficient slack will be created to move more quickly and implement them faster. And there is always a danger that pre-announcing tax cuts will defer economic activity (though not, of course, investment) until the lower taxes come into effect.

The twenty-four policies which are discussed in further detail in the following chapters are as follows:

Proposal 1: A flat tax. The flat tax proposal is to replace all taxes on employment and income with a single flat tax, with the current tax allowance (indexed). Disguised income taxes that are charged as taxes on business and wealth or transactions are also abolished, though distributions from businesses and capital gains (except for long-term entrepreneurs) will be covered by the flat tax.

Proposal 2: Abolition of National Insurance. National Insurance (NI) contributions will be abolished, in Year 1 for employees and between Years 2 and 10 for employers. Because of the need to pay for the abolition of employees' NI, the initial flat tax rate is set at 30 per cent, but this will be reduced to 25 per cent by Year 15 and to 20 per cent by Year 20.

Proposal 3: Non-dom tax reform. Reinstate the pre-2024 tax regime for so-called 'non-doms'.

Proposal 4: Abolition of all stamp duties. We propose that in Year 3, stamp duty is abolished for all transactions.

Proposal 5: Abolition of inheritance tax. We propose that in Year 3, inheritance tax is abolished.

Proposal 6: Abolish corporation tax on retained earnings and abolish long-term capital gains tax. We propose that in Year 4, corporation tax on retained earnings (currently 25 per cent) is halved and in Year 5 fully abolished. We also propose that in Year 4, capital gains tax on entrepreneurial gains held for more than five years is abolished with anti-avoidance provisions to prevent abuse.

Proposal 7: Raise public sector productivity. We propose that a target be set to raise public sector productivity by 2 per cent per annum, reversing the post-Covid fall in productivity.

Proposal 8: Freeze welfare spending on sickness benefits in real terms. Our proposal for welfare spending is to freeze the spending level on sickness benefits in real terms from its 2025–26 levels, which is already 11 per cent higher in real terms than in 2021–22. In practical terms, this will mean that additional potential claimants will have to compete with existing claimants.

Proposal 9: Raise the pension age and remove the 'triple lock'. We propose raising the pension age with life expectancy, including implementing the existing plans at the earlier of the proposed dates and to replace the triple lock with simple indexation of pensions to prices.

Proposal 10: Increase spending on infrastructure. We have allocated 2.5 per cent of GDP by 2045–46 to additional public funding for infrastructure, raising it from its current level of approximately 5 per cent of GDP to 7.5 per cent.

Proposal 11: Raise defence spending. We propose raising the amount spent on defence to 5 per cent of GDP within twenty years.

Proposal 12: Change the remit of the Monetary Policy Committee to target nominal GDP and pay more attention to the exchange rate and the pace of monetary expansion. We recommend that the Monetary Policy Committee targets the growth of nominal GDP, while paying explicit attention to the sterling exchange rate especially against the dollar and to the pace of monetary expansion.

Proposal 13: Limit budget deficits and bring down the debt ratio. We recommend these additional fiscal requirements: that the ratio of the deficit to GDP should be on a path to fall to below 2 per cent by 2029–30 and that policy should aim at gradually reducing the debt-to-GDP ratio to 60 per cent by 2043–44.

Proposal 14: Ensure the consequences of new regulations are fully understood and ensure that sunset clauses remove redundant regulations. The regulatory process should be reformed as above to ensure that regulations cannot be implemented without proper consideration of their full effects. And as a matter of course, 'sunset clauses', where a regulation is dropped if its continuation cannot be justified, need to be incorporated within all regulations.

Proposal 15: Reform planning so that residential and commercial buildings are easier to construct. Planning needs to be substantially reformed to ensure that residential and commercial buildings can more easily be built.

Proposal 16: Streamline infrastructure planning. For large projects of national importance, we recommend streamlined planning that will reduce planning delays by at least 75 per cent.

Proposal 17: Reverse the tax increases on landlords and anti-landlord legislation. To improve the supply of rental housing in the UK and offset the damaging impact of recent legislation, the government should restore the tax and legislative position for private landlords to that which existed pre-2015.

Proposal 18: Adopt 'smart net zero'. Policies to achieve environmental objectives should be implemented at minimal economic cost and only when cost-justified.

Proposal 19: Labour market liberalisation. Adjust legislation to make it easier for employers to hire and dismiss employees and scrap the Employment Rights Bill if it becomes law.

Proposal 20: Bring down the minimum wage as a share of the median wage. Adjust the minimum wage level by returning it to its 2023 level in relation to the median wage (61 per cent) by freezing it until this ratio is reached.

Proposal 21: Improve road infrastructure, paid for by the introduction of road user charges. We've already proposed increased infrastructure spending, particularly on roads. In addition, road user costs should be frozen at their current level in real terms. In time, all road usage taxes should be scrapped and replaced by road user charges on the basis set out below. Road user charges should not be additional to existing road taxes.

Proposal 22: Push through and extend the trade deals with the US and India and create a CANZUK free trade area. The government should fully implement the deals with the US and India and seek to develop them further to enhance trade in services. We propose that His Majesty's government (HMG) prioritises creating a CANZUK free trade area.

Proposal 23: Leave the EU Carbon Border Adjustment Mechanism and encourage further trade liberalisation under CPTPP. We recommend that the UK does not adopt the European Carbon Border Adjustment Mechanism, and we recommend encouraging further liberalisation under the Comprehensive and Progressive Agreement for Trans-Pacific Partnership (CPTPP), including its extension to trade in services.

Proposal 24: Liberalise trade in services. Our research shows that 67.7 per cent of UK exports measured by value add (excluding the import content in exports) is now composed of exports of services. We recommend that the UK focus much of its trade negotiations on trade in services to reflect the new reality of UK trade becoming much more based on services, negotiating with its trading partners to reduce non-tariff barriers on such trade.

Lord Petitgas told us, 'Can you fix all this by being incremental, or do you have to go baseball bat? I think you have no choice. You have to go baseball bat. I think this is a situation where you have to go hard.'

We estimate that these proposals will after twenty years add 28.8 per cent to GDP, pulling the UK up from a projected forty-ninth place in the world GDP per capita league table to nineteenth place. The growth plus net cuts from planned spending of £111 billion at 2025–26 levels of income and prices will pay for the cost of the tax cuts plus a reduction in planned borrowing of £46 billion. For more details of the economic arithmetic see Annex 1.

CHAPTER 8

UK TAXATION

'You have to go back to Nigel Lawson to see a Chancellor who has actually thought about tax in the round, and who was interested, genuinely interested, in reform.'

– LORD MACPHERSON OF EARL'S COURT

The first kingdom is low taxation.

As we point out in Part I: 'The goal of taxation is to have a tax system that collects the requisite revenues to fund government while doing the least damage to the economy.'

To create the conditions for stronger economic growth and more jobs, while treating taxpayers fairly, the government must reform taxes to make them lower, simpler and more transparent.

This section first looks at the economic evidence that lower taxes boost growth; it then proposes an approach towards achieving a flat tax, eventually at a 20 per cent rate (though initially at 30 per cent), and finally it shows what needs to be done to achieve the tax programme suggested.

HOW IS THE UK TAXED?

Table 11 shows the current and forecast sources of tax revenues in the UK taken from the Office for Budget Responsibility's analysis of the 26 March 2025 Spring Statement.

It shows clearly that roughly three quarters of tax revenues for 2025–26 are forecast to emerge from four taxes: income tax, National Insurance contributions, value added tax and corporation tax.

TABLE 11: BREAKDOWN OF UK TAXES[1]

		£ billion						
		Outturn	Forecast					
		2023–24	2024–25	2025–26	2026–27	2027–28	2028–29	2029–30
Income tax[*]		277.4	310.0	330.7	356.0	378.5	385.3	398.1
of which:	Pay as you earn	239.0	266.2	283.6	295.8	307.2	317.2	328.8
	Self-assessment	42.7	49.7	53.3	61.9	68.4	72.0	76.2
	Other income tax	-4.2	-5.9	-6.1	-1.8	2.8	-4.0	-6.8
National Insurance contributions		179.1	167.8	200.6	206.9	212.9	219.5	226.2
Value added tax		168.9	171.3	180.4	187.5	195.8	202.7	211.1
Corporation tax[†]		90.8	95.6	99.4	103.4	108.0	112.8	118.1
of which:	Onshore	88.1	93.7	97.1	101.9	107.1	112.2	117.3
	Offshore	2.7	1.9	2.3	1.5	0.9	0.7	0.8
Petroleum revenue tax		-0.4	-0.4	-0.3	-0.2	-0.1	-0.1	-0.1
Fuel duties		24.8	24.4	24.4	27.0	27.3	27.3	27.0
Business rates		29.3	31.8	33.7	37.3	37.6	38.2	39.2
Council tax		44.5	47.7	50.2	52.8	55.6	58.5	61.5
VAT refunds		28.1	29.2	31.6	32.2	33.3	34.0	34.9
Capital gains tax		14.5	13.3	19.7	19.4	20.2	23.1	25.5
Inheritance tax		7.5	8.4	9.1	10.0	11.7	13.3	14.3
Property transaction taxes[‡]		12.8	15.0	15.7	18.8	21.6	24.4	26.5
Stamp taxes on shares		3.2	4.2	4.4	4.5	4.7	4.9	5.1
Tobacco duties		9.0	8.1	8.1	8.1	8.1	8.0	8.0
Alcohol duties		12.5	12.4	13.0	13.7	14.3	15.0	15.7
Air passenger duty		3.9	4.2	4.7	5.4	5.8	6.1	6.5
Insurance premium tax		8.4	8.9	9.2	9.3	9.5	9.7	9.9
Climate change levy		1.9	1.9	1.9	1.9	1.8	1.8	1.8
Bank levy		1.5	1.3	1.3	1.3	1.3	1.3	1.3
Bank surcharge		1.5	1.1	1.1	1.1	1.2	1.2	1.3
Apprenticeship levy		3.8	4.1	4.2	4.4	4.5	4.6	4.8
Digital services tax		0.7	0.8	0.9	1.0	1.1	1.1	1.2
Other HMRC taxes[§]		9.9	10.3	10.4	10.6	11.4	11.9	12.3
Vehicle excise duties		7.7	8.2	9.1	9.6	10.0	10.5	11.1
Licence fee receipts		3.7	3.8	3.9	4.0	4.1	4.1	4.2

[*] Includes PAYE, self-assessment, tax on savings income and other minor components, such as income tax repayments.

[†] National Accounts measure.

[‡] Includes stamp duty land tax, devolved property transaction taxes and the annual tax on enveloped dwellings.

[§] Consists of landfill tax (ex-devolved), aggregates levy, betting and gaming duties, customs duties, diverted profits tax, soft drinks industry levy, residential property developer tax, the Carbon Border Adjustment Mechanism, vaping tax and plastic packaging tax.

Environmental levies	9.9	11.9	12.1	14.7	14.6	14.5	14.8
Emissions Trading Scheme	6.0	3.5	2.6	2.5	2.5	2.1	1.7
Energy profits levy	3.1	2.7	3.2	2.3	1.9	1.7	1.7
Electricity generator levy	1.2	1.0	0.7	0.1	0.0	0.0	0.0
Other taxes	11.1	13.5	15.5	15.6	16.0	16.4	16.7
National Accounts taxes	**976.2**	**1,016**	**1,102**	**1,161**	**1,215**	**1,254**	**1,300**
Interest and dividends	43.8	43.5	41.3	42.2	43.5	44.8	46.5
Gross operating surplus	75.9	79.3	83.5	85.8	88.9	91.8	94.4
Other receipts	2.6	2.7	3.1	3.3	3.4	3.6	3.6
Current receipts	**1,099**	**1,141**	**1,229**	**1,292**	**1,351**	**1,394**	**1,445**

Source: OBR Spring Statement Economic and Fiscal Outlook 2025 Annex A

HOW DOES THE UK COMPARE WITH OTHER COUNTRIES?

The OECD measures tax (and other government receipts) as a share of GDP for all qualifying economies[2] and its latest comparison is shown in Table 12.

The increase has taken the UK from being below the OECD average historic tax burden to significantly above.

TABLE 12: GENERAL GOVERNMENT TOTAL TAX AND NON-TAX RECEIPTS AS A PER CENT OF NOMINAL GDP[3]

Country	Average 1997–2007	2025	Change
Australia	35.9	35.7	-0.2
Austria	49.6	52.3	2.8
Belgium	49.4	50.2	0.8
Canada	41.5	42.5	1.0
Czechia	38.8	40.9	2.2
Denmark	54.8	49.9	-4.9
Estonia	36.7	43.0	6.3
Finland	52.7	53.7	1.0
France	51.1	51.6	0.5
Germany	44.7	47.1	2.4
Greece	40.1	47.7	7.6
Hungary	43.0	42.7	-0.3
Iceland	46.2	43.5	-2.6
Ireland	35.0	24.6	-10.4

Israel	...	37.1	...
Italy	44.3	46.7	2.4
Japan	29.9	38.0	8.1
Latvia	36.0	44.5	8.5
Lithuania	34.9	39.3	4.3
Luxembourg	43.2	46.4	3.2
Netherlands	43.6	42.3	-1.2
New Zealand	37.1	38.5	1.4
Norway	56.0	61.6	5.6
Poland	40.4	43.9	3.6
Portugal	39.9	44.3	4.4
Slovak Republic	38.1	43.0	4.9
Slovenia	44.4	46.0	1.6
Spain	38.8	42.5	3.7
South Korea	27.1	34.7	7.6
Sweden	54.5	48.3	-6.2
Switzerland	32.6	33.5	0.9
United Kingdom	36.2	42.0	5.8
United States*	33.1	31.6	-1.4
Euro area 17	45.4	46.5	1.1
Total OECD	36.9	38.1	1.2

Source: OECD Economic Outlook December 2024 Statistical Annex

Data refer to the general government sector, which is a consolidation of accounts for the central, state and local governments, plus social security.

But the UK's tax competitiveness position is even less attractive than the OECD data for its tax burden would indicate.

Every year, the Tax Foundation compares the tax competitiveness of the main economies. This index attempts to measure the extent to which tax distorts economic decisions, especially at the margin, and affects investment decisions by international businesses.

Lord Macpherson of Earl's Court told us, 'I think 80 per cent of our revenue comes from income tax, social insurance and VAT ... The rest is all irrelevant and probably counterproductive.'

As recently as 2017, the UK ranked fourteenth and above all its major large competitors.[4] But since then, the relative position has declined. In

---

* Excludes the operating surpluses of public enterprises.

the latest comparison, the UK now ranks as low as thirty-fourth out of the thirty-eight countries studied and behind all major competitors.[5]

Looking at the subcomponents of the index, the only area where the UK scores well is in its cross-border tax rules, though this score predates the 2024 change in rules for 'non-doms' (foreign residents not domiciled for tax purposes, who were liable for tax on their UK incomes but not on their international incomes).

We have taken into account the UK's declining tax competitiveness in putting forward our main proposals.

The Tax Foundation found the following strengths of the UK tax system in 2024:

- The UK provides full expensing for business investments in machinery at above-average cost recovery for investments in intangible assets.
- The UK has a territorial tax system exempting both foreign dividend and capital gains income without any country limitations.
- The UK operates the broadest tax treaty network in the OECD with 131 countries.

However, the Tax Foundation highlighted the following weaknesses:

- The top personal income tax rate on dividends is 39.35 per cent, well above the OECD average (24.7 per cent).
- The real property tax burden is the highest in the OECD.

The VAT at a rate of 20 per cent applies to less than half of the potential consumption tax base, and the VAT exemption threshold is 2.5 times as high as the OECD average.

Lord Macpherson of Earl's Court said, 'You can raise taxes a bit and get away with it, but if you make a habit of it, there comes a point when people just say, enough is enough.'

This contrasts with Estonia, which has been top of the tax competitiveness index for the past eleven years. Estonia's tax competitiveness is based on four key features:

- It has no corporate income tax on reinvested and retained profits (and a 14–20 per cent corporate income tax rate on distributed profits). This means that Estonia's corporate income tax system allows companies to reinvest their profits tax-free.
- It has a flat 20 per cent tax on individual income. The tax is not applied in the case of distributed dividends that have already been taxed with a corporate income tax (see above).
- Its property tax applies only to the value of land, rather than to the value of real property or capital.
- It has a territorial tax system that exempts 100 per cent of foreign profits earned by domestic corporations from domestic taxation, with few restrictions.

Clearly, the UK has some distance to go to match the Estonian system.

THE 24/7 GROWTH PLAN FOR THE UK

Taking the evidence from the very best academic literature on the relationship between the level and type of taxation and economic growth, what sort of tax system should we be aiming for in the UK to increase economic growth?

This section describes a tax system which we calculate would provide a major boost to growth.

INCOME TAX

Proposal 1: A flat tax. The flat tax proposal is to replace all taxes on employment and income with a single flat tax, with the current tax allowance (indexed). Disguised income taxes that are charged as taxes on business and wealth or transactions are also abolished, though distributions from businesses and capital gains (except for long-term entrepreneurs) will be covered by the flat tax.

Proposal 2: Abolition of National Insurance. National Insurance contributions will be abolished, in Year 1 for employees and between Years 2 and 10 for employers. Because of the need to pay for the abolition of employees' NI, the initial flat tax rate is set at 30 per cent, but this will be reduced to 25 per cent by Year 15 and to 20 per cent by Year 20.

George Osborne told us, 'On income tax, what I actually wanted to do was take [the top rate of] income tax from fifty pence back to forty pence.'

The details are below.

In Year 1, all rates of income tax are replaced by a flat tax of 30 per cent and employees' National Insurance contributions (currently 8 per cent) are abolished.

In Year 1, reinstate the pre-2024 Spring Budget rules for non-domiciles.

Between Years 2 and 10, employers' National Insurance contributions (currently 15 per cent) are gradually abolished.

In Year 10, the flat rate of income tax is reduced to 25 per cent and in Year 15 to 20 per cent.

The flat tax will be charged on incomes above the current tax allowance of £12,570 which should be indexed from 2026–27.

This generates huge benefits of simplicity and incentives, especially as the welfare budget can be replaced with proper incentives to work.

The current system of tax is set out in Table 13.

TABLE 13: PERSONAL INCOME TAX BANDS FOR 2025–26

Band	Taxable Income	Tax Rate
Personal allowance	Up to £12,570	0 per cent
Basic rate	£12,571 to £50,270	20 per cent
Higher rate	£50,271 to £125,140	40 per cent
Additional rate	Over £125,140	45 per cent

However, the personal allowance is phased out on taxable incomes above £100,000 at a rate of £1 for every £2 of income until it reaches zero. This creates a marginal tax rate of at least 60 per cent and in many cases more because various allowances such as childcare are also phased out at the same income level.

On top of this, employers and employees pay National Insurance contributions which are in effect a further tax on incomes or employment. The system for employees is set out in Table 14. There is anecdotal evidence that some employees are now refusing pay rises that would take their income above the £100,000 taxable income threshold.

Sir Vince Cable said, 'The tax structure as you move up beyond £100,000 is very uneven, and there's a sort of group of people who are paying exceptionally high marginal rates over a range of about £100,000, and then it drops again.'

TABLE 14: EMPLOYEES' NATIONAL INSURANCE BANDS FOR 2025–26[6]

Your pay	From 6 April 2025 to 5 April 2026
£242 to £967 a week (£1,048 to £4,189 a month)	8%
Over £967 a week (£4,189 a month)	2%

Source: Gov.uk

For employers, the rate varies but a standard rate for much of employee income is 15 per cent.

EXPERIENCE OF COUNTRIES WITH FLAT TAXES

TABLE 15: COUNTRIES WHICH HAVE HAD OR STILL HAVE FLAT TAXES SINCE THE SECOND WORLD WAR[7]

Country	Year of introduction	Rate	Notes
Jersey	1940	20%	
Hong Kong	1947	16%	Initial rate 10 per cent in 1948; replaced by progressive tax at rates 2 per cent to 17 per cent in 2024
Guernsey	1960	20%	
Isle of Man	1970	22%	Basic tax with a lower rate of 10 per cent up to £6,000 Isle of Man £
Jamaica	1986	25%	Originally 33 per cent – higher rate tax of 33 per cent from 2016
Tuvalu	1992	10%	
Estonia	1994	21%	Originally 26 per cent
Guyana	1994	30%	Replaced with 28 per cent and 40 per cent rates in 2017
Latvia	1995	25%	Progressive rates from 2018
Belize	1995	25%	
Grenada	1996	30%	15 per cent lower rate from 2014

Lithuania	1996	24%	Originally 33 per cent; replaced with progressive rates from 2019
Russia	2001	13%	Higher rate of 15 per cent from 2021
Serbia	2003	14%	
Iraq	2004	15%	
Slovakia	2004	19%	Higher rate of 25 per cent from 2013
Ukraine	2004	15%	Originally 13 per cent
Saudi Arabia	2004	20%	Only on non-nationals (locals subject to zakat)
Georgia	2005	12%	
Romania	2005	16%	
British Virgin Islands	2005	8%	Payroll tax, plus mandatory social security
Turkmenistan	2005	10%	
Kazakhstan	2006	10%	
Trinidad	2006	25%	Higher rate of 30 per cent from 2017
Albania	2007	10%	Replaced with two rates 13 per cent and 23 per cent in 2014
Iceland	2007	36%	Replaced by progressive rates in 2010
Kyrgyzstan	2007	10%	
North Macedonia	2007	10%	
Mongolia	2007	10%	Higher rates of 15 per cent and 20 per cent from 2023
Montenegro	2007	15%	
Bulgaria	2008	10%	
Czech Republic	2008	15%	Effective rate 20 per cent; changed to 22 per cent in 2013. Replaced by two rates 15 per cent and 23 per cent in 2021
Timor-Leste	2008	8%	
Moldova	2008	18%	Lower rate of 7 per cent
Mauritius	2009	15%	
Bolivia	2009	13%	
Belarus	2009	12%	Raised to 13 per cent 2015; higher rate of 25 per cent from 2024
Bosnia	2009	10%	
Seychelles	2010	15%	Higher rates of 20 per cent and 30 per cent from 2018
Hungary	2010	15%	Started at 16 per cent and reduced to 15 per cent
Paraguay	2010	10%	
Greenland	2013	37%	
Madagascar	2014	20%	Lower rates introduced in 2021
Azerbaijan	2014	14%	Additional taxes in the oil sector
Anguilla	2020	6%	Solidarity tax
UAE	2023	9%	On business income only

The most widely quoted example of a flat tax is that of Hong Kong, which introduced a tax rate of 10 per cent in 1947. The rate has varied, but for most of the period since the rate was set, the system has been a generally flat one.

Hong Kong, of course, has achieved astonishing economic growth since 1947. One would suspect a significant part of it is to do with the flat tax.

Jersey and Guernsey are not technically part of the UK but are Crown Dependencies with flat taxes. Jersey's GDP per capita had risen to $74,989 in 2023, compared with the $49,284 estimate for the UK for the same year.[8]

The Isle of Man, also a self-governing Crown Dependency and not part of the UK, has a tax regime with a 10 per cent basic rate and a 20 per cent higher rate and a 0 per cent rate for companies. Its GDP per capita in 2022 was $94,300.

Lord Macpherson of Earl's Court said, 'A flat [tax] is maybe going a bit too far but definitely a tax system which has little differentiation.'

Our analysis of the transition economies above shows how much faster growth has been in the economies with lower tax rates. Although they are not always exactly the same economies that have flat taxes, there is considerable overlap.

Table 15 sets out the list of all countries with or which have had flat taxes. The bulk of them have had strong growth while they have had flat taxes. Notably, the predictions by the International Monetary Fund (IMF) and other economists that flat taxes would lose revenues have been confounded.[9] It is notable that a number have given up flat taxes and introduced higher or lower rates. But most of these countries have only done so after their economies have already been boosted by flat or low taxes.

What is clear is that flat or low taxes are positive for generating economic growth.

NON-DOMS

Proposal 3: Non-dom tax reform. Reinstate the pre-2024 tax regime for so-called 'non-doms'.

Boris Johnson told us, 'I was proud to say that London was to the billionaire as the jungles of Sumatra are to the orangutan – it's their natural habitat, and it was the place to be.'

The tax regime for the so-called 'non-doms' (non-domiciled residents of the UK who have certain tax exemptions of which the most important is that they are allowed to pay tax on a remittance basis rather than being taxed on their worldwide income) was changed in the April 2024 Budget introduced by Chancellor Jeremy Hunt and further changes were announced in the subsequent October 2024 Budget introduced by the incoming Chancellor Rachel Reeves.

This section looks at the potential impact if the earlier regime were reinstated. It examines studies of the international mobility of wealthier taxpayers and uses them to estimate the impact on both tax revenues and GDP.

It concludes that using the elasticities from international studies, the central estimate of the impact of abolition of the 2024 changes would be for HMRC to gain £5 billion* in revenues and for GDP to rise by 0.5 per cent.†

So, perversely to some minds, abolishing the tax change would *raise* revenue *and* GDP.‡

The industries especially affected would be banking, oil, car production and professional football.

About a fifth of top-earning bankers used to take advantage of the non-dom regime.

Meanwhile, using past elasticities suggests that more than half the 371 overseas players in the Premier League in 2024 would leave the UK (205 players) following the abolition of the regime, although a more detailed analysis of the alternative opportunities in football brings this number down to fifty to eighty.

The best-known study of the impact of taxation of non-doms is the LSE/Warwick study,[10] which has been widely quoted for its conclusion that tax changes would be unlikely to affect migration. The study estimates that the abolition of the non-dom regime would only cause seventy-seven non-doms to leave and that the additional revenue raised would be £3.6 billion.

Unfortunately, this study is flawed and provides only very partial

---

*   This compares with lower annual estimates from Cebr, which take less account of the impact on GDP: 'Impact of changes to the UK non-domiciled regime', Cebr, 6 May 2025, https://cebr.com/reports/impact-of-changes-to-the-uk-non-domiciled-regime/

†   This assumes that extra income would be potentially taxed at 45 per cent.

‡   A new study by Cebr assesses the revenue loss if 50 per cent of non-doms leave at £12.2 billion. This makes our £5 billion look cautious.

evidence to support its contention. Its analysis relates only to the 2017 tax changes, which, though substantial, mainly applied to longer-term settled migrants of a kind unlikely to be affected by a changed tax regime. Moreover, the tax changes were unlikely to lead to much movement of people.

Boris Johnson said, 'I'm afraid I'm going around the world and I'm meeting more and more refugees. It really is like eighteenth-century France. They're fleeing the encumbrance of the Labour purges. They're all going. Dubai is now the nineteenth biggest British city.'

As the accountants RSM pointed out commenting on the LSE/Warwick study:[11]

> Unfortunately, this ignores the context of the 2017 changes. These were accompanied by a series of reforms which allowed affected non-doms to reorganise their affairs in advance of the new rules taking effect. The overall effect of the 2017 changes was to allow non-doms to remain UK resident after losing the remittance basis without being taxed on foreign income and gains, provided that they restructured their wealth in the form approved by the legislation.

In fact, the bulk of the income affected by the 2024 abolition of non-dom status is held by those non-doms who are likely to have been in the UK for fewer than five years. Clearly, such people are likely to be much more sensitive than the long-term residents covered by the 2017 changes, both in coming to the UK and leaving the UK, to changes in the fiscal climate.

An additional weakness of using the LSE/Warwick study is that it only looked at one side of the equation – the tendency of non-doms already in the UK to leave with respect to tax changes. But equally important is likely to be the impact on whether they decide to come to the UK. The LSE/Warwick study does not consider this.

THE PRESENT REGIME

Those who are resident but not domiciled in the UK used to be allowed to elect for the remittance basis of taxation – essentially, they are taxed on their earnings in the UK but not on those from outside the UK.

The remittance basis of taxation was a choice available to individuals whose 'domicile' (essentially their home country) is not the UK, who do not have a 'domicile of origin' (their domicile status inherited at birth from their parent) in the UK and who have been UK tax resident for fewer than fifteen of the previous twenty tax years. These individuals could elect not to be taxed in the UK on foreign income and gains so long as they are not 'remitted' to the UK. The claim could be made for free for the first seven years of UK residence, but after that an annual remittance basis charge (RBC) must be paid (£30,000 for those resident in at least seven of the previous nine tax years and £60,000 for those resident for at least twelve of the last fourteen tax years).

The Office for National Statistics (ONS) estimated[12] that there were 68,800 individuals claiming non-domiciled taxpayer status in the UK on their Self-Assessment (SA) tax returns in the tax year ending 2022.

The LSE/Warwick study estimated that in total, the non-doms had at least £10.9 billion in offshore income and gains.

Lord Petitgas said:

> The OBR hypothesis on non-doms was a 1.5 per cent attrition rate. What would be your guess of the resi non-doms who've left this country? Forget the rich Brits who are leaving, just the resi non-doms? It's 50 per cent, and of the top bracket more. Now you're talking about a massive exodus of tax dollars.

But interestingly, the non-doms used to pay in total £12.4 billion in tax and National Insurance contributions,* an average of £158,163 per non-dom taxpayer. This would imply that their UK taxable income was £27.6 billion, which in turn would imply that their contribution to UK GDP was around £46 billion.

All studies agree that mobility of wealthy people with respect to tax regimes is increasing for a range of reasons.[13] Most of the estimated

---

* The *Financial Times* estimate (which only takes account of income tax and is for 2022–23) is £8.9 billion: 'Tax paid by UK non-doms rose to £8.9bn in 2022–23', *Financial Times*, 9 July 2024, https://www.ft.com/content/7c36e942-b59b-492b-a64b-6ca331e7a960. Grossing up for National Insurance contributions and updating to 2024/25 GDP would be consistent with the higher figure.

elasticities have been calculated on data from the mid-2010s and conclude that the elasticity then was between one and two, probably at the higher end.

The elasticity of footballers for example has been estimated at 1.4; that of inventors at 2.3 and that of entrepreneurs at 1.6.

Data currently available on millionaires and billionaires leaving or not coming to the UK suggests that the elasticity of mobility is likely to be at the high end of the possible range.

Currently, the UK is facing a major net outflow of 'millionaires', with an alleged 10,800 lost in 2024 alone.[14] There is little data on the amount of tax paid by these people, but if one takes as a basis those who earn more than £500,000 a year (HMRC estimate that for 2024–25 there were 90,000 individuals in the UK earning that amount, paying on average £580,000 in tax),[15] the annual tax loss from their exodus would be £6.2 billion.

Stopping this and indeed turning it round would transform tax revenues. Survey evidence suggests that tax is the motivation for the bulk of the exodus,[16] so tax changes to encourage talented and wealthy people to work and invest in the UK would be likely to have a disproportionately beneficial impact.

Richard Gnodde said, 'I'm amazed how many people have left. A surprising number. I think the government's got absolutely no idea. Because you don't have to tell anyone you leave, you just stand up and go.'

Moreover, the number of countries that have non-dom tax regimes is increasing. It is no longer just Switzerland and Spain (the Spanish regime was established to attract a particular footballer and is commonly called the 'Beckham Law'). Malta, Portugal, Greece and Italy have all established or enhanced such regimes. In addition, looking further afield, Hong Kong and Singapore have highly attractive tax regimes for high earners while the UAE and even more so Saudi Arabia are making tempting if often selective offers.

BANKING AND THE PREMIER LEAGUE
According to a different LSE/Warwick report based on the same research:[17]

More than one in five top-earning bankers has benefited from non-dom status, according to a new LSE and University of Warwick report. Non-doms also make up a sizeable share of top earners – those in the top 1 per cent, earning over £125,000 – in other industries, with two out of five top earners in the oil industry and one in four top earners in the car industry having claimed non-dom status at some point. One in six top-earning sports and film stars living in the UK have claimed non-dom status, with an average income of £2 million each.

Clearly, since many of these industries are footloose, there is a potential threat to the whole industry if a substantial proportion of top earners relocate out of the UK.

It is worth noting that part of the UK bid for international sporting events normally includes offering not just non-dom treatment but complete tax-free status (e.g. for the Olympics, the UEFA European Championships and the UEFA Super Cup).

In reality, the lack of alternative options means that the 205 football players likely to be affected by the abolition of the non-dom status estimated from income elasticity data is probably an overestimate. Consulting with specialist experts on football,* and allowing for the fact that whereas in banking the opportunities to move abroad are considerable while those in football are limited, suggests that the real number of football players who would be able to find alternative clubs is more likely to be between fifty and eighty, of whom about twenty would be top stars, the rest players reaching the latter stages of their careers. And probably the move would be gradual, as contracts came to an end.

One of the best rules of taxation is for tax authorities not to be too greedy. Given the amount of revenue that the UK tax authorities currently earn from non-doms, it would seem highly risky to abolish non-dom status. The central estimate is of no change in taxes directly received from non-doms and a reduction of £5 billion in revenues from

---

* We are grateful to Paul Miller, banker and former central defender for Tottenham Hotspur and England, who has helped this part of the analysis.

other taxes with a loss of 0.5 per cent of GDP and it is hard to see why putting this amount of economic activity at risk makes sense.

STAMP DUTY

Proposal 4: Abolition of all stamp duties. We propose that in Year 3, stamp duty is abolished for all transactions.

A wide range of economists have consistently argued against stamp duties on both property and other transactions.[18] Stamp duty on share transfers makes the UK economically unattractive compared with other financial centres. Lord Lamont of Lerwick said:

> I think stamp duty on properties is a very bad tax. It interferes with two markets, the property market and the labour market. It's a major disincentive to mobility. And even at the top end, I can't believe this isn't a huge disincentive, and I think it probably ripples through the whole system.

Currently, they are charged at 0.5 per cent on share transfers and for property the rates set out below.

TABLE 16: STAMP DUTY LAND TAX BANDS FOR RESIDENTIAL PROPERTY FOR 2025–26

Property Purchase Price Bands	Stamp Duty Rate
Up to £125,000	0 per cent
£125,001 to £250,000	2 per cent
£250,001 to £925,000	5 per cent
£925,001 to £1,500,000	10 per cent
Over £1.5 million	12 per cent

For stamp duty on shares, a standard result is that reached by the Centre for Policy Studies:[19]

> Independent modelling by the Oxera consultancy for the Centre for Policy Studies – the first full analysis of the impact of the tax since the

financial crisis – shows that abolishing stamp duty on shares could be expected to lead to a permanent increase in GDP of between 0.2 per cent and 0.7 per cent in the long run.

Lord Lamont of Lerwick told us:

> It doesn't really hit the average punter very much, but it does reduce the liquidity of the market and trading in the market. And I do think the decline of the London Stock Exchange is one of the most worrying things that's happened in recent years. I would be personally inclined to look at abolishing stamp duty on shares, and it doesn't raise much.

PROPERTY TRANSACTION TAXES

An analysis by the economic consultancy Cebr in 2020 concluded that the continuation of the stamp duty 'holiday' for properties worth less than £500,000 would have the following results[20]:

- Extending the stamp duty holiday would be close to fiscally neutral or potentially even fiscally positive, with the new tax revenues generated by higher consumption and housing market activity recouping between £2.3 billion and £4.1 billion. In the upper-bound estimate, this leads to a fiscal surplus of £139 million associated with a permanent extension of the stamp duty holiday.
- Holding property prices and transaction numbers constant, extending the stamp duty holiday would lead to a £3.9 billion decline in revenues from Stamp Duty Land Tax (SDLT), Land and Buildings Transactions Tax (LBTT) and Land Transactions Tax (LTT).
- However, our analysis shows that the reduction in the rate of stamp duty would lead to 37,000 additional property transactions taking place each year, generating £266 million in revenues annually.
- If the stamp duty holiday were to be made permanent, HMRC's derived elasticities suggest that future UK house prices would be on average 1.3 per cent higher than they otherwise would have been. Moreover, the structure of the SDLT schedule means that the percentage

change in prices would be greater for higher value properties, leading to a 1.9 per cent increase in households' collective property wealth. These higher property values would have a positive effect on SDLT, LBTT and LTT receipts, generating £256 billion in additional revenues each year.

- Our analysis further shows that the increase in house prices would lead to an estimated 0.36 per cent to 0.75 per cent increase in household consumption. This additional economic activity would generate estimated tax revenues of up to £2.9 billion per year.
- Making the stamp duty holiday permanent would reduce UK households' collective stamp duty burden by £3.4 billion each year. In our lower-bound estimate, we assume that this will stimulate a further £1.0 billion of consumption, generating £290 million in tax revenues each year. In our upper-bound estimate, aggregate consumption rises by £2.0 billion per year, leading to a £561 million increase in tax revenues.
- Finally, by increasing the value of capital gains from the sale of residential properties, a permanent extension of the stamp duty holiday would generate an estimated £124 million in capital gains tax revenues in the first year, with this amount diminishing in future years.

These results are estimated to come from merely an extension of a 'holiday' on stamp duties on lower priced residential properties. There appears to be little information about the impact of abolishing all stamp duties and equivalent taxes on all properties, but there can be little doubt that the economic impact must be a considerable multiple of the Cebr calculations of partial abolition set out above.

INHERITANCE TAX

Proposal 5: Abolition of inheritance tax. We propose that in Year 3, inheritance tax is abolished.

Speaking with the then Prime Minister, Rishi Sunak, in January 2024, Nadhim Zahawi said:

> Abolish inheritance tax, because you need to do something if you want it to turn, to make the weather, and it'll be such a big thing. And I know what people will say. They'll say, only 4 per cent of estates pay. Actually, it's 4 per cent of estates every year, so in a parliamentary term, cumulatively, that's a much bigger percentage of the nation. The average estate is usually four because there's brothers, sisters and relations. So again, the number is much bigger. And whenever we've flown the kite at the Adam Smith Institute, people love it. He said, 'I can't afford it – I want to cut National Insurance' … I said, 'I've got another idea for you, which would pay for it, and you should announce the two together. I would announce you're abolishing inheritance tax on the one hand, and you're abolishing non-doms' … And his ears pricked up. I said what I would do, because it had become such a toxic term, and because Labour and Rachel Reeves had landed it really hard as an opposition campaign, is to replace it with an enterprise residency. You say we're going to do what Europe's doing, and Europe is Italy, and we're going to beat them, because we're going to double this. She was at 100, go for 250 and it will pay for abolishing inheritance tax, which is about £7 billion. And he turned to his PPS, and said, 'I really like that.' And I said, 'Great,' and left it with him. He recused himself from the policy making, gave it to Jeremy [Hunt] … And one of the things I wanted to do, which I never got around to do, was to change the Treasury sort of orthodoxy, from linear modelling to dynamic modelling. They refused to do it right. They gave Jeremy this thing. They said, 'Well, if you want 2.7 billion saved, abolish non-doms,' and that's where we end up in this crappy mess in the end, where we lost our supporters and we lost the election.

The Growth Commission in 2024 looked at inheritance tax in some detail.[21] The text below is heavily influenced by the results of its study which was commissioned by one of this book's co-authors.

The initial revenue expected to be raised from inheritance tax in 2025–26 is £9.1 billion. The Growth Commission special study[22] compared this with cutting income tax by an amount, initially reducing revenues by the same amount and cutting corporation tax by an equivalent amount.

FIGURE 46: USING EX ANTE FISCAL HEADROOM FROM ABOLISHING INHERITANCE TAX TO CUT DIFFERENT TAXES: IMPACT ON GDP PER CAPITA

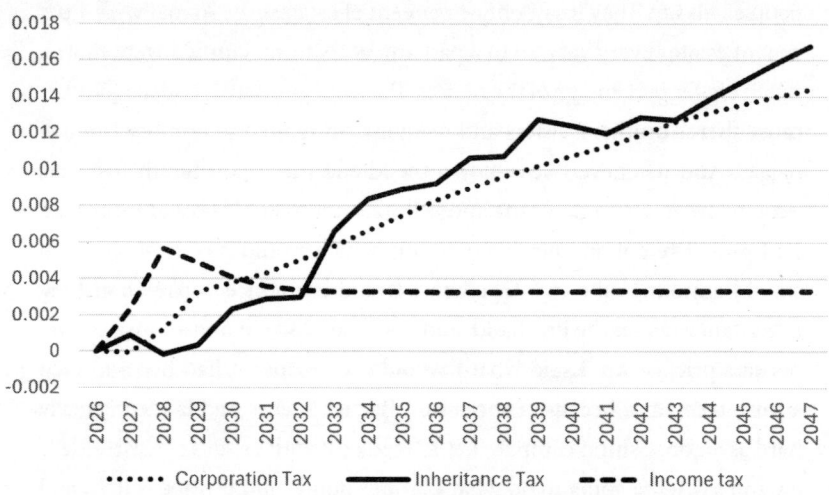

Source: Research by Cebr for the Growth Commission for 'The Spring Growth Budget 2024', Figure 19

The same ex ante amount could be used to reduce the basic rate of income tax by 1p and the higher rates by 2p; or it could be used to reduce the headline rate of corporation tax to 22 per cent from 25 per cent.

The results of the comparison are shown in Figure 46. Cutting both inheritance tax and corporation tax ultimately boosts GDP per capita by more than cutting basic rates of income tax and indeed both boost the economy in the long term by enough to generate much more tax revenue than they initially 'cost'. With the basic rate of income tax, there is an ultimate gain to GDP per capita, but it is smaller than the gain from cutting higher rates of income tax or from cutting inheritance tax or corporation tax.

A study by accountants UHY Hacker Young[23] showed that like for like, the UK and Ireland had the highest inheritance taxes in the world, with a sample estate of $3 million being subject to 26 per cent inheritance tax in Ireland and 25.8 per cent in the UK compared with an EU average of 14 per cent and a global average of 7.7 per cent.

The research indicates that abolition of inheritance tax after twenty years would keep 4,300 people in the country who might otherwise have left. Obviously, these would be disproportionately high-net-worth individuals. Even the US system, which is very much less onerous, is attracting migrants from the UK.*

The research indicates that abolition of inheritance tax would boost employment of older people substantially, leading to a 1.1 per cent boost to employment (though much of this would be part-time).

And the research suggests that investment would also be boosted because of what in effect would be a lower effective cost of capital, resulting from more savings left in the country and a lower total effective tax rate. Indeed, the reduction in the effective cost of capital is the biggest single element boosting economic growth.

Of course, the other side of the coin is increased inequality – the direct benefits of abolition will be received especially by the better-off groups. But it is clear that using inheritance tax to reduce inequality is a very expensive way of doing so.

Moreover, surprisingly few of the really rich actually pay inheritance tax – they either use trusts to avoid it (and to stop their inheritees spending their inheritance wastefully!) or they go abroad to one of the many places where there is no such tax.

CORPORATION TAX

Proposal 6: Abolish corporation tax on retained earnings and abolish long-term capital gains tax. We propose that in Year 4, corporation tax on retained earnings (currently 25 per cent) is halved and in Year 5 fully abolished. We also propose that in Year 4, capital gains tax on

---

* This is almost certainly an underestimate – more recent evidence suggests that mobility of taxpayers has increased.

entrepreneurial gains held for more than five years is abolished with anti-avoidance provisions to prevent abuse.

George Osborne told us, 'For an open trading economy that wants to be a home to international corporations, a very low corporation tax is a fantastic advert. It's a kind of global advertisement in the way that Ireland demonstrated.'

The current mainstream rate of corporation tax is 25 per cent, though there are lower rates for companies with low profits.

The capital gains tax system for 2025–26 is:

- 24 per cent on residential property
- 24 per cent on other chargeable assets
- 32 per cent on carried interest
- 10 per cent if you are a sole trader or partnership and your gains qualify for Business Asset Disposal Relief

A standard conventional result of tax analysis is that corporate taxes are especially damaging to growth. Hence a revenue-neutral reduction of corporate taxes paid for by higher personal taxes will boost growth. In other words, corporate taxes damage growth by more than other taxes. This might seem intuitively obvious to some but yet policy, especially in the UK in recent years, has been to load tax increases on companies rather than households.

George Osborne said, 'We took it [corporation tax] down to 19 per cent, we legislated to take it down to 17 per cent and then a Conservative government completely reversed all of that and put it back up.'

The Growth Commission study reported in Figure 46 supports this. A study by the National Institute of Economic and Social Research (NIESR) in 2024[24] also concludes: 'A rise in the corporation tax rate leads to a severe and negative initial fall in GDP. Potential output also decreases. This leads to lower productivity, higher inflationary pressures and deteriorating economic circumstances in the long run.' OECD cross-country studies have consistently confirmed the damaging impact of corporate taxes. The most recent highlights the negative impact on business investment.[25]

The evidence seems to suggest that our proposal of abolishing corporation tax on retained earnings would generate a considerable boost to both growth and especially business investment.

CAPITAL GAINS TAX

Our proposal for capital gains tax is that it is abolished as a tax but that capital gains will fall into the single tax net except for entrepreneurs for whom we propose abolition of the tax for holdings of more than five years, with appropriate anti-avoidance provisions.

Richard Gnodde told us, 'We spend too much time talking about rule changes. Financial incentives are more important. The tax system, I'd simplify it for sure. There's so much talk here about the UK equity market. Well, why don't you eliminate commissions, stamp duty and possibly abolish capital gains tax on equity ownership?'

The Growth Commission developed a bespoke model to calculate the economic impact of this using its own macro model as the base.[26] The bespoke model shows that abolition of capital gains tax could create a dramatic increase in savings, investment and entrepreneurial activity, boosting GDP by 3.8 per cent over twenty years. This is a massive uplift and reflects the fact that a very high proportion of entrepreneurship in the UK is buttressed by the fact that a significant proportion of an entrepreneur's capital gains can be retained even after tax.

To put this in context, the boost to GDP is about three times that of a boost from a reduction in employers' National Insurance contributions with an equivalent ex ante cost.

TAX COMPLIANCE

Over the last thirty-five years, the UK tax code has grown from 1,500 pages to 22,000 pages.[27] The increase has made the system much more complex.

Until recently, there has been no data available in the UK about the costs that tax compliance places on taxpayers. But a report by the National Audit Office (NAO)[28] has now given a hint about what these costs might be.

The NAO report estimates that the cost to HMRC of raising tax in 2022–23 was about £563 million to raise £8.3 billion of tax. But rather more importantly, it estimates that the cost of compliance for business alone (and it states that this is almost certainly an underestimate) was £15.4 billion for the same year.

A simple single flat rate of income tax would dramatically reduce tax complexity and eliminate many of the compliance costs.

CONCLUSION

Lord Petitgas made an illuminating comment about tax and mobility:

> If I'm an entrepreneur here, and I work my butt off here, when they sell their company, they're going to go to Dubai. They're going to hang out in Dubai for a while. They keep their house, keep their passport. There's no plague, the roads are going to be sort of clean and the UK is going to carry on.

We have been very circumspect in our calculations of the impact on GDP of our tax proposals; they have been evaluated singly rather than as a package and we have not taken full expectations into effect. The estimated effects are based on analysis for the 2020 Tax Commission and for the Growth Commission, both of which presented credible tax estimates.
So it is highly likely that the estimated impact set out in Annex 1 is well below what might actually happen.

But our approach is deliberately to be cautious about the assumed benefits of our proposals. If our numbers turn out (as we suspect) to be too low, the programme can be accelerated. On the other hand, we live in difficult times and it makes sense to be chary.

The estimated effects of the tax changes and their costs are set out in Annex 1, together with the growth effects and the spending changes. This shows that the tax changes alone contribute 12.7 percentage points to the 28.8 percentage point boost to growth which we expect the 24/7 Growth Plan to generate.

CHAPTER 9

UK GOVERNMENT SPENDING

'We need to get back to being a country that can live within its means.'
– George Osborne

The second kingdom is restrained government spending.
As we point out in Chapter 1:

Government spending should be limited, as best as is possible, to providing products and services that government alone produces more efficiently than the private sector. These categories frequently include the judiciary, military, police, highways, schools and some other highly specialised activities. The role government plays in how it spends its revenues is central to prosperity. A government that is too small will definitely hold back prosperity, as will a government that is too large.

Government, like any other provider of goods and services, has an optimal size: for spending, the correct size of government should occur at that point where the benefits of the next pound spent is just above the damage done by the next pound collected in taxes.

And in conjunction with spending restraint, government workers should be incentivised to act in the public interest. In other words, teachers who teach well should be paid more than teachers who don't teach well. This is the key to ensuring government spending is aligned to the North Star of economic growth.

This section looks at UK government spending and how we propose to reorientate it to meet the objectives set out in Chapter 1.

Our Growth Plan requires both savings in public expenditure and higher levels of spending on defence and necessary infrastructure. This chapter shows where the savings can be made.

It starts by examining what the government spends on what, looks at recent trends and comparisons with other countries, looks at trends for productivity and for spending on welfare and finally discusses our proposals for both savings and extra spending, to reorientate spending and best support the British people and the growth of the economy.

SPENDING AT PRESENT

Correlli Barnett's *The Lost Victory: British Dreams, British Realities 1945–1950*[1] describes how, while other countries were engaged in post-war reconstruction, the UK tried to build 'the new Jerusalem', a welfare state which the country could not afford. As a result, by the mid-1950s, other countries had renewed their industry and now could start to afford to introduce their welfare states. The UK achieved its welfare state earlier but at the cost of failing to renew its economy. Oddly (to some), the outcome is that because of higher growth, those countries which waited to build their welfare state until they could afford it now have a welfare state that provides better services, partly because they can afford to spend more and partly because in the UK the public sector is plagued by particular problems of productivity.

In effect, the UK has again made the same mistake post-Covid – while other countries quickly scaled back spending from the high levels reached during the pandemic, the UK did rather less. Moreover, much of the UK higher post-Covid public spending financed either increased public sector inefficiency or unsustainable growth in welfare; at least the post-Second World War welfare state provided new or improved services.

Details of government spending are given in Table A.7 of the Office for Budget Responsibility's Economic and Fiscal Outlook Annex A.[2] We have calculated defence spending using the percentages of GDP set out in the Prime Minister's speech of 25 February 2025.[3] This is shown in Table 3.

Lord Macpherson of Earl's Court said:

It's a tyranny of the baseline. It's a tyranny of what you've inherited. There have been governments which have thought quite hard about this. I think in the late period of the John Major government, they were committed to reducing public spending to 35 per cent of GDP, having got into 40 per cent of GDP.

The key items of spending are health, education, welfare, investment and debt interest, with defence spending starting to catch up.

TABLE 17: GOVERNMENT PLANNED SPENDING IN CASH TERMS TO 2029–30[4]

	£ billion						
	Outturn	Forecast					
	2023–24	2024–25	2025–26	2026–27	2027–28	2028–29	2029–30
Public sector current expenditure (PSCE)							
PSCE in RDEL	422.7	450.7	481.0	498.0	513.3	528.3	543.7
PSCE in AME	670.3	681.8	710.6	731.3	752.2	777.0	807.4
of which:							
Welfare spending	296.4	313.0	326.1	342.1	348.8	358.5	373.4
Locally financed current expenditure	62.3	66.5	68.9	70.5	73.6	77.2	81.1
Central government debt interest, net of APF*	106.7	105.2	111.2	111.4	117.9	124.2	131.6
Scottish government's current spending	42.9	46.5	48.2	49.6	50.4	52.1	53.5
EU financial settlement	7.7	0.9	1.5	0.8	0.3	0.5	0.1
Unfunded public service pensions	5.1	1.6	-0.1	-0.4	-0.9	-2.4	-3.6
Company and other tax credits	9.7	10.4	11.1	11.3	11.6	12.0	12.3
BBC current expenditure	4.1	4.4	4.1	4.2	4.3	4.3	4.3
National Lottery current grants	1.2	1.4	1.4	1.3	1.2	1.2	1.2

---

* Includes increases in debt interest payments due to the APF.

General government imputed pensions	1.7	1.8	1.9	1.9	2.0	2.0	2.1
Public corporations' debt interest	0.5	0.5	0.5	0.5	0.5	0.5	0.5
Non-domestic energy support	0.6	0.0	0.0	0.0	0.0	0.0	0.0
Domestic energy support	3.8	0.0	0.0	0.0	0.0	0.0	0.0
Funded public sector pension schemes	17.5	18.3	19.2	20.1	21.0	22.0	23.0
General government depreciation	58.2	62.3	66.5	68.8	71.5	74.1	76.5
Current VAT refunds	24.0	25.3	27.7	28.1	29.2	29.8	30.7
Environmental levies	12.1	13.2	13.3	15.9	15.9	15.8	16.1
Other PSCE items in AME	12.1	10.1	9.2	6.5	6.6	6.7	6.8
Other National Accounts adjustments	3.5	0.4	-0.4	-1.3	-1.5	-1.8	-2.3
Total public sector current expenditure	**1,093.0**	**1,132.5**	**1,191.5**	**1,229.3**	**1,265.5**	**1,305.3**	**1,351.2**
Public sector gross investment (PSGI)							
PSGI in CDEL	96.6	102.9	111.3	118.0	124.1	125.3	126.9
PSGI in AME	40.4	43.2	44.4	42.2	41.2	40.8	41.0
of which:							
Locally financed capital expenditure	9.8	10.3	9.4	8.5	8.4	8.3	8.4
Public corporations' capital expenditure	13.9	13.9	13.0	13.9	14.1	14.3	14.4
Student loans	10.0	9.0	8.5	8.1	8.0	8.0	8.0
Funded public sector pension schemes	0.7	0.7	0.7	0.7	0.7	0.7	0.7
Scottish government's capital spending	5.7	5.8	6.3	6.5	6.8	6.9	7.0
Tax litigation	0.0	0.7	2.0	0.5	0.5	0.5	0.5

Other PSGI items in AME	1.2	2.6	4.4	3.7	2.5	2.0	1.8
Other National Accounts adjustments	-0.9	0.1	0.0	0.1	0.1	0.1	0.1
Total public sector gross investment	**136.9**	**146.1**	**155.7**	**160.1**	**165.3**	**166.2**	**167.9**
Less public sector depreciation	-65.2	-69.4	-74.1	-76.4	-79.1	-81.6	-83.9
Public sector net investment	71.7	76.6	81.5	83.7	86.2	84.5	84.0
Total managed expenditure	**1,230**	**1,279**	**1,347**	**1,389**	**1,431**	**1,471**	**1,519**
Memorandum items							
Non-welfare current spend	796.6	819.5	865.4	887.2	916.7	946.8	977.8
Welfare spend	296.4	313.0	326.1	342.1	348.8	358.5	373.4
Defence spend*	68.8	71.9	74.8	80.6	83.7	86.8	90.1
Infrastructure	136.9	146.1	155.7	160.1	165.3	166.2	167.9

Source: Office for Budget Responsibility

RDEL (Resource Departmental Expenditure Limit) and CDEL (Capital Departmental Expenditure Limit) are components of a government department's Departmental Expenditure Limit (DEL), which sets the maximum amount of money that can be spent.

The OECD data in Table 18 below show that the UK traditionally spent slightly less than the OECD average but had caught up by the pre-Covid year of 2019. Since Covid, UK spend has remained 3–4 percentage points of GDP above the OECD average. We started the twenty-first century[†] with the ninth lowest public spending share of GDP out of thirty-two OECD countries and now have only the eleventh lowest share, having overtaken public spending in Israel and New Zealand.

Note that this was before the October 2024 Budget and subsequent measures which boosted public spending on our estimates by £57 billion, or 1.8 per cent of GDP.[‡]

---

[*]   Authors' calculations

[†]   Average spending 1997–2007.

[‡]   Authors' calculation, comparing OBR Economic and Fiscal Outlook March 2024 with same data for March 2025.

TABLE 18: OECD COMPARISON OF GENERAL GOVERNMENT SPENDING AS A PERCENTAGE OF GDP BY COUNTRY[5]

	Average								
	1997–2007	2019	2020	2021	2022	2023	2024	2025	2026
Australia	34.2	36.1	47.1	39.9	37.4	37.8	39.1	39.7	39.6
Austria	51.9	49.1	57.4	56.1	53.1	52.6	56.3	56.7	56.8
Belgium	50.1	51.8	58.5	54.9	52.3	53.3	54.5	54.9	54.6
Canada	40.5	40.6	52.4	45.5	40.6	42.1	44.7	44.4	44.2
Czechia	42.5	40.4	46.2	45.0	43.0	43.9	43.0	43.2	42.6
Denmark	52.9	49.8	53.3	49.4	44.9	46.8	46.5	47.5	47.4
Estonia	35.8	39.2	44.8	42.2	40.0	43.7	44.0	44.4	46.6
Finland	49.6	52.6	56.5	55.1	52.6	55.9	57.6	57.4	57.3
France	53.9	55.3	61.7	59.5	58.4	56.9	57.1	57.0	56.6
Germany	47.3	45.5	51.2	50.8	49.1	48.4	49.5	49.8	50.4
Greece	46.5	47.7	59.3	56.7	52.8	49.5	48.0	47.7	47.7
Hungary	49.4	45.8	51.0	48.1	48.7	49.2	46.9	46.9	44.7
Iceland	44.8	43.5	51.0	49.4	46.6	45.2	46.2	46.4	46.6
Ireland	33.3	23.9	26.6	23.6	20.6	22.7	23.5	23.3	22.8
Israel	...	39.3	45.5	40.7	37.5	40.0	43.2	41.9	41.3
Italy	47.2	48.4	56.8	56.0	54.9	54.0	50.6	49.8	49.9
Japan	35.7	38.4	45.7	43.6	42.9	40.2	39.2	39.6	39.4
Latvia	37.3	39.7	44.3	46.5	44.2	43.7	45.7	47.7	48.2
Lithuania	37.7	34.6	42.3	37.3	36.3	37.4	39.5	42.3	42.9
Luxembourg	40.8	43.2	47.1	42.5	44.2	46.8	47.3	46.4	45.9
Netherlands	44.5	42.1	47.8	45.9	43.3	43.2	43.9	44.6	45.1
New Zealand	34.5	38.3	44.5	43.0	41.0	40.7	40.3	39.8	39.7
Norway	45.0	51.1	57.5	47.1	38.1	46.7	49.3	51.6	51.2
Poland	44.5	41.5	47.8	43.6	43.3	46.9	49.5	50.2	51.1
Portugal	44.2	42.5	49.1	47.3	43.9	42.3	42.8	44.1	44.1
Slovak Republic	43.7	40.6	44.5	44.9	43.0	48.0	47.1	47.8	49.0
Slovenia	46.7	43.8	51.8	49.9	47.7	46.5	46.8	47.7	47.6
Spain	39.2	42.0	51.4	49.5	46.4	45.4	45.4	45.3	44.9
South Korea	25.4	32.0	35.9	35.4	37.1	35.2	36.2	37.7	37.5
Sweden	53.6	49.7	53.0	50.1	49.0	49.3	50.0	49.7	49.9
Switzerland	33.3	33.2	38.4	35.7	32.8	33.2	32.9	32.9	33.2
United Kingdom	37.8	40.8	52.3	47.9	46.1	46.8	46.3	47.3	46.5
United States*	36.3	38.4	47.4	45.4	38.4	39.2	39.3	39.2	39.2
Euro area 17	47.6	47.0	53.6	52.1	50.1	49.6	49.6	49.6	49.7
Total OECD	39.5	40.7	48.3	46.0	42.4	42.5	42.7	42.8	42.7

Source: OECD Economic Outlook EO116 Statistical Annex Table 29

Data refer to the general government sector, which is a consolidation of accounts for the central, state and local governments, plus social security.

---

* These data include outlays net of operating surpluses of public enterprises.

Table 18 shows that the rise in public spending as a percentage of GDP in 2020 was at 11.5 per cent, well above the OECD average of 7.7 per cent, but as Figure 47 (taken from the same source) shows, the sustained rise, comparing 2024 with 2019, was much higher than in any other G7 economy.

WHY HAS THE RELATIVE RISE IN UK PUBLIC SPENDING TAKEN PLACE?

The relative rise in UK public spending between 2019 and 2024 shown in Figure 47 might be seen as surprising given that the country was governed by a centre-right political party, the Conservative Party, with a solid majority for the entire period.

FIGURE 47: RISE IN PUBLIC SPENDING AS A PERCENTAGE OF GDP 2019–24

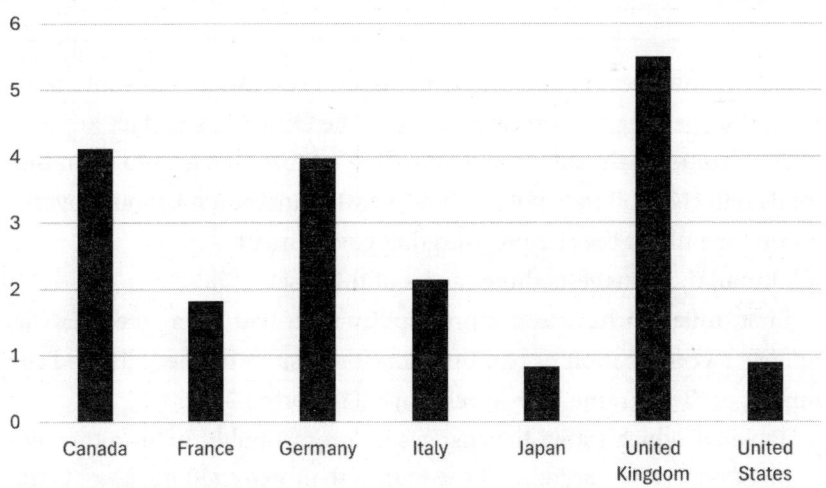

Source: OECD[6]

Boris Johnson said, 'There needs to be some way of doing more to restrain public expenditure in this country. It's terrible.'

We have examined this quite carefully.

The first point is that the rise appears to have been largely unplanned.

TABLE 19: CHANGING FORECASTS OF PUBLIC EXPENDITURE £ BILLIONS[7]

	Outturn 2019–20	2020–21	2021–22	2022–23	2023–24	2024–25	2025–26
Total managed expenditure March 2021	885.2	1,140.9	1,053.3	992.3	1,030.1	1,068.7	1,111.5
Total managed expenditure November 2023				1,151.4	1,222.3	1,236.8	1,264.5
Total managed expenditure March 2025					1,229.9	1,278.6	1,347.2
Overrun March 2021 to November 2023				159.1	192.3	168.1	153.1
Overrun November 2023 to March 2025					7.6	41.8	82.7
Total overrun March 2021 to March 2025					199.9	209.9	235.7

Source: OBR Economic and Financial Outlooks, March 2021, November 2023 and March 2025, mainly from Annex A, Table A.7 from each publication

Table 19 shows how planned total managed expenditure has kept creeping up, surpassing the forecasts given by the OBR in its Budget Reports. Even if some of the additional spending in the March 2025 spending totals reflects deliberate policy choices by the incoming Labour government, the bulk of the rise predates that government.

Our analysis suggests three causes of this rise.

First, inflation has risen more rapidly than had been forecast. This reflects a combination of bad inflation forecasting by the OBR and the impact of the Ukraine War which started in spring 2022.

Table 20, which shows the changes in forecast public expenditure as a share of GDP, takes account of the higher-than-expected inflation. It still shows public spending overruns AFTER INFLATION of over £70 billion.

The second cause of the public spending overrun has been a sharp fall in public sector productivity.

There is a clue in Figure 48. This shows the ONS's estimates for movements in public service productivity since 1997. The latest data for 2024 shows public service productivity down 4.2 per cent from the 2019 average.[8] As the chart indicates, the recent data shows public service productivity at best flatlining and an unsympathetic observer might observe that the latest data seems to show public service productivity declining again after an initial post-Covid bounceback.

TABLE 20: CHANGING FORECASTS OF PUBLIC SPENDING AS A PERCENTAGE OF GDP[9]

	Outturn 2019–20	2020–21	2021–22	2022–23	2023–24	2024–25	2025–26
Total managed expenditure March 2021	39.8	54.4	46.5	41.8	41.9	41.9	41.9
Total managed expenditure November 2023				45.0	44.9	44.1	43.4
Total managed expenditure March 2025					44.7	44.4	45.0
Overrun March 2021 to November 2023				3.2	3.1	2.2	1.5
Overrun November 2023 to March 2025					-0.2	0.3	1.6
Total Overrun March 2021 to March 2025			-		2.8	2.5	3.1
Total Overrun March 2021 to March 2025 in £bn					77.1	73.3	92.8

Source: OBR Economic and Financial Outlooks, March 2021, November 2023 and March 2025, mainly from Annex A, Table A.7 from each publication, with the levels of GDP calculated from Tables A.3

Kwasi Kwarteng told us, 'I think the thing that people have consistently failed to do in government – and we did as well with Liz Truss – is to reduce spending. That's the really challenging thing, and nobody seems to have any interest in doing that.'

It is well known that measuring public service productivity is difficult (the challenges of measuring productivity in the public sector are well known from the Atkinson review[10]), so it behoves any analyst to be cautious about placing too much weight on the productivity data alone.

But the spending overruns indicated in Tables 19 and 20 are real, whether caused by declining productivity or higher spending. And the comparative data shows that the growth in the cost of spending in the UK is high by international standards.

There is also data indicating that satisfaction with public services has fallen sharply, which would be unlikely if the rise in public spending had been mainly in the quality or quantity of services delivered rather than simply a fall in productivity. For example, the British Social Attitudes Survey in 2024[11] showed dissatisfaction with the NHS at 52 per cent compared with 25 per cent in 2019 despite inputs for the sector up 15 per cent in real terms between the two periods.

FIGURE 48: PUBLIC SERVICE PRODUCTIVITY SINCE 1997

(index, 1997 = 100)

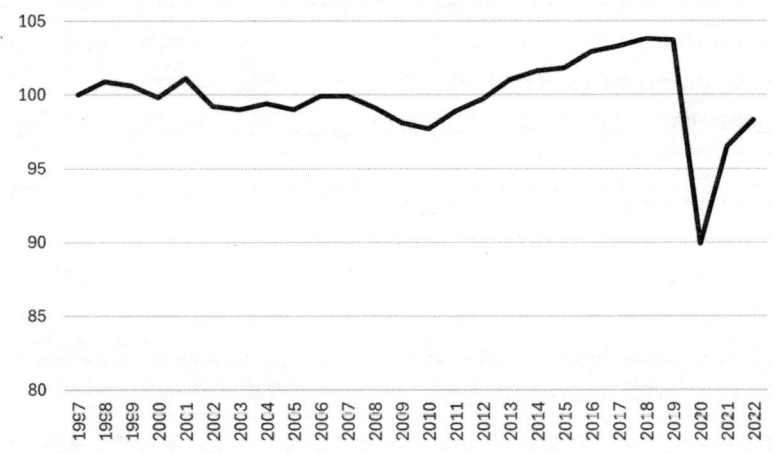

Source: ONS

The productivity data also provide detail of productivity for some individual public services. These are shown in Table 21. Note that the main area recording a significant improvement is social security administration. There must be some doubts about whether the measured change is realistic given the issues noted below under welfare since there appears to have been both a rise in welfare claims (which create an apparent improvement in efficiency) and a reduction in the level of scrutiny of health benefit claimants.

TABLE 21: CHANGE IN PRODUCTIVITY FOR VARIOUS GOVERNMENT SERVICES 2019–22[12]

Government Services	Productivity 2019–22
Healthcare	-9.9%
Education	-5.1%
Adult social care	4.1%
Social security administration	16.2%
Children's social care	-5.0%
Public order and safety	-11.5%
Tax administration	-3.3%

Source: ONS

Proposal 7: Raise public sector productivity. We propose that a target be set to raise public sector productivity by 2 per cent per annum, reversing the post-Covid fall in productivity.

Lord Wolfson of Aspley Guise said:

I think with government expenditure, there is one incredibly powerful principle that could radically transform the whole of the public sector, which is that the public sector should have no more constraints on its action than the private sector. So all of the sweeping rules they have on purchasing, recruitment, HR, all of those things should be swept away, and, say, look, the public sector is going to be run without all of the constraints that progressively, politicians of every colour have added to public employment to try and achieve social aims and all of those things serve to undermine the effectiveness of the organisations that deliver public services.

We accept that it will take time to turn round the problem of public sector inefficiency. But efficiency rose by not far short of 1 per cent per annum in the mid-2010s from a higher peak. There is evidence from, for example, the Passport Office that proper management attention can ensure that efficiency will rise.[13]

We propose a target of increasing overall efficiency in the public service sector by 2 per cent per annum. Even with this target, it will take untill 2027 for public service productivity simply to return to its pre-Covid level in 2019.

WHY PUBLIC SECTOR PRODUCTIVITY HAS FALLEN

A range of possible explanations have been put forward for the fall in public sector productivity.

The House of Lords debated the subject on 9 October 2024.[14] The explanations put forward in the debate were:

- pervasive working from home
- lack of delegation
- duplication
- restrictive practices
- underinvestment
- chopping and changing investment plans
- too many administrators and not enough managers
- lack of empowerment of staff to make useful improvements

Interestingly, the debate placed less emphasis on issues like the following:

Poor management. Generally, productivity is the responsibility of managers and if it falls, the primary blame should fall on them. It is not encouraging when managers spend their time blaming everything and everyone but themselves.

Impact of diversity, equality and inclusion (DEI). The increasing weakness of management has coincided with the growth of DEI consciousness within government. Whether or not this rise is justified by other benefits, it is likely that it has been associated with the creation or enhancement of a range of management difficulties. This creates a variety of problems such as managers being selected for reasons other than managerial competence; poor-performing staff using DEI to make it difficult to sack them; increased costs when outside suppliers are forced to satisfy disproportionate DEI requirements, which very often inhibit tendering by the best suppliers; and managers being diverted from the primary delivery requirements of their jobs by DEI requirements.

Experience of small business tendering for public sector projects shows how DEI requirements imposed on suppliers also put smaller firms at a disadvantage when tendering for public projects compared with large (and expensive) firms with comparably large human resource departments to produce reams of forms claiming to have DEI policies. This not only adds to cost but, probably rather more importantly, reduces competition. As one study puts it:

> Empirical focus on the challenges SMEs encounter when tendering for public sector contracts has yielded valuable insights. It has revealed how the economic 'rules of the game' differ between the public and private spheres of the economy and why SMEs often struggle to establish themselves in the public sector marketplace as a result.[15]

Impact of trade unions. According to the official government report on trade union membership statistics,[16] 'The overall proportion of employees who are members of trade unions is significantly higher in the public sector relative to the private sector. 12.3 per cent of private sector employees belonged to a trade union, compared to 49.2 per cent of public sector employees in 2023.'

In the private sector, trade union membership has declined to its current low level, possibly reflecting its unsuitability to a modern information-based economy, where jobs are individualised. Since productivity performance in the private sector has not been stunning either, it seems unlikely that trade unions are the only inhibitor of productivity in the public sector (though there have been highly publicised instances, especially in the rail industry, where trade union resistance is holding back public sector productivity – for example the refusal even to allow the testing of ninety trains because 'the windscreen wipers are too large'[17]).

But if trade unions inhibit future improvements in productivity, they might well become an issue to be dealt with.

Of the other potential causes mentioned in the House of Lords debate, some discussion is necessary.

Working from home. Management that is weak or that has lost morale often resorts to using visual evidence of performance to assess those who might be slacking. While working from home has both advantages and disadvantages in the private sector, in the public sector where performance is less easy to measure, the lack of visual evidence resulting from employees working from home seems to have had a much more damaging impact on performance. There is anecdotal evidence of public sector employees being paid for more than one job while claiming to 'work' from home. There is also evidence from a group of whistle blowers with a combined experience of fifty years working in social services that 25 per cent of Kent County Council social workers are using working from home to enable their alcoholism.[18]

Underinvestment in technology. It is often claimed that the reason that the public sector is inefficient is underinvestment in technology. It certainly appears to be true that public sector processes have been behind those in the private sector in being automated. But a simple comparison of spending on IT between the public and private sectors does not show clear signs of failure to spend on IT in the UK public sector compared with elsewhere in the economy.

Input–output statistics are available for 2020, but because that year was affected by Covid, it is better to analyse those for 2019.[19] We compare the shares of spending on various IT categories[20] for the public service sector with comparable parts of the private sector.

The comparison shows that public services[21] spending on products of these sectors as a share of its own value added in 2019 was 3.54 per cent compared with an economy-wide figure of 2.49 per cent, although the equivalent figures for education[22] were 1.06 per cent and for health[23] 1.77 per cent. For the public sector as a whole, therefore, actual spending on technology was 42 per cent higher in relation to value added than for the whole economy.

Except in education and possibly health, the figures do not provide clear evidence of significant underinvestment in spending on technology, in fact the contrary.

Boris Johnson told us:

What I would recommend is that we really use AI to send an inferno, a destructive inferno, through the legal profession and the consultants and all the environmental people and immolate them, because what they're doing is totally unnecessary, and it's incredibly costly, and it's stopping things being built and stopping things getting done in the UK.

It seems likely, though, that further increased investment in technology could both reduce costs and improve performance in the public sector. Cebr's report for Virgin Media Business[24] showed 'continued investment in hybrid working technology, digital services and better use of data in the public sector could add £100 billion to UK GDP by 2040'.

Turning round productivity in the public sector is likely to take time and serious effort. Our Growth Plan allows time for productivity to be raised.

If the public sector's performance cannot be turned around, the tax-payer cannot be expected to fund ever-growing comparative inefficien-cy. Activities which in other countries may be carried out by the public sector (and which could be carried out better in theory in the UK by the public sector) might have to be removed from the public sector to the market sector where only those that can pay their way will continue. But making the public sector more efficient through raising productivity would be substantially preferable to this.

The current government has talked about public sector productivi-ty difficulties, but its actions do not seem to the level of concern that has been highlighted in speeches. Indeed, some of its proposals like the Employment Rights Bill[25] and its public sector pay settlements without productivity strings are likely to intensify public sector productivity problems.

WELFARE

The third driving force behind the growth in public expenditure in the UK has been the scale of the increase in welfare payments, as shown in Figure 49.

FIGURE 49: RISE IN PLANNED WELFARE SPENDING IN £ BILLIONS[26]

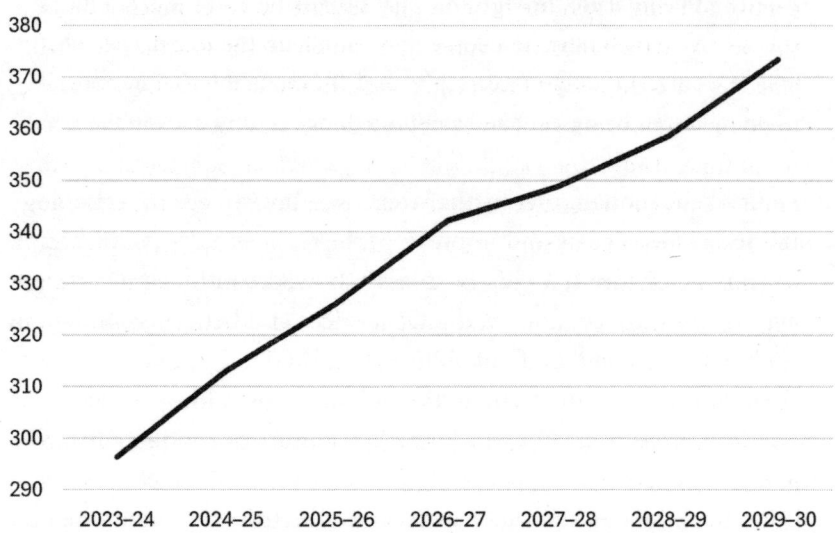

Source: OBR Economic and fiscal outlook Annex A, Table A.7, March 2021, March 2023 and March 2025 Supplementary fiscal tables – expenditure

Comparing the forecasts made in 2021 with those in 2025, the increase in forecast welfare spend for 2025–26 is £34.4 billion. This is not a result of policy changes – if anything, policies have become theoretically less generous over the period. Instead, it reflects take-up and specifically take-up of sickness benefit.

Sir Jeremy Hunt MP said:

> The cost of benefits is counted as annually managed expenditure, which means that the Treasury picks up the bill whatever it is, and the Department for Work and Pensions has no budget for the overall cost of the benefits bill. So they have a budget for their staff but not for the overall cost of the benefits bill. The reason for that is because if you go back to the 1970s, the argument was, well, no government can control the levels of unemployment because it's kind of cyclical, so we can't have a budget for that. So if there are another million people unemployed, then the Treasury needs to cough up another million people's worth.
>
> This is supposed to be a positive thing, but it's a disaster for two

reasons. First of all, the Department for Work and Pensions has no incentive to bring down the benefits bill, because however much it costs, they just send their bill to the Treasury. Secondly, the bit that they do have a budget for is the cost of DWP employees, and so that incentivises them to do as few face-to-face checks as possible, because face-to-face checks mean time. And if you can do these things with an automated system or on the phone, it's quicker, and so the way to raise productivity for the DWP is to process as many claims as quickly as possible, irrespective of whether the answer is yes or no. But obviously, it's much quicker to say yes, because no one complains if you apply for benefits and the answer is yes ... I do not understand why we have decided as a society that we have to have a budgetary limit on how much we spend defending the nation, a budgetary limit on how much we spend saving people who are at death's door from illness, and no budget for how much we spend on benefits. It seems to be a completely extraordinary set of priorities.

The Institute for Fiscal Studies (IFS)[27] has pointed out the scale of the increase in spending on working-age health-related benefits, from £36 billion in 2019–20 to £48 billion in 2023–24. Meanwhile, official forecasts expect this spending to increase further to £63 billion in 2028–29 (all in 2024–25 prices).

Total health-related benefits spending for all ages rose from £52 billion in 2019–20 to £65 billion in 2023–24.

What appears to have been the biggest single driver for the increase in working-age spending has been the increasing caseload: from 2.2 million in 2019–20 to 3.2 million in 2023–24 for disability benefits (39 per cent growth) and from 2.5 million in 2019–20 to 3.2 million in 2023–24 for incapacity benefits (28 per cent growth).

Sir Jeremy Hunt said:

If we got the benefits bill down to 2019 levels, that is £49 billion a year. For £1 billion a year, you could double the number of people treated for anxiety or depression by the NHS. So [for] a tiny fraction of the savings, you could pretty much double our mental health treatment. The truth is that many people are genuinely suffering mental illness.

The IFS also shows that the rapid growth in health-related benefits seems to be largely a UK phenomenon. Its analysis points out that

> the number of claimants of similar benefits in most similar countries with available data (Australia, Austria, Canada, Germany, Ireland, the Netherlands, Sweden and the US) has in fact slightly fallen over the same period. There have been small percentage increases in claims in France and Norway. Denmark was the only other country with available data that saw a significant increase and, at 13 per cent, even that was considerably smaller than the increase in health-related benefit claimants in the UK (where claimants for disability benefits have increased by more than 30 per cent).

Self-assessment of health has indicated a deterioration in health[28] but not on the same scale as the increase in disability claimants.

The IFS study also indicated that the reasons for the rise in the number of claimants was a mix of increased new claimants and fewer people coming off benefits.

It also indicated that, compared with previous benefit claimants, new claimants tended to have different characteristics:

> First, they are younger. The number of new awards made to under-40s has grown by 150 per cent (from 4,500 a month in 2019–20 to 11,500 in 2023–24); growth for 40- to 64-year-olds was 'only' 82 per cent (11,000 a month to 20,000 a month). Second, current new claimants are more likely to claim due to mental health problems (including learning, social and behavioural conditions). In 2019–20, 28 per cent of all new awards were primarily for mental health conditions (3,900 claims a month); that figure now stands at 37 per cent (12,100 a month), a 9 percentage point increase. Only 2 percentage points of this rise is accounted for by the increasing rate of claims among younger individuals – there has been a marked rise in claiming for mental health reasons at all ages. Third, new claimants are slightly more likely to be women, whose share of new claims has grown from 55 per cent in 2019–20 to 58 per cent in 2023–24.

The IFS study also noted that increased health benefit claims were correlated with areas of previous high levels of health benefit claims:

> Broadly, the growth in claims has been fastest in areas that already had a large number of claimants. For example, in Merthyr Tydfil and Blackpool, around 15 per cent of 16- to 64-year-olds were in receipt of a health-related benefit before the pandemic. Now that figure is around 19 per cent. Conversely, in Windsor & Maidenhead and Wokingham, around 3 per cent were receiving one of these benefits before the pandemic, and now around 4 per cent are.

It is tempting to conclude from the IFS data, both the international comparisons and the evidence of correlation with areas where claims have traditionally been high, that a proportion of the rise in health benefits claims could be reduced with better welfare management.

Proposal 8: Freeze welfare spending on sickness benefits in real terms. Our proposal for welfare spending is to freeze the spending level on sickness benefits in real terms from its 2025–26 levels, which is already 11 per cent higher in real terms than in 2021–22. In practical terms, this will mean that additional potential claimants will have to compete with existing claimants.

PENSIONS

Proposal 9: Raise the pension age and remove the 'triple lock'. We propose raising the pension age with life expectancy, including implementing the existing plans at the earlier of the proposed dates and to replace the triple lock with simple indexation of pensions.

Meanwhile, the UK pension age, currently sixty-six, is set to rise to sixty-seven between 2026 and 2028 and to sixty-eight between 2044 and 2046. Experience from Japan is that a rising pension age can make a significant contribution to the economy and a recent paper drawing on this experience shows the potential benefits.[29]

Lord Macpherson of Earl's Court told us:

My problem with our basic income [pension] is that it's rising at a faster rate than the net wages of people who are financing it, and you've got more old people. And so if it were left to me, you would set it every sort of twenty years and then up-rate it just by wages, because it's seriously costing money.

INFRASTRUCTURE

Proposal 10: Increase spending on infrastructure. We have allocated 2.5 per cent of GDP by 2045–46 to additional public funding for infrastructure, raising it from its current level of approximately 5 per cent of GDP to 7.5 per cent.

In our supply-side analysis, we have argued for increased resources to be devoted to housing, transport and energy.

While much of this is likely to be generated in the private sector, it would be prudent in our funding calculations to make provision for some public sector funding.

The UK lacks adequate infrastructure. This partly reflects planning difficulties but also too often when economies in public spending have had to be found, cuts in spending on infrastructure have provided the bulk of the savings. A result is that the UK is short of roads, power stations and housing. The UK needs to build more infrastructure in each of these areas.

Boris Johnson said:

They teach the British handling of HS2 in Chinese universities as an example of the failure of democracy and the catastrophic inability of politicians to get things done. I've just flown in from California to meet you. We were delayed coming in by half an hour, and there was a guy sitting next to me who's going crazy, because the only way he has of getting from Heathrow to Manchester is to get another plane, which is mad.

The biggest impact on the provision of public sector infrastructure is likely to result from simplifying the planning system (see Chapter 11). Our section on planning draws attention to a range of current practices that impede infrastructure development and add massively to its cost. The National Infrastructure Commission's cost drivers report[30] argued that costs could be reduced substantially:

> Industry has suggested that changes ranging from optimising design through to using more efficient construction methods could reduce the outturn costs of some projects by as much as 20 to 40 per cent. The Commission concludes that harnessing these opportunities system wide could translate to reductions of between ten and 25 per cent of outturn costs across a portfolio of enhancement projects.

A Boston Consulting Group estimate points out the high cost of infrastructure in the UK, quoting an 'average cost for a flat road in the UK is £8.45 million per km, compared with a European average of £5.77 million per km and £4.22 million per km in France, according to BCG'.[31] Andrew Bailey said:

> I did a visit to Scotland, to Orkney, and they have one of the major North Sea oil terminals for bringing the oil in, still operating. It was opened in, if I remember rightly, in 1967, when the North Sea oil industry was getting going. They took me there, and they said that it was built in under two years, and they said you'd never be able to do it now. And the great irony was, there was a plaque up on the wall which revealed the name of the identity of the minister who had opened it. It was the Minister of Technology at the time – Tony Benn. [This was the] Harold Wilson period, when the emphasis was on getting investment in the economy, getting investment in infrastructure. So despite Tony Benn's politics, they did it. Now it would not happen – under any government.

The savings from improved planning and spending procurement will mean that the additional money allocated will permit even higher spending in real terms.

DEFENCE SPENDING

Proposal 11: Raise defence spending. We propose raising the amount spent on defence to 5 per cent of GDP within twenty years.

Defence spending is widely believed to have beneficial effects on innovation and stimulating the economy.* The government has increased its defence spending in 2025–26 from 2.2 per cent to 2.5 per cent, but with international trends, this seems nowhere near sufficient to meet likely future defence needs in a world where the US pulls back from helping defend Europe.

CONCLUSION

Although the Growth Plan looks to spend money more efficiently and to encourage an increased proportion of those on sickness benefit back to work, within twenty years a considerable proportion of the savings from both in cash terms are expected to be swallowed up in increased defence spending and infrastructure spending. The key point is that an initially reduced budget aimed at boosting growth can then be increased again when the economy can afford higher spending.

The details and financial implications of the spending changes which we propose are set out in Annex 1.

---

* In Ethan Ilzetzk, *Guns and Growth: The Economic Consequences of Defense Buildup*, Kiel Report No. 2, February 2025, the Kiel Institute for the World Economy argues that a 1 per cent rise in the share of defence spending raises total national productivity by as much as 0.25 per cent through its impact on innovation and R&D.

CHAPTER 10

UK MONETARY POLICY

'We have a single mandate. We have a hierarchy of objectives. That's what distinguishes us from the Fed. Actually, the ECB [European Central Bank] is in a pretty similar situation. So we have what I tend to call a hierarchical mandate. And the hierarchy is this – the language is important here – it's price stability, and then the language says and subject to that, it's cast in terms of aligning with the other economic policy objectives of the government.'

– ANDREW BAILEY

The third kingdom is sound money.

As we point out in Part I:

There is little that can bring an economy to its knees faster than unsound money, unhinged paper currencies and the accompanying inflation and high interest rates that invariably attend bad monetary policy. A key function of a sound numeraire, such as the UK pound or the US dollar, is to provide a stable valued medium of exchange where all participants know what that numeraire's value is and also what its value will be. Secular inflation and excessively high interest rates destroy the information content of the unit of account and damage markets in the present and capital markets where future goods and services are exchanged. Unsound money is a major cause of poverty, despair and economic underachievement, while sound money is the antidote.

This section of the plan sets out the details of how to optimise this for the UK.

It looks first at monetary policy and exchange rate policy, then fiscal policy. Finally, it sets out the policy details of how to ensure sound money.

MONETARY AND EXCHANGE RATE POLICY

UK history before 1997 has varied between maintaining a gold standard, an exchange rate policy and a monetary policy.

The UK targeted the gold standard from 1717* to 1931, with the exception of the period from 1914–25. The UK suspended convertibility into gold at the end of July 1914 during the financial crisis that was associated with the beginning of the First World War. The country returned to the gold standard in April 1925 under Winston Churchill as Chancellor of the Exchequer. The decision to do so proved highly controversial.†

After the Wall Street Crash, the Smoot–Hawley tariff and the collapse of Creditanstalt, the UK government was forced off the gold standard in September 1931.

During the Bretton Woods period, the UK followed a fixed exchange rate policy from 1944 until the collapse of the system in 1971. The exchange rate was devalued twice during this period, in 1949 from $4.03 to $2.80 and in 1967 from $2.80 to $2.40.

Andrew Bailey told us:

I think the history of governments taking decisions on monetary policy over the years was not a particularly happy story. Now, quite a lot of that was down to the UK being unable to decide what regime it wanted to follow in the post-Bretton Woods period. We alighted, after the painful experience of the European Exchange Rate Mechanism, on domestic

---

*   The effective start of the UK being on the gold standard was in 1717 when Isaac Newton, then Master of the Royal Mint, fixed the gold–silver exchange rate. The UK formally joined the gold standard in 1821 after the Napoleonic Wars. See Angela Redish, 'The evolution of the gold standard in England', *The Journal of Economic History*, Vol. 50, No. 4, 1990, pp. 789–805.

†   The major critic was John Maynard Keynes, who wrote a polemic called 'The Economic Consequences of Mr Churchill' shortly after in the same year: https://www.economicsnetwork.ac.uk/archive/keynes_persuasion/The_Economic_Consequences_of_Mr._Churchill.htm

price stability and inflation target, which I think is the right thing for this economy.

For most of the period since the end of the Bretton Woods system in August 1971, the UK has tried to have some kind of monetary policy framework, not always successfully.

From the five years from the collapse of Bretton Woods until the Labour government in 1976 was forced to appeal for support from the International Monetary Fund, the UK lacked a formal monetary policy. Arguably, this would have been exposed anyway, but the oil crisis of the mid-1970s left the country even more bereft. The initial deal with the IMF signed in December 1976 contained conditions for limits on domestic credit expansion, which gradually morphed into monetary targets as the consensus view shifted towards them.

Monetary targets were perceived to be too restrictive in the early 1980s and political disputes during the 1980s between Prime Minister Margaret Thatcher and her Chancellors led to a policy of shadowing the Deutsche Mark. But inflation again got out of control and effectively monetary policy had to be tightened again.

Because of the feeling that monetary targets had been discredited, the long-standing debate about monetary targets and exchange rate targets swung back to a fixed exchange rate policy from October 1990 to September 1992, when the UK was a member of the European Exchange Rate Mechanism.* This ended in such a traumatic ejection on 16 September 1992 that in the subsequent thirty-three years, there has been relatively little support for the UK returning to a fixed exchange rate policy.

Is now the time to reconsider a fixed exchange rate policy for the UK?

The first point to make is that a fixed exchange rate policy doesn't in itself guarantee stability – it merely ties the country to the exchange

---

* Technically, the major factor that eventually caused the UK to leave the European Exchange Rate Mechanism was German unification. This and the resultant inflationary fears meant that German interest rates were too high for a UK economy that had already been in recession for a number of years and that might otherwise be recovering but for high interest rates resulting from ERM membership. Meanwhile, the French President, Mitterrand, had decided to hold a referendum on the Maastricht Treaty that was in danger of being lost (in the end, there was a 'petit oui' driven by large majorities in favour in various far-flung dependencies). The speculation in the week before the French referendum affected all ERM members but particularly the UK, which was seen as most vulnerable.

rate of another country or country grouping. If that country or country group is unstable, its instability may be passed through to the UK.

At present, while US policy appears volatile and the EU has some major economic difficulties, it might not appear to be a good time to tie the UK currency to either the dollar or the euro.

Moreover, academic studies point to the relatively high interest rate sensitivity of the UK economy[1] and in particular in its large real estate sector compared with some other economies (particularly those in Europe).[2] Since arbitrage means that a fixed exchange rate policy translates into interest rates approximately equal to those in the base currency plus (or minus) a risk premium, there are potential dangers for a highly interest rate sensitive economy like the UK being tied to the interest rate policy of another economy with a different sensitivity.

On the other hand, because the exchange rate and particularly the dollar exchange rate is an important factor driving the prices of imported goods into the UK, it is clearly a highly relevant factor in determining inflation.

Moreover, there are ways of implementing an exchange rate policy such as a 'crawling peg' that might have fewer downsides than the UK has faced when following an exchange rate policy.

We propose that exchange rates and particularly the dollar exchange rate need to be taken into account in monetary thinking. But for a country with the UK's unusual exposures and sensitivities and with the UK's history of traumatic exchange rate crises, we step back from recommending further fixed exchange rates.

We recommend that the Monetary Policy Committee pays particular attention to the exchange rate and especially the dollar exchange rate as an advance indicator of potential inflationary problems.

RECENT CONDUCT OF MONETARY POLICY

Monetary policy has to be sufficiently rigorous to ensure that policy is not inflationary. The current monetary policy rules and processes have failed to achieve this.

We are conscious that any monetary policy rule can be difficult to operate in complicated international circumstances such as the period of extreme monetary policy volatility around the world during the past three years.

But even allowing for both the uncertainty generated by unexpected circumstances and external shocks like Covid and the Ukraine War, we believe that the UK Bank of England Monetary Policy Committee (MPC) has made major mistakes which appear to have been reflected in the emergence of high inflation which was initially persistent, though the reversal of monetary policy has now turned the trend on the transitory elements of inflation.

Andrew Bailey said:

> We appear in front of Parliament regularly. That's very important that we are held to account for the decisions that we take. We're not always popular. We're not meant to be always popular. That's clear. That's partly why we are independent ... So I am strong in the view that the system works for us.

MONETARY TARGETING

Because this inflation was predicted in advance by a range of experienced outside observers to whom the MPC has appeared to pay little or no attention, it is hard to escape the view that the problems of the MPC reflect structural causes about how the committee is constituted.

To correct these, we recommend two policy changes.

There should be an obligation on the Chancellor to ensure that appointments to the MPC reflect a wide range of economic views about monetary policy and that this obligation should be monitored by the Treasury Committee of the House of Commons.

Although we would be cautious about recommending a fixed monetary target, we would recommend that in normal times, the MPC should aim to keep the growth in the UK money supply (M4) within a range consistent with low inflation. Currently, this would probably imply a range of between 1.5 and 4.5 per cent per annum growth.*

But more important is ensuring the right policy objective.

POLICY OBJECTIVES

Currently, policy is set based on an inflation objective. This is set in a letter of instruction from the Chancellor of the Exchequer to the governor of the Bank of England.[3] The current inflation target is 2 per cent for the consumer price index, with the governor having to write an open letter to the Chancellor if inflation overshoots or undershoots by 1 per cent, explaining why and what is being done to bring inflation back to target and over what timescale.[4]

The Bank of England also has a subsidiary policy since 2021 of 'helping to facilitate the achievement of net zero emissions',[5] but this has (presumably deliberately) been kept as an institutional target (mainly affecting financial reporting) rather than relating directly to the mandate of the MPC which concerns inflation alone. Climate change has only been mentioned in MPC minutes insofar as there are potential downside costs and boosts to inflation in future relating to climate change or measures to mitigate climate change.

Lord Lamont of Lerwick said:

It doesn't matter how determined a Chancellor may be in his wish to beat inflation if you have the Prime Minister breathing down your neck all the time saying, 'Why not [cut interest rates]? When's the next one?' Mrs Thatcher was not immune from behaving like that herself. What we don't really know about central bank independence is whether the great moderation in inflation, which has coincided since independence

---

* Tim Congdon, one of the UK's leading monetarists, has recommended that this implies the governor of the bank should write an open letter if monetary growth becomes negative or exceeds 7 per cent, explaining why the MPC judges that such rates of growth if they occur would not be either inflationary or disinflationary: https://committees.parliament.uk/writtenevidence/120080/pdf/

of the Bank of England and the adoption of inflation targeting, whether this was caused by China rather than bank independence. It may be that some of what we think was appropriate monetary policy was actually just caused by Chinese imports being cheaper.

The advantage of inflation targets is that the prime purpose of monetary policy is to prevent inflation getting out of control. The implicit model for inflation is that rising inflation bids up inflationary expectations which means that the costs of bringing inflation back under control become considerable compared with any potential losses from holding inflation down in the first place. So, in theory, targeting inflation directly is the best way of minimising the losses from inflation instability over the long term. This is backed up by academic evidence.[6]

But the UK experience of inflation targeting throws up two problems. The first is that it does not deal with the instability generated through asset booms and busts. This, of course, was the problem exemplified by the global financial crisis (GFC).

A longish period of inflation targeting around the world had failed to prevent asset price bubbles emerging that, when they burst, created huge problems for the world economy.

The second has been that while monetary policy has been fairly effective at managing demand-pull inflation, it has not been as successful in restraining supply-push problems.

Underpinning this problem is the issue of groupthink, where so many in official posts in the UK share a prevailing Keynesian consensus which does not pay sufficient attention to monetary influences on demand and on inflation. We look at groupthink among those working for the public sector and consider how this might be reduced in Part III of this book.

NOMINAL GDP

Proposal 12: Change the remit of the Monetary Policy Committee to target nominal GDP and pay more attention to the exchange rate and

the pace of monetary expansion. We recommend that the Monetary Policy Committee targets growth of nominal GDP, while paying explicit attention to the sterling exchange rate especially against the dollar and to the pace of monetary expansion.

The concept of targeting money GDP is generally associated with the Nobel Prize-winning economists James Meade[7] and James Tobin.[8] In this section, we discuss the advantages and disadvantages of the proposal.

In the UK, it was strongly supported by the eminent economics commentator Sir Samuel Brittan from the mid-1970s until his death in 2020, most cogently in his *Financial Times* columns on 1 July 2010[9] and 13 July 2013.[10]

More recently, it has been resuscitated in an excellent Institute of Economic Affairs (IEA) booklet by commentator Damian Pudner.[11] One of the co-authors of this book has also made a contribution[12] to the discussion of this issue.

The idea is that rather than having a target for inflation, the MPC should have a target for the growth in GDP in cash terms – this is not the real GDP, which is a concept with which we are familiar, but the actual cash amount of growth before being deflated for inflationary effects to give the real GDP growth figure.

Arguably, in a world free from shocks, inflation targeting is operationally easier than targeting nominal GDP, where the data is available late and is subject to revision.

But in a world that is subject to major asset price fluctuations and to unpredictable supply-side shocks, it is at least arguable that targeting nominal GDP, with a careful watching eye on asset prices, exchange rates and the growth in money supply, can provide a better framework for stability than simply looking at CPI inflation.

The weakness of targeting inflation alone is that in practice with either asset price shocks or supply-side shocks, policy makers have substantial discretion about how they respond. By contrast, a policy of stabilising nominal demand through nominal GDP targets builds in a greater level of both transparency and predictability.

Given that both the asset price issues that were associated with the

GFC and the supply-side issues associated with Covid and then the Ukraine War were international issues, it behoves one to be cautious and not to overestimate the extent to which targeting nominal GDP in the UK could have prevented demand and other fluctuations.

But it seems likely that a nominal GDP policy regime with less discretion and more transparency could have limited the scale of inflation, demand and interest rate fluctuations with their associated output losses.

PROBLEMS WITH NOMINAL GDP TARGETING

Nominal GDP targeting is not without its problems, which is why in more stable times we might be more cautious about recommending it. The biggest of these is that the data appear late and are subject to considerable revision. More fundamental are what specific targets and bands to choose and how to cope with past under- or overshoots.

In current circumstances, our proposed rate of growth of nominal GDP would be about 5 per cent in cash terms with a band of plus or minus 2 per cent. This would permit growth of 3 per cent real and 2 per cent inflation.

We would be flexible about coping for overshoots depending on their reason and whether they risk inflation becoming endemic. That is the real curse which one wants to avoid since when inflation becomes embedded, eliminating it is highly costly.

FISCAL TARGETS

The current official targets have been described in the current iteration of the Charter for Budget Responsibility,[13] which states:

The Charter is structured in two parts:[14]

- Chapter 3 'The government's fiscal policy framework' contains the Treasury's objectives, principles, and the mandate for fiscal policy;

the required contents of the Treasury's annual Budget Report; the Treasury's policy for the management of the national debt; the required contents of the Treasury's annual debt management report and the debt management remit; and the technical detail underpinning the operation of the fiscal lock

- Chapter 4 'The role of the Office for Budget Responsibility' contains guidance to the OBR on its role and the duties it shall perform within the fiscal policy framework. A Memorandum of Understanding will be agreed between the OBR, the Treasury and other government departments as appropriate, setting out how the relationship between these institutions will work in practice under normal circumstances

And:

In order to achieve the above objectives, the Treasury's mandate for fiscal policy is that:[15]

- the current budget must be in surplus in 2029–30, until 2029–30 becomes the third year of the forecast period. From that point, the current budget must then remain in balance or in surplus from the third year of the rolling forecast period, where balance is defined as a range: in surplus, or in deficit of no more than 0.5 per cent of GDP
- this range will support the government's commitment to a single fiscal event every year by avoiding the need for policy adjustment at forecasts outside of fiscal events. If the range is used between fiscal events, the current budget must return to surplus from the third year at the following fiscal event

3.7 The Treasury's mandate for fiscal policy is supplemented by:

- a target to ensure debt, defined as Public Sector Net Financial Liabilities (PSNFL), is falling as a share of the economy by 2029–30, until 2029–30 becomes the third year of the forecast period. Debt should then fall by the third year of the rolling forecast period

3.8 To ensure that expenditure on welfare remains sustainable, the Treasury's mandate for fiscal policy is further supplemented by:

- a target to ensure that expenditure on welfare is contained within a predetermined cap and margin set by the Treasury

In volatile bond markets, our view is that these targets are insufficiently rigorous to meet the objective of sound money.

Proposal 13: Limit budget deficits and bring down the debt ratio. We recommend these additional fiscal requirements: that the ratio of the deficit to GDP should be on a path to fall to below 2 per cent by 2029–30 and that policy should aim at gradually reducing the debt-to- GDP ratio to 60 per cent by 2043–44.

These should still permit substantial tax cuts over the period, provided that public spending remains under control and that supply-side policies are also followed.

FISCAL HEADROOM

Within these enhanced rules, there is still scope for cutting taxes (or increasing expenditure).

The best way to create fiscal headroom is to grow the economy, which creates increased scope for further fiscal action later. Our proposals will do that.

But the 2 per cent of GDP target for 2029–30 would permit £60 billion of headroom by that date, even if the economy did not grow any faster than in the base case.

We would recommend using this gradually, with about £15 billion of net tax cuts in 2024–25 and a cautious approach with an eye to looking for further fiscal dividends as the benefits of the tax cuts come through.

Bearing in mind that we think a debt crisis is highly likely, we would encourage a cautious long-term approach.

CONCLUSION

Sound money is not something theoretical; it is a critical plank of the 24/7 Growth Plan. Not only will it make the economy more stable, itself a contributor to growth, but it will also permit faster non-inflationary growth as a result of the confidence it generates, both in the UK and abroad.

By in effect guaranteeing the value of money, our sound money programme enables savers to save without the fear of their assets being eroded by inflation and to invest knowing that the fruits of investment will be returned in currency that has value. It also enables all economic agents to have confidence in the future.

CHAPTER 11

UK REGULATORY POLICY

'What we had in the previous government was a one-in, one-out rule,
which I changed to the one-in, two-out rule. Then Theresa May comes
along and just scraps it. Things like that are built to discipline the system.
I think having a sunset clause on all new business regulation, so it just
automatically expires after a period, is a good thing.'
– Sir Sajid Javid

The fourth kingdom of macroeconomic policy is avoiding excessive regulation.

As we point out in Part I:

Regulations cover an enormous area of economic activities and take on a vast array of forms. But from a 60,000-foot perspective, the principles become a lot clearer.

We all know we need government regulations over a wide range of activities. People can't be free, for example, to choose to drive on the left side of the road one day and then change their minds and drive on the right side of the road the next. Transparency rules, traffic rules, judicial rules etc. are all critical to the well-functioning of a prosperous market economy.

Excessive regulation can also be stifling to economic prosperity and growth. In all, regulations should be directed to the specific externalities at hand and avoid as much as possible unintended deleterious consequences and collateral damage. Given the lack of proper incentives, regulations have spun way out of control. As a general rule, regulations and oversight have been justified by overstating benefits and understating costs. As such, to align to the North Star of economic growth, oversight should be to optimise and simplify the amount, extent and timing of regulations.

Enacting regulations should be difficult and require as much political oversight as possible. Independent boards, committees and agencies, unless legislatively authorised, should not be allowed to impose regulations on their own authority. Virtually every regulation should have a sunset provision where its effects can be evaluated before it is renewed, removed or reformed.

This section sets out the 24/7 Growth Plan to achieve supply-side improvements to the economy to boost growth. It looks at cross-cutting issues such as regulatory compliance costs and the growth duty of regulators before focusing on four specific issues:

- Reducing environmental constraints on planning to allow more and more flexible building while freeing up the rental market to allow people to move to the jobs they want;
- Replacing the current net zero plans with smart net zero plans that reduce the damage done to the economy from ideological and over-aggressive plans to achieve net zero, to focus on energy policy with the aim of bringing down the price of energy to make the UK economy competitive by removing excessive environmental requirements and by building the appropriate infrastructure;
- Making labour markets work more effectively and flexibly, both reducing the barriers to working and also ensuring sufficient flexibility to enable people to increase their productivity by moving to jobs where they are most productive; and
- Enabling the infrastructure that the economy needs to be built – from power stations to transport – by reducing planning obstruction and providing the necessary finance.

REGULATORY COMPLIANCE COSTS

It appears that an important factor holding down UK growth is not only the extent of regulation itself but also the costs imposed on the economy in complying with them.

One of the authors has had quoted comparative figures for the cost of taking on board a new corporate client from a key investment bank: 'In Hong Kong it is $75; in London about $10,000.'[1]

More generally, the huge and relatively recent growth in the compliance cost of regulation in the financial services sector is illustrated by the LexisNexis annual survey,[2] which shows that this cost had risen to £38.3 billion by 2024 and that this total had risen by about a third since 2021. Moreover, this growth in compliance costs seems to have had little impact on the extent of money laundering (the main alleged target of much of the increased financial regulation), which the UK's National Crime Agency estimates to have risen to between £36 billion and £90 billion a year.[3]

For the economy as a whole, the total cost of regulation has been estimated as having grown by £143 billion (then 6 per cent of GDP) owing to the increase in regulation since 2015.[4] The Employment Rights Bill currently under consideration is estimated by the government itself to be likely to impose further compliance costs of up to £5 billion.[5]

To achieve economic growth at a pace that will generate significant gains in living standards, we need to unblock the economic arteries that have been gradually clogged up over recent years by a range of regulations.

Sir Tony Blair thinks that government is constantly regulating, and if you turn away for a minute, you will find someone somewhere is putting another piece of regulation in place. He likes the idea of measuring regulation against a North Star and tried to create a large bill on deregulation.

Not only is the compliance burden of regulations excessive and disproportionate to the aims of the regulation but the process for imposing regulations is seriously flawed.

In the US since the Reagan administration, regulatory assessment has been embedded in the regulatory process with mandatory cost-benefit analysis.[6] While such assessments are also compulsory in the UK, and overseen by the Regulatory Policy Committee, in practice these assessments are often of low quality and self-serving,[*] delivered too late for parliamentary scrutiny (possibly deliberately) and generally not acted upon.[7]

---

[*] A good example of this is the £5 billion estimate of regulatory costs imposed by the Employment Rights Bill, which to most expert observers fails to include major cost implications.

Proposal 14: Ensure the consequences of new regulations are fully understood and ensure that sunset clauses remove redundant regulations. The regulatory process should be reformed as above to ensure that regulations cannot be implemented without proper consideration of their full effects. And as a matter of course, 'sunset clauses', where a regulation is dropped if its continuation cannot be justified, need to be incorporated within all regulations.

It is possible to build on the existing structure in the UK to help roll back those regulations where the costs are excessive in relation to benefits and to prevent the imposition of new regulations. It should be mandatory that regulatory impact assessments are properly carried out and placed before Parliament before any regulation is imposed; the Regulatory Policy Committee already certifies in retrospect those assessments that are fit for purpose or otherwise, but these assessments should be part of the legislative process and carried out before new regulations come before Parliament.

There also needs to be a rolling process of regulatory reform where existing regulations are scrutinised and, if they damage the economy, scrapped.

REGULATION AND THE GROWTH DUTY

Both the previous Conservative government and the current Labour government have highlighted regulators' growth duty. The growth duty was imposed in the 2015 Deregulation Act and came into force in 2017. It requires regulators exercising a specified regulatory function, to do so in a way which ensures that regulatory action is taken only when it is needed and that any action taken is proportionate.

The growth duty was extended in 2024[8] but in practice weakened, by replacing growth with 'sustainable growth'. In practice, this allows regulations which do not promote economic growth to be promoted if it can be argued that they are positive for the environment. As we point out below, normal cost-benefit analysis already takes into account environmental benefits and to take further into account additional somewhat speculative environmental benefits in the name of sustainability is double counting.

The requirement for sustainability should be removed from the growth duty, which should also be made subject to parliamentary scrutiny.

PLANNING AND HOUSING

The first area where the UK's supply side needs to be improved is planning and housing. To its credit, the Labour government elected in 2024 has made this a priority. But it has already had to scale back its targets from building 1.5 million new homes to 1.2 million and may fail even to achieve this.

Part of the weakness of the government's approach is that it appears to assume that the bulk of the resistance to new building reflects so-called NIMBYs who oppose building in their local area. Clearly such resistance exists, and to the extent that increased housebuilding is not matched by adequate infrastructure provision, the resistance has a degree of genuine social justification. But it is not just the resistance of NIMBYs but also the increase and complexity of planning regulations, mainly for environmental reasons, that has reduced the scale of building and hence held back the economy. The current government is starting to legislate to deal with some of the blockages but at this stage seems unlikely to achieve more than a partial impact on the current inertia.[9]

UK planning regulation has dramatically increased in complexity in recent decades. The impact has been very little progress reducing the shortage of houses, as a result of which house prices have continued to rise (though falling slightly in real terms) despite high interest rates.

Sir Tony Blair thinks that the biggest risk for the government now is that it sets out a very bold ambition on planning, which we should have, but that the actual legislation doesn't really perform the task. Therefore, it is difficult to work out how you put together the legislation that does the trick.

There are three areas where the country's planning rules especially damage the economy:

- They lead to an artificial shortage of housing, exacerbated by net migration, keeping house prices and rents high, reducing disposable incomes and reducing labour mobility and hence productivity.

- They impede commercial developments and hence commercial activity.
- They make new infrastructure very hard to build, leading to backlogs in many areas, especially transport and energy.

HOUSING

The CBI/RICS task force on planning, 'Shaping the Nation',[10] estimated that the capital cost of the excess price of houses caused by planning restrictions was £78 billion at 1987 values, causing an annual loss to the economy of 1.9 per cent of GDP.

Studies in different countries show significant crowding-out effects from high house prices, damaging the growth of the rest of the economy. In the US, a very detailed micro study looking at bank branches found that a one-standard-deviation increase in house prices in areas where a bank has branches reduced lending growth to firms that borrow from the same bank by 42 per cent. The total investment undertaken by the affected firms fell by 21 per cent.[11] Similarly, a study from China showed that based on data from manufacturers in 172 Chinese cities, a 50 per cent increase in property prices would raise borrowing costs, reduce investment and productivity and result in a 35.5 per cent decline in the firms' value-added output.[12]

The economist Liam Halligan in his book *Home Truths*[13] and in his evidence to the House of Commons Housing, Communities and Local Government Committee has recommended additional measures to support housing, including the charging of penal rates of council tax on land with planning permissions which have not been built on and a 50–50 rule for sharing the value of property uplift from planning permissions between the local authority and the developer.[14]

RETAIL AND HOSPITALITY

The McKinsey study commissioned by Gordon Brown when he was Chancellor attributed the bulk of the 40–50 per cent of the productivity differential in the hospitality and retail sectors in the UK compared with the US to the inefficiencies and lack of competition caused by the planning system.[15] This implies a loss of productivity in these sectors alone equal to about 3 per cent of GDP.

OTHER SECTORS

In general, we recommend the adoption of an Australian-style zoning system for planning, with the presumption that planning applications should be successful provided that they are in line with zoning.

Lord O'Donnell said:

> We wrote papers in the Treasury on planning reform for decades – what was wrong, what should be changed etc. – and in the end, every time there's a new piece of legislation, you end up tacking on some environmental regulations, some other regulations, and you end up with this mess which is static in a world that's very dynamic.

PLANNING AND HOUSING RECOMMENDATIONS

Sir Vince Cable told us:

> The only point in modern British history when we were growing at over 3 per cent was in the 1950s and early '60s, and that was on the back of post-war reconstruction and large-scale house building. And I guess the one sector of the British economy where you could produce rapid growth would be in housing if we could reproduce that experience.

Proposal 15: Reform planning so that residential and commercial buildings are easier to construct. Planning needs to be substantially reformed to ensure that residential and commercial buildings can more easily be built, unlocking economic activity.

George Osborne said 'I would sweep away a lot of the planning controls. You know, planning is a form of socialism. It tells you what you can do with your property. I'm all for protecting really historically beautiful buildings and so forth, but there aren't that many of them.'

We recommend speedier resolution of planning issues. This can be accomplished by a range of policy tools. First, we advocate the concept of a trusted developer for whom expedited planning is possible.

Sir Sajid Javid said:

We've got too much green belt in this country. It's gone up four times in the last thirty years. It's just ridiculous. It's far easier to designate something as green belt than it is to take it out. And even if you took 5 per cent of the green belt out, you would have so much more land available for development, for housing. It'll be a housing boom. You could stop the rate of acceleration of house prices. Houses, over time, will become more affordable, and it will just unleash so much production and development.

Second, where a planning application is in line with the zonal planning system, we advocate an expedited review where if a decision is not made within weeks, planning permission is deemed to have been granted.

The UK mainly has a discretionary, regulatory approach to planning, as opposed to a zoning approach, though Simplified Planning Zones moderate this. A good example of how to regulate a Simplified Planning Zone is Slough Trading Estate, one of the UK's most successful industrial estates[16] and one of the two Simplified Planning Zones currently operating in the UK. Proposals for increasing zonal planning were made in 2020[17] but so far have failed to develop momentum. These need to be resuscitated.

The UK should apply concepts like outline planning permission for known and trusted entities. The 2020 paper does envisage automatic outline planning processes and suggests some ideas typically found in zonal approaches to planning. It also advocates the greater reliance on technology and electronic submissions as opposed to the paper-based system still used in UK planning.

A one-stop shop for planning processes would also simplify the process. There does need to be a much simpler process for analysing the environmental effects and the specific role of statutory consultees.

At the moment, since statutory consultees have no growth duty and only a prudential concern, there is no incentive for them to move quickly or to consider economic effects in their submissions. There is also no incentive to input their views on a timely basis and the reality is their comments very often come in at the latest possible stage, slowing the process down considerably (quite possibly deliberately).

Local councils are also deeply concerned about the possibility of judicial review and this creates a culture where it is easier to say no to development than to allow it. Once again, if courts were required to consider the economic growth impact of proposed development, this would shift the burden regarding planning processes and judicial review.

INFRASTRUCTURE

Proposal 16: Streamline infrastructure planning. For large projects of national importance, we recommend streamlined planning that will reduce planning delays by at least 75 per cent.

A recent analysis points out that 'the average cost for a flat road in the UK is £8.45 million per lane km compared to the European average of £5.77 million'.[18]

The bulk of this difference in costs reflects the UK's planning system. It has been reported that[19]

> the planning documentation for the Lower Thames Crossing, a proposed tunnel under the Thames connecting Kent and Essex, runs to 360,000 pages, and the application process alone has cost £297 million. That is more than twice as much as it cost in Norway to actually build the longest road tunnel in the world.

RENTAL HOUSING

Proposal 17: Reverse the tax increases on landlords and anti-landlord legislation. To improve the supply of rental housing in the UK and offset the damaging impact of recent legislation, the government should restore the tax and legislative position for private landlords to that which existed pre-2015.

Both the current government and its predecessor have increased the tax burden on rental housing and have weakened the position of landlords in coping with unsatisfactory tenants.

The result appears to be one of the worst examples of the law of unintended consequences – landlords appear to be moving out of the rental market and rents are rising sharply. The negative consequences of populist measures to make life difficult for landlords and apparently more favourable for tenants is one of the relatively few areas where almost all economists agree.

Evidence of negative effects abounds: 'The UK has a supply problem not a landlord problem'[20] is a typical quote. A study by the Deposit Protection Service[21] shows that legislation and taxation are the most widely quoted concerns by landlords who are withdrawing from the market.

Academic studies have shown the negative impact of restrictions on landlords on the supply of rental properties – e.g. in San Francisco, where the supply reduced by 15 per cent[22] and rents rose by more than 5 per cent compared with what had been expected.[23] A study by Rettie & Co. for the British Property Federation of the emergency freeze announced on Scottish rents in 2022 based on independent interviews with property investors indicated that the policy risked causing major supply imbalances.[24]

The Cambridge Centre for Housing and Planning Research found that tax changes reduced purchases by prospective landlords by nearly 40 per cent.[25]

SMART NET ZERO AND ENERGY

Boris Johnson said:

[On] net zero, we went far too fast. And I've got to be honest about that;

I got carried away by the idea that the sustainable and renewable forms of energy could fill the gap. When the price went up and the Ukraine thing happened, it was obvious that that wouldn't work. And I think we did allow some more hydrocarbons, but I think what you've got to do now is just say, you've got to see. You've got to be like St Augustine. You've got to say, 'We will be chaste, but not yet.'

Proposal 18: Adopt 'smart net zero'. Policies to achieve environmental objectives should be implemented at minimal economic cost and only when cost-justified.

The UK has adjusted its energy usage and supply to reduce its carbon emissions dramatically, with territorial carbon emissions down 53 per cent since 1990. However, much of this has reflected deindustrialisation. As a result, the UK's carbon footprint has fallen by only 22 per cent[26] over roughly the same period since displaced deindustrialised production has simply been shifted abroad, often to less environmentally friendly locations. Moreover, the bulk of this reduction of the carbon footprint itself has resulted from the replacement of coal by gas for electricity production, although the development of renewables is now starting to have an impact.

At the same time, world energy consumption continues to rise – in 2023 by 2.2 per cent.[27]

So, in effect, the UK's relatively aggressive net zero policies have had surprisingly little impact on its carbon footprint, often with deindustrialised production shifting to less green producers, while the economic costs to the UK have been considerable.

Moreover, while hitherto the economic cost of deindustrialisation has been cushioned by the ability to replace industry with the production of services at minimal energy cost, it is widely expected that future generations of the service sector will become increasingly industrialised and will themselves become energy-intensive.

Sir Tony Blair thinks that China will build, or authorise the building of, almost as much new, coal-fired energy this year as the whole stock of Europe.

The International Energy Agency report on data centres and artificial intelligence[28] points out that already

> in large economies like the United States, China and the European Union, data centres account for around 2–4 per cent of total electricity consumption today. But because they tend to be spatially concentrated, their local impact can be pronounced. The sector has already surpassed 10 per cent of electricity consumption in at least five US states. In Ireland, it now accounts for over 20 per cent of all electricity consumption.
>
> For comparison, large data centres can have a power demand equivalent to that of an electric arc furnace steel mill. However, steel plants are less likely to be clustered in the same geographic area.

The UK has the most expensive industrial electricity in the world according to the International Energy Agency, whose figures are quoted in Figures 50 and 51 from HMG.

Lord Hammond of Runnymede said:

> The public has been misled, shall we say, over the cost of decarbonisation, and if they were told the facts, I think they would choose a different route … The point for me is that if you look at the cost curves, the cost of decarbonising by 2060 or 2070 is dramatically lower than the cost of decarbonising by 2050. Fully decarbonising by 2050 means replacing capital assets which are not yet life-expired.

Removing coal from the energy mix has happened now; while the scope for reducing the UK's carbon emissions by shifting its industry offshore is much diminished and, in any case, this often increases total worldwide carbon emissions, since relatively clean UK production is displaced to less carbon-efficient locations.

Moreover, the UK has survived deindustrialisation with some pain only through the growth of the service sector. But it is now likely that the service sector, with increased dependence on data centres and AI, will become increasingly energy-intensive.

FIGURE 50: COMPARATIVE ELECTRICITY COST IN 2024 – MEDIUM INDUSTRIAL CONSUMERS P/KWHR[29]

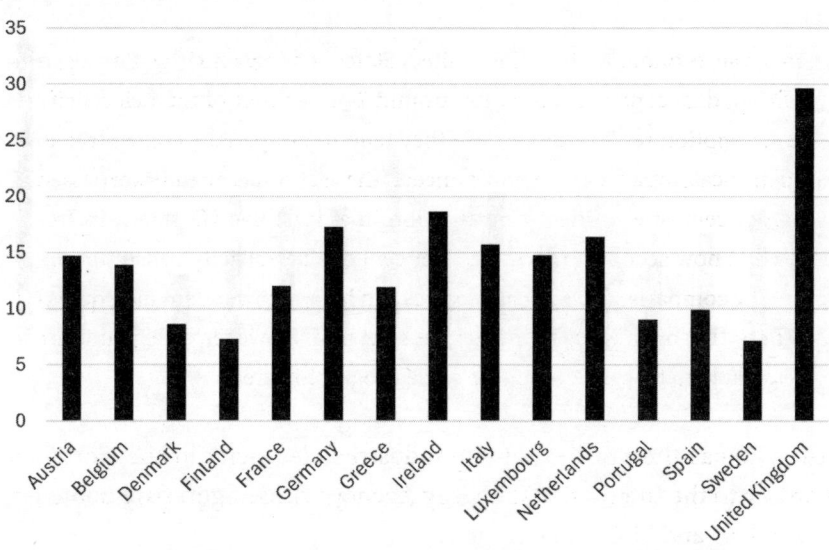

Source: Gov.uk

Net zero is an important policy but the current approach does remarkably little for the environment at huge economic cost.

Stephen Phipson, CEO of MakeUK, told us:

> We are now very uncompetitive … Japan is looking at this saying, why do we continue in Sunderland? The costs are about 50 per cent more expensive than mainland Europe. And if you look at today's rate, it's twenty-eight pence per kilowatt hour for electricity in this country, compared to six pence in the United States. There's a direct correlation. There's a direct correlation, as you will know, between industrial energy costs and output and performance.

Figure 50 shows how high the UK's energy costs are compared with those elsewhere in Europe for medium users. And Figure 51 shows how the excess cost of electricity in the UK is an especially serious problem for the largest users.

FIGURE 51: COMPARATIVE ELECTRICITY COST IN 2024 – LARGE
INDUSTRIAL CONSUMERS P/KWHR

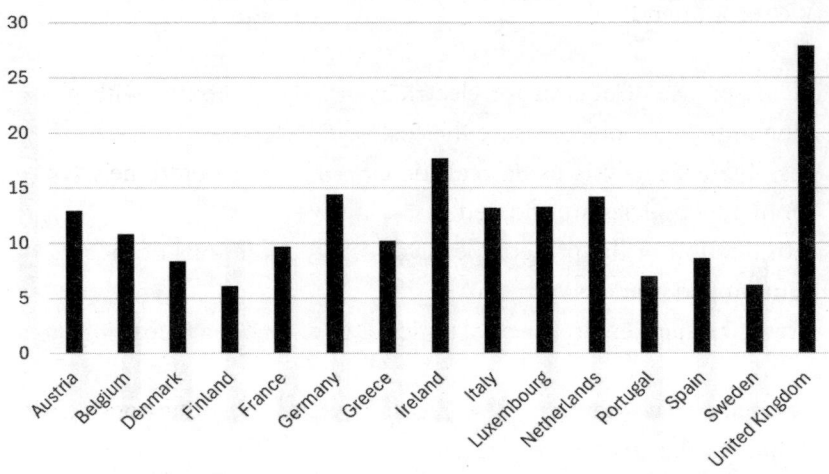

Source: Gov.uk

Many of those whom we consulted believed that if energy costs continue in the UK to be internationally uncompetitive, the whole of UK manufacturing would eventually leave the UK. And some pointed out the urgency of sorting this.

The Stern review of climate change policy calculated an implicit shadow price of CO_2 in 2000 of £18 per tonne of CO_2 equivalent.[30] This would translate to a price of £33.25 in August 2024.[31] Other values can be used, however – for instance, the 'social cost of carbon' estimated by the US government[32] in 2022 was £48.54. Whichever quasi-scientific measure is used, however, gives a very much lower shadow price than that currently used by HMG – £255.40 at 2022 prices[33] – which is calculated working backwards from official policy and the shadow price necessary for the policy to be cost-justified.

The cost–benefit analysis of the impact of the proposed ban on fossil-fuelled new car sales in 2030[34] showed that even using the government's guidance for the shadow price of carbon, the costs outweighed the benefits five times; using the US government shadow price of carbon halves the value of the benefits and the costs are ten times the benefits rather than five times in the base case.

Net zero needs to be replaced by smart net zero which takes account of the least harmful way of achieving the policy objective.

We recommend:

- increased use of nuclear for electricity supply, combined with planning improvements to ensure the cost is kept down
- cost–benefit analysis using realistic carbon prices before new environmental policies are adopted
- introduction of the pro-competitive recommendations of the Competition and Markets Authority[35]
- a review of past environmental policies to see if they are cost-justified

We estimate that adopting these recommendations could boost GDP per capita by 2.2 per cent by 2045.

LABOUR MARKET

Boris Johnson said:

> There were RV parks, and places by the river for people to sit and have picnics, and my family and I were all swimming in the river full of snakes – it was quite scary – but there were no Americans there, because the Americans have only got two weeks holiday a year, and if it was Britain, the sun was out and the river was warm, this place would be swarming. All the parks would be full. Everybody would be bunking off.

Proposal 19: Labour market liberalisation. Adjust legislation to make it easier for employers to hire and dismiss employees and scrap the Employment Right Bills if it becomes law.

A further area where the UK needs major reform is its labour market.

The policies where the UK scores badly in the model, based on estimates of the economic impact of its labour market,[*] include:

---

[*] This is based on the Growth Commission's modelling of supply-side constraints.

- minimum wage
- associational right
- paid annual leave
- notice period for redundancy dismissal
- severance pay for redundancy dismissal
- labour force participation rate
- restrictions on overtime work
- redundancy dismissal permitted by law

Calculations have suggested that if the UK were to optimise* its score in labour market flexibility, it could expect an associated increase of between 4.6 and 5.1 per cent in GDP per capita. It may not be practical to implement all the policies that might bring the UK into line with high-performing Far Eastern economies, but even catching up with Australia is estimated to be likely to raise GDP per capita by 1.9 per cent.

The following policies would contribute to that gain in GDP per capita that correlate to the factors listed above:

- lower notice period and reduced compulsory severance pay for re-dundancy dismissals
- efforts to improve labour force participation rate
- eliminate restrictions on overtime work by deleting the EU Working Time Directive from the UK statute book
- allowing firms to dismiss employees more easily if business conditions require it

Meanwhile, an Employment Rights Bill is currently under consideration in Parliament that would impose additional costs on employers of up to £5 billion according to the government's own calculations. Progress on this bill should be halted or, if passed, it should be repealed.

On the Employment Rights Bill, Anna Leach told us:

---

* This represents the GDP per capita increase from an improvement in the sub-score to the same level as the best performing country. The lower end of the range is the result from a model which controls for both country- and time-fixed effects, whereas the higher end of the range is given by the model with country-fixed effects.

There's just this desperation from DBT [Department for Business and Trade] trying to find evidence that this is going to deliver a productivity improvement, when all the evidence is that it doesn't. And OBR are sitting in on the calls now. OBR already said they expected to be negative and [they haven't] even done the analysis yet. They're pretty confident that it's negative.

THE MINIMUM WAGE

Proposal 20: Bring down the minimum wage as a share of the median wage. Adjust the minimum wage level by returning it to its 2023 level in relation to the median wage (61 per cent) by freezing it until this ratio is reached.

When the minimum wage was introduced in the UK in 1999, few opposed it, including even the Conservatives then in opposition. But since then, the minimum wage has risen dramatically as a percentage of the median wage from the initial 46 per cent in 1999. Its current rate of 66 per cent of the median wage is the highest in the advanced economies and well above the OECD average of 54 per cent.

The case for a minimum wage is to prevent exploitation when employers have too much control in the labour market; the case against it is that it increases the cost base for employers. In some circumstances, this is unaffordable and jobs are destroyed – often those of the most marginal members of the labour force with physical or mental disabilities or new migrants. In other circumstances, the costs are passed on and lead to higher inflation which requires higher unemployment to squeeze it out.

Sir Sajid Javid explained the interaction between welfare benefits and work:

I think we should use more stick than carrot. In general, a lot of the benefits that we have are just far too generous. And there's plenty of work out there. There's plenty of opportunities, and we just need to make it more of an incentive for people to go out and get those jobs.

But one senior businessman we interviewed told us:

The problem is, where do you stop? At what point do you say, it's one of those figures where poverty is defined as being a percentage of a number that's constantly moving. So as absolute wages go up, you always end up with the same number of people in poverty, which is the people who are on whatever it is, 50 per cent of the average wage.

Where a minimum wage can have a positive effect is if it is paid for by higher productivity. But productivity performance in the UK has deteriorated since the minimum wage started rising sharply, so there seems scant evidence of this potentially favourable outcome occurring. The idea of higher wages causing a rise in productivity is controversial: had the theory applied generally, Britain in the 1970s with its aggressive trade unions and high wage inflation would have been the most productive country in the world – in reality, it was one of the least productive of the major economies.

The most comprehensive academic research on the effects of a minimum wage, an international study in 2019, concludes 'recent work helped identify how this impact may vary by the level of the minimum wage. Across US states, the best evidence suggests that the employment effects are small up to around 59 per cent of the median wage.'[36]

Two different econometrically estimated models have been used to analyse the impact of the minimum wage. A micro model suggests that scrapping the minimum wage would add 1.36–1.49 per cent in GDP per capita. Its macro model suggests that reducing the minimum wage from 66 per cent of the median wage to 61 per cent would in twenty years' time add 0.8 per cent to GDP per capita. This reduction to 61 per cent is our proposal, which would still leave the minimum wage higher than the 60 per cent proposed for the EU and the rate of 55–60 per cent proposed by the trade union advisory committee to the OECD.

TRANSPORT INFRASTRUCTURE

Proposal 21: Improve road infrastructure, paid for by the introduction of road user charges. We've already proposed increased infrastructure spending, particularly on roads. In addition, road user costs should be frozen at their current level in real terms. In time, all road usage taxes should be scrapped and replaced by road user charges on the basis set out below. Road user charges should not be additional to existing road taxes.

We advocate taking action to reduce losses on the rail sector which currently are greater than the total spending on roads. Ultimately, if the trade unions make rail unaffordable, the system should be pared back and the land thus released should be turned into roads.

The quality of transport infrastructure is an important arterial sector which has a significant impact on GDP per capita. There has been much debate in the UK on the quality of its rail sector, but we should note that most passenger journeys and most freight journeys in the UK are made by road.

This is because of the lack of granularity of the public transport system – it can only be used for journeys between specific origins and destinations, which means that for most journeys, a mix of modes is likely to be required.

The UK scores particularly badly for transport infrastructure, mainly due to its lack of roads and their inferior quality.

Modelling suggests a potential boost of between 0.68 per cent and 0.75 per cent in GDP per capita.* The UK scores particularly poorly in this sub-variable with a score of 4.9 in 2019, compared to Singapore's peak performance 1.8 points higher.

Rail contributes much less than road to the UK economy yet consumes a disproportionate amount of resources. Much of this appears to reflect the aggressive trade unions in the sector which have reduced productivity and also driven up rail drivers' pay. According to ASHE data available in August 2024, train and tram drivers earned a median annual salary of £63,807 in 2023 despite having their training paid for them (and a salary while they are being trained). The equivalent pay for airline pilots in 2025 was £72,000 and in general they have to pay for their own training.

The latest official data from the Office of Rail and Road shows that the

---

* Using the Growth Commission micro model.

cost of rail in 2023–24 was £25.4 billion, while fares and other charges raised £11.0 billion[37] so that rail has to be subsidised to make up the difference. By comparison, road users[38] paid in the same year £7.8 billion in vehicle excise duty, £24.8 billion in fuel duties and very roughly £5 billion in road user charges,* fines and official parking charges while total expenditure on the road system was £13.3 billion.

With regard to roads, improving road infrastructure can unleash significant GDP per capita benefits. East–west connections are as important as north–south connections and improving links among towns and cities in the UK that do not involve London-centric networks will be important.

Ultimately, it is unlikely that modern modes of propulsion can be implemented without moving to a more modern system of financing roads through user pricing.

Another report on road pricing[39] identified two major constraints to its introduction:

- After many years where governments have appeared to be anti-motorist (evidenced in the taxes on motoring being well in excess of the spending on road transport), road users do not trust governments to impose additional charges on road users – hence the ongoing reaction against any increase in fuel duty.
- There might be a temptation for the government to create an artificial shortage of road space to help maximise the user price that could be charged and most road users are suspicious that the government would thus abuse any power it had to charge based on scarcity.

It also suggested solutions to these problems through the following:

- A user authority representing those who pay for and use the roads only, to oversee the road pricing mechanism and ensure the money (other than that paid to the government as set out below) is spent on roads.

---

* Estimate based on a range of sources.

- A 'Barnett' formula working out the share of the road-pricing revenue that should be taken by the government.
- The rest of the revenue should be reinvested in improving the road network.

Subsequent calculations suggested that these reforms could raise capacity by at least a third and reduce accidents by 90 per cent. It also calculated a potential gain to GDP of 3 per cent.

CONCLUSIONS

The range of planning, housing, rental, energy, environmental, labour market and transport reforms described above will make a potentially massive difference to GDP – in twenty years' time, our cautious estimate is that such supply-side measures add 16.3 percentage points of the 28.8 percentage points that our proposals will add to GDP.

This is a huge gain and one that the country should aim for.

The full details of our supply-side proposals and their impact on GDP growth are shown in Annex 1.

CHAPTER 12

UK TRADE POLICY

'We have embassies with a commercial arm in pretty much every country on the planet. They could have done more to support the case of British goods and British services overseas, but they put their diplomatic role somewhat ahead of their trade role when it comes to support in many instances.'

– ANDY HALDANE

The fifth kingdom of the Growth Plan is free trade.
As we state in Part I:

> Going back as far as records have been kept, trade has been as important as any factor in creating prosperity and economic growth. There are some things that one country produces better and more efficiently than other countries. And likewise, those other countries produce products and services more efficiently than the first country. Each country in its turn would be foolish in the extreme if it didn't realign its production to export those products it makes more efficiently than its trading partners, while importing those products its trading partners produce more efficiently than it does. This is called 'comparative advantage' or 'the Ricardian gains from trade' and is a win-win-win for all participants.

Attempts to restrict trade have a cost, though sometimes temporary costs can be justified to the extent they generate leverage to help reduce trade barriers elsewhere. A country's leverage will depend on what it can offer as a potential market.

As a medium-sized economy, the UK has a degree of leverage, but its main potential gains from trade are likely to result from increased unrestricted trade.

Andy Haldane said, 'I think it's fair to say that our own governments of various stripes have not been as front foot in supporting British business into overseas markets as some other governments around the world.'

This section looks at the potential gains from trade from trade agreements with the US, EU, India, the Trans-Pacific Partnership and a potential CANZUK free trade area. It looks specifically at the potential damaging impact of joining the European Carbon Border Adjustment Mechanism and finally considers the scope for expanding trade in services where the UK has a comparative advantage.

Proposal 22: Push through and extend the trade deals with the US and India and create a CANZUK free trade area. The government should fully implement the deals with the US and India and seek to develop them further to enhance trade in services.

TRADE WITH THE US

A trade deal between the US and the UK, the US–UK Economic Prosperity Deal, was agreed on 8 May 2025.[1]

This incorporates a wide range of agreements on tariff levels for most goods, including more than $700 million in ethanol exports and $250 million in other agricultural products like beef, a regime for car exports and special regimes for trade in steel and aluminium.

It commits the countries to work together to enhance industrial and agricultural market access. It closes loopholes and increases US firms' competitiveness in the UK's procurement market. It ensures streamlined customs procedures for US exports. It establishes high standard commitments in the areas of intellectual property, labour and environment.

It maximises the competitiveness and secures the supply chain of US aerospace manufacturers through preferential access to high-quality UK aerospace components and creates a secure supply chain for pharmaceutical products.

There are substantial provisions in the treaty covering standards:

The United Kingdom and the United States each confirms its intent to accord to conformity assessment bodies of the other treatment no less favorable than that it accords to conformity assessment bodies located in its own territory. Treatment under this paragraph includes procedures, criteria, fees, and other conditions relating to accrediting, approving, licensing, or otherwise recognizing conformity assessment bodies.

Both countries intend to build on an existing set of Mutual Recognition Agreements (MRAs) by negotiating additional agreements, as appropriate, across certain industrial goods and advance toward an agreement on services domestic regulation.

The United Kingdom and United States intend to discuss the principles and criteria used in order to recognize a standard as an international standard. The United Kingdom and the United States will further commit to discuss respective applicable standards for mutually agreed sectors of interest and, within those specified sectors, to agree which of the other's relevant domiciled standards development organizations (SDOs) currently meet recognized international principles.

Increasing Digital Trade

(a) Both countries confirm that they will negotiate an ambitious set of digital trade provisions that will include within its scope services, including financial services.

(b) Both countries confirm that they will negotiate provisions on paperless trade, pre-arrival processing, and digitalized procedures for the movement of goods between our countries.

The importance of standards is often not fully understood. A report written by one of the co-authors for the British Standards Institute showed how improved and more internationally consistent standards has boosted UK GDP growth by 0.4 per cent per annum.[2] An unpublished report using similar methodology showed how the impact of opening up China to international standards might boost Chinese GDP by nearly 7 per cent fifteen years forward.

We recommend that the UK fully implements the free trade deal with the US and extends the deal already negotiated to include increased mutual recognition of standards and freer trade in services.

TRADE WITH INDIA

HMG signed a trade deal with India, the world's fourth largest economy, on 6 May 2025.[3] The deal is estimated to boost trade, currently £42 billion, by £25.5 billion by 2040 and UK GDP by £4.8 billion by the same year.

Responding to the deal, Bill Winters CBE, group CEO of Standard Chartered and co-chair of the India–UK Financial Partnership, said, 'The India–UK Free Trade Agreement is a significant achievement. It will create new opportunities for UK and Indian businesses, enable greater access to one of the world's largest and most dynamic markets, and drive growth and innovation across the India–UK corridor.'[4]

Clearly, given these figures, the deal is just a start of a process of liberalisation. But as with the US deal, we welcome the deal and recommend that the UK fully implements it and negotiates further extensions, particularly applying to services. Although India currently is an economy that is roughly the same size as the UK, most forecasts including ours have it reaching about the same size as the US in the second half of this century.

CANZUK FREE TRADE AREA

We propose that HMG prioritise creating a CANZUK free trade area. This proposal is for free trade and mutual recognition of standards, plus political alignment between the three former dominions (Australia, Canada and New Zealand) and the UK. It has been enabled as a result of Brexit.

There are few major problems that would make such a deal difficult, but it has been opposed by some in the UK on the grounds that it would complicate a reversal of Brexit.

The UK and Australia already have a comprehensive agreement, even allowing for mutual recognition of legal qualifications, and Australia and New Zealand have an even more comprehensive agreement.

Proposal 23: Leave the EU Carbon Border Adjustment Mechanism and encourage further trade liberalisation under CPTPP. We recommend that the UK does not adopt the European Carbon Border Adjustment Mechanism, and we recommend encouraging further liberalisation under CPTPP, including its extension to trade in services.

TRADE WITH THE EU

An updated agreement with the EU has been negotiated. Some of the elements of this are subject to continued discussions, but an element of the updated agreement with the EU is reported to be the incorporation of the UK into the European Carbon Border Adjustment Mechanism (CBAM).

The Growth Commission has recently published a very full analysis of why such tariffs introduced in the name of net zero are damaging to the UK economy.[5]

The EU's CBAM will lead to the imposition of a tariff on the imports of these competing products where the carbon costs are lower.

The UK CBAM is a targeted tariff which is intended to apply to the following emission-intensive industrial goods imported to the UK:

- aluminium
- ceramics
- cement
- fertiliser
- glass
- hydrogen
- iron and steel

To prevent leakage, the UK government would apply a liability through the CBAM on a country-by-country basis. This liability will depend on the carbon dioxide (CO_2) emissions intensity of the imported good and the difference between the carbon price applied from the country of origin (if any) and the price if the good had been produced in the UK.

The estimated cost of CBAM is a loss of 3 per cent of GDP.[6]

It is not clear that CBAM is consistent with other trade deals which the UK is trying to achieve, including those with the US and India. Moreover, currently, trade remedies exist under the World Trade Organization rules which provide mechanisms for coping with genuine dumping of goods made using internationally agreed non-compliant processes and such mechanisms should be sufficient for UK policy purposes.

TRADE WITH OTHER COUNTRIES

Rishi Sunak MP said, 'I'm a believer in free trade. That's a minority opinion these days. But although I took Britain into the CPTPP because I thought that was a good thing, the world has changed, rightly so in some regards, because the security environment has changed.'

The UK joined the Comprehensive and Progressive Agreement for Trans-Pacific Partnership (CPTPP) in December 2024, becoming the first European country to join this trade bloc. CPTPP now includes twelve countries: Australia, Brunei, Canada, Chile, Japan, Malaysia, Mexico, New Zealand, Peru, Singapore, Vietnam and the UK.

The main contents of the CPTPP are:

- Free trade: The agreement aims to eliminate tariffs on 99 per cent of goods traded between member countries typically over a seven-year period.
- Rules of origin: It provides a single set of rules of origin, allowing for content from any CPTPP country to be cumulated.
- Investment and trade: The agreement also covers aspects like investment liberalisation, government procurement and intellectual property.

Proposal 24: Liberalise trade in services. Our research shows that 67.7 per cent of UK exports measured by value add (excluding the import content in exports) is now composed of exports of services. We recommend that the UK focus much of its trade negotiations on trade in services to reflect the new reality of UK trade becoming much more based on services, negotiating with its trading partners to reduce non-tariff barriers on such trade.

Most trade agreements focus on goods, while fewer concentrate on the service sector. Yet, as Figure 52 shows, services now account for the bulk of UK exports. The latest data (on 29 July 2025) shows that they comprise 59.2 per cent of total exports of goods and services for the twelve months to May 2025 compared with 40.8 per cent for exports of goods.[7]

Moreover, since exports of goods tend to have a much higher import content, this is especially the case when the value added generated by these exports is measured and the share is even higher. Assuming the ratios for import contents are as they were in 2022 when the most recent input–output tables were produced, the value added generated by exports of services in the twelve months to May 2025 was 68.6 per cent of the total value added generated by exports of goods and services, while that of goods was 31.4 per cent.

FIGURE 52: UK ANNUAL EXPORTS OF GOODS AND SERVICES IN £ BILLIONS

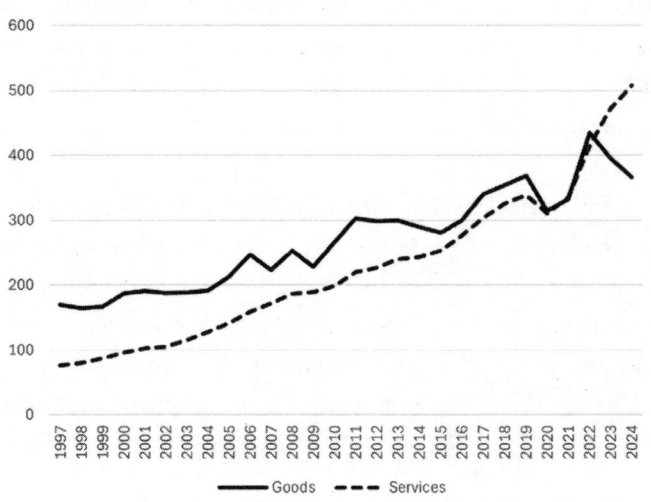

Source: ONS

Normally, trade in services is not subject to tariffs (though the US has suggested tariffs on products not carried in US-made and registered ships). But it is heavily subject to non-tariff barriers.

CONCLUSION

Although the UK is widely seen as a relatively free trading economy, in practice we fall far short of that ideal. Obviously, as trade is a two-way street, solving all our trade problems is not entirely within the competence of the UK government. Nevertheless, there are many improvements which are within our control and the potential gains from this are on a scale worth achieving – we estimate that our proposed trade improvements that can be costed would make up 4.5 percentage points to the 28.8 percentage points total boost to GDP from the 24/7 Growth Plan.

We should aim to achieve these gains.

PART III

THE POLITICS OF ECONOMIC GROWTH

Putting a sensible plan together may seem hard. But getting it implemented is generally rather harder. As former European Commission president Jean-Claude Juncker wrote (quoted by Lord Hammond in his interview with us), 'We all know what to do, but we don't know how to get re-elected once we have done it.'[1] Yet there is in fact statistical evidence from EU member states that governments that try for reform are not significantly any less likely to be re-elected than those that do not.[2]

We have based our plans for implementation on the results of thirty-four interviews with a wide range of people with extensive experience of UK politics and the links between politics and business, including five of the eight living former Prime Ministers and nine of the eleven living former Chancellors. The full list of interviewees – the dramatis personae, if you like – are listed below. We are grateful to each and every one of them for their time and their openness.

The interviews were wide-ranging and covered topics from why the UK is suffering an economic malaise to ways in which growth could be kickstarted. But the prime focus was on the political and institutional obstacles to growth that would have to be overcome if the UK economy were to be revitalised.

Part III of the book begins with a discussion of the economic reasons for the UK's low growth as seen by our interviewees (Chapter 13); then it looks at their views about the political reasons for low growth (Chapter

14) and finally at their assessment of the political obstacles that have to be overcome to enable an economic renaissance (Chapter 15).

The quote which perhaps best sums up the thesis of our book and the economic situation we are in comes from David Giampaolo, CEO of Pi Capital, who came to the UK from the United States and made London his home:

> What I've observed over the last thirty-five years … is the profound impact technology has had and is going to have going forward. And I think it would be very difficult for any country to be prosperous without its ability to somehow capture two key things. One is they're going to have to make decisions which are longer term than typically exist in a democratic environment, around healthcare, education, infrastructure – things that, by definition, are large and take five, ten, fifteen, twenty years, both from a vision and an implementation point of view. And I believe the world has become more and more unequal in every sense – from income inequality, education inequality, opportunities inequality – but that the most prosperous areas are where capital and talent flow. And therefore, in order for the United Kingdom to be prosperous and grow and benefit all, it has to still be a magnet for capital and for talent, and they're joined at the hip.
>
> So, what are the policies that attract capital and attract talent? And you get into all sorts of policies which are around regulation, taxation, other incentives and infrastructure which make living there pleasant, be it schools and universities and culture and so on and so forth. To me, the UK has many of these attributes and virtues, but they seem to me to be declining, wasting, not being leveraged. And political decision-making seems to get even more short term … You're making no investment for the future … At best, you're trying to stand still, which is impossible. You're either going forward or backwards. There is no status quo.

THE INTERVIEWEES

Andrew Bailey: Governor of the Bank of England 2020–present, CEO of the Financial Conduct Authority 2016–20.

Sir Tony Blair: Prime Minister 1997–2007, MP for Sedgefield 1983–2007.

Sir Vince Cable: Business, Innovation and Skills Secretary 2010–15, MP for Twickenham 1997–2015, 2017–19.

Lord Cameron of Chipping Norton: Prime Minister 2010–16, MP for Witney 2001–16.

Lord Chartres: Bishop of London 1995–2017.

Lord Clarke of Nottingham: Chancellor of the Exchequer 1993–97, MP for Rushcliffe 1970–2019.

Jamie Dimon: Chairman and CEO of JPMorganChase 2006–present.

Jonathan Geldart: Director general of the Institute of Directors, an advocacy group on behalf of company directors in the UK over the past century, 2019–present.

David Giampaolo: CEO of Pi Capital, an investment network for high-net-worth individuals based in London and around the world, 2002–present.

Richard Gnodde: Vice chairman of Goldman Sachs January 2025–present. Previously CEO of Goldman Sachs International 2006–25. Gnodde recently announced he was moving away from London to Milan.

Andy Haldane: Chief executive of the Royal Society of Arts 2021–25. Previously, chief economist at the Bank of England 2014–21.

Lord Hammond of Runnymede: Chancellor of the Exchequer 2016–19, MP for Runnymede & Weybridge 1997–2019.

Rupert Harrison: Chair of the Council of Economic Advisers, HMT, 2010–15, George Osborne's chief economic adviser 2006–10.

Sir Jeremy Hunt MP: Chancellor of the Exchequer 2022–24, MP for Godalming & Ash (formerly South West Surrey) 2005–present.

Sir Sajid Javid: Chancellor of the Exchequer 2019–20, MP for Bromsgrove 2010–24.

Boris Johnson: Prime Minister 2019–22, Mayor of London 2008–16.

Kwasi Kwarteng: Chancellor of the Exchequer 2022, MP for Spelthorne 2010–24.

Lord Lamont of Lerwick: Chancellor of the Exchequer 1990–93, MP for Kingston-upon-Thames 1972–97.

Anna Leach: Chief economist at the Institute of Directors 2024–present.

Clare Lombardelli: Deputy governor for monetary policy of the Bank of England 2024–present, chief economist for the OECD 2023–24.

Lord Macpherson of Earl's Court: Permanent Secretary to the Treasury 2005–16.

Lord O'Donnell: Cabinet Secretary 2005–11, Permanent Secretary to the Treasury 2002–05.

Lord O'Neill of Gatley: Commercial Secretary to the Treasury 2015–16. Lord O'Neill worked for Goldman Sachs between 1997 and 2013.

George Osborne: Chancellor of the Exchequer 2010–16, MP for Tatton 2001–17.

Lord Petitgas: Special adviser to Rishi Sunak on business and investment 2023–24, having been international head at Morgan Stanley 2018–22.

Stephen Phipson: CEO of MakeUK, the main organisation that represents manufacturing in the UK, 2017–present.

Sir John Rose: Chief executive of Rolls-Royce 1996–2011.

Sir Tom Scholar: Permanent Secretary to the Treasury 2016–22.

Rupert Soames: Chairman of the Confederation of British Industry, one of the largest representative groups for business in the UK, 2024–present.

Lord Stevens of Birmingham: Chief executive of NHS England 2014–21.

Rishi Sunak MP: Prime Minister 2022–24, MP for Richmond & Northallerton (formerly Richmond (Yorks)) 2015–present.

Liz Truss: Prime Minister 2022, MP for South West Norfolk 2010–24.

Lord Walney: Former political spokesman for Gordon Brown while Brown was Prime Minister, 2008–09.

Lord Wolfson of Aspley Guise: Chief executive of the retailer Next 2001–present.

Nadhim Zahawi: Chancellor of the Exchequer 2022, MP for Stratford-on-Avon 2010–24.

The interviews were conducted off the record, on the understanding that we would seek approval for any material we wanted to use. Some of our interviewees signed off their quotes unamended. Others made small changes or asked us to paraphrase their remarks. A few asked to remain anonymous. All of the conversations were informative, and we are grateful to each and every one of the people we spoke to.

CHAPTER 13

THE ECONOMIC REASONS
FOR LOW GROWTH

We asked our interviewees about the reasons for the UK's slow growth. Their responses were a mix of big-picture reasons and specific reasons. The big-picture reasons were often linked to recent events – the global financial crisis, Brexit and Covid. But they also touched on wider themes such as a loss of ambition as a country, the loss of faith in markets and the lack of appreciation for entrepreneurs and wealth creators. There were also specific factors such as low productivity, worklessness, high taxation, high spending and overregulation.

All of these themes are explored below, but perhaps the most comprehensive and eloquent analysis for the UK's weak growth performance was given to us by Richard Gnodde, vice chairman of Goldman Sachs, who previously served as CEO of Goldman Sachs International:

> If we go back two or three decades, the country was in a pretty good place on many of these measures, but we slipped. How we dealt with the financial crisis – the nationalisation, for want of a better word, of some of the banks – how long it took for the government to get out of the banking sector [was] way too long. We said to government, as long as the government owns one share in your bank, that the whole country's got a right to comment on your bank. The US did a much better job – they were sort of in and out – because they realised they were not in the business of allocating capital and banking. So, the financial crisis is part of it. Brexit, Covid – you put all that together over the last fifteen-plus years, I think we've lost a lot of our drive and thrust.
>
> And I put those issues on the table because, in one sense, they're now in the rear-view mirror, but I think they did impact how people operate

and think economically. They created huge uncertainty. The financial crisis created uncertainty. Brexit clearly created uncertainty. In the end, if part of the solution to productivity is both public and private investment, that doesn't happen at scale if there's a lot of uncertainty.

And then there's the level of interest rates. This country has carried higher interest rates than others for most of this period, and that obviously makes investment more challenging.

Maybe the country does start with a structural sector disadvantage – less tech than the US, for example. The lack of investment in tech and driving tech is an issue.

The whole trade component, obviously. Brexit was a massive negative for that. Everybody has been talking about an India trade deal today, and everybody's eyes are focused on a trade deal with the US. We need to do a trade deal with Europe. That's our big trading partner. Europe is our neighbour.

And then there's the question about being dynamic in a commercial sense. And it feels to me that people here are quite good – maybe as good as anywhere – in terms of starting a business. There are lots of businesses. The question is the ecosystem – is it dynamic enough? Does the system support them in a dynamic way so that they can actually grow these businesses and they don't move somewhere else when they've grown them?

The labour market here is something that one has to spend a lot of time on and really has to understand, and I'm certainly no expert on it … I was with someone today – an entrepreneur whose wealth will be measured in the tens of billions, out of Asia, but he does a fair amount of business here – and he says people here, when he talks to some of these companies, they come to work one and a half days a week. The balance is work from home – that cannot be the way forward. Having a job is a privilege to be respected, as should be those who create the jobs.

The long-term sickness stats in this country are terrible. The whole benefits, disability, welfare system – how do we incentivise people to get back to work? So, I think labour market composition is an interesting one, because it is obviously a challenge here. And, of course, net migration has been strongly positive. But the question is whether the make-up of that migration is what we want? Is it students bringing big families? Pre-Brexit, when you needed an extra plumber, some guy from Poland got on a train and was working as a plumber here the next day. And when you didn't need him, he went home. So, I think the sort of flexibility or the elasticity of the labour market has changed completely in the last decade here. So, really the question is, are we attracting and are we getting the right skilled workers? Are we attracting the right people?

I think those are some of the challenges. I think about the last fifteen years, and I can see how one gets here. I go back to the financial crisis, Brexit, Covid – each of these are huge events – the uncertainty that's resulted, the cultural piece. Those are some of the problems.

GLOBAL FINANCIAL CRISIS

The global financial crisis (GFC) hit the UK especially because of its dependence on the financial sector and on property – the two sectors that were most affected. The interviewees agree on its importance but disagree about the nature of the impact.

On how the GFC affected the UK economy, Lord Petitgas said:

The GFC really was the start of the stigmatisation of capitalism. [The stigmatisation] is not a British thing. The British were more vulnerable to the stigmatisation even than the Americans, (a) because the City of London is so important and (b) because capitalism was more successful in the UK than anywhere else in Europe. Europe is a more socialist environment, so the UK had already become more than halfway towards America in terms of its capitalism, and the GFC hits it even more. But the UK is also a European country, so the minute you start stigmatising capitalism, you have a natural reversion to our natural state, which is that we don't really like it anyway.

The stigmatisation of capitalism comes in different ways. It comes in risk aversion – more regulation. Not only does the state grow, so does the belief that the state is very important. And Covid, in my mind, magnifies that, because there's a view that actually the state is a provider. We go back to Clement Attlee – the NHS, the post-war period. And I think you've got to understand this whole issue of vaccines etc. between Europe and the US. Europe will always put safety above freedom, because of the wars. This idea that the state is actually making things more safe for me is something that people actually believe. People were not happy, and some of them revolted, but in the end, even somebody like Boris [Johnson] ended up falling into that because the pressure is too great to go for safety over freedom. And I think Covid was probably the last nail in this whole idea of the stigmatisation of freedom. So now we get to this situation where you've got risk aversion and low investment.

There are other reasons for low investment in my view, which is that capital itself has also lost its weight during that period [since the GFC]. I think there was a sense of Wall Street, capital return, magnification of EPS [earnings per share] accretion, dividends, capital returns are more important than investment in plant and machinery because you can actually get that elsewhere. And higher returns are directly linked to higher compensation, so incentives got somewhat screwed up, not just in the City and Wall Street but also in the corporate world. I'm not saying these are the reasons why investment is less, but I think there's no question in the UK, every statistic you'll see is that investment in the UK in both the public sector and the private sector has been less than anywhere else in the world.

George Osborne highlighted how an outsized City meant the UK was particularly hit by the GFC:

One is the more prosaic economic historian argument that Britain had a very outsized banking sector, so it was particularly hit by the financial crash. And some of the clean-up was not quite as severe as countries that actually went bust like Iceland or Ireland. But nor were we big enough like the US to absorb it and move on. So … if you were an economic historian, you wouldn't be that surprised by UK GDP over the last fifteen years.

Andy Haldane discussed UK underinvestment post-GFC:

> So, interesting fact for you – there has not been a single pound in net terms lent to UK businesses by UK banks since the global financial crisis … We have become very risk-averse off the back of the financial crisis – [a] very risk-averse banking system. It is encouraged – I would say over-encouraged – to be risk-averse … What was right at the time of excessive risk taking – '08 – is not right today, at a time when risk taking is too low rather than too high. There's a risk culture aspect to it, but there's also a missing middle. That is to say there is money for start-ups. The problem comes at the point of scaling up – what's sometimes called the valley of despair – when you try and take your £10 million business to be a £500 million business, to be a £10 billion business.

Andrew Bailey thinks that productivity is a bigger factor behind weak growth than the GFC:

> If you go back to the period before the financial crisis, the potential growth rate of the UK economy was somewhere in the sort of order of 2–2.5 per cent a year. Gordon Brown had a great objective to get it up to 2.5 – and he did for a bit – but it was always in that order. If you look at the period since the financial crisis, it's been in the order of 1 to 1.5, roughly. Covid, obviously, is a very volatile period, but if you look through all of that, it's 1 to 1.5, and that's probably about where it is today. And then if you ask the question, well, what has accounted for that fall? It looks like it's much more productivity than it is labour supply, in terms of the change that fits with a pretty weak investment story … There's a danger in saying what I've just said, that therefore causality is assigned to the financial crisis, and it commonly is in a lot of the commentary. I'm not so convinced about that myself. I'm not suggesting that the financial crisis was good for anything, by the way, and I'm sure it did have a role

to play. But I think if you look at TFP [total factor productivity], for instance, it was probably beginning to come off a bit before the financial crisis.

BREXIT

Some of the interviewees blamed Brexit for the UK's weaker economic performance. Others pointed out that the UK had failed to take advantage of Brexit opportunities.

Boris Johnson considered what should have been done post-Brexit:

We should never have dropped the Planning Bill. Rishi [Sunak] totally watered it down by the end, and it was gone. We should not have dropped the infrastructure plans. We should never have put taxes up in the way that we did … I don't want to blame the Treasury, but I kept waiting for Rishi to kind of pupate into this Lawsonian figure that I thought he was going to be.

What we should have done is put a big 'Invest Here' flag on Britain, and we should have cut corporation tax, or something like that, probably corporation tax below Irish levels, and just said, 'This is it, the Brexit dividend' …

The trouble with Brexit was, it was a great fight, and we won, and it was very, very difficult. But what we didn't do enough was to have a single big 'Buy Here' sign to the rest of the world. You know, we should have. We should have done that …

I kept thinking that Rishi wanted to do things like that, but he was basically just captured by the Treasury. The Treasury hated everything. They hated Brexit. They hated the idea of tax cuts. They hated that they had no plan for growth. They were hopeless. That's right and I think something like that really would have worked, because I remember meeting a bunch of investors in Florida, and they were all saying, you know, 'Brexit is great. We love it. But, you know, what's the big sell?' We didn't have that. And I think given time, we would have done it, but it was not to be.

On Brexit, Rishi Sunak said:

> I voted for it, I supported it, I think it's a good thing. I was always of the view that the benefits of Brexit are lots of incremental things that happen over time, some of which we've done, some of which we haven't done. And that remains my case.
>
> I was rereading my old paper, that one of the benefits of Brexit was having control of trade policy. And as someone who believed in that, that nimbleness was going to be of value in signing new trade deals, I think if we're going to be self-critical as Brexiteers, you have to probably acknowledge, given the world that we're in, where free trade is less of a thing, and actually the world is, for [the] right reasons, focused more on security. That is probably less valuable than we thought it was right at the time. I mean, it's still a good thing and a positive thing. It probably has slightly less value in the world, arguably. But that said, it's helped us with the US and [we've] been able to do this deal with them quicker than others. So, straight away, there's some benefit there.
>
> But I know the benefit of Brexit to me is the regulatory flexibility in a world where innovation drives growth. I always thought that was incredibly valuable. That is not a politically salient argument whatsoever, and will not help anyone win an election, and requires a general argument ... where you can convince a society that if you want a dynamic, capitalist growth-oriented economy, you know that means being pro-innovation and pro-risk. But that requires a cultural mind shift in the UK and communications, which is very tough, right? It's not an argument that is easy to win with the country.

George Osborne said the following should be done now to rectify the Brexit 'rupture':

> There is no doubt ... that Brexit was a massive rupture. And whether you think it was going to lead to better things in the end for the economy, it nevertheless absorbed an enormous amount of time and energy and caused great disruption to trade patterns between the UK and the Continent ...

You've got to sort out the kind of trading relationship with the EU, because that is a mess. And this is not to relitigate Brexit, but in the politics after Brexit, the kind of drive was for the complete separation. And so we actually have a less engaged trading relationship with our largest single bloc than we do with lots of other countries around the world. And that's obviously not sensible. I would step back into all of that mess and say, we've got to have a better kind of trade and services agreement with our European neighbours.

Lord O'Donnell thinks the EU has become more protectionist without the UK:

We have thrown away our wonderful trade deal with our number one trading partner, the EU. I mean – gun, head, shoot – that, to me, is just crazy … My argument always on Brexit was you have to realise that the EU has got all sorts of problems because it's a Franco-German run job. But the one group – and I used to belong to the Economic Financial Committee – that was central banks and treasuries, there we had the free traders. We were the liberalisers … And the EU, without the UK, is a much more protectionist vehicle … Without us, the EU's got worse, no question. And there's no voice in there that's arguing for freer trade and liberalisation of markets.

On rejoining the single market, Sir Vince Cable said:

There are various things which I feel quite strongly about but which are very controversial and would land you in a political dog fight. I think leaving the European single market has imposed major costs, because that was regulatory alignment. It was a very good form of trade liberalisation. It was originally brought in by Margaret Thatcher. She subsequently criticised her own policy, but it actually was very effective in exposing British exporters to more competition and helped with our growth. And I think we've now spent the best part of ten years in an endless argument about, should we be in Europe or not in Europe? Should we be having liberalisation with America or not? Or with China or not?

And Britain is sort of paralysed because we can't get these debates out of our system. You know, people defending historic positions. So, trade policy priorities have got to be [considered, but] it requires a new generation to think about these things anew. That's certainly one very big, difficult area …

If we were being strictly rational in the UK, we would realign ourselves with the European Union's single market and customs union. And we don't have to join Europe politically but having advantage, basically, in the way that the United States has a single market, Canada has a sort of single market, we should be part of that structure. That's certainly my view.

On the idea of either rejoining the EU or working more closely with the United States, Franck Petitgas said:

On the EU, in my view, either we go all the way through with this freaking Brexit thing – which means we are going to do what we talked about with the regulators etc., and we're going to get out of the Court of Justice and all this stuff – or if you're not going to do it, you know what? Rejoin the ******* thing. OK? Because it's a joke. We are paying too much for not being in EU … I think Brexit has been an extremely expensive game for the UK. It's probably one of the biggest, biggest costs, and for no benefit, that's the problem. No benefit is the problem. Get the benefit. Just do something about it … Either you rejoin the EU in some way or we have to do something with America.

COVID

Although the productivity and growth slowdowns date from the GFC, Covid marked an intensification of the drop in the UK's relative performance.

On Covid, and the level of lockdown, Boris Johnson said:

Covid was a total nightmare, and I'm sure that this inquiry[1] will say that the biggest single problem is ... [that the government] were not locking down everybody sooner and harder and, you know, everywhere or not at all. No, that's what they will say. The inquiry will be totally left-wing rubbish, and it will be totally rubbish ...

One of my joys in life is giving speeches to large American audiences. I talked to 800 American cardiologists, you know, doctors, and they all said that lockdown had gone way, way too far. So, you watch this inquiry, they will attack me for not locking down hard enough or soon enough. Yeah, they will, and they will attack me for being too cavalier. That's what they will say.

On the furlough scheme, George Osborne said:

I don't actually think we did the Covid furlough very well ... In the US (not that it was particularly well thought through, because it was kind of two administrations just trying to win elections), they, by sending cheques to everyone, didn't really trap anyone in employment and they allowed a bit of creative destruction. People left jobs and new companies were created and other companies went to the wall ... In the US, it was a kind of straightforward cash support for the fact that a business was shut or the shops were shut. Whereas in the UK, it was a kind of loan that's all very complicated and the furlough scheme for individuals in the UK meant that people were paid to stay in the same job, so when the pandemic ended, it was like you had sort of frozen in aspic the economy for two years and you hadn't allowed, you know, the normal process of company creation and collapse to take place ... It's ironic because I think the furlough scheme is kind of held up as a great kind of British achievement. I understand the kind of requirement for it; I understand the sort of political [reasoning] ...

To begin with, everyone thought, you know, I might die for this thing. I mean, it was pretty scary. But once you had a vaccine – which was in Britain's case being deployed by January 2021 – you should have started to pull back all the programmes and they were allowed to continue, including the monetary easing [which] continued for another year.

On growth under the last Conservative government, pre-Brexit and Covid, one of our interviewees pointed out:

> [In] the post-2010 period, the UK actually performed well. It basically grew as fast as the US and was joint top in the G7 ... From 2016, we pushed ourselves into a period of deep uncertainty for at least three years, and it's clear that the impact of that uncertainty was pretty major, particularly on business investment, and that was probably avoidable had we managed the post-Brexit situation better. But those three years were clearly chaos and had a clear economic impact. And then, just as we're coming out of that period, we're hit by Covid, which obviously is a global shock, but the UK opts for a particularly restrictive version of both lockdowns. And I think that there's a mixed legacy from this, from the kind of the interventions and the furlough scheme, for example, which I think was very innovative and probably was good for human welfare and kept a lot of people in work. But it was very different from the US experience, where the US response to Covid was a very big spike in unemployment, and then in the recovery from Covid a big reallocation of people across roles and industries. The UK effectively froze people in roles and industries with the furlough scheme, and therefore we've had much less [of a] kind of vibrant reallocation and creative destruction process after Covid than the US. So, I think that since 2016, there have been a series of reasons why UK economic performance is impacted by some very idiosyncratic and largely self-inflicted issues, and so it's very hard to use that period as a kind of benchmark for what trend growth could or should be in the UK.

LACK OF AMBITION

George Osborne highlighted our lack of ambition as a country:

> I think the second [reason for low economic growth] has been a kind of lack of ambition ... There's been no consensus on the right that

prioritising enterprise in the economy was the thing that we should do. And we've had all sorts of other objectives, be it sovereignty, or immigration control, or net zero, or whatever it happens to be. And without getting into the politics of all of those different things ... the economy was not put first for a long period by Conservative governments who were in power for almost all of this period. And certainly, you could argue not put first by the Labour government.

LACK OF FAITH IN CAPITALISM AND MARKETS

Lord Wolfson discussed our lack of faith in free markets:

I think the real problem is a lack of faith in free markets and the rule of law as being the primary engines of growth ... I think we've lost faith in the ability of individuals – individual people and individual companies – to create success and talked ourselves into the belief that somehow government intervention is necessary in order to achieve prosperity, when, in my view, quite the reverse is true, in almost all bar one case. That's my starting point: free markets and the rule of law are the bedrock of prosperity. It doesn't guarantee success – in the same way that good health doesn't guarantee happiness – but it's almost impossible to be happy without your health, and it's almost impossible for an economy to be successful without free markets and the rule of law. So, all the things that have been done over the last twenty-five years to undermine free markets and the rule of law are things that have detracted from the UK economy.

I think there are two battles. I think the most important one – which is the one that free market liberals will win eventually – is that actually free markets and the rule of law are not barbaric means of suppressing the poor and serving the rich, which I think is how it's been characterised. And, secondly, that we have the wherewithal already within the global position of the UK economy. We're slap bang in the middle of the world's time zone. Our first language is the world's second language. This should be a successful country, and it's not. And it's one of those terrible features of the British economy that all too often we end up making a problem. We then try to correct the problem and we make the problem worse.

LACK OF APPRECIATION FOR WEALTH CREATORS

On honouring wealth creators, Boris Johnson said:

You won't really get growth out of the UK economy in the way that you've got growth in the United States ... until you change the mindset, because fundamentally, all these things are very important – skills, infrastructure, housing – they're all incredibly important for productivity, but in the end, the big, big switch is psychological, and in the UK, we just don't have the same admiration for wealth creation or the same culture of wealth creation ... You will not find, you know, the scenes at the inauguration of Donald Trump. Whatever you think about them, [they] were an amazing celebration of capitalism and entrepreneurship. I mean those guys, whatever you say about Elon and Zuckerberg and Mr and Mrs Bezos, you know, they came up with brilliant ideas to improve the lives of ordinary people, right, with Amazon and iPhones and God knows what. They're not like Saudi princelings who would be given oil franchises or Russian oligarchs. These are geniuses, right? And we don't have that in the UK. We don't. Part of the reason we don't have that ... is we don't have a culture of honouring them and extolling them ... We don't have that same attitude to wealth creation.

Richard Gnodde said:

There's a culture of envy ... There's a challenged relationship from the, let's say, if I can use these words loosely, the sort of have-nots. Let's say the bottom 5 per cent versus the top 5 per cent. But even between, let's say, the top 5 per cent versus the next 5 per cent down – the next 5 per cent down, they're envious of the top 5 per cent, even though that might be their destination. There's too much looking left and right.

How's everyone else doing? Is it fair or not? As opposed to, this is what it takes to get into that top 5 per cent. Let's get it done. There's an expectation that everyone should be there, but there's no understanding of what it takes. There's no respect for what it takes. The sacrifices. Maybe they took some big risks. Maybe they went bankrupt three times. Maybe a whole lot of stuff happened to them. Maybe they've sacrificed some parts of their life that to you are very important. Better to say, OK, well, I'm happy I did what I did. Good luck to them for doing what they did …

Frankly, I actually think in Europe, many European countries are [in] a different place, because they feel much more comfortable. Actually, with their core value system, which is maybe a bit more socialist. I'm not saying it's a good system, but I think they are more comfortable with where they are. Of course, everyone would rather have more than less. But I think their family structure, their social life, their community – obviously, every country's got its issues – but I think this country is well known for having this issue. The less well-off don't like the rich. Remember, as well as being wealth creators, they are often job creators and capital allocators. Important to have.

Lord Chartres said the following on the Good Samaritan:

The Samaritan was not only a businessman; he was also an outsider, so it would be a Sikh businessman. Lady Thatcher, whom I knew quite well and buried, was notorious for claiming – so her enemies said – that there's no such thing as society. That's nonsense. Of course, she believed utterly in the relationships, the small platoons, the families. What she was objecting to is the idea that there was some extraordinary amorphous body somewhere, and you could, as a society, say to people, look, live precisely as you choose to live, follow your bent, follow your will and we will pay the bill for the disasters. Now, no society is rich enough to issue that invitation, but that is precisely the invitation [that] will be issued: live as you will, and we will pay the bill for the disasters. That's insane and will be unsustainable very soon.

LOW PRODUCTIVITY

All the current or ex-Bank of England interviewees and Vince Cable (who worked as a professional economist before going into full-time politics) focused on the UK's weak productivity.

Andy Haldane discussed underinvestment and low productivity being the reason for low growth:

> When it comes to the recipe for growth, I am of the view that the recipe for growth is in some respects quite similar to the recipe for baking a cake. In other words, if it is to be done successfully, you need to combine a range of ingredients in the right proportions, mixed in the right way. So, people say, what is the single most important thing that could be done to get growth going? … It's a bit like saying what is the single most important ingredient when baking a cake? [When] the single most important ingredient [is] missing, the cake doesn't rise. And when I turn that metaphor to the UK plc, we are short on a number of the raw ingredients which have yet to be brought together into a coherent recipe … I think the ingredients of which the UK is short are fairly well known, and … in some ways, this is no more than taking us through the arithmetic of a standard growth model.
>
> We have underinvested structurally in physical capital for the greater part of thirty years. One diagnostic on that will be that the capital stock per worker here in the UK is about half the size it is in France or Germany, and that's the fruits or forbidden fruits of thirty years of investing significantly less than those and many other G7 countries. That underinvestment problem is not distinctive or unique to the public or private sector. We have sat below the investment levels of our competitors along both the public investment and private investment … The arithmetic of that is, if you have your average worker operating with a suboptimal supply of capital, they will be less productive. And that is part of the story of UK plc, we invested too little. Our capital stock is too low relative to international competitors, and that has been a significant contributor to our productivity malaise.

Productivity, as best we can tell, has been crabbing sideways for the better part of two decades, and to some extent that's a global phenomenon, but we have underperformed even our international competitors and the US very significantly so over that period. That is, to some significant extent, a story of physical capital. It's not entirely a story of physical capital, because mirroring that has been underinvestment in our human capital as well as the skills and experience of our workforce. Again, the numbers are very revealing. We sit towards the bottom of the G7 and OECD tables when it comes to the investment we're making in people – education, skills and healthcare ...

Within the skills bucket, the biggest deficiencies exist for those who don't go to university – the half of young people who don't go to university that are developing vocational as distinct from academic skills. Our education skills system is two lanes. It's bifurcated. There is a fast lane and there is a slow lane ... The bifurcation starts early in the educational life, but it manifests itself most obviously at age eighteen in the half of young people who go to university – they're, to a significant extent, on the educational high road. And those that don't who, by and large, then find themselves on the educational low road. We have a well-developed path for those that go through university and graduate ... but for those that don't go, vocational training and skills pathways are far fewer, far less well developed and there's been far less investment in them over at least fifty years, and that manifests itself in a low skill base and therefore low levels of productivity and low levels of pay for people in that category. So, when I tell the story of the UK, I can tell a story of two people, those on the educational fast lane and those on the educational slow lane.

When considering the distribution of productivity in the UK across businesses, Andy Haldane said:

That too is rather bifurcated. We have a large upper tail of high-productivity businesses. There's one dimension at the very beginning. They have levels of productivity that stand very favourable in comparison with our international competitors. In fact, that upper tail and levels of productivity is sometimes 30 per cent above the upper tail in France, Germany, the US, which begs the obvious question, how can it be then that average productivity levels in the UK are 20–30 per cent below those self-same countries? The answer is, because we have an offsetting long tail of businesses where productivity is slow, low and stalled – a long and lengthening tail of those businesses which mirrors the bifurcated pattern we've seen in skills as well.

The third dimension of this is the spatial dimension. In other words, where they're located – if they're located in some places where productivity is high and rising, which tend to be those places where the high-skilled workers live and where the high-productivity businesses are located, or on the flip of that are the places without those things.

There are always shades of grey within that picture – the tale of two workers, a tale of two companies, a tale of two cities – but it's not the worst way of thinking about how it is we've found ourselves in this position.

On the role of tech in productivity and growth, Andrew Bailey said, 'We, like many other countries, have got a population that is, on average, ageing, so in terms of contribution to labour supply, we are not going to see a major change on that front, then the importance of productivity growth becomes even greater.'

In terms of productivity and low private sector investment, Clare Lombardelli highlighted:

The lack of growth and the lack of productivity is obviously the driver of many of the problems that we see, but it's actually broader ... This has been the thing that has constrained real living standards and, over the long period, gives a sense that 'no longer do we see each generation doing better than the previous' ... This is not a UK-specific problem. If you look across advanced economies, the outlier is the US. Other advanced economies, certainly of a decent size, have all got the same, right, which is very, very low productivity growth. And it's the US that is the outlier ... Those are countries that have very different sizes of the state, investment in the private sector, investment in the public sector, skills and talent policies, immigration policy and all of that. So you've got to say that this isn't just about the role of government in both its size and its nature; it's about broader things ... I actually think the pre-global financial crisis period for the UK, the ten to twenty years running up to that, was unusual, and that was more of an outlier, because that was when you saw this ICT adoption happening ... There's a question about, can you sustainably get back to that level now? There's a set of questions about new technologies [like] AI, and there will be a surge with adoption. But I do think that pre that period was when we were really seeing most firms adopting ICT; you can only replace your production line once.

If you break down productivity into various different ways of looking at the economy ... [and] compare manufacturing and services, this is very interesting. So even in the US at the moment, it's not manufacturing productivity that's increasing, it's services productivity that's increasing. Now, you would think that's a very good story for the UK, because we're a very high-service economy. And if that's where you can see the growth, there's potential there. I do think there are a few things where you look at the UK compared to other countries that are worth drawing out and will play a role. It's very hard to attribute causation, but we do tend to have lower levels of private sector investment than other countries, and this has been going on for a very long time ... And some of that will, no doubt, be about incentives, but a lot of it will be about culture.

If you look at the way in which business, government [and] citizens interact in, say, Germany or other European countries with higher levels of private sector investment, they are a bit different. But we do see consistently lower levels of private sector investment in the UK. There's a really interesting discussion about adoption. The UK is actually at the technology frontier ... but a lot of firms are not. And so there's a real question about innovation, the adoption of technology ... There's also, if you break it down, some really interesting questions about firm size ... Large firms tend to be more productive. They tend to do more investment. The UK has a lot of small firms. A lot of micro firms [find it a] lot harder to do investment, to be adopting from frontier technologies and those sorts of things. I mean, some do, some small firms are unbelievably innovative. Of course, everyone starts as a small firm, but I do think there's some interesting questions there. But I would say this is very much not a UK-specific problem. It is an advanced economy problem. And in a way, you expect it, right? This is convergence. This is what you sort of expect.

Vince Cable highlighted that underlying growth is consistent and falling productivity has resulted in low growth:

I started my life teaching economics in the late '60s, early '70s, and [even then] books were appearing on why Britain grows so slowly relative to Japan, Germany, Italy and so on, and the debate has continued over the years. I think... the slightly depressing conclusion which I drew is that even when you've had radical changes of government with a very different political agenda – we had highly interventionist governments that believed in five-year planning in the 1960s, and then in the '80s, we had Margaret Thatcher with a totally different approach – the unnerving conclusion is actually that the underlying rate of growth didn't change in one iota. And particularly the productivity, which most economists look at, total factor productivity, remained on a very steady, unchanging trend for about fifty years, and then there was a sudden kink in 2008 when any growth in productivity stopped, and we've effectively ground to a halt since 2008.

WORKLESSNESS

Worklessness is, of course, both a cause and a consequence of slow growth. Our interviewees commented on both.

Lord Cameron said:

Growth does include, for instance, fundamental welfare reform. You can't grow the economy if you've got 8 million people on out-of-work benefits, who otherwise could work. So welfare is a fundamental productivity issue. And the other thing I think Conservatives should do is never talk about immigration without talking about welfare. Because, of course, one of the reasons we keep having to suck in more people is that we are leaving 8 million of our own working-age citizens not working. So, to me, welfare is one of the really big growth issues. We won't grow the economy if we're leaving a large part of our country out of work.

Boris Johnson said, 'In my view, you need to study the [tax cuts which] have the most powerful incentives. But the burden is far too high, and the reward for not working is also too high.'

On the UK's worklessness post-Covid, Lord O'Neill commented:

At the most basic, it depends on the growth of the labour force. A particular problem that we've had since Covid, which is bizarrely unique to the UK, [is that] we've lost nearly a million people out of the workforce. It's a staggering [and] arguably should be the number one policy issue at the moment. Unfortunately, I don't think there's a lot of real, objective evidence as to precisely why, but it's pretty weird, because no other G7 countries [have] got so much worklessness …

Most conventional economists would say our growth trend would be two, two and a quarter-ish. And over that period [during the Blair government], we actually averaged that, but it was all because of huge labour force growth and productivity was extremely weak. Since Covid, we've got both. We've got dreadful productivity and a declining workforce. You couldn't make it up to be any worse … But the fundamental new problem is the labour force itself … The actual and probably, dare I say, self-perception of mental health. Self-diagnosis of mental health has grown. The way society has developed is seemingly … like a lot of people struggle more about stuff and, secondly, linked to aspects of the welfare system, are able to declare themselves as suffering from mental health, therefore subject to benefits or welfare payments. I think it's greatly involved with the interplay of those things myself and other things that are legacies of that have become more specific about state handouts, that have grown more through time. Classic stuff, people find it less rewarding to work for low value-added jobs … I don't know if it's an important policy focus as it should be, but if I were driving things, I'd have loads of people working on it.

On worklessness, Lord Clarke said:

The thing they do have to tackle is the welfare system, which gives incentives to people who stay out of work, if you feel like it, if you find the whole idea of having a job boring. Having to go to the same place at nine o'clock every morning, just as if it was a school. Being in trouble if you're late. You can't leave until five o'clock. And then, as long as you work out how to get your PIP and your incapacity benefits, you'll wind up on about the same as you'd get if you did that job on a minimum wage. So you've got to think there's some other good reason for doing it. My opinion is that there are other good reasons for doing it, in the national interest and in the point of view of the person. I think it has a tremendous effect on the motivation and lifestyle and ambitions of a person to have a job. But even the most miserably routine job can lead on to other things and keeps you in social contact with other people. These youngsters are settling down to a lifetime of not working. Too high a proportion become quite a problem for society as a whole. You've always had families like that, and unless they do something to get the financial incentives restored to get into work, as opposed to living on benefits, the terrible problem will continue. How can you do it without damaging the genuinely permanently incapable and incapacitated for whom these quite generous systems were quite rightly designed? We are going to have problems when the newspapers find an individual who's blind and got one leg, who's lost so much a year because he somehow can't satisfy the PIP tests, because he's less likely to know where to find the answers to the telephone questions on the internet. The eighteen-year-old lad who's competing with him will know exactly where to find the right answers.

On where the government should start politically, Richard Chartres said:

I think we start with immense sympathy for the 987,000 [young NEETs (not in education, employment or training)]. I'm just thinking in very practical terms, of course, because I think that there are groups of people now who are alive to the insanity of the way in which we're living and are banding together to do something else and to live as best they can, in a rather negative environment. But I think generally and politically, hammering home the fate of the 987,000 with the greatest sympathy [is of great importance]. Nobody's attacking them, but they are actually the fruit of the society we've built. I think there's a present opportunity to actually demand that we reflect on something, and it's right at the heart of this welfare debate that the Prime Minister is having. At the moment, he's rowing back from some of his social welfare reforms because there is huge opposition in the Labour Party. Now is the moment to really spread stories, do inquiries, do research into how the fifth of a whole generation came to be in the situation that we know they're in. I think that we need an immense amount of telling reportage – statistics don't move people – [and] on the whole, academic research into why these things are. We need some very vivid examples of the tragedy that is unfolding before us now. We need filmmakers. 'Cathy Come Home' was a famous film which prompted the conscience of a whole generation and caused us to think about victims, the vulnerable. That's very good. What we need to do now is talk about something that's much less popular – the waste of people who aren't free but actually have been given a deluded vision of what freedom is.

HIGH TAXATION

By far the most widely quoted specific cause of low growth cited was high taxation.

On tax complexity and uncertainty, Richard Gnodde said:

I think the tax system here is a combination of at least two things. It is way, way, way too complicated. And the tax burden is just way too high. I talk to global entrepreneurs, because they spend more time focused on the nuts and bolts of this stuff, and the complexity of the tax system here is just crazy. That's just its operation. And then, secondly, it's too burdensome, obviously.

When asked if it is adversarial, Gnodde replied:

> Well, first of all, I think it's uncertain. So, I'm an oil company. Russia/
> Ukraine happens, or something happens. I have one or two bumper
> years, and then, out of nowhere, I get a windfall energy tax. Or the
> banks, there's a special bank tax. You're never sure if you're actually
> really having a good period in an after-tax sense. Well, those guys can
> afford it now, so we're going to have a special one-off. Maybe it's not a
> one-off but a windfall tax or a levy. So it's adversarial in that sense.
>
> Two, I think it's retroactive. They're always tinkering. And I think that's
> both from an individual's point of view but also from a corporation's point
> of view. I mean, there's one thing making a decision, knowing that you're
> operating in a high tax environment; it's another thing operating in that
> environment. And you think you've actually made some after-tax income,
> and then suddenly it turns out not to be after-tax income, because they
> change the rules on you. That is definitely adversarial, yes.

Sir Jeremy Hunt highlighted the need for tax cuts:

> I am a believer that high growth needs lower taxes. And there are lots of
> economists who say it depends what the taxes are, and if you increase
> VAT or income tax, that is not as damaging as increasing business taxes.
> But there are two reasons why I fundamentally believe that you need
> lower taxes. First of all, because, by definition, lower taxes by the state
> means a bigger private sector, and a private sector is the engine that cre-
> ates wealth. That's one really important reason. And the second reason
> is a cultural one, that basically lower tax societies are more dynamic
> because they send a signal to people that you will be able to keep more
> of the fruits of your efforts.

Even Sir Tony Blair, a Labour Prime Minister, argued that if you look at
the levels of direct taxation for people, they're really very high, and in
historical terms, they'd be considered extremely high, and people feel
they're getting taxed highly.

He pointed out that the state spends quite a lot of money, and the outcomes aren't good. There is a real desire to untie that knot. And he thinks, in the future, we've got to end up with much lower rates of taxation.

He concluded that the single thing that we could do to change the way people look at growth is around the taxation system and to re-educate people that there is a work incentive aspect to taxation that can't be ignored. He also pointed out that the need for incentives meant also looking at the welfare system and that the economies that are emerging as successful are where they're much more looking at taxation.

On Rachel Reeves picking the wrong tax rise, Ken Clarke said:

The global economy is in crisis, so Rachel's problems are huge. I had high hopes for Rachel, but so far, she's doing very badly. She had to raise taxes and control public spending when she came in – just as I did, just as Geoffrey Howe did, and he started on the margin – but she chose the wrong tax. And she's decided to carry on borrowing a lot so she can call it investment. This is why I don't think she's making very much progress.

HIGH SPENDING

Most interviewees linked high tax rates with high spending.

David Cameron looked at the need for spending control:

Part of it will have to be tight public spending control. I'm a fiscal conservative, because ultimately you've got to grow the economy faster than you're growing public spending. You've got to hold back public spending, and you've got to have a balance, and that will help you to cut taxes.

On the causes of high spending, Boris Johnson said:

We've more or less flatlined since '08, unlike the United States of America, and we have a situation in which the state is pre-empting the biggest share of national income since the end of the Second World War ...

We've been through the nightmare of Covid, which necessitated, according to all expert opinion, a massive expansion in the size of the functions of the state, and we haven't got back out of it at all. And we are still spending prodigious amounts on welfare, which we haven't properly reformed. And there's no doubt that the animal spirits of Britain's entrepreneurs are being choked and restrained.

Lord Lamont focused on the need to restrain spending to cut the national debt:

The starting point, I think, has got to be that the country is hugely indebted – nearly 100 per cent, or about 100 per cent of GDP forecast, with a projection on certain assumptions from the OBR that by 2070, it could be 270 per cent of GDP. I mean, that is a terrifying extrapolation. Now, there are all sorts of reasons why it probably won't happen, but it still concentrates the mind, so I think the first priority in economic policy has to be stability and financial probity. And people don't like this, and they think, 'Oh, well, we can get rid of the constraints of debt to GDP, just by growing it'll go away.' But actually, the whole time you play that game – and Liz Truss played it a bit – you are exposed to risk, and I think the bond markets have become a more important factor than they have been for some years. So I'm certainly not against growth, obviously, and I'm not against tax cuts to get growth, but I do believe in balanced public finances and the reduction of debt. Even Reeves is right in saying, stability has to come before anything else. The trouble was, she was talking a lot of nonsense about instability that didn't really exist and exaggerated the problems she had. But no, I do very strongly think this, that a lot of people just think there's a self-financing, easy route to growth, and I don't think it is.

Where does growth come from? Well, I think the traditional conservative view is the right one. Growth comes from a myriad of things, but it comes primarily from individuals, from companies, from someone with ideas. Mrs Thatcher once said, 'The purpose of the Conservative Party was to advance extraordinary people.' Well, maybe a rather bold way of putting it, but I think there's something in that, and it doesn't come from the state. Growth doesn't come from the state by and large. And so what we've got to find are the ways that we incentivise and encourage. It's not just incentives; it's a cultural thing as well.

On the pressure for higher spending, Ken Clarke said:

The reasons we don't get [growth at 2–3 per cent] is because it's absolutely essential that you borrow another 100 billion or so for investment
in infrastructure (so-called), [by] which you mean investment in seats,
where Reform is a close second to Labour. Levelling up is a desirable
economic policy itself if they can keep it to infrastructure, and it doesn't
leave the silly local political gimmicks that the local politicians insist on
spending it on. It won't do that much harm, but it's no good pretending
that it doesn't create a borrowing problem in a phase when all the public
services are screaming out for more money and lobbying in a way they
always do …

I'm sure the main problem here is you cannot continue to run substantial deficits every year when you're already at about 100 per cent of
GDP total debt and rising with high interest rates … [Reeves] needs to
have a 1981 Budget or two, and be backed by her Prime Minister, and I
think he will. None of her colleagues will back her, but the naysayers
were slaughtered.

Richard Chartres said the following on the size of government:

It's perfectly clear that one of the ways in which we play the electoral
game here is by employing the electorate in a vast number of bureaucracies. I've seen figures that suggest the government employs more people
north of the Humber than the government employed in Bulgaria in the
worst days of the communist dictatorship. So you've got the expansion of
the inspectorate office jobs at the expense of … the personal energy, the
delight that comes in well-run small businesses. But, of course, almost
everything that has happened very recently is extremely discouraging
to small businesses – not only the tax burden but also the Employment
Rights Bill, which I personally think will be very deleterious for small

businesses. So I delight in small businesses. We need more and more of them, and there are people with gumption and abilities, and it ought to be easier to employ people and easier to say goodbye to them when they don't fit. It ought to be positively encouraged to invest in apprenticeships, whereas now, if you do take them seriously, people go off somewhere else. It isn't very cost-effective for a small business to think about apprenticeships, so there are all sorts of problems there which can actually be susceptible to legislative means. But unfortunately, we seem to be going in the other direction, that the only employment that is really growing is the machine: is the inspectorate, is the surveillance state, is the extraordinarily regulated state – unbelievable. So if you want growth, I wouldn't be putting all your eggs in multiplying the bureaucracies.

OVERREGULATION

There were numerous comments about the impact of regulation. On reforming regulation, Simon Wolfson said:

On regulation, everyone wants a bonfire of regulations. My view is that with a few limited exceptions, that plan will never ever deliver anything … I want a moratorium on all new regulation for five years … Because actually coping with existing regulation, the vast majority of regulation is about form, not substance. And once you've written systems and got people sat there filling out the forms, it's not that expensive. The big problem with regulation is adapting to new regulation, so stemming the flow of new regulation would be enormously beneficial.

Tony Blair also pointed out the problems caused by regulation and the House of Lords, arguing that he had found that the government is constantly regulating, and if you turn away for a minute, you would find someone somewhere is putting another piece of regulation in place.

He liked the idea of measuring it against a North Star. He had tried to do a kind of omnibus bill around deregulation. He pointed out that the House of Lords could also be a real problem; because no political party had a majority there, it's sometimes quite hard for a government to drive their policy through both Houses.

ECONOMIC HISTORY 101

Former Chancellor Ken Clarke gave a compelling overview of the UK economic growth since the 1990s, and the significant difference before and after the global financial crisis:

> I followed Norman Lamont, and Black Wednesday, and I was remarkably orthodox in my economic policy. I'd been on the Economic Affairs Committee of governments. I've been at Employment, I've been at DTI [the Department of Trade and Industry] and I stuck to the basic principles, a pretty orthodox fiscal policy aimed to balance the Budget over the cycle. I think the economic cycle was inevitable, which meant you raised rates once growth looked like [it was] turning into a boom, and you lowered rates once it slowed down or looked like it was turning to a bust, and I followed that consistently. I also used monetary policy solely for the purpose of controlling inflation and because of the background circumstances and things that were going on internationally.
>
> It sounds very straightforward and simple, but the politics, of course, is the whole point of the job of Chancellor of the Exchequer – you're constantly under political pressures and demands as you react to unexpected events to deviate from those basic principles. I didn't deviate, and the result was that John Major's government should have won the '97 election, because the only subject we led on was the economy, and 'the economy, stupid' is usually what determines elections. But unfortunately, the party and the Cabinet had caused so many other problems for John that we were thrown out. And in order to make sure that they were going to win, Blair and Brown simply killed off our attempts to campaign on our economic success by simply saying they wouldn't change anything. And Gordon stuck to that. He borrowed and spent a bit more money than I would have done, but he stuck basically to the same principles. And the whole thing, I think, was the great normality, the period

some have called the Clarke/Brown chancellorship. And sadly, it came to an end with the 2008 financial crash. It wasn't really Gordon's fault. It was mainly the bizarre, absurd, disgraceful behaviour in the American markets. And I think Western economies – most of them, certainly ours – have never recovered from the 2008 crash.

No one has ever succeeded in reverting to fiscal responsibility, combined with monetary policy now exercised by the Bank of England. We've been hit by things that have kept the economy stagnant and in constant damage. We've had Covid, we've had Brexit, we've had the Russians' invasion of Ukraine, the breakdown in the rules-based international order, which we were putting together in the 1990s in trade and economic policies, and the WTO [World Trade Organization] came along in my time with all that, and we remain in an extremely fragile, dangerous position. Meanwhile, successive governments have piled up debt. I used to tease my Eurosceptic critics behind me by pointing out that I stuck to the Maastricht criteria, and I used to defend them, saying it's not because I'm a Europhile, it's because they're basic economic common sense if you believe in free markets – 60 per cent of GDP total debt, never more than the 3 per cent annual deficit. They're among my firm rules, I would say, and I gave Budgets saying I have met them. And the idea that you could have a level of debt in most of the countries in the Western world you have now [was unthinkable]. The dominant problem we are facing, among many at the moment, is that we are in a debt crisis, [with] constant fragility and danger in the financial markets. One day, we'll get back to common sense, but I am quite fearful of the present situation.

CHAPTER 14

THE POLITICAL REASONS
FOR LOW GROWTH

The previous chapter gave interviewees' views of the economic reasons for low growth. But our interviewees also had views on the political issues that affect economic decisions. Some of their comments related to the constrains imposed by operating from a democracy rather than an autocracy. But many of the others related to how government works at both the political level and the official level. The quotes below summarise the key points.

GROWTH IN A DEMOCRATIC
SOCIETY VS AN AUTOCRACY

Lord Hammond highlighted that politicians know how to generate growth but prioritise electoral success:

> I quote Jean-Claude Juncker, who said that almost all politicians in Europe know what needs to be done, they just don't know how to get re-elected after they've done it. And that's the problem with the UK economy ... Over the years, we've built up layer upon layer upon layer of, if you like, varnish over our economy, which stops it from breathing, stops it from functioning properly, but every layer of that varnish creates vested interests, whether they're benefit recipients, professionals enjoying protected status, who will fight to the death to avoid it being stripped away. And in a democracy, that gives you a problem, because you can only do what you need to do with the consent of the electorate. Actually, in a parliamentary system, it's even worse than that. You, first of all, can only do it with the consent of your own backbenchers who are

busy looking at the views of the electorate, their electorate in particular. I think the Chinese would say that what they have done could not have been done in a democratic system. They can bulldoze, sometimes literally, roadblocks to economic growth. We have to negotiate every single step of the way with the electorate ...

Political parties, by their nature, try to survive and get re-elected. And clearly telling people harsh truths, except in very specific circumstances, doesn't get you re-elected ... Our hole is deep, both in terms of taxation and in terms of incentives not to work or to be able not to work. And it isn't obvious how you can reverse that within the democratic consensus. Political realism: you don't get elected by telling people hard truths, it's as simple as that. Everybody says politicians should be more honest, and then when you're honest with them, they say, 'I'm not voting for you.'

Boris Johnson highlighted the link between voting and higher government spending:

We are facing a very serious problem because it looks as though democracies cannot deal with the consequences of the franchise that they created, because the franchise wants ever greater public spending, and it's not economically advisable, and so that's why – back to the cultural point – the first and most important job is to educate people about things like the Laffer curve but also about wealth creation and the primacy of wealth creation. Unless you have that, unless you throw that psychological switch, all the rest of the stuff is going to be for nought.

When asked whether you can have growth in a modern democracy, Jim O'Neill said:

[This is] something I've thought about a lot ... I think they can have [growth] for periods ... I have observed over the forty years of my professional career, and the thirty years of it really following China closely. They can tackle big things that hit them so much easier than we can. It looks to me like they might have dealt with their property crisis way better than Japan. Name me a democracy that's dealt with an overvalued property issue well. I think the only one that I'm aware of that has done is Singapore, which isn't really a democracy. So I find that very interesting. You know, most people in the States knew that was an idiotically overvalued housing market, but did anybody want to really try and do anything about it? ... So I think there is definitely something that makes it easier, if you're not a democracy, to identify and just think, you know, we can see that, unless we deal with that, there's going to be a problem ... I don't know whether you call this democracy or not, but I always thought the buy-in with the Chinese people was that we don't really care about this nonsense. If you let us aspire, and we can have our families, wealth, income and health doubling every decade, we don't care. So there's an implicit buy-in – whatever you idiots want to do with the system, we're fine. And the dilemma is that it is now threatened by the scale of this control. I think it's very unstable.

On growth in a democracy, David Giampaolo said:

I think the time has come where you have to ask the question, what is democracy? What is the question of democracy? What is the definition of democracy? I think you have to start there ... We're being boiled like a frog ... How do companies go bust? They go bust slowly, and then quickly. The number of people I speak to who have no idea the true perilous state of the country, the finances, the deficit, its inability to fund itself, its inability to grow its way out etc. – they'll only find out when the lights go off ... These things are rarely linear. You have tipping points, and tipping points go in both directions. You can have good ones and bad ones. But I'm thirty-five years here. I came here with a suitcase and knew no one, and I do mean no one, and I came for a couple of years with an entrepreneurial idea and a little backing to bring health and fitness to this country, and I got really lucky – right place, right time. Unbelievable work ethic. And I stayed because I like it. I stayed. I met a girl. I stayed. I had a couple of kids, and I've been here thirty-five years, and I've created other businesses. But I'm looking y'all in the eyes, and I'm telling you I'm remarried for ten years, and my wife and I are having conversations that never happened before, about where are we going to live? Are we going to stay here? And that's tragic.

THE BRITISH STATE

Former Prime Minister Liz Truss, who challenged the 'system' and suffered the system's revenge, is eloquent on its role in the UK's decline:

I think the problem in Britain has been over 100 years in the making. That's how bad the situation is. And it was really the Northcote–Trevelyan so-called 'reforms' of the 1850s that brought in the permanent bureaucracy. That is where the start of Britain's economic problems were. Even by the early twentieth century, we had an elite in Britain whose number-one focus wasn't the prosperity of the people of Britain. Their focus was on things like prestige. It was on the sort of moral value of the British idea, but it was not on how do we ensure the future prosperity of the people of Britain? And I think what has transpired since is a continuation and development of that mistaken ethos that really started in the nineteenth century. And one of the key moments it got worse was the establishment of permanent bureaucracy.

I think it got a lot worse after the Second World War, and in particular the establishment of the National Health Service, the Beveridgian welfare state, as well as the Town and Country Planning Act 1947 which is probably, I think, the most economically damaging piece of legislation that has ever been passed. And obviously I haven't really gone into things like the nationalisation of industry and all those kinds of things that happened, but that sort of socialist idea of state planning still has not been removed from the British system.

Looking back at the Thatcher government, I think that did enough to unleash certain aspects of the economy to keep the whole failed model going for longer. This is no criticism of Mrs Thatcher, because I don't think that the Establishment of this country would have allowed this to happen, but she didn't fundamentally return Britain to having the ability for businesses of all natures to thrive. And, in fact, by unleashing the City, what we've created is the financialisation of the economy, which actually enabled a lot of things to be covered up, like the decline in manufacturing, the decline in other areas of service industries etc.

Things got even worse in the 1990s. Mrs Thatcher actually started creating some of these terrible government agencies, but the quangofication of Britain was turbo-charged by Tony Blair and Gordon Brown. Whether it was outsourcing the monetary policy to the so-called independent Bank of England, i.e. unaccountable Bank of England, whether it was the Migration Advisory Committee, the Climate Change Committee, that essentially parcelled out different bits of economic responsibility to different organisations, not to mention the regulators. There are, even according to the government, about 440 quangos – quasi-autonomous non-governmental bodies – most of which have some kind of economic role.

What Labour also did is put the Civil Service Code on a statutory footing. It was previously enshrined in secondary legislation, but it became primary legislation. So Gordon Brown hard-wired the bureaucracy. Of course, [George] Osborne made that even worse with the creation of the Office for Budget Responsibility, which outsourced fiscal policy.

One of the things I would say from my experience in office is all of these bodies got more and more powerful, and they've actually started co-opting the private sector. For example, the Bank of England pays huge rates of interest to the commercial banks. The commercial banks are now dependent on the Bank of England. So this has created a sort of orthodoxy where nobody wants to challenge the system, because they are part of the system. So whether it's green energy companies, whether it's commercial banks, whether it's housing organisations, all of these companies have become dependent on the state. So even though officially, Britain spends 44 per cent of GDP on the state, I think a lot more of our GDP is actually controlled by the state, and so you've essentially got a massive set of vested interests.

And the big challenge in Britain, which I tried to deal with, is how on earth do you take them on? This is not a neutral thing, where you've just got to persuade people, you've got to roll the pitch. These people are fighting for their entire existence, and believe me, they're prepared to fight extremely dirty.

VESTED INTERESTS

Truss also pointed out that the 'system' is backed up by vested interests. But she wasn't the only former Prime Minister to point this out.

On policies vs politics, Liz Truss said:

> The problem isn't the policies. I could tell you what the policy should be in five minutes. We all know what the policy should be. That's not the problem. The problem is, why has Britain for the last 150 years pursued the wrong policies? And the answer is, it's not just people are wrong-headed. There are vested interests who are benefiting from bad policies being pursued, and those are the people that are going to fight like hell.

Tony Blair pointed out how vested interests made change difficult, making the point that every time you try to make a change, you've got various vested interests that will stand in the way. He argued that there's always an anxiety that anything that's about reducing taxes is necessarily going to be regressive rather than progressive and people would not see the bigger picture – that the most progressive thing you can do is have a really well-functioning economy.

On Budget lollipops, Gus O'Donnell commented:

> This is the reason I'm here. I think this is a magnificent project. I think this is really, really important. And I think you're talking to someone, if I could be blunt, who's failed. Because in the years I've been in the Treasury, we've written the same papers multiple times, and we've had Conservatives/Labour/coalitions, and generally the problems are much the same. I go from my first Chancellor – Nigel Lawson – all the way through, basically. It goes back to Jim Mirrlees's paper on tax reform – you know, broader base, lower rates, just fundamentally simple. Every

single Budget we get lollipops, what Chancellors call lollipops – a special exemption for this or special tax relief. If you look at the back of the Treasury document [at] the tax reliefs, it's billions, absolutely billions. Evaluation of those, approximately zero.

When asked how this happens, O'Donnell continued:

Because every time you put papers to Chancellors – whatever kind – these things involve losers, and the losers scream, and the winners keep quiet. And politically, it's incredibly hard to get them to move on those things … And so you get things where, basically, they do things which most of us would say were pretty crazy, short-term political gains. I mean, winter fuel allowance – classic. Gordon Brown kept it as quiet as possible for as long as possible, because you knew that once you do these things, it's very hard to take them away. I think we've observed the problems that happened. So there's this ratchet [and] you get a bad policy, and it's so hard to kill bad policies. It's so hard to kill bad projects.

MEMBERS OF PARLIAMENT

Senior ministers, businesspeople and officials believe that lack of understanding of economics among MPs and indeed elsewhere in government is a serious problem.

On the lack of foundational understanding of economics, Tony Blair pointed out that there was a lot of basic ignorance among the political class as to what the facts are around tax, spending and growth and the relationship between all of them. He thought that there was an absence of what he called foundational facts, where people take a step back and look at the system from first principles and say, 'Well, what are we actually trying to achieve here, and what's the best way of achieving it?'

In terms of MPs acting as a brake on growth, Rishi Sunak commented:

The political system that we're in is responsive to people wanting to prioritise other things over growth – [and it] is a big roadblock. That

manifests itself with individual MPs. We are, in general, a lightly regulated country. Of course we can make improvements, but on any international index, we're going to come towards the better end of that. The
one exception is planning. There's a lot of focus on housing, for obvious
reasons, but from an economic growth perspective, I've never been massively persuaded that building more houses will add to GDP every year
– more construction activity is more labour mobility etc. It's all good.
It's not a bad thing for growth. But the bigger reason planning blocks
long-term sustainable growth is infrastructure and those types of developments, and again, that is a political system and a devolved planning
system where everyone in their area is like, 'No, I don't want the HS2
carving up my garden, thanks very much. Please put it underground.'

On MPs' knowledge of economics, Gus O'Donnell observed:

I think more understanding among MPs of the basic economics would
be great. There's no training to be an MP ... These are basic truths we're
talking about ... You can have nuances around them – the right and the
left – but basic stuff, I think, would be really important, because they are
the decision-makers.

Sir John Rose commented on the business knowledge of people in
government:

One of the things I found really interesting early on, and it's really clear
today, is that, essentially, government doesn't understand business.
There isn't a single businessperson in the Cabinet or among the ministers in the current government. When Brown was Prime Minister, I
literally went to his office and took him through a presentation on how
businesses make decisions – what influences their investment decisions,
employment decisions and so on. Because he had no idea – he came
up through politics. Civil servants are very similar. Occasionally, you
get a businessman who goes in as an appointee, and his only point of
influence is about the minute before he makes the decision to be an
appointee, because after that, you've got no constituency, so you get

ignored. So the introduction of businessmen into the system has been poorly handled, I think. So there's an education process required.

PARLIAMENT

A number of interviewees made the point that compared with a presidential system (the interviews were carried out in the aftermath of President Trump's whirlwind reforms in the first months of his second presidency), a parliamentary system constrained ministers.

On pushing things through Parliament, David Cameron said:

The best bit of Trump is that he had a set of plans that had been rolled out through executive orders. He probably pushed it further than he was able to, but it was the most successful bit. We need to have an equivalent to that now. It should be easier, because you can pass through Parliament things much quicker than you could ever get through Congress, and in our Parliament, we don't have earmarks – you get in very little pork in Britain or anything like that.

The British constitution can be summed up in eight words: What the King enacts in Parliament is law. That's it. That's the constitution. So it should be possible with emergency legislation and everything else. It's got to go through both Houses, it's signed by the King, that's it. But it's no good unless you've worked out what the actual impediments are. What are the things holding back growth? Well, there's an inability to build infrastructure, an inability to build houses, an inability to employ, an inability to reform, get people off welfare and into work, the difficulties of getting investment underway, the difficulties of raising capital etc. All the different things. And under each one, you have your plan for the things we're going to change to make it happen.

Once you start in government, once you're in the system, you're going to be covered in, 'Oh, Prime Minister, come and meet this person. Come and do that, and come and share this.' And this is why you've got to have a plan that you can roll into government with a really clear idea of who's going to do what.

On how Parliament makes things difficult, Jeremy Hunt said:

> I think there are two big constraints that you cannot avoid. One of them is the requirement for a parliamentary majority to get Budgets passed by the House of Commons and laws through the House of Commons. This is the constraint that tripped up Keir Starmer [on welfare reform], and that is just a requirement in a democracy, that you can pass your laws.

Rishi Sunak said the following on how he effectively operated without a parliamentary majority:

> Many things I would like to have done I did not have the space to do because all of these things are incredibly hard and require an enormous amount of political capital. I started with minus political capital, and we had the immediate crisis of inflation being where it was, and everything else, so our immediate priority was to sort all of that stuff out. Planning was a case in point. I became Prime Minister, and four weeks later, there's a massive Conservative rebellion on a planning bill. So when your party's tearing itself apart, you've had four Prime Ministers, two leadership elections, you're not able to tell your party, 'Oh, by the way, you've got it all wrong on tax. I'm going to tell you you're wrong on that, whether you like it or not.' But you can't pick a fight with them on absolutely everything. So there's a case in point about what you were dealing with at that moment.

Kwasi Kwarteng suggested that growth is easier in a presidential system:

> In a presidential system, it's a lot easier. It's never easy, but they're ring-fenced in a way that a parliamentary leader or Prime Minister isn't. If you look at the United States, in order to get rid of a President, they've either got to die or be impeached, and impeachment is even rarer than them dying in office. Whereas a parliamentary leader, you've always got MPs to satisfy. And we all know that Tory MPs have a particular predilection for getting rid of the leader. So Liz/Boris/May, they were all essentially removed by MPs, whereas a President is essentially insulated

from that. And that's why I think a presidential model is a kind of a top-down system where the President can lay down the law. There'll be political blowback, but their political lives aren't necessarily deeply intertwined with what they're trying to do.

GOVERNMENT DEPARTMENTS AND THE ROLE OF MINISTERS

Some of the interviewees commented on how the departmental structure of Whitehall inhibited change (see also later comments on the role of the Treasury and a Prime Minister's Department).

On Whitehall departments and spending cuts, Boris Johnson said:

One of the problems is the way Whitehall is structured. Each department is a barony, where the Secretary of State estimates his or her own personal worth and success by the budget he or she wields. And so one of the difficulties is trying to change that mindset, and trying to get them to focus on value for money, rather than their estimating their own importance by, you know, 'I'm defence, I got 50 million,' 'I'm social security, I've got 150 billion' ... I used to sit them down and say, we've got to kill the sacred cows ... I want you to go through all your budget lines, and you've got to find all the things that are the relics of some defunct politician, because virtually everything that's public spending is all legacy stuff ... There'll be people who've come up with some scheme for, you know, a war on this or that, that's employing people across local or national government, whether in the public or the private sector, and it'll be a total waste of money. It's all about the egos of the politicians concerned, either at a local or national level. And the difficulty is getting those people to go through their budgets and kill the things they don't want. And the Treasury was never strong enough in doing that.

Andy Haldane highlighted the following on the quality of ministers:

I think the two issues – there's a question of skill, and a question of will.

Again, speaking candidly, the current crop of Cabinet ministers and supporting civil servants, do they know how to deliver on the sort of agenda and things we've been talking about today? I don't know, it's still early in a parliamentary term, but I would say [there are] odds against [them] in terms of the pure personnel currently on both sides. That's partly just a question of relative inexperience in knowing how the knee bone connects to the thigh bone to get things done. And there's a question of [political] will – is there enough? … People are saying the right things, but I've heard at least half a dozen governments of different hues utter identical words over the last twenty years, setting some sort of targets, but failing to deliver, and that's often been a question of will, rather than skill. Does that leave me hopeful overall? Well, I think we might be at a point where for both of the main parties, unless they do something rather bigger and bolder and braver and brassier, they risk irrelevance actually, and that's quite a potent force for doing something more decisive.

On non-executive ministers and the Great Repeal Bill, Liz Truss said:

One very important thing that people do not understand about the British government is that ministers are not actually executives. So the Chancellor is not an executive. The Permanent Secretary for the Treasury is the executive, and the Chancellor is the sort of chairman figure who can kind of veto things, but they don't actually run the department.

There's two things that need to happen. The first thing is variously described as a Great Restoration Bill or a Great Repeal Bill. You've got to repeal all of the acts that created all of these bodies – the Bank of England Act 1998, the Constitutional Reform Act 2005, the Constitutional Reform and Governance Act 2010, the Climate Change Act 2008, the Town and Country Planning Act 1947 – there's a massive swathe.

The second thing is within that legislation, there will be pieces of legislation that remove the power of the bureaucracy. And you basically say, right, the Permanent Secretary to the Treasury is now going to be appointed by the Chancellor. Now the Permanent Secretary to the Home Office is going to be appointed by the Home Secretary. The Home Secretary reports into the Prime Minister.

CIVIL SERVICE

There were a range of views about the extent to which the civil service constrained government.

Sajid Javid thought the civil service could be managed with strong leadership:

> I definitely think it can be managed. You know, 'the civil service' is the excuse that poor ministers use when they're incapable. They blame the civil service ... By and large, what the civil service wants more than anything is direction. They're not terribly political, they have their own personal views, but they will take direction, and they will act on direction. And they like ministers that are going to get on top of the details and make decisions.
>
> In the UK, so many ministers are afraid to make decisions, because a decision means a trade-off, and they don't like the one aspect of that trade-off, so they decide not to make their decision. And I always felt not making a decision is actually a decision in itself. It has consequences. And most ministers don't understand that. So I think if you went in and said, 'You know what? Let's go in and have a massive reform of the civil service,' I think you will have a massive distraction in the end and it will take you years to recover from [it]. The alternative is to work with the civil service, to give proper direction, proper guidance.

David Cameron said the following on dealing with the civil service:

> I think what Starmer is realising is he set the right priority, which is growth, but he's not making everything else subservient to it. Mistake number one. Mistake number two is he thinks that if I just give the orders to the civil service that I want growth, they'll come up with ideas. I'll then put the ideas in place, and it'll happen. And I think what he'll find is it'll just sink into a mush of stuff. They're not not on side. They're just not implementers. They love giving you policy options and talking about policy issues. Their weakness is the implementation. So I think you have to work out your implementation plan as much as you can

in advance and then bring in some people to help you implement it alongside and with the civil service. But try to work out what you have to do in terms of law changes on the inside, and then work out what can be done from the outside.

The reason free schools were successful is they were outside the control of the government. To give you a small example [of setting up something outside the control of government], when I set up the world's first genomics programme, which was the first time we had 100,000 genome sequences for a population genomic programme, I announced it, sent the civil service off to set up a 100,000 genomes world-beating database. Six months later, I asked them how is it getting on? Nothing, and literally nothing had happened. That's why we set up Genomics England, which was a private sector company. We set up a company and said, 'You go and organise this.' And then it all worked out. That's why implementation doesn't mean simply, here are the plans, you open with them. You've got to work out what primary legislation, what secondary legislation, what requires new bodies, what requires bodies to be abolished, what requires regulations to be changed, what requires new personnel. It's sort of every piece of the jigsaw and then also thinking, in as much as you know, who's dealing with this, what are the weak points, and how is this done? ...

I cut the civil service by a third, since I, unlike both parties now, did actually care about shrinking the state. And everyone thinks I was a 'wet' Tory, but I was a Treasury man, and so we did it by having the worst policy ever, but it does work. You just have to remove people from stuff, because it just stops the problem getting worse. It's about policies. In the end, you end up with lots of bad people, no good new people, but it's a good way to start. But you know, like everything else, you have to make it part of your plan. It has to be, and the Prime Minister and the Chancellor have to be hand in glove. Everyone wants to spend more money, apart from the Chancellor, including the Prime Minister. You can't have that.

On paying civil servants more upfront and unfunded pensions, Gus O'Donnell said:

I was head of the civil service. I tried with Chancellors of all colours, different parties, to change the system whereby if you're a civil servant, you get most of your pay after you stop working ... You name me an incentive structure system that says it's really smart to pay people actually below the market rate all the time they're working and then give them most of their money when they've left. And you're young, you've got fifty people applying for every single fast-track job in the civil service. We get great people in, but after a while they can't afford to stay because they want to get on the housing ladder, they want to start a family and the good ones go off to the private sector. The only ones that stay are the bad ones, and the ones who've got the Bank of Mum and Dad ... This is crazy because if you're an up-and-coming civil servant, you want to get on the housing ladder. You want a mortgage. You go to someone for a mortgage, and they say, 'What are you paid?' There's no question asking you what your pension is. Your pension is totally irrelevant. So we are stopping them from getting a mortgage. So it's pretty crazy all around ... If I said this to George Osborne, he'd say, 'OK, so the increased pay is going to show up in my deficit, and the reduction in my future pension liabilities is going to show up in a reduction in debt?' No, Chancellor, it's not, because the accounts do not include unfunded liabilities. And so he says, 'Well, that's crazy. Why don't we put them in?' Absolutely, Chancellor, I've been trying to do this for a long time. By the way, when we publish the next debt numbers, you're going to have a fit, because the unfunded public sector tax liability is huge. Can you imagine? This is a question of how rational markets are in this sense, and they think that the markets will be completely spooked by this.

Liz Truss said the following about the civil service:

I don't think people quite understand how poor the civil service is, how much they are wired to be part of the attitude we're talking about. I just think it's impossible to deliver the types of policies that we're discussing without changing the senior civil service, and by that, I mean the top three layers of the civil service, as well as making everybody else hire- and fireable. So everybody from the tea lady, frankly, otherwise you'll have people in the system who are trying to sabotage it. Even under this Labour government, Foreign Office civil servants have threatened to walk out because they're not pro-Palestine enough. There are not just Sir Humphrey types who resist things in the civil service. There are activists who are actively promoting a neo-Marxist agenda. That's what we've got …

The other difference with Thatcher is that the bureaucracy was not as bad then, because you hadn't had all these Blairite laws passed, so not as much power had been outsourced. It was easier to replace senior officials. I've spoken to people in the Thatcher administration who had their lot of trouble with the civil service, but it was nowhere near as bad. It's a bit like what Trump found – in Trump One – that people had been radicalised and deliberately placed by people like Obama. I think Thatcher was dealing with a less hostile bureaucracy. Organisations like the Bank of England were just Machiavellian, which I don't think she had, to the same extent. The night before the mini-Budget, they announced the sale of gilts. When the LDI [liability-driven investment] crisis happened, they blamed it on the mini-Budget …

Ultimately, Thatcher did not succeed in dealing with British bureaucracy, and I think that is the fundamental British problem … I actually think dealing with the British bureaucracy is more important than introducing a flat tax … It's the size of the state that is the problem, the size of reach of the state.

NO. 10

Different interviewees had different views about whether the Prime Minister needed a more powerful office – those who had been Prime Minister thought this should be the case, those who had been Chancellor but not Prime Minister disagreed. Rishi Sunak, who had been both Chancellor and Prime Minister, sided with the other former Prime Ministers.

On an Office of the Prime Minister, Liz Truss commented:

A very important thing that also has to happen is spending needs to be taken out of the Treasury and put in the Office of the Prime Minister, very much like the OMB [Office of Management and Budget] works in the United States, so the Treasury becomes essentially a debt management and taxation function and in charge of regulation. I would definitely get rid of the so-called Business department, but the Treasury should be much more akin to the role of the American Treasury with the OMB put in the Office of the Prime Minister. I think that is very important because essentially the Prime Minister is the chief executive, doesn't have the hire and fire powers and they also don't have the budgetary powers. What kind of chief executive is that?

David Cameron said:

The problem is not that the Treasury is too strong. It's that the Treasury and the other departments don't work together. You know, basically the Prime Minister thinks they're in charge. They make an announcement, and then everyone goes away and frustrates it. I think we need some machinery changes. I think the Cabinet Office becomes the Prime Minister's Office effectively. I created the National Security Council, which the Prime Minister chairs. In the National Security Council, the national security adviser has a bit of the Cabinet Office working for him, inside the Prime Minister's Office. You have sitting around the table all the departments – whether it's aid or foreign policy or defence or Home Office – so everyone is there and owns the decision and has to implement the decision. I think we need to do the same [with growth]. Because I think the trouble is the economic policy is left to the Treasury, who do want growth, but they have a hostile relationship with the other departments, and so you come up with growth plans, and then it just goes into a Treasury vs departments fight and nothing happens. So I think the Prime Minister fundamentally has to chair two meetings, the National Security Council and a sort of economic growth council. And the economic growth council needs to be Treasury-led, dominated and chaired by the Prime Minister, with the other departments, and that should be the driving force behind this implementation plan.

What departments do is they take decisions and then just talk about the analysis; there's no collective work. You say to the Home Secretary, 'I'd like to see the figures for how many foreign offenders we've returned in the last month,' and they go, 'Well, I'm sorry, I can't share them.' You'd fire these people in the private sector. You've got to have a system where there's one set of information that's collectively shared. There's no department silos. You've got to try and break that pattern, and it's amazing how bad that is.

On the idea of an expanded Office of the Prime Minister with spending powers, Norman Lamont said:

I hadn't really thought of it as the single proposition you put forward. Normally, it's two separate propositions. One, that the power of the Prime Minister should be increased with an ever-larger Cabinet Office. And two, there ought to be – as in the US or Germany – a separate Economy Minister or Budget Minister, and the Treasury is just left signing the cheques. Well, I think it's a monstrous idea. Obviously, a Prime Minister needs to have resources in terms of information, knowledge and people who know what they're talking about. It's amazing how Mrs Thatcher managed with very few. And I think the whole scene has altered massively since I was in government, with social media. I see you need a lot of people to deal with social media, but what seems to be happening, anecdotally, from everything I've heard over the years, is there are a lot of young people sort of telling Cabinet ministers what they should do on the basis of an idea they've developed themselves in No. 10, which more often than not, just gets floated and then rejected and creates a lot of problems. If you want to have outsiders in No. 10, I think they need to be people of experience, with real expertise, not just communication strategists, of whom there seems to be a very large number. That's what I think about No. 10. [And] people are always saying expenditures should be separated from the Treasury, because nobody's in favour of controlling expenditure except in a theoretical way. And it's always, 'Oh, there's no imagination. It's too short term. What about a little seed money? You know, just oil the wheels, get it going. Oh, it'll pay for itself.' The Treasury are not unimaginative people, but someone needs to keep an eye on spending.

Rishi Sunak said the following on a beefed-up No. 10:

> David and Tony didn't have the experience that Gordon and I had. It's odd coming from the Treasury into No. 10, because you have a department of 1,400 people, or whatever it is, or 1,000 people that work for you, and you also have less to do, in a sense. And then you move into this building, with like 200 people, and you have like twenty times more things to do every day. Like that is an odd adjustment. You're constantly having to work through people, which is not ideal.

HM TREASURY

The interviewees were divided on whether the Treasury was an obstacle to growth.

From a Department for Business, Energy and Industrial Strategy (BEIS) perspective, Kwasi Kwarteng said:

> Let's not be cute about this, everything economically is done through the Treasury. BEIS were essentially like a business development, client outreach, customer outreach department. We had a lot of say in policy – broad policy – but we weren't writing any cheques, and we had no input at all into fiscal policy. And a lot of the levers that you have are regulatory and fiscal, and BEIS obviously has some oversight on the regulation, but insofar as the regulation has an impact fiscally, the Treasury ultimately has the say ... I think Gordon Brown centralised the Treasury to an absurd degree. And I think that's been a big problem, actually, to growing the economy, because, essentially, they've got a kind of ledger book, cash accounting, almost like, I would say, a Victorian accounting approach, and it means it's very hard to get investment, very hard to get tax cuts that are not fully funded. So even if you do want to boost the

economy in that way, there's a lot of reluctance in the Treasury. And people like Nick Macpherson think the Treasury is this golden, Rolls-Royce machine. But actually there is an argument – and I've subscribed to it – that it's that thinking that's actually impeded growth and not helped it. And from a BEIS Secretary of State point of view, that was pretty much the impression I had …

[The Treasury are] not geared to drive growth. I think the assumption was that growth just happens, and for much of the twentieth century, it kind of did. And then once the growth happens, then the government has the luxury to tax it and pay for the welfare state. The growth was a given, but now it's no longer a given. I don't think the state has been that smart in trying to figure out how to get it back. It's a very odd thing, actually, because that sort of non-interventionist approach vis-à-vis growth you'd associate more with a kind of classical liberal, Victorian, nineteenth-century view. But we've built this huge welfare state – which they didn't have yet – so you'd think we'd be more interested in driving growth than is the case.

On the problem with the Treasury, Vince Cable said:

The issue to pursue with the Treasury is this whole problem of borrowing to invest. Let me just give you a concrete example. In this country, Royal Mail was, until I was in government, publicly owned, and it was basically, as an industry, becoming obsolete. I mean, we don't use stage coaches anymore, and in the world of emails, people are not using letters and postage stamps. They desperately needed to invest in diversification and moving into parcels, for example, so that they could handle Amazon's distribution etc. But the Treasury simply would not allow them to borrow to invest. It was a publicly owned enterprise, but they wouldn't allow them to invest, and it was in terrible decline. They also had difficult trade unions. So I privatised it. It was terribly controversial and very unpopular. But the reason I did it was not actually an ideological thing about private versus public, it was that it was the only way they could raise any capital.

OBR

Although the Office for Budget Responsibility (OBR) has come under some criticism, Jeremy Hunt, who had had some run-ins with the office, believed that with hard work, the OBR could be made to work effectively.

Jeremy Hunt said the following on the bond markets and the fiscal rules and how to work with the OBR:

> The second constraint [to pro-enterprise policies] is the markets. When I became Chancellor, that second constraint was the one that I had to think about, because we had a big problem with our gilt yields. The markets did not like the fact that my predecessor, Kwasi Kwarteng, had announced tax cuts without corresponding spending cuts, and they thought that that was fiscally irresponsible, and therefore our gilt yields rose, and that started to have a knock-on effect on all sorts of other things, and that persuaded Liz Truss herself that she had to change direction. And I don't think she would have done that otherwise. I think, actually, in exactly the same way that Trump realised he had to change direction when it came to his tariffs, I think that the markets are a fact of life that we all have to work with, but I think it is perfectly possible to get to the kind of dynamic enterprise-led economy that all of us want in a way that is consistent with what markets will accept ...
>
> There's been a lot of discussion about fiscal rules, and I have given some thought to this, and my early conclusion is that there is only one fiscal rule that we really need to have, which is that, over the course of a cycle, public spending needs to grow more slowly than the economy. That is something that Chancellors need to adopt as a way of making sure we don't bankrupt ourselves ...
>
> The childcare reforms I introduced cost £4 billion a year, but they also helped a lot of parents get back to work, because childcare is so expensive, a lot of mums in particular were quitting their jobs. So I asked the OBR to score the GDP impact, and then the cost, in terms of tax revenues, of having more parents in work, and because these are a very productive group of people, because they're in their thirties and forties,

it's like a very productive part of your life, the GDP impact reduced the cost from £4 billion to £600 million a year only … This was the first time the OBR had ever used dynamic scoring.

JUDICIARY

A number of the interviewees were concerned about judicial activism. On the judiciary and judicial review, David Cameron commented:

The reason all these growth plans that governments have announced haven't worked is that as soon as they hit the reality of dozens of regulators, judicial reviews, parliamentary amendments [and] other duties that governments decide to put in place, as soon as they hit all these other things, they don't make it across nowhere. You've got to explain that's the problem. And therefore we need to make growth the priority. Everything else is subservient, point one. Policies aren't enough – you need the plan to implement them, point two. You need to have the people who are going to be able to see that through. And you need to work out what the obstacles are going to be in advance and try and remove them, and that might include some quite profound changes to the way our judicial legal systems and appeals works. I don't know the answer, obviously, but I know that's the question …

The great irony is that all over the world, special economic zones have been set up with not only English law but English judges. Dubai's International Financial Centre is the most successful in the world. I regularly play tennis with an English judge who sits in Kazakhstan, in Astana. Bhutan is trying to set one up. Everyone is copying English law, and they're doing it because of the consistency and case resolution. But our judicial review system seems to fur up our planning permission and regulatory system.

On judicial activism, Rishi Sunak said, 'The judiciary, over time, has clearly just become a mission creep of judicial activism. Notably, the Next equal pay case being Exhibit A.'

CHAPTER 15

HOW TO NAVIGATE A PRO-GROWTH AGENDA POLITICALLY

Perhaps the most helpful insight from our interviewees was the advice from people who had climbed to the top of the greasy pole on how to implement a pro-growth agenda. A number of common themes emerged – the importance of leadership, making growth the number-one priority, preparation in opposition, the importance of thinking long term and avoiding short-termism, good communications and continuity.

IMPORTANCE OF LEADERSHIP

Tony Blair both surprised and impressed us in his interview when he explained that in many ways, the political problems were surmountable. And he was supported by some of the other former Prime Ministers. He pointed out that the key was leadership, arguing the need to get the relationship between leadership and the led correct. He pointed out that they say the job of the leader is to do what the people want, but it's not. He argued that the job of leadership is to set out what you think that people need and persuade them that that's what they want. He argued that people want a lot of things, and that while the public has a right to be inconsistent in what it wants, you can't produce policy on that basis. He contrasted this with Margaret Thatcher in the '80s; when he was coming and working his way up and couldn't work out why on individual policies she had polled badly, but she kept on winning elections. And then came to the conclusion that the reason was because people thought 'Yeah, but you put her all together, there's a clear direction, and basically we support it.' He pointed out that if you asked the public in a detached way about one specific policy, especially if the media was saying it's all a terrible idea and we should be doing so-and-so – the result was likely to be negative. But putting it all together, and giving a clear direction for the country, would get a more positive response. He was convinced that pro-growth policies were a perfectly sellable proposition. He thought that the country wanted it, because either conventional politics would produce an answer to this problem or unconventional politics would dismantle the system.

On the need to level with people, Boris Johnson said:

> Yes, I think it can be done. I think you need to level with people. And I used to have fantastic arguments about that. So our old friend [Dominic] Cummings, you know, he was basically a sort of national socialist, right? That was one of the problems. He said the NHS would basically be fire-hosed with money and corporation taxes. His argument was that any-thing for business was bad juju with the public, and you shouldn't do it.

MAKE GROWTH THE NUMBER-ONE PRIORITY

David Cameron was also optimistic about the ability to change the mindset of voters, as was George Osborne.

On getting back to growth, now versus the 1970s, David Cameron commented:

> There's no one particular thing. It's not like the 1970s, when it was simple. There was this sense that if only we could roll back the frontiers of the state, cut taxes, rebelieve in the economics of the marketplace and freedom, then everything would follow from that. And I think Margaret Thatcher, and the team around her, ran a brilliant, intellectual campaign to make that happen, and it was successful.
>
> I think this time around, that's necessary, but it's sort of bigger than that, because it's not just the private sector economy that isn't working. It's that nothing is working properly. But you need to have an absolutely joined-up plan before you come into government for how you change every single thing that would help you get your growth rate from 1 per

cent to 3.5 per cent. And there isn't a single thing to make this happen. It's like, why aren't broadband speeds better? Why can't we build telephone masts? Why does infrastructure take so long? Why can't we build more houses? Why is the planning system so slow? Why can't government see that certain projects in healthcare and genomics and things like that really drive growth? Why is it that market access agreements aren't being negotiated in the way that they should? Why is it that taxes on wealth creation are so high? It's everything, and the crucial thing, the most important thing is, if you're Prime Minister, you're very lucky if you achieve one thing, but if you want to do one thing, everything else has to be subservient to it. And so Starmer is right in a way saying growth is the priority, but he hasn't made it the top priority. It's only when you say, I want growth and everything else is subservient. So I'll have to U-turn on non-doms. I'll have to scrap my renters' rights bill, because it's going to screw up the housing market. I'll have to change my workers' rights bill or get rid of it all together. Everything must be subservient to getting growth moving. So I think it's a similar nature to what the Thatcher team did at the end of the '70s, but it's way more comprehensive, and the government will only succeed if it plans in advance, down to the minutest detail, every rule, every regulation, every regulator that needs to be changed, every personality that needs to be altered, every planning policy that needs to change …

Go back to the '70s, there was this sense that you had to adopt some free market ideology … Everything followed from that. I think this time it is more complicated. It's about anything that gets in the way of the ability of investors to invest, employers to employ, entrepreneurs to start up businesses. You know, anything gets in the way of making those things, it needs to go. Obviously, you're going to have to have a smaller state, you're going to have to spend less because you can't go on spending and borrowing as we are. But that's the consequence, as well as the cause.

George Osborne said, 'I would prioritise economic growth. But when I say prioritise for economic growth, I mean take the necessary hard decisions to put prioritising enterprise, business development, business expansion and wealth creation over other goals that you have in a society.'

PREPARE IN OPPOSITION

The interviews were carried out after President Trump had burst into office with a wide range of initiatives, and the level of preparation in advance had clearly impressed some of our interviewees, who pointed out that if you had not done so, it would be very unlikely that you could impose the policies that were economically necessary to generate growth.

On the need to have a clear plan in opposition, David Cameron highlighted:

> You have to have a very clear plan before you get into office about which regulations are in the way, and how you're going to change, because I would say with most governments, the things they invent outside government work. The things they try and invent in government often don't work. I'll give you a very good example. We decided to do our version of charter schools – they're called free schools here. They were set up by private sector and other organisations, but they provided a free education effectively inside the state sector. They were an amazing success. But when we came up with the idea, everyone in the education world said no one would build them, no one would want them, no teachers would teach in them, no parents would want to send their children there. Everyone was against them, but we set them up, and they had a huge success. When we were in government, we said, let's do the same thing for young offenders institutions, for youth prisons. How many did we build? Zero. Literally none. Because once you're in the system, the system just sort of covers you in goo.
>
> It's really important that you've worked out exactly what you want when it comes to the regulators. There's a bunch of regulations, for instance, to do with house building, about biodiversity and offsets and nature regulations and bats and newts and all the rest of it. And you've got to get that to work. You've got to work out which regulations need to change and who could be the regulator. Who will help me do that? These organisations have quite a lot of quasi-institutional, quasi-judicial power, and you've also got to think about the process of judicial review,

and how to reform that. So it's a really big project, because you'll often find that, OK, we've got a plan, we're going to change this regulation, we're going to change this regulator, we're going to have this new rule, and six months, a year down the line, nothing's happened, because you're just furred up in the courts with objections to it, so you work out and deal with all those things.

Government has become more difficult partly because we made it more difficult, but we've got to try and find a way to fix that. You have to work out literally day one, week one, month one, which laws and rules to come for. You know what normally happens? You write a manifesto, you get into office and you give the manifestos to the civil servants, and they turn it into laws, and the laws grind out, and it all goes through slowly. So this time around, you really need to work out not just what's the policy of the manifesto, but what is the implementation plan for turning that policy into a reality. The manifesto is obviously the bit that explains what the aims and the goals are, but there needs to be a whole backup programme of literally what you're going to change and how you're going to change it. This also applies actually to the whole migration issue, where governments just keep getting stuck on this position of thinking you've changed the rules, but then the courts unwind and change them and all the rest of it.

Cameron continued, considering Keir Starmer's lack of pitch-rolling in opposition:

The other mistake Starmer made is they obviously knew they were going to have to do some of these things. They said nothing before the election. We announced before 2010 a two-year public sector pay freeze in opposition. What nutter does that? But it meant we had permission. We announced £6 billion in-year cuts in 2010 before the election. OK, it wasn't enough, but it was a clear direction of travel. And so therefore you felt you had permission. And so this new government does not have permission to take the difficult decisions by having explained how bad the situation is, how desperate our fiscal situation is, how bad our growth situation is, in order to get the permission to take the action.

On entering government from opposition, Kwasi Kwarteng said:

> I think the best governments tend to be ones that are formed in oppo-
> sition, because they've got the time to think. I'm not talking about this
> Labour government, but generally, they've got the time to think about
> what they're going to do and how they're going to do it, and I think,
> in my experience, we kind of rushed into stuff, and then we panicked
> when things went wrong. And I think there's too much lurching around,
> actually, in British politics to get long-term answers.

Ken Clarke said the following on preparing for government and winning
a second election:

> Margaret [Thatcher] took over after the Winter of Discontent with a
> bust economy. And she had spent her time with the help of Keith
> Joseph, studying Hayek, deciding what needed to be done with the full
> support of the key people, two people she depended on most, Geoffrey
> Howe and Nigel Lawson. We didn't put much of it in our election man-
> ifesto – a very toned-down version – because you weren't going to get
> elected if you told people what you're going to do, like upsetting the
> unions. We started as soon as we got here … I think Geoffrey Howe's
> 1981 Budget was the most hated or unpopular that I ever heard, and
> it was an absolutely essential Budget, but it was hated even by half the
> Cabinet members. By halfway through the parliament, we'd done all
> the things we wanted to do. We were well over twenty points behind
> in the polls. And from then on, people suddenly started saying, 'Well,
> it seems to be working. Actually, the unions aren't running everything,
> and perhaps they shouldn't be.' Then what helped admittedly – General
> Galtieri had a drink too many and invaded the Falklands. And then,
> most important thing of all, the Labour Party appointed Michael Foot
> as their leader. But in 1983, [Thatcher] achieved a much bigger majority
> than she'd had in '79. It was a fantastic election in 1983, and we'd done it
> by doing what this government needs to do in the national interest, the
> things that we believe to be right for the standing of the country in the

world, greater safety and security of the country and for the medium- to long-term health of our economy. We thought it would have the right effect, and we bloody well did it.

Rishi Sunak said the following on the difficulty of attempting pro-growth policies twelve years into governing:

It's not complicated, right? Win an election with a majority and have a party that agrees. Yes, we do need to deregulate and not have legislative targets for the environment and net zero etc. etc. And we should scrap the Habitats Directive, and we should not have the Equal Pay Act work like this. It's clearly mad, if that's how it's affecting companies. And you just need your party to agree with that, and pass the bill in Parliament, then crack on with it, right? The [Conservative] Party disagrees on all those things. And obviously, I wasn't in a position that won an election with a majority, but if you had you could do all that ...

This was very particular to my circumstances. Keir Starmer unquestionably had more power than most US Presidents have. A British Prime Minister, with a majority, has more power than a typical US President. Executive and legislature are fused. But my circumstances were not like that, at the tail end of the situation, with no functioning majority. A brand new British Prime Minister, without question, has the legislative power to do this and face everyone down and pass the legislation and take and get what they want done.

Perhaps unsurprisingly, civil servants seemed less impressed by the preparation for government from opposition.

As Gus O'Donnell said on the current government's predicament:

So the nonsense this government's got itself stuck in is in their manifesto, they committed themselves to not changing income tax, corporation tax or VAT. So the big levers are all gone. So we end up doing dumb things ... The problem with manifestos is they get written in opposition.

THINK LONG TERM/AVOID SHORT-TERMISM

At the risk of saying what is obvious, it is easier to run a country with sensible solutions if governments can avoid being pushed around by short-term distractions.

On the damage of short-termism, and Trump's effectiveness, Tony Blair pointed out the damage of short-termism, arguing that it was the mistake you can easily make in politics – to believe that you know people's instinctive reactions to things, or what they say, or opinion polls and everything. He thought it was like with social media – and this is one of the reasons he thought that Trump was successful in America, not simply because of his use of social media but actually his ability not to surf the wave of every passing bit of public opinion but to have the wave break over him. He pointed out that it was an important thing in politics, because people could say, 'OK, so I know where that guy is, and I'll follow that.' He contrasted that with those perceived to be swerving all over the place, so that in the end, even if the voters liked one particular manoeuvre, they would say, 'Well, you're not leading.'

On the Conservatives lurching around, Kwasi Kwarteng commented:

If I asked you, what was the organising theme of those fourteen years [of Conservative government], you wouldn't be able to tell me the answer. That was because we were literally being buffeted around. Someone said to me that having all those different leaders means that it's much harder to get a consistent line, because each leader thinks, 'Oh, I'm the leader. I've got to impose my May-ism or Truss-ism or Johnson-ism' or whatever it is. And so, by having a new leader, you're changing the direction, or at least the messaging, which means that it's harder to get consistency. So the political instability led to a world where the Tories were all over the place. And so I don't think anybody could describe what we were trying to do across those fourteen years. And, of course, you're being buffeted by Brexit and Covid and stuff, but there didn't seem to be any principles. And ironically, the one woman who did have principles, lasted the least time. And that was because I just don't think her approach was right. I don't think our approach was right. I don't think it was sensible.

To avoid short-termism, Ken Clarke said:

> As Chancellor, what you're trying to do is to judge everything you're doing by what you want the effect to be in two, three, four years' time. Damn tomorrow morning's *Daily Express* front page. Quite often in government, the steps you have to take are unpopular. Under Margaret, I never had a popular policy. I had just tremendous battles. She never really noticed opinion polls, and she never read any newspaper. She had this clear, principled view of what she very strongly always felt was needed … What you're trying to do is make yourself consistent and predictable. The problem comes if you've made a mistake, if you're wrong and the combination of weapons you're using and policies you chose don't go well. But that's when you have to be quick on your feet and U-turn quickly.

On whether a pro-growth policy is feasible, Andy Haldane said:

> I think there's a broadly shared diagnosis of what isn't working as well as it might. There's even a broadly shared prescription about what might be done differently to unlock this potential, which takes it back to political will. Is there the political will to make choices which carry short-term political cost? Most of what we're describing is at least a five-, more likely a ten- or fifteen-year project … All of these things could be done, [but] that's different from will they be done?

On running a successful business, John Rose said, 'I ran a decent business by having a view on the long term and sticking to strategy and being consistent.'

Lord Macpherson said the following on how governments run:

> Governments can have sensible ideas, but they tend to introduce changes piecemeal but then lose interest because they just can't keep the focus

on the right issues ... Politicians get rewarded for announcing things, but they're never around long enough to be accountable for the consequences. It's a real problem. Governments announce a new growth policy every two years. And we largely know what causes growth – skills and investments, a sensible tax system, innovation, things like that. And if the government ever had the attention span that it focused on something for, say, fifteen years, it might actually change the underlying growth rate by 0.1 per cent. But everybody always thinks you can impact growth overnight, and it discredits politicians in the process.

Anna Leach highlighted how political short-termism puts off businesses:

It's just bandwidth. Everything just gets more complicated. There are policies being added to complicate it all the time. And yes, politicians always want it. They want to announce something new, and then it disappears five minutes later, and businesses just can't keep up, so they give up trying to engage with government support for businesses.

Simon Wolfson called for a long-term approach:

I can give you the remedy. I can't tell you how you're going to get it to the patient. It comes down to leaders who are determined to do this, and who can spend the time explaining things and get the bad headlines tomorrow. You shouldn't worry about bad headlines tomorrow. Only worry about what happens in five years. So if you ask me, what should the Conservative Party focus on today? My answer is that they should be focusing on what we need to do so that at the end of our first term in office, the country is a better place than it was when we took it over. That's the question they should be asking. But the question they jump far too quickly to is, how do we get into office? And then they ask, how do we get more popular tomorrow, and what happens on Sunday? But I think, unfortunately, the nature of Britain is that you have to reach crisis point before you have the strength of leadership required to talk sense to people. And then when you do talk sense to people, lo and behold, they make the right choice. I mean, always. So the real answer is political courage, determination, good organisation.

GOOD COMMUNICATIONS

Most of the politicians thought that presenting a narrative made it easier to fit what might in the short run look like harsh decisions into an over-riding policy that might obtain support.

David Cameron highlighted the need for good communications:

> You've got to have a narrative. The point about politics is the narrative you have has got to back up what you're doing. And this is where Trump succeeds, particularly on the deportation point. 'This is the problem: the border, the wall, the fact that so many people are coming in.' So when people see the detailed implementation of deportation, they go, 'Of course, you're doing that, because your big picture is this.' And we need to provide the big picture that growth isn't working because there's too much regulation, there's too much control. No one can invest, no one can build anything. The system's broken. We're going to mend it. So when you start smashing things up, they go, 'Of course, you're smashing things up, because you told us it was broken and it needs to be.' I think you need to describe this problem and have the narrative right from the beginning, but then it'll help you justify the difficult things.

Norman Lamont said the following on how Margaret Thatcher delivered her message in opposition and Rab Butler's approach to living standards:

> The electorate were fed up with dustbins in the streets being unemptied. They were fed up with reading about British Leyland being ruined by militant trade unions, who were then bailed out by the government. There was a strong public reaction. But Mrs Thatcher didn't say we're going for growth. She just said, 'We're restoring sanity, we're stopping borrowing. Borrowing is merely deferred taxation.' She didn't

concentrate on growth. And in those days, people didn't so much talk about growth in the abstract way that we do today. I mean, it's rather odd. We moved from growth to GDP per capita growth, which is nearer what people did talk about, which was living standards. Rab Butler, for example, set out an ambition to double living standards. It was reckoned that with growth returning to the economy, rationing being abolished and more goods coming on the market, living standards were improving and that this could continue with stability over several decades. So I think it was over twenty-five years, they were going to double living standards.

Ken Clarke considered how government communications now work, compared to the 1980s:

Debates have become sillier and more personalised. We don't get many political issues in the newspapers or on the television. Now it's all personalities and press releases and scandals when people fail to keep their sex life secret, and all this kind of gossip, and all that ... We were miles behind in the polls in the first part of Margaret's governments, because we were doing what we had to in the national interest, and the public wanted a quiet life. We were 20 per cent down in the polls. We handled it. We came through this. It all began to work. And people began to listen to what we say, and they began to say, 'Well, perhaps somebody had to do some of this.' Nowadays, you're not allowed to do that. In No. 10, there are half a dozen twenty-year-olds who are in charge of media relations and campaigning, and they will tell you when you've got to go out on a Sunday morning to do the interview. Only two or three Cabinet ministers will be asked – the ones who will learn the slogans – and the other Cabinet ministers have to get permission before they go out and get their speeches cleared. It's all very mechanically organised by a rather lightweight group of people who've no experience of doing anything before they got this job and are dominated by trying to get a decent headline in the *Daily Mail* tomorrow morning. Yet it cuts across the way you should govern the country – it's no way to govern the country at all.

On dealing with the 24-hour media, Tony Blair said that you had to engage with it but that you have to engage with it without being in thrall to it. You couldn't be in modern politics today without an effective social media operation. It would just be an incompetent thing. But he also thought that politicians needed to understand that people were very paradoxical about social media, pointing out that they used it, they fuelled it, but they distrusted it at the same time. He argued that if politicians showed no consistency in their approach, then it would not work. He pointed out that the public like to see people stand up for something, as in their own lives, in their own friends, those they respected are the people that stand for something. So he concluded that the politics was easier than people think even though a lot of people think it's very difficult. He didn't think the politics was difficult. What was difficult, because this was always what's difficult about governing, was getting the deep policy right.

IMPORTANCE OF CONTINUITY

The importance of communicating a consistent narrative is matched by the need for continuity of approach.

On the need for a cross-party approach to growth, John Rose said:

> Highest on my list of things [to encourage economic growth] is trying to get some sort of cross-party agreement on what we need to do – decision-making in a way that some managed democracies like Singapore have been able to do. Even places like Abu Dhabi, where you're not constantly being whipsawed by changes in the political climate. So having something that people generally bought into, and were prepared to back across party lines, would be a very fine thing.

Tony Blair ascribes his success to a strong centre and continuity of policy, arguing that his government was lucky because it had a strong centre and didn't really disturb the basic settlement for the Thatcher period, which gave a continuity of policy.

CONCLUSION

Concern about how the country is run is not new. The 1854 Northcote–Trevelyan report[1] on the civil service argued:

It would be natural to expect that so important a profession would attract into its ranks the ablest and the most ambitious of the youth of the country; that the keenest emulation would prevail among those who had entered it; and that such as were endowed with superior qualifications would rapidly rise to distinction and public eminence.

Such, however, is by no means the case. Admission into the Civil Service is indeed eagerly sought after, but it is for the unambitious, and the indolent or incapable, that it is chiefly desired. Those whose abilities do not warrant an expectation that they will succeed in the open professions, where they must encounter the competition of their contemporaries, and those whom indolence of temperament or physical infirmities unfit for active exertions, are placed in the Civil Service, where they may obtain an honourable livelihood with little labour, and with no risk; where their success depends upon their simply avoiding any flagrant misconduct, and attending with moderate regularity to routine duties and in which they are secured against the ordinary consequences of old age, or failing health, by an arrangement which provides them with the means of supporting themselves after they have become incapacitated.

It may be noticed in particular that the comparative lightness of the work, and the certainty of provision in case of retirement owing to bodily incapacity, furnish strong inducements to the parents and friends of sickly youths to endeavour to obtain for them employment in the service of the Government; and the extent to which the public are consequently burdened, first with the salaries of officers who are obliged to absent themselves from their duties on account of ill health, and afterwards with their pensions when they retire on the same plea, would hardly be credited by those who have not had opportunities of observing the operation of the system. It is not our intention to suggest that all public servants entered the employment of the Government with such views as these; but we apprehend that as regards a large propor- tion of them, these motives more or less influenced those who acted for them in the choice of a profession; while, on the other hand, there are probably very few who have chosen this line of life with a view to raising themselves to public eminence. The result naturally is that the public service suffers both in internal efficiency and in public estimation.

Our interviewees for this book are generally agreed that the UK is in trouble and possibly heading for a financial crisis.

This is backed up by the projections from Cebr in Annex 1, which show the UK dropping from twenty-fourth in 1998 to twenty-sixth in 2007 to thirtieth in 2024 to a projected forty-sixth in 2050 in the world GDP per capita league table,[2] being overtaken by countries like Poland (2034) and Turkey (2043).

There is a sense of fiscal crisis, backed up by the OBR's risks and sus- tainability report,[3] which concludes:

The UK's public finances have emerged from a series of major global economic shocks in a relatively vulnerable position. At the end of 2024, the UK government's deficit stood at 5.7 per cent of GDP, around 4 per- centage points higher than the advanced-economy average. This is the third highest among 28 advanced European economies, and the fifth highest among 36 advanced economies (after France, Slovakia, the US, and Israel). At 94 per cent of GDP, UK government debt is the fourth highest among advanced European economies, and the sixth highest among advanced economies (after Japan, Greece, Italy, France, and the US).[4] And with its ten-year bond yielding 4.5 per cent at the end of June, the UK government faces the third-highest borrowing costs of any ad- vanced economy after New Zealand and Iceland.

It appears that the UK public sector has lost the ability to do anything that requires management – the evidence is in the length of time and costs it takes to develop infrastructure, the extent of potholes, the length of waiting lists for various public services, the burgeoning list of welfare claimants, the increasing prevalence of crime and the loss of control over borders. The public sector rate of sickness absence is 2.8 per cent compared with 1.9 per cent in the private sector.[5] In the past three years, the public sector has lost more than 3 million days of work through strike action[6] and an analysis by the ONS showed that public sector workers were five times as likely to be on strike as private sector workers.[7] Meanwhile, productivity trends in the public sector have been especially unimpressive, with public sector productivity virtually unchanged since 1997,[8] while productivity for the whole economy has risen by 26.9 per cent.[9] Since Covid, market sector productivity has risen by 3.3 per cent[10] while public sector productivity has actually fallen by 4.6 per cent.[11]

REASONS FOR OPTIMISM

Given this state of affairs, one might have expected our interviewees to be full of gloom and doom. And to be fair, some were. But the majority were not and believed that it would be possible to generate change and that indeed there was an appetite for change to a much more growth-oriented economic policy.

Tony Blair detected an appetite for change, arguing that the good news was that there is an appetite to break out of old ways of thinking. He pointed out that a reason for President Trump's election in the US was that people sensed that he would actually get things moving now, that there would be change. He thought that people could agree or disagree with some of the changes but that the desire for the system to be fundamentally altered was very, very strong. But one of the things he had learned about governing was that, in the end, it was about policy and that is the most important thing. He thought that the question you should start with is, what's the right answer? And that you should leave all the ideology to one side and just look at that.

George Osborne noticed a political opening for a pro-growth party:

There's a gap in the market for someone who's got a credible plan to grow the British economy. I would humbly suggest the Conservative Party gets back to what it's normally elected to do, which is put the economy first and put people's prosperity first and come forward with a credible, deliverable, practical plan ... Obviously you've got to have something to say on immigration or whatever, but that is not going to be the reason why people vote Conservative over Reform. And it might put people off voting Conservative over Liberal Democrat, which is the other big problem they've got. But what is lacking is [a plan for growth] – the Labour government doesn't have it, the Liberal Democrats don't have it, Reform doesn't have it and the Tories don't currently have it. They don't have a plan for the economy ... And I would humbly suggest the Leader of the Opposition should spend less time talking about toilets and more time talking about taxes. You know, that would be our overall kind of strategy. [Kemi Badenoch] spends an odd amount of time telling me I shouldn't go into the trans toilet ... If I was a woman, I wouldn't want a man in my toilet, but it's not the only topic.

Boris Johnson called for a Thatcherite revolution:

What this country needs, basically, is a massive new Thatcherian revolution and a new kick in the pants. And I think it's actually happening. The one good thing about Labour is it's so bad, so bad that I think there's ... a chance of all this happening. And I think the public – as more and more young people are so pissed off with not being able to get housing – they're genuinely looking at Reform, in a way that they would never have done before. There is an opening, I think, for a 1979-style change at the next election. That's what I think. But whether we'll find the formula for [it], I don't know.

Clare Lombardelli sees huge potential for the UK economy:

I'm very optimistic. I think there's a huge amount of opportunity and potential in the UK economy. We have a history that is [all about] developing frontier and technologies ... [and] pretty open and deep trade. All of these things are fantastic for productivity, for improvements there, so there's a huge amount of opportunity here.

Andy Haldane is also a 'super-optimist':

I am a super-optimist about the UK. I think it is pregnant with a huge amount of potential, and I'm frustrated we haven't been able to unlock more of it. And I know that because I spent the probably larger part of my working life travelling around the UK, meeting businesses, speaking to businesses. I met many brilliant people, with many brilliant businesses, with many brilliant ideas, in all four corners of the UK. So I know it's there. Opportunity is knocking. And the question then becomes, what have been the blockers or the barriers to unleashing more of that potential, which I know to be there, and all the assets that we know are there in spades. They certainly include language and rule of law. They certainly include our university and research base. They certainly include real comparative advantage across at least half a dozen sectors. They do include an appetite for entrepreneurship, at least at start-up level. The list could go on, but that's enough by way of raw ingredients to think there's a huge amount there to be done to unlock that potential.

And David Giampaolo hopes that political survival will spur the government to take the tough decision necessary for growth:

If you think about the instincts of politicians – I want to get elected, I want to stay elected. They're not going to get elected or stay elected if they don't address this low growth, no growth, low productivity thing, and none of the policies out there are really addressing it ... I think that somebody has to make tough decisions, hard decisions, and there are going to be winners for the UK to prosper as a whole. The political class is going to have to make tough decisions, which, by definition, are going to adversely affect some, but if you don't make these tough decisions, you will adversely affect everybody.

THE FIVE KINGDOMS OF ECONOMIC GROWTH

It is for this reason that we began this book with the basics – what is actually needed to run an economy – the five kingdoms set out in Part I: low taxes, small government, sound money, regulations that don't impose more costs than benefits, and free trade.

Incentives are the key. In an increasingly mobile world, where entrepreneurship, talent and capital can move rapidly, the impact of incentives for good or bad has greatly increased. This means that the effect of anti-growth policies is multiplied up. But the good news is that it also means that the effect of pro-growth policies is also likely to be greater than that assumed using out-of-date estimates of elasticities.

THE 24/7 GROWTH PLAN

We move on from the five kingdoms to propose in Part II the 24/7 Growth Plan, which consists of twenty-four proposals that we have carefully costed and analysed. We estimate that they will produce 7 per cent additional growth within five years (over and above the government's current, optimistic, growth predictions) and an additional 28 per cent within twenty years.

According to the modelling, the 24/7 Growth Plan would also eliminate borrowing within a decade and bring the debt ratio down to around 60 per cent of GDP within twenty years compared with the 96 per cent in 2028–29 projected by the OBR Budget Report and the 270 per cent of GDP projected by the OBR risks and sustainability report.

This plan is robust and, on the basis of past evidence, if implemented, will generate the growth – indeed the economic effects have been estimated conservatively.

HOW TO GET THERE

We recounted our interviews with key economic decision-makers and business leaders in Part III. Among others, they included five of the eight living former Prime Ministers and nine of the eleven living former Chancellors. All thirty-four interviewees gave us high-level advice on how to implement pro-growth policies.

What emerges is substantial agreement about what needs to be done:

i. Show leadership
ii. Prepare well
iii. Get electoral buy-in
iv. Either reform the civil service or get the key tasks carried out by bodies outside government
v. Make growth the absolute priority

Leadership was quoted most frequently by the former Prime Ministers who decried the excessive concern with short-term headlines. 'They are behaving as if there will be an election tomorrow – but there won't be for another four years,' claimed one of them. They criticised the failure to use the electoral cycle to do economically beneficial things that might have political drawbacks. This was combined with the suggestion that clarity, consistency of purpose and clear communication of the longer-term goals were necessary to get buy-in from both Whitehall and Parliament.

The Trump example was frequently quoted as showing the benefits of preparation. 'If you don't get your homework done before you come to office, it's really hard to get much direction once you are sucked into the system,' said one interviewee.

Most of those who offered political advice suggested that to make radical economic change happen, it was necessary to obtain electoral buy-in. Their concept was of an election where the need for change had been fully communicated to the electorate and voted for by the public.

But an economic crisis, though not to be wished for, might also generate the same public desire for a change of path.

Among former Prime Ministers of different backgrounds, there was clear frustration with officialdom. However, they were divided on whether having a fight with Whitehall to generate reform was worth the political capital, given the possibility of sidelining civil servants and the scale of the challenges to be faced.

THE NEED FOR CHANGE

There seems a degree of agreement that change is necessary. Some seemed resigned to the UK gradually sliding down the world league table and losing relative prosperity and influence, as set out in the Cebr forecasts. Those witnesses tended to advocate fairly minor policy remedies for low growth.

But others – the majority – thought that in the modern world of mobile talent, this option no longer applies. Once talented and entrepreneurial people see that your economy is failing, they start first to look elsewhere and then move elsewhere. The slide forecast by Cebr may turn out much worse than predicted, so significant policy change is required to ameliorate the economic malaise.

This book sets out the North Star of economic growth and explains how incentives create prosperity through growth. And it then uses those principles to outline a robust, carefully costed plan to turn the UK around.

It is up to the electorate and political leaders to ensure it gets implemented.

ANNEX 1: COSTING THE 24/7 GROWTH PLAN

INTRODUCTION

This section costs the 24/7 Growth Plan.

It looks at the impact on tax and expenditure totals without behavioural change and then separately at the impact of the behavioural change estimated to result from each policy. This is then used to estimate the impact on GDP growth and hence on induced tax revenues. Please note that the proposed timing of the measures is indicative. The programme will have to be imposed with an eye on the extent to which it has achieved credibility in the financial markets. We have put forward a conservative approach, but if it becomes clear that the programme has achieved credibility (which it probably will), it will make sense to accelerate it. In particular, it is always a risk to propose future tax cuts in advance of implementation. History tells us that this can create problems as transactions get delayed until the cuts are implemented.

METHODOLOGY

The sums are done using a standard methodology developed for a range of bodies and explained in some detail below.

The static costs or gains from policy changes are first assessed assuming behaviour is unchanged.

Then behavioural models are used to estimate the impact on GDP. The tax model is an updated version of that used for the 2020 Tax Commission.[1] The model for estimating the supply-side changes is taken from the Growth Commission's 'Autumn 2024 Growth Budget' report[2] and the estimates are based on that report.

Using a standard (if cautious) fiscal drag elasticity of 1.5, the estimated impact of the growth on tax receipts is measured. This allows the net impact on tax, spending and borrowing to be estimated. These are set out in the tables below. (All totals are calculated from unrounded data.)

TAX CHANGES

Table 22 shows the gross cost (ex ante – meaning that these costs haven't yet been ameliorated by the impact of the growth engendered by the tax proposals set out in Chapter 8 as part of the 24/7 Growth Plan):

- In Year 2, all rates of income tax are replaced by a flat tax of 30 per cent and employees' National Insurance contributions (currently 8 per cent) are abolished with phasing in during Year 1.
- In Year 1, reinstate the pre-2024 Budget rules for non-domiciles.
- Between Years 2 and 10, employers' National Insurance contributions (currently 15 per cent) are gradually abolished.
- In Year 3, stamp duty is abolished for all transactions and inheritance tax is abolished.
- In Year 4, corporation tax on retained earnings (currently 25 per cent) is halved and in Year 5 fully abolished.
- In Year 4, capital gains tax on entrepreneurial gains held for more than five years is abolished, with anti-avoidance provisions to prevent abuse.
- In Year 10, the flat rate of income tax is reduced to 25 per cent and in Year 15 to 20 per cent.

Table 22 estimates the total static fiscal cost of the tax changes at constant levels of GDP (i.e. before taking into account the impact of behavioural changes). It shows a potential cost building up to £514 billion a year in the absence of behavioural changes in the final year. But that figure of course does not measure what would actually happen because tax cuts generally incentivise growth, shown in the tables below.

TABLE 22: FISCAL IMPACT OF TAX CHANGES

Static costs of policy	Year 1	Year 2	Year 3	Year 4	Year 5	Year 10	Year 15	Year 20
Flat rate of tax at 30%	0	4	12	12	12	12	12	12
Flat rate of tax at 20% (additional to 30%)						38	96	241
Reintroduce non-dom status	-5	-5	-5	-5	-5	-5	-5	-5
Abolish employees' NI phased in	35	70	87	105	122	140	201	201
Abolish stamp duty		10	20	20	20	20	20	20
Abolish CT on retained earnings				15	31	31	31	31
Abolish CGT for long term entrepreneurial investment				1	1	2	3	5
Abolish IHT			9	9	9	9	9	9
Total tax cuts	30	79	123	157	191	248	367	514

PUBLIC SPENDING

The cuts in taxes are paid for by higher growth and by savings in public spending. Looking at public spending:

- Public sector productivity is improved by 2 per cent each year, after the fall of 8 per cent since pre-Covid.
- The welfare budget is frozen at its 2024–25 level in real terms.
- As savings become available, both infrastructure and defence are prioritised. By Year 20, both are 2.5 per cent of GDP higher, bringing UK defence spending to 5 per cent of GDP.

Table 23 estimates the fiscal impact of public spending changes proposed.

TABLE 23: FISCAL IMPACT OF PUBLIC SPENDING CHANGES (£ BILLIONS)

	Year 1	Year 2	Year 3	Year 4	Year 5	Year 10	Year 15	Year 20
Productivity in public spending	35	52	69	87	104	121	138	156
Freeze welfare	13	29	36	46	55	75	95	115
Additional infrastructure spend				10	20	40	60	80
Additional defence spend				10	20	40	60	80
Total public spending net savings	48	81	105	112	119	116	113	111

Table 24 estimates the additional impact on GDP from the supply-side and trade policy measures proposed.

The supply-side improvements are:

- remove excessive environmental restrictions on planning
- targeting net zero at a similar pace to other advanced economies so that UK companies are not at a disadvantage from excessively rigorous green policies
- reforming labour markets to make working easier
- removing both tariff and non-tariff restrictions on international trade
- measures to improve productivity, mainly in the public sector

The trade policy measures costed are:

- remove trade restrictions on imports and on trade in services
- do not implement CBAM, the EU's system of carbon border taxes

TABLE 24: SUPPLY-SIDE MEASURES AND THEIR IMPACT ON GROWTH (BOOST TO GDP PER CENT)

	Year 1	Year 5	Year 10	Year 15	Year 20
Reduced environmental restrictions on building	0.2	0.6	2.5	3.9	5.4
Make energy prices more competitive	0.1	0.8	1.9	2	2.2
Smart net zero	Effects scored under energy prices				
Labour market reforms	0.5	1.5	1.8	2.3	2.7
Return minimum wage to 60% of median wage	Effects scored under labour market reforms				
Welfare reforms		0.6	0.9	1.2	1.6
Productivity improvements in public sector (not scored under public spending)	0.2	1	2.5	3.4	4.4
Improved infrastructure and road pricing	Not scored				
Total	1	4.5	9.6	12.8	16.3
	Year 1	Year 5	Year 10	Year 15	Year 20
Trade policy measures and their impact on growth (boost to GDP per cent)					
Removing trade restrictions	0.3	0.9	1.2	1.4	1.5
Avoiding CBAM	0	1.5	3	3	3
Other measures					
Reduce borrowing ratio to GDP	Not scored				
Restrain monetary growth with nominal GDP target	Not scored				

IMPACT ON BORROWING

Table 25 examines how the mix of higher growth, public spending economies and tax cuts is forecast to impact on borrowing. It shows that in every year, borrowing is predicted to be lower. This is important because lower borrowing is an ingredient in the sound money policies necessary to encourage confidence.

TABLE 25: CHANGES TO BORROWING AT OBR FORECAST 2025–26 LEVELS OF INCOMES AND PRICES

	Year 1	Year 2	Year 3	Year 4	Year 5	Year 10	Year 15	Year 20
Extra tax from higher GDP	5	11	22	53	88	244	339	449
Savings from reduced public spending	48	81	105	112	119	116	113	111
Total extra tax and reduced spending	53	92	127	165	207	360	452	560
Gross cost of tax cuts	30	79	123	157	191	248	367	514
Reduction in borrowing	23	13	4	8	16	112	85	46

Table 25 translates the net impact estimated in Table 24 into the impact on actual borrowing based on the OBR's March 2025 projections (the base borrowing assumption is that borrowing continues to fall at the pace set out in the last two years of the OBR projection).

It shows that the plan implies that the UK runs budget surpluses from the tenth year of the Growth Plan. This is what happens in other growth economies and the surpluses could be invested in a sovereign wealth fund.

TABLE 26: IMPACT ON BORROWING

Costs and gains at OBR forecast 2025–26 levels of incomes and prices £bn								
	Year 1	Year 2	Year 3	Year 4	Year 5	Year 10	Year 15	Year 20
Reduction in borrowing	23	13	4	7	16	112	85	46
Planned borrowing at 2025–26 incomes and prices	118	94	75	69	64	37	10	-17
Actual borrowing after 24/7 plan	95	81	71	62	48	-75	-75	-63

IMPACT ON GDP

Table 27 quantifies the GDP impact of the 24/7 Growth Plan. It shows that the impact of the measures is expected to build up to a boost to GDP of nearly 30 per cent in twenty years.

TABLE 27: ADDITIONAL GROWTH (GDP VS BASE) IN PER CENT

	Year 1	Year 2	Year 3	Year 4	Year 5	Year 10	Year 15	Year 20
From tax	0.4	1.0	1.2	2.0	2.3	6.4	8.9	12.5
From supply-side reforms	1.3	2.0	3.0	4.0	4.5	9.6	12.8	16.3
Total additional GDP	1.7	3.0	4.2	6.0	6.8	16.0	21.7	28.8

Table 28 shows how this affects the growth rate, based on the current OBR forecasts. It shows GDP growth averaging above 3 per cent.

TABLE 28: GDP GROWTH (ANNUAL PER CENT) BEFORE AND AFTER THE 24/7 GROWTH PLAN

	Year 1	Year 2	Year 3	Year 4	Year 5	Year 10	Year 15	Year 20
OBR growth forecast per annum	1.9	1.7	1.8	1.8	1.8	1.8	1.8	1.8
Additional growth from 24/7 Growth Plan	1.7	1.3	1.2	1.8	0.8	1.8	1.1	1.4
Resulting growth	3.6	3	3	3.6	2.6	3.7	2.9	3.2

If the 24/7 Growth Plan is implemented, our estimate is that it will raise UK GDP per capita in 2050 from a projected $74,832* to $96,383.† This would raise the UK's position in the world's GDP per capita league table from a projected forty-ninth position to nineteenth.

This is a huge gain – and it would transform the political position of any government that implemented it. For example, the UK would not fall behind Poland in 2034 as projected or behind Turkey in 2043. For those who want the UK to remain in the premier league of the world, it is essential to adopt this plan.

---

*   At 2017 international dollars PPP.
†   Projections commissioned from Cebr for this book based on the 2025 World Economic League Table.

ANNEX 2: WORLD ECONOMIC LEAGUE TABLE PROJECTIONS

For this book, we have specially commissioned world league table experts, the consultancy Cebr, to translate their world economic league table forecasts, WELT 2025,[1] into forecasts of GDP per capita to 2050. They have produced these forecasts for each year to 2050, and we include a table showing the forecasts for 2024, 2030, 2040 and 2050.

TABLE 29: WORLD GDP PER CAPITA (PPP) LEAGUE TABLE

Rank	2024		2030		2040		2050	
	Country	GDP per Capita	Country	GDP per Capita	Country	GDP per Capita	Country	GDP per Capita
1	Singapore	$132,570	Guyana	$151,422	Guyana	$193,396	Guyana	$241,745
2	Luxembourg	$131,596	Singapore	$145,125	Singapore	$173,107	Qatar	$204,782
3	Ireland	$113,869	Luxembourg	$132,202	Qatar	$161,430	Singapore	$204,688
4	Macao SAR	$112,631	Macao SAR	$129,234	Macao SAR	$158,027	Macao SAR	$188,351
5	Qatar	$102,271	Qatar	$126,039	Ireland	$142,266	Ireland	$164,339
6	Norway	$91,130	Ireland	$123,179	Luxembourg	$138,360	Brunei	$152,217
7	Switzerland	$83,521	Norway	$96,152	Brunei	$117,593	Luxembourg	$143,145
8	Brunei	$80,669	Brunei	$91,286	UAE	$108,764	UAE	$139,411
9	United States	$75,494	Switzerland	$87,051	Norway	$105,292	Malta	$133,756
10	Denmark	$74,570	UAE	$83,979	Taiwan	$103,289	Taiwan	$130,291
11	Guyana	$73,445	United States	$81,939	Malta	$98,969	Lithuania	$115,540
12	Netherlands	$71,880	Taiwan	$81,034	Switzerland	$98,963	Romania	$114,061
13	San Marino	$70,664	Denmark	$79,400	United States	$91,795	Norway	$114,017
14	Taiwan	$69,997	Netherlands	$75,755	Hong Kong	$90,346	Switzerland	$112,314
15	Iceland	$69,544	San Marino	$74,645	Denmark	$88,101	Hong Kong	$111,294
16	UAE	$67,824	Malta	$73,252	Netherlands	$83,316	United States	$102,837
17	Hong Kong	$66,083	Hong Kong	$72,990	San Marino	$82,854	Poland	$99,280
18	Belgium	$64,662	Iceland	$70,973	Lithuania	$81,183	Denmark	$97,403
19	Malta	$64,450	Belgium	$67,960	Iceland	$77,783	Croatia	$94,779
20	Austria	$64,062	Sweden	$67,914	Cyprus	$76,970	Slovenia	$93,635

21	Sweden	$63,547	Austria	$66,438	South Korea	$76,114	Cyprus	$93,580
22	Germany	$62,355	Germany	$65,356	Romania	$75,976	Hungary	$93,262
23	Australia	$61,557	Australia	$65,106	Sweden	$74,587	South Korea	$92,262
24	Bahrain	$57,966	Cyprus	$63,334	Austria	$74,214	Georgia	$91,793
25	Finland	$56,524	South Korea	$61,713	Belgium	$73,866	San Marino	$91,729
26	Canada	$56,093	Finland	$60,892	Australia	$73,695	Netherlands	$91,660
27	France	$56,039	Bahrain	$59,614	Poland	$73,605	Czech Republic	$89,637
28	South Korea	$55,158	Canada	$59,590	Germany	$72,860	Turkey	$89,419
29	Cyprus	$54,726	France	$58,798	Slovenia	$72,367	Latvia	$88,757
30	**UK**	**$54,475**	Lithuania	$57,057	Czech Republic	$71,626	Serbia	$87,117
31	Italy	$53,811	**UK**	**$57,004**	Finland	$70,764	Iceland	$85,834
32	Saudi Arabia	$52,557	Czech Republic	$56,868	Croatia	$68,993	Moldova	$85,320
33	Czech Republic	$49,921	Saudi Arabia	$56,771	Bahrain	$67,494	Austria	$82,755
34	Slovenia	$48,931	Italy	$56,351	Hungary	$67,302	Bulgaria	$82,755
35	Spain	$47,903	Slovenia	$55,960	Saudi Arabia	$66,722	Australia	$82,379
36	Lithuania	$47,697	Poland	$55,182	**UK**	**$65,620**	Finland	$82,306
37	Israel	$47,444	Israel	$53,674	France	$64,548	Estonia	$82,235
38	New Zealand	$47,371	Romania	$51,108	Canada	$63,801	Sweden	$81,549
39	Japan	$46,374	Spain	$50,359	Israel	$63,326	Germany	$81,521
40	Poland	$45,733	Croatia	$50,235	Italy	$62,638	Belgium	$80,293
41	Kuwait	$43,731	New Zealand	$49,815	Turkey	$62,407	Saudi Arabia	$77,412
42	Puerto Rico	$43,643	Japan	$49,568	Latvia	$62,179	Panama	$75,829
43	Croatia	$42,726	Hungary	$48,534	Estonia	$62,114	Bahrain	$75,285
44	Aruba	$42,649	Aruba	$47,955	Bulgaria	$59,238	Israel	$75,232
45	Estonia	$42,327	Portugal	$47,003	Spain	$58,828	Slovak Republic	$74,973
46	Portugal	$42,225	Estonia	$46,909	Slovak Republic	$58,653	**UK**	**$74,832**
47	Russia	$41,585	Puerto Rico	$46,014	Portugal	$57,142	Dominican Republic	$74,772
48	Romania	$41,266	Slovak Republic	$45,889	Panama	$56,970	Malaysia	$74,705
49	Hungary	$40,949	Russia	$45,444	Malaysia	$56,629	France	$70,878
50	Slovak Republic	$40,102	Kuwait	$44,625	Georgia	$55,885	Seychelles	$70,215
51	Greece	$37,761	Latvia	$43,564	Serbia	$55,772	Italy	$69,645
52	Latvia	$37,366	Panama	$43,556	New Zealand	$55,734	Portugal	$69,263
53	Kazakhstan	$36,716	Malaysia	$42,948	Japan	$55,592	Spain	$68,739

54	Panama	$36,574	Kazakhstan	$42,733	Aruba	$55,196	Canada	$67,680
55	Oman	$36,312	Bulgaria	$42,701	Seychelles	$53,884	Montenegro	$66,334
56	Malaysia	$36,208	Turkey	$42,531	Russia	$53,766	China	$65,682
57	Turkey	$35,631	Greece	$41,861	Kazakhstan	$52,436	North Macedonia	$65,342
58	Seychelles	$35,085	Seychelles	$40,893	Greece	$50,805	Kazakhstan	$64,099
59	Bulgaria	$34,697	Suriname	$38,226	Puerto Rico	$50,666	Aruba	$63,115
60	The Bahamas	$33,047	Oman	$37,356	Dominican Republic	$49,472	Maldives	$62,802
61	Uruguay	$30,944	Serbia	$35,885	Kuwait	$48,480	Russia	$62,434
62	Maldives	$30,515	Uruguay	$35,283	Maldives	$47,023	Mauritius	$61,929
63	Trinidad and Tobago	$30,295	Maldives	$35,241	Montenegro	$47,012	New Zealand	$61,731
64	Chile	$29,697	The Bahamas	$34,226	Suriname	$46,950	Greece	$61,677
65	St Kitts and Nevis	$28,627	Georgia	$33,776	China	$45,596	Armenia	$61,515
66	Belarus	$28,473	Trinidad and Tobago	$33,583	Moldova	$45,337	Japan	$61,414
67	Montenegro	$27,932	Montenegro	$33,382	Mauritius	$45,259	Suriname	$61,090
68	Mauritius	$27,342	Mauritius	$33,115	North Macedonia	$44,474	Puerto Rico	$57,255
69	Serbia	$27,234	St Kitts and Nevis	$32,857	Uruguay	$43,730	St Kitts and Nevis	$54,760
70	Antigua and Barbuda	$26,774	Chile	$32,820	Oman	$42,712	Albania	$54,407
71	Costa Rica	$26,298	Dominican Republic	$32,329	St Kitts and Nevis	$42,438	Uruguay	$53,524
72	Argentina	$25,744	Belarus	$31,988	Armenia	$40,981	Costa Rica	$53,398
73	Dominican Republic	$25,645	Costa Rica	$30,638	Costa Rica	$40,297	Kuwait	$51,763
74	Georgia	$24,860	Argentina	$30,481	Trinidad and Tobago	$39,968	Oman	$47,996
75	North Macedonia	$24,353	China	$30,396	Chile	$39,770	Chile	$47,537
76	St Lucia	$24,139	North Macedonia	$30,306	Argentina	$38,340	Kosovo	$47,309
77	China	$23,835	Antigua and Barbuda	$28,906	Belarus	$37,207	Argentina	$47,247
78	Turkmenistan	$23,639	Armenia	$26,752	Albania	$36,683	Trinidad and Tobago	$47,056
79	Thailand	$22,179	St Lucia	$26,240	The Bahamas	$35,973	Bosnia and Herzegovina	$46,745
80	Mexico	$22,059	Turkmenistan	$25,382	Antigua and Barbuda	$33,766	Vietnam	$46,498

81	Azerbaijan	$21,980	Albania	$25,025	Bosnia and Herzegovina	$32,862	Egypt	$45,694
82	Gabon	$21,218	Thailand	$24,954	Thailand	$31,876	Bhutan	$45,140
83	Armenia	$20,552	Moldova	$24,213	Kosovo	$31,825	Mongolia	$45,008
84	Brazil	$19,594	Azerbaijan	$23,892	Egypt	$31,766	Ukraine	$44,830
85	Barbados	$19,409	Mexico	$23,276	Ukraine	$31,243	Belarus	$42,917
86	Albania	$19,132	Bosnia and Herzegovina	$23,022	Mongolia	$31,015	Thailand	$40,649
87	Bosnia and Herzegovina	$18,978	Gabon	$22,002	Bhutan	$30,079	Antigua and Barbuda	$39,725
88	Suriname	$18,919	Brazil	$21,968	St Lucia	$29,640	India	$39,197
89	Colombia	$18,909	Barbados	$21,803	Vietnam	$29,407	The Bahamas	$39,192
90	Equatorial Guinea	$18,565	Ukraine	$21,590	Turkmenistan	$28,384	Indonesia	$38,442
91	Egypt	$18,255	Mongolia	$21,554	Azerbaijan	$28,201	Philippines	$37,617
92	Grenada	$17,973	Colombia	$21,347	St Vincent and the Grenadines	$27,642	St Vincent and the Grenadines	$36,802
93	St Vincent and the Grenadines	$17,452	Kosovo	$21,345	Mexico	$26,804	Palau	$33,951
94	Ukraine	$17,388	Egypt	$21,237	Indonesia	$26,788	Grenada	$33,838
95	Islamic Republic of Iran	$17,222	Grenada	$20,794	Grenada	$26,570	Botswana	$33,596
96	Botswana	$16,749	St Vincent and the Grenadines	$20,780	Brazil	$26,563	St Lucia	$33,276
97	Mongolia	$16,706	Bhutan	$19,741	Barbados	$25,930	Azerbaijan	$32,931
98	Kosovo	$16,696	Paraguay	$18,843	Colombia	$25,868	Bangladesh	$32,301
99	Paraguay	$16,357	Dominica	$18,766	Palau	$25,209	Colombia	$31,669
100	Moldova	$16,299	Botswana	$18,546	Botswana	$24,971	Turkmenistan	$31,619
101	Dominica	$16,184	Vietnam	$18,451	Gabon	$24,151	Brazil	$31,220
102	Peru	$15,729	Indonesia	$18,372	Paraguay	$24,004	Barbados	$30,412
103	Algeria	$15,545	Palau	$18,152	Dominica	$23,650	Mexico	$30,139
104	Palau	$14,840	Islamic Republic of Iran	$17,722	India	$23,252	Paraguay	$30,129
105	Indonesia	$14,567	Peru	$17,260	Philippines	$23,243	Dominica	$29,760
106	Vietnam	$14,371	Algeria	$16,894	Islamic Republic of Iran	$21,850	Cabo Verde	$28,574
107	Bhutan	$14,297	Fiji	$16,358	Fiji	$21,332	Fiji	$27,846
108	Fiji	$14,174	Libya	$16,328	Peru	$20,069	Uzbekistan	$26,589

109	Ecuador	$14,073	Equatorial Guinea	$15,906	Bangladesh	$19,637	Gabon	$26,106
110	South Africa	$13,772	Ecuador	$15,378	Cabo Verde	$19,264	Islamic Republic of Iran	$24,505
111	Iraq	$13,535	Guatemala	$15,151	Guatemala	$19,139	Guatemala	$24,237
112	Belize	$13,482	Belize	$14,175	Libya	$19,116	Peru	$23,436
113	Sri Lanka	$13,172	Philippines	$14,159	Algeria	$18,805	Djibouti	$22,959
114	Libya	$13,103	Iraq	$13,944	Uzbekistan	$18,350	Libya	$21,563
115	Guatemala	$13,044	South Africa	$13,808	Ecuador	$17,183	Algeria	$20,730
116	Tunisia	$12,584	India	$13,639	Iraq	$17,105	Iraq	$20,677
117	El Salvador	$11,547	Eswatini	$13,286	El Salvador	$16,333	El Salvador	$20,622
118	Eswatini	$11,316	El Salvador	$13,246	Eswatini	$15,392	Ecuador	$19,912
119	Philippines	$10,621	Sri Lanka	$13,233	Djibouti	$15,135	Cambodia	$19,854
120	Jamaica	$10,585	Tunisia	$13,092	Belize	$15,114	Morocco	$18,938
121	Namibia	$10,420	Cabo Verde	$12,891	South Africa	$14,625	Eswatini	$17,815
122	Uzbekistan	$10,297	Uzbekistan	$12,715	Sri Lanka	$14,459	Kyrgyz Republic	$17,646
123	Cabo Verde	$10,053	Jamaica	$11,621	Morocco	$14,429	Côte d'Ivoire	$17,459
124	Bolivia	$9,935	Bangladesh	$11,528	Tunisia	$14,083	Sri Lanka	$16,239
125	India	$9,878	Namibia	$11,300	Jamaica	$13,713	Jamaica	$16,233
126	Jordan	$9,661	Morocco	$11,057	Equatorial Guinea	$13,492	Guinea	$16,127
127	Nauru	$9,555	Jordan	$10,952	Jordan	$13,289	Belize	$16,118
128	Morocco	$9,377	Djibouti	$9,973	Cambodia	$13,213	Jordan	$16,103
129	Angola	$8,867	Bolivia	$9,641	Namibia	$12,614	South Africa	$15,489
130	Lao PDR	$8,576	Nauru	$9,447	Kyrgyz Republic	$12,447	Marshall Islands	$15,194
131	Bangladesh	$8,563	Lao PDR	$9,006	Côte d'Ivoire	$12,113	Tunisia	$15,086
132	Djibouti	$7,706	Kyrgyz Republic	$8,839	Marshall Islands	$11,608	Ghana	$14,981
133	Nicaragua	$7,650	Cambodia	$8,825	Ghana	$11,337	Kenya	$14,200
134	Timor-Leste	$7,288	Nicaragua	$8,714	Timor-Leste	$11,017	Namibia	$14,096
135	Mauritania	$7,258	Angola	$8,440	Nicaragua	$10,986	Nicaragua	$13,922
136	Cambodia	$7,196	Ghana	$8,424	Kenya	$10,322	Timor-Leste	$13,840
137	Kyrgyz Republic	$7,193	Côte d'Ivoire	$8,334	Nauru	$10,304	Ethiopia	$13,585
138	Ghana	$7,062	Marshall Islands	$8,194	Guinea	$9,603	Honduras	$11,477
139	Tonga	$6,733	Mauritania	$8,147	Lao PDR	$9,514	Equatorial Guinea	$11,399
140	Côte d'Ivoire	$6,726	Timor-Leste	$8,091	Honduras	$9,261	Nepal	$11,397

141	Honduras	$6,692	Tonga	$7,611	Bolivia	$8,899	Pakistan	$11,183
142	Kenya	$6,267	Kenya	$7,582	Tonga	$8,776	Nauru	$10,986
143	Samoa	$6,236	Honduras	$7,468	Ethiopia	$8,701	Rwanda	$10,984
144	Marshall Islands	$6,111	Samoa	$7,043	Pakistan	$8,592	Tajikistan	$10,488
145	Pakistan	$5,916	Pakistan	$6,655	Angola	$8,326	Lao PDR	$10,267
146	Tuvalu	$5,858	Tuvalu	$6,533	Nepal	$8,318	Tonga	$10,144
147	Nigeria	$5,789	Nigeria	$6,039	Tuvalu	$8,044	Tuvalu	$9,764
148	Republic of Congo	$5,622	Tajikistan	$6,021	Tajikistan	$7,952	Senegal	$9,407
149	São Tomé and Príncipe	$5,450	Nepal	$5,935	Samoa	$7,724	Benin	$9,074
150	Myanmar	$5,005	Republic of Congo	$5,887	Nigeria	$7,707	Nigeria	$8,736
151	Tajikistan	$4,940	São Tomé and Príncipe	$5,791	Mauritania	$7,176	Tanzania	$8,485
152	Cameroon	$4,881	Guinea	$5,771	Rwanda	$7,164	Samoa	$8,457
153	Nepal	$4,761	Myanmar	$5,475	Senegal	$7,019	Bolivia	$8,377
154	Zimbabwe	$4,465	Cameroon	$5,457	Cameroon	$6,745	Cameroon	$8,334
155	Senegal	$4,465	Senegal	$5,209	Republic of Congo	$6,716	Angola	$8,094
156	Micronesia	$4,042	Ethiopia	$5,025	Benin	$6,575	Republic of Congo	$7,616
157	Benin	$3,967	Zimbabwe	$5,016	São Tomé and Príncipe	$6,387	Zimbabwe	$7,181
158	Guinea	$3,896	Benin	$4,744	Zimbabwe	$6,183	São Tomé and Príncipe	$7,161
159	Zambia	$3,748	Rwanda	$4,506	Tanzania	$6,151	Uganda	$7,018
160	Tanzania	$3,638	Zambia	$4,474	Myanmar	$6,147	Myanmar	$7,011
161	Ethiopia	$3,592	Tanzania	$4,405	Zambia	$5,655	Zambia	$6,963
162	Comoros	$3,392	Micronesia	$4,264	Uganda	$5,239	Togo	$6,479
163	Rwanda	$3,356	Uganda	$3,926	Micronesia	$4,857	Mauritania	$6,225
164	Uganda	$3,241	Comoros	$3,793	Togo	$4,736	Sierra Leone	$5,723
165	Papua New Guinea	$3,144	The Gambia	$3,479	Comoros	$4,538	The Gambia	$5,699
166	Kiribati	$3,105	Togo	$3,452	The Gambia	$4,472	Comoros	$5,434
167	The Gambia	$3,074	Sierra Leone	$3,451	Sierra Leone	$4,416	Guinea-Bissau	$5,198
168	Sierra Leone	$2,966	Papua New Guinea	$3,395	Guinea-Bissau	$4,078	Micronesia	$5,166
169	Togo	$2,895	Kiribati	$3,314	Papua New Guinea	$3,889	Burkina Faso	$4,652

170	Lesotho	$2,891	Guinea-Bissau	$3,201	Burkina Faso	$3,616	Papua New Guinea	$4,408
171	Guinea-Bissau	$2,729	Lesotho	$2,927	Kiribati	$3,576	Mali	$4,156
172	Haiti	$2,669	Burkina Faso	$2,848	Mali	$3,391	Sudan	$4,008
173	Vanuatu	$2,611	Mali	$2,761	Sudan	$3,256	Kiribati	$3,816
174	Chad	$2,589	Sudan	$2,640	Lesotho	$3,082	Niger	$3,383
175	Burkina Faso	$2,509	Haiti	$2,615	Solomon Islands	$2,684	Lesotho	$3,249
176	Mali	$2,473	Chad	$2,585	Niger	$2,611	Somalia	$3,155
177	Solomon Islands	$2,306	Solomon Islands	$2,455	Chad	$2,573	Liberia	$3,120
178	Sudan	$2,062	Vanuatu	$2,418	Somalia	$2,542	Madagascar	$3,119
179	Niger	$1,748	Niger	$2,031	Haiti	$2,531	Solomon Islands	$2,950
180	Madagascar	$1,731	Liberia	$2,025	Liberia	$2,445	Mozambique	$2,685
181	Liberia	$1,670	Madagascar	$1,920	Madagascar	$2,444	Democratic Republic of the Congo	$2,640
182	Somalia	$1,623	Democratic Republic of the Congo	$1,786	Mozambique	$2,369	Haiti	$2,614
183	Democratic Republic of the Congo	$1,592	Mozambique	$1,773	Vanuatu	$2,311	Chad	$2,550
184	Malawi	$1,515	Somalia	$1,765	Democratic Republic of the Congo	$2,173	Yemen	$2,483
185	Yemen	$1,500	Malawi	$1,649	Yemen	$2,015	Malawi	$2,419
186	Mozambique	$1,486	Yemen	$1,551	Malawi	$2,001	Vanuatu	$2,198
187	Central African Republic	$1,145	Central African Republic	$1,155	South Sudan	$1,473	South Sudan	$1,846
188	Burundi	$880	South Sudan	$1,069	Central African Republic	$1,175	Central African Republic	$1,218
189	South Sudan	$660	Burundi	$872	Burundi	$852	Burundi	$924

NOTES

INTRODUCTION

1 'Supplementary forecast information release', OBR, 30 January 2025, https://obr.uk/docs/dlm_uploads/Non-doms-supplementary-release-Jan-2025.pdf

2 See, for example, 'Analysing Singapore's 2025 general elections', Australian National University, 26 May 2025, https://www.anu.edu.au/events/analysing-singapores-2025-general-elections

3 There are literally thousands of reports on the impact of AI. We have focused here on: 1) 'The Impact of AI on the Labour Market', Tony Blair Institute for Global Change, September 2024; 2) 'The Economic Potential of Generative AI', McKinsey and Co., June 2023; 3) 'Gen AI and the Future of Work', IMF, January 2024; 4) 'Artificial Intelligence and Its Potential Effects on the Economy and the Federal Budget', Congressional Budget Office, December 2024; and 5) Daron Acemoglu, 'The Simple Macroeconomics of AI', MIT Shaping the Future of Work Initiative, May 2024, as well as the co-authors' own experience.

4 'The impact of AI on UK jobs and training', Department for Education, November 2023, https://assets.publishing.service.gov.uk/media/656856b8cc1ec500138eef49/Gov.UK_Impact_of_AI_on_UK_Jobs_and_Training.pdf

5 Andrew Buck, 'Ecommerce Market Size by Country', MobiLoud, 3 July 2025, https://www.mobiloud.com/blog/ecommerce-market-size-by-country

6 'Artificial Intelligence', Business.gov.uk, https://www.business.gov.uk/campaign/grow-your-tech-business-in-the--uk/artificial-intelligence

7 'Next Generation UK 2024', British Council, 2024, https://www.britishcouncil.org/research-insight/next-generation-uk-2024

8 Thomas Piketty, *Capital in the Twenty-First Century*, Harvard University Press, 2013.

9 E.g. the distinguished inequality scholar Sir Anthony Atkinson (see https://www.tony-atkinson.com/the-15-proposals-from-tony-atkinsons-inequality-what-can-be-done/0 or the IMF study https://www.imf.org/en/Publications/WP/Issues/2017/07/24/Why-Is-Labor-Receiving-a-Smaller-Share-of-Global-Income-Theory-and-Empirical-Evidence-45102). Also see Douglas McWilliams, *The Inequality Paradox*, Overlook Books, 2018, by one of the co-authors of this book.

CHAPTER 1

1 See especially his seminal article 'An Exploration in the Theory of Optimal Income Taxation', *Review of Economic Studies*, Vol. 38, No. 114, February 1971, pp. 175–208.

2 Ibid., p. 207.

3 'Government Spending Details for 1910 in percent GDP', usgovernmentspending.com, https://www.usgovernmentspending.com/year_spending_1910USpn_24ps2n

4 OECD Economic Outlook Statistical Annex, estimate for 2024, https://www.oecd.org/en/topics/sub-issues/economic-outlook/oecd-economic-outlook-statistical-annex.html

5 Total wealth estimate from Table Z1, Federal Reserve Bank, public debt estimate from https://fiscaldata.treasury.gov/americas-finance-guide/national-debt/

6 Steve H. Hanke and Alex K. F. Kwok, 'On the Measurement of Zimbabwe's Hyperinflation', *Cato Journal*, Vol. 29, No. 2, 2009, https://www.cato.org/sites/cato.org/files/serials/files/cato-journal/2009/5/cj29n2-8.pdf

7 'BCV admits hyperinflation of 53,798,500% since 2016', *Venezuela Al Dia* (in Spanish), 28 May 2019.

8 'Argentina Economic Outlook: June 2025', BBVA Research, 26 June 2025, https://www.bbvaresearch.com/en/publicaciones/argentina-economic-outlook-june-2025/

9 Theodore Roosevelt, Banquet Speech, Dallas, Texas, 5 April 1905.

CHAPTER 2

1 Adam Smith, *The Wealth of Nations*, Vol. I, Liberty Fund Facsimile, p. 16.

CHAPTER 3

1　See Tax Foundation evidence to the House of Representatives: https://taxfoundation.org/testimony/federal-tax-complexity-costs-reform/

2　'General Election 2024: Reform UK propose big cuts in income, inheritance and corporation taxes', Chartered Institute of Taxation, 18 June 2024, https://www.tax.org.uk/general-election-2024-reform-uk-propose-big-cuts-in-income-inheritance-and-corporation-taxes

3　For a deeper discussion of these concepts, see James Gwartney and Richard Stroup, 'Labor Supply and Tax Rates: A Correction of the Record', *The American Economic Review*, Vol. 73, No. 3, June 1983, pp. 446–51.

4　IRS Statistics of Income, Table 3.4: Returns with Modified Taxable Income: Tax Classified by Both the Marginal Rate and Each Rate at Which Tax Was Computed, https://www.irs.gov/uac/soi-tax-stats-statistics-of-income

5　Originally authored by Arthur B. Laffer, Jeanne Sinquefield and Brian Domitrovic.

6　Thomas Piketty, Emmanuel Saez and Gabriel Zucman, 'Distributional National Accounts: Methods and Estimates for the United States', *Quarterly Journal of Economics*, Vol. 133, Issue 2, May 2018.

7　For a mathematical derivation of the 'Ellipse', see Victor A. Canto, Douglas H. Joines and Arthur B. Laffer, 'Taxation, GNP and Potential GNP' presented at the American Statistical Association, San Diego, California, 14–17 August 1978.

8　Victor A. Canto, Douglas H. Joines and Arthur B. Laffer, 'Tax Rates, Factor Employment, and Market Production', 1981.

9　Bruce Bartlett, 'Supply-Side Economics: "Voodoo Economics" or Lasting Contribution?' Laffer Associates, 11 November 2003.

10　Published in *The Selected Letters of John Galbraith*, 2017.

11　Martin Gardner, *Knotted Doughnuts and Other Mathematical Entertainments*, W. H. Freeman & Co Ltd, 1986, p. 260

12　Martin Gardner, 'Mathematical Games: The Laffer curve and other laughs in current economics', *The Scientific American*, print edition, December 1981.

13　N. Gregory Mankiw, *Principles of Economics*, Cengage, 2008, p. 169.

14　N. Gregory Mankiw, 'On Supply-Side Economics', gregmankiw@blogspot.com, 2 July 2007.

15　Dylan Matthews, 'Where does the Laffer curve bend?', voices.washingtonpost.com, 9 August 2010.

16　Paul A. Samuelson, *Economics: An Introductory Analysis*, McGraw-Hill, 1967, p. 343.

17　Heller in JEC, *Twentieth Anniversary of the Employment Act of 1946*, 1966, p. 66.

18　Edmund Burke, 'Speech on American Taxation', *Select Works of Edmund Burke*, Vol. 1, Liberty Fund, 1999, p.237.

19　William F. Buckley, 'The Laffer Curve Revisited', *Palm Beach Post*, 29 July 1980.

20　John Maynard Keynes, *The Collected Writings of John Maynard Keynes*, Cambridge University Press for the Royal Economic Society, 1973, p. 159.

21　Smith, *The Wealth of Nations*, Vol. II, p. 367.

22　James M. Buchanan and Dwight R. Lee, 'Politics, Time, and the Laffer Curve', *Journal of Political Economy*, August 1982, p. 818.

23　Zagorin, 'The Laffer Curve', *Time*, 29 March 1999, p. 112.

24　'Reagan's Legacy', *WSJ*, 23 January 1989.

25　Miller, 'Arthur Laffer, the Man Who Loved Tax Cuts', *Bloomberg Businessweek*, 13 November 2014.

26　'A Dozen Who Shaped the '80s', *Los Angeles Times*, 1 January 1990.

27　'The Heroes, Villains, Triumphs, Failures and Other Memorable Events', *Institutional Investor*, July 1992.

28　Ronald R. Reagan, 'Remarks during a Teleconference', 2 March 1983.

29　David Ricardo, *On the Principles of Political Economy and Taxation*, Liberty Fund, 2004, p. 172.

30　Based on *The Compleat Statesman, or, The Political Will and Testament of Cardinal Richelieu*, Vol. II, R. Bentley (ed.), University of Michigan Digital Collections, 1695, pp. 110–11, https://quod.lib.umich.edu/e/eebo/A57249.0001.001?rgn=main;view=fulltext

31　Patrick J. Purcell, 'Geographic Mobility and Annual Earnings in the United States', *Social Security Bulletin*, Vol. 80, No. 2, 2020.

32　Jonathan F. Pingle, 'A Note on Measuring Internal Migration in the United States', *Economics Letters*, Vol. 94, No. 1, 2007, pp. 38–42. William H. Frey, 'The Great American Migration Slowdown: Regional and Metropolitan Dimensions', Brookings Institution, 2009, https://www.brookings.edu/wp-content/uploads/2016/07/1209_migration_frey-1.pdf

33　US Bureau of Transportation Statistics, 'Annual US motor vehicle production and domestic sales', https://www.bts.gov/content/annual-us-motor-vehicle-production-and-factory-wholesale-sales-thousands-units

34　Arthur B. Laffer and Wayne H. Winegarden, 'The Economic Consequences of Tennessee's Gift and Estate Tax', Laffer Associates, November 2011.

35 Part of a booklet produced by Nato in 1998, repeated in Julian Cooper, 'Russian Military Expenditure: Data, Analysis and Issues', Swedish Defence Ministry, 2013.

36 Sabina Silajdžić and Eldin Mehić, 'How Effective Is Tax Policy in Attracting Foreign Direct Investments in Transition Countries?', *Central European Business Review*, 2022, pp. 19–39.

37 Ulrich Blum, 'The Eastern German Growth Trap: Structural Limits to Convergence?', *Intereconomics*, Vol. 54, No. 6, 2019, pp. 359–68, https://www.intereconomics.eu/contents/year/2019/number/6/article/the-eastern-german-growth-trap-structural-limits-to-convergence.html

38 Jörg Bibow, 'No. 67A, 2001. The Economic Consequences of German Unification: The Impact of Misguided Macroeconomic Policies', https://www.levyinstitute.org/pubs/hili67a.pdf

39 *The World Factbook 1990*, CIA, 1990.

40 Blum, 'The Eastern German Growth Trap'.

41 IMF data.

42 James Cloyne, 'What are the Effects of Tax Changes in the United Kingdom? New Evidence from a Narrative Evaluation', CESifo Working Paper No. 3433, Center for Economic Studies and ifo Institute, 2011.

43 Christina D. Romer and David H. Romer, 'The Macroeconomic Effects of Tax Changes: Estimates Based on a New Measure of Fiscal Shocks', *American Economic Review*, Vol. 100, No. 3, June 2010, pp. 763–801.

44 OBR Forecast Evaluation Report, October 2014, https://obr.uk/box/effect-of-the-additional-rate-of-income-tax-on-receipts/

45 'The 50p tax – good intentions, bad outcomes', Cebr, 2011, https://conservativehome.blogs.com/files/cebr-report---final.pdf

46 'Did cutting the 50p rate of tax raise £8 billion?', Full Fact, 4 March 2016, https://fullfact.org/economy/did-cutting-50p-rate-tax-raise-8-billion/

47 Robert J. Barro, 'Economic Growth in a Cross Section of Countries', *Quarterly Journal of Economics*, Vol. 106, Issue 2, 1991, pp. 407–43.

48 Gerald W. Scully, 'What is the Optimal Size of Government in the United States', National Centre for Policy Analysis report no. 188, November 1994.

49 Livio Di Matteo, *Measuring government in the 21st century*, Fraser Institute, 2013, https://www.fraserinstitute.org/sites/default/files/measuring-government-in-the-21st-century.pdf

50 Alex Durante, 'Reviewing Recent Evidence of the Effect of Taxes on Economic Growth', Tax Foundation, 21 May 2021, https://taxfoundation.org/research/all/federal/reviewing-recent-evidence-effect-taxes-economic-growth/

51 This is mainly taken from Chapter 7 'Inequality and Growth', pp. 126–37 of McWilliams, *The Inequality Paradox*, which in turn quotes from Table 16 in Patrick Minford, 'Tax and Growth: Theories and Evidence', in Philip Booth (ed.), *Taxation, Government Spending and Economic Growth*, Institute for Economic Affairs, London, November 2016, pp. 105–21.

52 Barro, 'Economic Growth in a Cross Section of Countries', pp. 407–43.

53 Reinhard Koester and Roger Kormendi, 'Taxation, Aggregate Activity and Economic Growth: Cross-country Evidence on Some Supply-side Hypotheses', *Economic Inquiry*, Vol. 27, 1989, pp. 367–86.

54 Pär Hansson and Magnus Henrekson, 'A New Framework for Testing the Effect of Government Spending on Growth and Productivity', *Public Choice*, Vol. 81, 1994, pp. 381–401.

55 Paul Cashin, 'Government Spending, Taxes and Economic Growth', IMF Staff Papers, Vol. 42, No. 2, 1995, pp. 237–69.

56 Eric M. Engen and Jonathan Skinner, 'Taxation and Economic Growth', *National Tax Journal*, Vol. 49, 1996, pp. 617–42.

57 Willi Leibfritz, John Thornton and Alexandra Bibbee, 'Taxation and Economic Performance', OECD Working Paper 176, 1997.

58 Alberto Alesina, Silvia Ardagna, Roberto Perotti and Fabio Schiantarelli, 'Fiscal Policy, Profits, and Investment', *American Economic Review*, Vol. 92, 2002, pp. 571–89.

59 Michael Bleaney, Norman Gemmell and Richard Kneller, 'Testing the Endogenous Growth Model: Public Expenditure, Taxation and Growth over the Long Run', *Canadian Journal of Economics*, Vol. 34, No. 1, 2000, pp. 36–57.

60 Stefan Folster and Magnus Henrekson, 'Growth Effects of Government Expenditure and Taxation in Rich Countries', Stockholm School of Economics Working Paper 391, 2000.

61 Andrea Bassanini and Stefano Scarpetta, 'Does Human Capital Matter for Growth in OECD Countries? Evidence from PMG Estimates', OECD Economics Department Working Paper 282, 2001.

62 Karel Mertens and José Luis Montiel Olea, 'Marginal Tax Rates and Income: New Time Series Evidence', *Quarterly Journal of Economics*, Vol. 133, Issue 4, 2018, pp. 1803–84. Owen Zidar, 'Tax Cuts for Whom?

Heterogenous Effects of Income Tax Changes on Growth and Employment', *Journal of Political Economy*, Vol. 127, No. 3, 2019, pp. 1437–72.

63 Zidar, 'Tax Cuts for Whom?', pp. 1437–72.

64 Alexander Ljungqvist and Michael Smolyansky, 'To Cut or Not to Cut? On the Impact of Corporate Taxes on Employment and Income', NBER Working Paper 20753, 2014.

65 Samara Gunter, Daniel Riera-Crichton, Carlos Vegh and Guillermo Vuletin, 'Non-linear Effects of Tax Changes on Output: The Role of the Initial Level of Taxation', NBER Working Paper 26570, 2019.

66 Anh D. M. Nguyen, Luisanna Onnis and Raffaele Rossi, 'The Macroeconomic Effects of Income and Consumption Tax Changes', *American Economic Journal: Economic Policy*, Vol. 13, No. 2, pp. 439–66.

67 James Cloyne, Nicholas Dimsdale and Natacha Postel-Vinay, 'Taxes and Growth: New Narrative Evidence from Interwar Britain', NBER Working Paper 24659, 2018.

68 Nazila Alinaghi and W. Robert Reed, 'Taxes and Economic Growth in OECD Countries: A Meta-analysis', *Public Finance Review*, Vol. 49, No. 10, pp. 3–40.

69 Jon Moynihan, *Return to Growth: How to Fix the Economy – Volume One*, Biteback, 2024 and Jon Moynihan, *Return to Growth: How to Fix the Economy – Volume Two*, Biteback, 2025.

70 Ibid.

71 I. Ball and G. Pflugrath, 'Government Accounting: Making Enron Look Good', *World Economics*, Vol. 13, No. 1, January–March 2012.

72 G. Leach, *The Negative Impact of Taxation on Economic Growth*, Reform, 2003.

73 Ibid.

74 Ibid.

75 Ibid.

76 Ibid.

77 Alinaghi and Reed, 'Taxes and Economic Growth in OECD Countries', pp. 3–40.

CHAPTER 4

1 John Cochrane, 'Negative Stimulus, 1946', 2 February 2012, http://johnhcochrane.blogspot.com/2012/02/negative-stimulus-1946.html

2 For a detailed examination of this, see Shigeru Fujita, Valerie A. Ramey and Tal Roded, 'Why Didn't the US Unemployment Rate Rise at the End of WWII?', NBER Working Paper 33041, October 2024, https://www.nber.org/papers/w33041

3 Larry Klein, 'A Post-Mortem on Transition Predictions of National Product', *Journal of Political Economy*, Vol. LIV, No. 4, August 1946.

4 Arthur B. Laffer, Jeanne Cairns Sinquefield and Brian Domitrovic, *Taxes Have Consequences: An Income Tax History of the United States*, Post Hill Press, 2022.

5 A more comprehensive treatment is in Arthur Laffer, 'The "Ellipse": An Explication of the Laffer Curve in a Two Factor Model', A. B. Laffer Associates, 28 July 1980, pp. 21–4, a published version of which appeared in the *Financial Analysts Journal*: Arthur B. Laffer, 'Supply-Side Economics', *Financial Analysts Journal*, September/October 1981.

6 See Arthur B. Laffer, 'The Truth About Redistribution', Laffer Associates, 16 October 2014. Also see: Casey Mulligan, *The Redistribution Recession: How Labor Market Distortions Contracted the Economy*, Oxford University Press, 2012.

7 Olivia Lang, 'Why has Germany taken so long to pay off its WW1 debt?', BBC News, 2 October 2010, https://www.bbc.com/news/world-europe-11442892

8 Jenny Cosgrave, 'UK finally finishes paying for World War I', CNBC, 9 March 2015, https://www.cnbc.com/2015/03/09/uk-finally-finishes-paying-for-world-war-i.html

9 'IRS Budget & Workforce', IRS, https://www.irs.gov/statistics/irs-budget-and-workforce

10 'School workforce in England', gov.uk, 6 June 2024, https://explore-education-statistics.service.gov.uk/find-statistics/school-workforce-in-england/2023

CHAPTER 5

1 Javier Andres and Ignacio Hernando, 'Does Inflation Harm Economic Growth: Evidence for the OECD', NBER Working Paper 60, 1997.

2 Earl J. Hamilton, *American Treasure and the Price Revolution in Spain, 1501–1650*, Harvard University Press, 1934.

3 Thomas J. Sargent, 'The Ends of Four Big Inflations', in *Inflation: Causes and Effects*, Robert E. Hall (ed.), University of Chicago Press, 1982, pp. 54–5.

4 The relationship between increases in tax rates and the increasing demand for gold in the first devastating

years of the Great Depression in the United States, 1929–33, is discussed in Chapter 5 of Arthur B. Laffer, Brian Domitrovic and Jeanne Cairns Sinquefield, *Taxes Have Consequences: An Income Tax History of the United States*, Post Hill Press, 2022.

5   See Douglas McWilliams, 'Strong Currencies the Swiss and German Experience', CBI Review, summer 1975.

6   For an explanation of currency boards, including a discussion of Johns Hopkins University Professor Steve Hanke's record of success in shaping them, see Brian Domitrovic, 'The Emerging International Currency Crisis: Currency Boards Can Stave It Off', Laffer Associates, 8 November 2018.

7   Statista.

CHAPTER 6

1   Junichi Suzuki, 'Land Use Regulation as a Barrier to Entry: Evidence from the Texas Lodging Industry', University of Toronto, Department of Economics, Working Paper 412, 2010.

2   McKinsey Global Institute, 'Driving productivity and growth in the UK economy', 1 October 1998. Cited by Gordon Brown in his Harvard University interview, https://sites.harvard.edu/uk-regional-growth/directory/gordon-brown/

3   Al Neuharth, 'Traveling Interstates is our Sixth Freedom', *USA Today*, 22 June 2006; US Department of Transportation.

4   'History of Smog', *LA Weekly*, September 2005, https://www.laweekly.com/history-of-smog/

5   Zen Vuong, 'SoCal's reduction in smog linked to major improvement in children's respiratory health', USC Today, 12 April 2016.

6   Jonathan H. Adler, 'Fables of the Cuyahoga: Reconstructing a History of Environmental Protection', *Faculty Publications*, 2002, p. 191.

7   United States Environmental Protection Agency.

8   'History of the Surgeon General's Reports on Smoking and Health', Centers for Disease Control, https://www.cdc.gov/tobacco-surgeon-general-reports/about/history.html

CHAPTER 7

1   Marc A. Miles, 'The Effects of Devaluation on the Trade Balance and the Balance of Payments: Some New Results', *Journal of Political Economy*, Vol. 87, No. 3, June 1979, pp. 600–620.

2   'Lifting 800 Million People Out of Poverty – New Report Looks at Lessons from China's Experience', World Bank Group, 1 April 2022, https://www.worldbank.org/en/news/press-release/2022/04/01/lifting-800-million-people-out-of-poverty-new-report-looks-at-lessons-from-china-s-experience

3   Mancur Olson, *Economics of the Wartime Shortage*, Duke University Press, 1963.

4   Ibid.

5   Ibid.

6   Ibid.

7   Ibid.

8   Jacob Abbott, *Peter the Great*, 1900, p. 82.

CHAPTER 8

1   OBR Spring Statement Economic and Fiscal Outlook 2025, Annex A.

2   'Economic Outlook', OECD, https://www.oecd.org/economy/outlook/statistical-annex/

3   OECD Economic Outlook December 2024, Statistical Annex, https://www.oecd.org/en/topics/sub-issues/economic-outlook.html#stat-annex

4   Kyle Pomerleau, Jared Walczak and Scott Hodge, '2017 International Tax Competitiveness Index', Tax Foundation, 31 October 2017, https://taxfoundation.org/research/all/global/2017-international-tax-competitiveness-index/

5   Alex Mengden, 'International Tax Competitiveness Index 2024', Tax Foundation, 2024, https://taxfoundation.org/wp-content/uploads/2024/10/International-Tax-Competitiveness-Index-2024-FV.pdf

6   'National Insurance rates and categories', gov.uk, https://www.gov.uk/national-insurance-rates-letters. Numbers relate to Category A.

7   This is originally based on research from the Fraser Institute (https://www.fraserinstitute.org/sites/default/files/Flat_Tax_Lessons_From_Abroad.pdf) but has been updated by the authors.

8   Data from the World Bank 'GDP per capita (current US$)' and the 'World Development Indicators'.

9   For example, P. D. Aligica and H. Terpe, 'The Flat Tax Experiment: The Romanian Case', 2005. The working paper predicted wrongly that the Romanian flat tax would fail to generate revenues, while IMF advice has almost invariably been against flat taxes.

10   Arun Advani, David Burgherr and Andy Summers, 'Reforming the non-dom regime: revenue estimates', CAGE Warwick LSE International Inequalities Institute, 2022.

11   RSM, https://www.rsmuk.com/insights/tax-voice/could-abolishing-tax-benefits-for-non-domiciled-individuals

12   'Statistical commentary on non-domiciled taxpayers in the UK', gov.uk, 17 July 2025, https://www.gov.uk/government/statistics/statistics-on-non-domiciled-taxpayers-in-the-uk/statistical-commentary-on-non-domiciled-taxpayers-in-the-uk--2

13   A. Esteller-Moré, A. Piolatto and M. D. Rablen, 'Taxing high-income earners: tax avoidance and mobility', in N. Hashimzade and Y. Epifantseva (eds), *The Routledge Companion to Tax Avoidance Research*, Routledge, 2018. This study is a meta study and summarises the conclusions of thirty-seven other studies.

14   'Why Millionaires Are Fleeing the UK Under Labour', 14 February 2025, https://www.blacktowerfm.co.uk/news/millionaires-are-fleeing-the-uk-under-labour

15   Data from HMRC Income Tax Liabilities Statistics Table 2.5.

16   Andrew Amoils, 'London's Wealth Exodus', Henley & Partners, https://www.henleyglobal.com/publications/henley-private-wealth-migration-report-2024/londons-wealth-exodus

17   'One in five bankers claims non-dom tax status', LSE, 7 April 2022, https://www.lse.ac.uk/News/Latest-news-from-LSE/2022/d-Apr-22/Non-doms

18   See, for example, Paul Johnson, 'Stamp duty is an economic nonsense', Institute for Fiscal Studies, 22 November 2016, https://ifs.org.uk/articles/stamp-duty-economic-nonsense

19   'Stamp duty on shares is "a tax on growth", new CPS modelling shows', Centre for Policy Studies, https://cps.org.uk/media/post/2024/stamp-duty-on-shares-is-a-tax-on-growth-new-cps-modelling-shows

20   'The Fiscal Impact of a permanent stamp duty holiday for Kensington Mortgages', Cebr, 21 December 2020, https://cebr.com/reports/the-fiscal-impact-of-a-permanent-stamp-duty-holiday-for-kensington-mortages/

21   'The Spring Growth Budget 2024', Growth Commission, 2024, p. 69, https://www.growth-commission.com/wp-content/uploads/2024/02/Final-PDF-Spring-Budget-24-1.pdf

22   Ibid.

23   'Inheritance Tax rates in G7 and EU countries ten times higher than emerging economies', UHY Hacker Young, https://www.uhy-fay.com/wp-content/uploads/2020/01/Impuesto-Sucesiones-Comparativa-English-Dec19.pdf

24   'Which Taxes are Best and Worst for Growth?', National Institute of Economic and Social Research, 30 May 2024, https://niesr.ac.uk/news/which-taxes-are-best-and-worst-growth

25   'How does corporate taxation affect business investment?', OECD, 19 July 2023, https://www.oecd.org/en/publications/how-does-corporate-taxation-affect-business-investment_04e682d7-en.html

26   'The Growth Budget 2023', The Growth Commission, November 2023, Annex 1, p. 84, https://mcusercontent.com/179072cbb29cf412c033c8542/files/b2a78cbb-cdcc-f675-e0e4-b87fb8d6351b/FINAL_Growth_Budget_2023_DIGITAL_SPREAD_1_.pdf describes the underlying model; 'Cebr's Immediate Reaction: Autumn Budget Briefing October 2024', Cebr, October 2024, https://cebr.com/wp-content/uploads/2024/10/Cebr-Briefing-Note-Autumn-Budget.pdf describes the underlying calculation.

27   'Report – Value for money', National Audit Office, 10 February 2025, https://www.nao.org.uk/reports/the-administrative-cost-of-the-tax-system/

28   'The administrative cost of the tax system', National Audit Office, 2025, https://www.nao.org.uk/wp-content/uploads/2025/02/the-administrative-cost-of-the-tax-system.pdf

CHAPTER 9

1   Correlli Barnett, *The Lost Victory: British Dreams, British Realities, 1945–1950*, Pan Books, 2001.

2   'Economic and fiscal outlook – March 2025', OBR, 26 March 2025, https://obr.uk/efo/economic-and-fiscal-outlook-march-2025/

3   'Prime Minister sets out biggest sustained increase in defence spending since the Cold War, protecting British people in new era for national security', gov.uk, 25 February 2025, https://www.gov.uk/government/news/prime-minister-sets-out-biggest-sustained-increase-in-defence-spending-since-the-cold-war-protecting-british-people-in-new-era-for-national-security

4   OBR Economic and Fiscal Outlook 2025, Annex A.

5   OECD Economic Outlook EO116 Statistical Annex, Table 29.

6   Ibid.

7   OBR Economic and Financial Outlooks, March 2021, November 2023 and March 2025, mainly from Annex A, Table A.7 from each publication.

8   'Public service productivity, quarterly, UK: January to March 2025', ONS, 28 July 2025, https://www.ons.gov.uk/economy/economicoutputandproductivity/publicservicesproductivity/bulletins/publicserviceproductivityquarterlyuk/januarytomarch2025

9   Ibid., with the levels of GDP calculated from Table A.3.

10 Anthony B. Atkinson, *The Atkinson review: final report. Measurement of government output and productivity for the national accounts*, Palgrave Macmillan, 2005.

11 'British Social Attitudes', National Centre for Social Research, https://natcen.ac.uk/british-social-attitudes

12 'Public service productivity: total, UK, 2022', Office for National Statistics, 27 March 2025, https://www.ons.gov.uk/economy/economicoutputandproductivity/publicservicesproductivity/articles/publicservicesproductivityestimatestotalpublicservices/2022, Worksheet 3. It is likely that these numbers might have been revised since this was published but updated information has not been published.

13 See, for example, Lizzie Dearden, 'How the failing Passport Office was transformed into Britain's most efficient public service', *The Telegraph*, 21 June 2024, https://www.telegraph.co.uk/news/2024/06/20/how-failing-passport-office-was-transformed/

14 'Public Sector Productivity', Hansard, 9 October 2024, https://hansard.parliament.uk/lords/2024-10-09/debates/3FBE01A8-6DBF-486D-8F6F-E3DFFAD26691/PublicSectorProductivity

15 Anthony Flynn, David McKevitt and Paul Davis, 'The impact of size on SME public sector tendering', https://core.ac.uk/download/pdf/147607838.pdf

16 'Trade Union Membership, UK 1995–2023: Statistical Bulletin', Department for Business and Trade, 29 May 2024, https://assets.publishing.service.gov.uk/media/665db15a0c8f88e868d334b8/Trade_Union_Membership_UK_1995_to_2023_Statistical_Bulletin.pdf

17 Frankie Elliott, 'Brand new £1 billion fleet of passenger trains has been sitting in storage for YEARS after trade union row over window wipers', MailOnline, 2 October 2024, https://www.dailymail.co.uk/news/article-13917839/New-trains-sitting-storage-trade-union-row.html

18 'Whistleblowers claim up to 25 per cent of KCC Social Workers are alcoholics', Shepwayvox, 3 December 2021, https://shepwayvox.org/2021/12/03/whistleblowers-claim-up-to-25-of-kcc-social-workers-are-alcoholics/

19 'UK input-output analytical tables: produce by product', Office for National Statistics, 20 February 2025, https://www.ons.gov.uk/economy/nationalaccounts/supplyandusetables/datasets/ukinputoutputanalyticaltablesdetailed

20 CPA_S95 Repair services of computers and personal and household goods; CPA_J63 Information Services; CPA_J61 Telecommunications services; CPA_J62 Computer programming, consultancy and related services; CPA_C26 Computer, electronic and optical products.

21 CPA_O84.

22 CPA_P85.

23 CPA_Q86.

24 'Three Years of Progress', Virgin Media O_2 Business, https://www.virginmediabusiness.co.uk/revolutionise-the-everyday/CEBR-report/

25 'Employment Rights Bill: factsheets', gov.uk, 18 October 2024, https://www.gov.uk/government/publications/employment-rights-bill-factsheets

26 OBR Economic and Fiscal Outlook, Annex A, Table A.7, March 2023 and March 2025 and March 2021 Supplementary fiscal tables – expenditure.

27 Eduin Latimer, Freddie Pflanz and Tom Waters, 'Health-related benefit claims post-pandemic: UK trends and global context', Institute for Fiscal Studies, September 2024.

28 Robert Joyce, Sam Ray-Chaudhuri and Tom Waters, 'The number of new disability benefit claimants has doubled in a year', IFS, 7 December 2022, https://ifs.org.uk/news/number-new-disability-benefit-claimants-has-doubled-year

29 'Demographic Impacts on Economic Growth', Growth Commission, 3 May 2024, https://www.growth-commission.com/2024/05/03/demographic-impacts-on-economic-growth/

30 'Government ushers in new era for UK infrastructure delivery', gov.uk, 1 April 2025, https://www.gov.uk/government/news/government-ushers-in-new-era-for-uk-infrastructure-delivery

31 'Reshaping British Infrastructure: Global Lessons to Improve Project Delivery', BCG, 7 February 2024, https://www.bcg.com/united-kingdom/centre-for-growth/insights/reshaping-british-infrastructure-global-lessons-to-improve-project-delivery

CHAPTER 10

1   Simon Stevenson, Patrick Wilson and Ralf Zurbruegg, 'Assessing the Time-Varying Interest Rate Sensitivity of Real Estate Securities', *European Journal of Finance*, Vol. 13, No. 8, 2007, pp. 705–15.

2   Alexey Akimov, Chyi Lin Lee and Simon Stevenson, 'Interest Rate Sensitivity in European Public Real Estate Markets', *Journal of Real Estate Portfolio Management*, Vol. 25, Issue 2, June 2019.

3   The latest letter of instructions is here: 'Monetary policy remit: Mansion House 2024', gov.uk, 15 November

2024, https://www.gov.uk/government/publications/monetary-policy-remit-mansion-house-2024/monetary-policy-remit-mansion-house-2024

4   This is the most recent of such letters at time of writing: https://www.bankofengland.co.uk/-/media/boe/files/letter/2024/governor-cpi-inflation-letter-march-2024.pdf

5   James Jackson, Daniel Bailey and Matthew Paterson, 'Climate-related risks to central bank independence', *New Political Economy*, Vol. 30, Issue 3, 2025. This article compares the Bank of England's policy with those of other central banks.

6   B. S. Bernanke and F. S. Mishkin, 'Inflation targeting: a new framework for monetary policy?', *Journal of Economic Perspectives*, Vol. 11, No. 2, 1997, pp. 97–116.

7   Sir James Meade, 'The Meaning of Internal Balance', *Economic Journal*, Vol. 88, No. 351, September 1978, p. 423.

8   James Tobin, 'Stabilisation Policy 10 years after', Brookings Papers, 1980.

9   'What comes after inflation targets', *Financial Times*, 1 July 2010, https://www.ft.com/content/14e20968-8545-11df-9c2f-00144feabdc0

10 'The real target that Carney should be aiming for', *Financial Times*, 11 July 2013, https://www.ft.com/content/b3f5d09e-e8ba-11e2-aead-00144feabdc0

11 Damian Pudner, 'Rethinking Monetary Policy: The case for adopting NGDP targeting in Britain', Institute of Economic Affairs, March 2025, https://iea.org.uk/wp-content/uploads/2025/03/IEA_NGDP-Targeting_Digital_V1.pdf

12 'Should the UK Adopt Money GDP Targets?', Gresham lecture, 19 November 2013, https://www.gresham.ac.uk/watch-now/should-uk-adopt-money-gdp-targets

13 'Charter for Budget Responsibility Autum 2024', HM Treasury, January 2025, https://assets.publishing.service.gov.uk/media/678fbb377bb65baf62c2ada8/Charter_for_Budget_Responsibility_Autumn_2024_Accessible.pdf

14 Ibid., para 2.3.

15 Ibid., paras 3.6 and 3.7.

CHAPTER 11

1   Discussion at meeting on financial regulation hosted by the Lord Mayor of London with Pascal Donahue, chair of Eurogroup of European Finance Ministers, 3 September 2024, Mansion House, London.

2   'The True Cost of Compliance', Oxford Economics, 24 July 2024, https://www.oxfordeconomics.com/resource/the-true-cost-of-compliance/

3   'Money laundering and illicit finance', National Crime Agency, https://www.nationalcrimeagency.gov.uk/what-we-do/crime-threats/money-laundering-and-illicit-finance

4   Douglas McWilliams and Shanker Singham, 'Making the UK more successful through better regulation', Growth Commission, September 2023, https://www.growth-commission.com/wp-content/uploads/2024/04/65159ed6cecf730bdf41ed66_Report-3-GC_FINAL.pdf

5   'Factsheet: Employment Rights Bill – Evidence and Analysis', Department for Business and Trade, https://assets.publishing.service.gov.uk/media/67f67154b7e44efc70acc404/employment-rights bill-analysis.pdf

6   McWilliams and Singham, 'Making the UK more successful through better regulation'

7   For evidence of this, see the Regulatory Policy Committee's own reports – e.g. 'Scrutiny of Government Impact Assessments', gov.uk, 17 December 2021, https://rpc.blog.gov.uk/2021/12/17/scrutiny-of-government-impact-assessments/

8   'Growth Duty: Statutory Guidance – Refresh', Department for Business and Trade, 21 May 2024, https://assets.publishing.service.gov.uk/media/66476caebd01f5ed32793e09/final_growth_duty_statutory_guidance_2024.pdf

9   'Government goes further and faster on planning reform in bod for growth', gov.uk, 26 January 2025, https://www.gov.uk/government/news/government-goes-further-and-faster-on-planning-reform-in-bid-for-growth

10 'Shaping the Nation: Report of the Planning Task Force', CBI, November 1992.

11 Andrew MacKinlay, Indraneel Chakraborty and Itay Goldstein, 'Housing Price Booms and Crowding-Out Effects in Bank Lending', *Review of Financial Studies*, Vol. 31, No. 7, 2018, https://finance.wharton.upenn.edu/~itayg/Files/realestatebubbles-published.pdf

12 Harald Hau and Difei Ouyang, 'How Real Estate Booms Hurt Small Firms: Evidence on Investment Substitution', *Swiss Finance Institute Research Paper No. 18–38*, May 2018, https://ssrn.com/abstract=3174761

13 Liam Halligan, *Home Truths: The UK's chronic housing shortage – how it happened, why it matters and the way to solve it*, Biteback, 2019.

14   'Written evidence submitted by Liam Halligan', https://committees.parliament.uk/writtenevidence/2743/pdf
15   McKinsey Global Institute, 'Driving productivity and growth in the UK economy'.
16   'Simplified planning zone', Slough Borough Council, https://www.slough.gov.uk/planning/simplified-planning-zone-spz
17   'Planning for the Future', Ministry of Housing, Communities and Local Government, 6 August 2020, https://www.gov.uk/government/consultations/planning-for-the-future
18   Raoul Ruparel et al., 'Reshaping British Infrastructure: Global Lessons to Improve Project Delivery', Boston Consulting Group, 7 February 2024, https://www.bcg.com/united-kingdom/centre-for-growth/insights/reshaping-british-infrastructure-global-lessons-to-improve-project-delivery
19   Guy Taylor, 'Lower Thames Crossing planning application becomes UK's longest every – at more than 350,000 pages, and costing almost £300m', City AM, 15 January 2024, https://www.cityam.com/lower-thames-crossing-planning-application-becomes-uks-longest-ever-at-more-than-350000-pages-and-costing-almost-300m
20   'How will the Renters' Rights Bill affect landlords' plans?', Investec, 3 March 2025, https://www.investec.com/en_gb/focus/prime-property/renters-rights-update.html
21   'The Private Rented Sector Review', Deposit Protection Service, December 2024, https://content-assets.computershare.com/eh96rkuu9740/6tQ5i4T56nUmPn37sDflhR/8664c1ba93f2500701fd3291f4cd5f69/DPS_The_private_rented_sector_review_2024.pdf
22   Rebecca Diamond, Timothy McQuade and Franklin Qian, 'The Effects of Rent Control Expansion on Tenants, Landlords, and Inequality: Evidence from San Francisco', National Bureau of Economic Research, January 2018, https://www.nber.org/system/files/working_papers/w24181/w24181.pdf
23   'The Impact of Rent Control on the Private Rented Sector', BPF, 24 May 2023, https://bpf.org.uk/our-work/research-and-briefings/the-impact-of-rent-control-on-the-private-rented-sector/
24   'Assessment of Rent Freeze', Rettie & Co., https://bpf.org.uk/media/6181/assessment-of-of-scotlands-rent-freeze-and-impacts.pdf
25   Michael Jones, Kathryn Muir, Chihiro Udagawa and Gemma Burgess, 'The impact of taxation reform on the private rented sector', Cambridge Centre for Housing and Planning Research, May 2018, https://www.landecon.cam.ac.uk/sites/default/files/2024-01/downloadtemplate_25.pdf
26   Data from 'Measuring UK greenhouse gas emissions', Office for National Statistics, 18 June 2025, https://www.ons.gov.uk/economy/environmentalaccounts/methodologies/measuringukgreenhousegasemissions
27   'World Energy Outlook 2024 Free Dataset', IEA, October 2024, https://www.iea.org/data-and-statistics/data-product/world-energy-outlook-2024-free-dataset
28   Thomas Spencer and Siddharth Singh, 'What the data centre and AI boom could mean for the energy sector', IEA, 18 October 2024, https://www.iea.org/commentaries/what-the-data-centre-and-ai-boom-could-mean-for-the-energy-sector
29   'International industrial energy prices', gov.uk, 30 May 2013, https://www.gov.uk/government/statistical-data-sets/international-industrial-energy-prices
30   'The Social Cost of Carbon and the Shadow Price of Carbon', Department for Environment, Food and Rural Affairs, December 2007, https://assets.publishing.service.gov.uk/media/5a7c0a4aed915d414762263f/background.pdf
31   'Inflation calculator', Bank of England, https://www.bankofengland.co.uk/monetary-policy/inflation/inflation-calculator
32   'Technical Support Document: Social Cost of Carbon, Methane, and Nitrous Oxide Interim Estimates under Executive Order 13990', Interagency Working Group on Social Cost of Greenhouse Gases, United States government, February 2021, https://www.energy.gov/sites/default/files/2023-04/57.%20Social%20Cost%20of%20Carbon%202021.pdf
33   See 'The Green Book (2022)', gov.uk, 16 May 2024, https://www.gov.uk/government/publications/the-green-book-appraisal-and-evaluation-in-central-government/the-green-book-2020 and associated documents.
34   'Economic impacts of the 2030 – 2040 bans on the sale of fossil fuel vehicles', Fair Fuel UK, https://fairfueluk.com/CEBR-2030-BAN/
35   'Energy market investigation: Final report', Competition and Markets Authority, 2016, https://assets.publishing.service.gov.uk/media/5773de34e5274a0da3000113/final-report-energy-market-investigation.pdf
36   Arindrajit Dube, 'Impacts of minimum wages: Review of the International evidence', HM Treasury, November 2019, https://assets.publishing.service.gov.uk/media/5dc0312940f0b637a03ffa96/impacts_of_minimum_wages_review_of_the_international_evidence_Arindrajit_Dube_web.pdf
37   'Train fair revenue rising slower than passenger journeys', Office of Rail and Road, 28 November 2024, https://www.orr.gov.uk/search-news/train-fare-revenue-rising-slower-passenger-journeys

38 'Economics', RAC Foundation, https://www.racfoundation.org/motoring-faqs/economics
39 'The Future of Road Transport: Abolishing Traffic Jams', Cebr, 10 July 2017, https://cebr.com/blogs/the-future-of-road-transport-abolishing-traffic-jams

CHAPTER 12
1 'General terms for the United States of America and the United Kingdom of Great Britain and Northern Ireland Economic Prosperity Deal', gov.uk, 8 May 2025.
2 'The contribution of standards to the UK economy', Cebr, April 2022, https://www.bsigroup.com/globalassets/documents/about-bsi/nsb/cebr/bsi-uk-final-report-1.2-apr22.pdf
3 'UK concludes trade deal with India', gov.uk, 6 May 2025, https://www.gov.uk/government/news/uk-signs-trade-deal-with-india
4 Ibid.
5 Shanker A. Singham, *The Impact of Carbon Leakage Mechanisms on Growth*, Growth Commission, October 2024.
6 'British households to become £2400 poorer from new EU-style tax', Growth Commission, 26 April 2024, https://www.growth-commission.com/2024/04/26/british-households-to-become-2400-poorer-from-new-eu-style-tax/
7 'Export statistics', gov.uk, https://www.gov.uk/government/statistics/uk-trade-in-numbers/uk-trade-in-numbers-web-version#export-statistics

PART III
1 Jean-Claude Juncker, 'The Quest for Prosperity', quoted in *The Economist*, 15 March 2007.
2 Johnny Munkhammar, *The Guide to Reform; How Policymakers Can Pursue Real Change, Achieve Great Results and Win Re-Election*, Timbro/IEA, 2007.

CHAPTER 13
1 The official inquiry into Covid, https://covid19.public-inquiry.uk

CONCLUSION
1 *Report on the Organisation of the Permanent Civil Service*, George E. Eyre and William Spottiswoode, 1854, https://www.civilservant.org.uk/library/1854_Northcote_Trevelyan_Report.pdf. The report was actually presented to Parliament in 1853.
2 At 2017 PPP values – based on IMF data.
3 'Fiscal risks and sustainability', OBR, July 2025.
4 'Fiscal Monitor', IMF, April 2025.
5 'Sickness absence in the UK labour market: 2023 and 2024', ONS, 4 June 2025, https://www.ons.gov.uk/employmentandlabourmarket/peopleinwork/labourproductivity/articles/sicknessabsenceinthelabourmarket/2023and2024
6 'Labour disputes; working days lost due to strike action; public sector (thousands)', ONS, 17 July 2025, https://www.ons.gov.uk/employmentandlabourmarket/peopleinwork/employmentandemployeetypes/timeseries/f8xz/lms
7 'The impact of strikes in the UK: June 2022 to February 2023', ONS, 8 March 2023, https://www.ons.gov.uk/employmentandlabourmarket/peopleinwork/workplacedisputesandworkingconditions/articles/theimpactofstrikesintheuk/june2022tofebruary2023
8 Because the public sector productivity figures have recently been revised to reflect quality improvements, there is currently no longer-term data on public sector productivity. The earlier data indicated a slight fall in public sector productivity from 1997 to 2022: see 'Public service productivity, UK: 1997 to 2022', ONS, 17 November 2023, https://www.ons.gov.uk/economicoutputandproductivity/publicservicesproductivity/articles/publicserviceproductivityuk/1997to2022
9 'Productivity flash estimate and overview, UK: January to March 2025 and October to December 2024', ONS, 15 May 2025, https://www.ons.gov.uk/employmentandlabourmarket/peopleinwork/labourproductivity/articles/ukproductivityintroduction/januarytomarch2025andoctobertodecember2024
10 Comparing 2024 with 2019, see ibid.
11 Comparing 2024 with 2019, see 'Public service productivity, quarterly, UK: October to December 2024', ONS, 8 May 2025, https://www.ons.gov.uk/economy/economicoutputandproductivity/publicservicesproductivity/bulletins/publicserviceproductivityquarterlyuk/octobertodecember2024. Please note that the public sector productivity figures have recently been sharply revised to take account of quality improvements; equivalent changes have not been made to the same extent for the private sector. So arguably these figures flatter the public sector.

ANNEX 1

1   The model and the modelling approach is described on pp. 27–30 of 'The Single Income Tax: Final report of the 2020 Tax Commission', TaxPayers' Alliance, May 2012, https://assets.nationbuilder.com/taxpayersalliance/pages/16357/attachments/original/1533563661/2020tc.pdf?1533563661

2   'The Autum 2024 Growth Budget', Growth Commission, 2024, https://www.growth-commission.com/wp-content/uploads/2024/10/FINAL-TEXT-GC_Autumn-Growth-Budget-2024.pdf. The models used and the costing approach are described in Appendices 1 and 2 of that report. The numbers for the impact of planning are different from those in the Growth Commission report because the impact of the policy already adopted (as estimated by the OBR in its March 2025 Economic and Fiscal Outlook) is subtracted from the estimated impact of the Growth Commission proposals.

ANNEX 2

1   GDP per capita at 2017 PPP dollars. 'World Economic League Table', Cebr, https://cebr.com/world-economic-league-table/

ACKNOWLEDGEMENTS

First and foremost, we'd like to acknowledge the people we interviewed: Andrew Bailey, Sir Tony Blair, Sir Vince Cable, Lord Cameron of Chipping Norton, Lord Chartres, Lord Clarke of Nottingham, Jamie Dimon, Jonathan Geldart, David Giampaolo, Richard Gnodde, Andy Haldane, Lord Hammond of Runnymede, Rupert Harrison, Sir Jeremy Hunt MP, Sir Sajid Javid, Boris Johnson, Kwasi Kwarteng, Lord Lamont of Lerwick, Anna Leach, Clare Lombardelli, Lord Macpherson of Earl's Court, Lord O'Donnell, Lord O'Neill of Gatley, George Osborne, Lord Petitgas, Stephen Phipson, Sir John Rose, Sir Tom Scholar, Rupert Soames, Lord Stevens of Birmingham, Rishi Sunak MP, Liz Truss, Lord Walney, Lord Wolfson of Aspley Guise and Nadhim Zahawi, who gave us such brilliant insight.

Secondly, our sincere thanks to those who have helped us make our ideas for this book a reality: Chantelle Hale, James Smith and Alex Wilson in Michael Hintze's office; Jillian Roney, Nicholas Drinkwater, Belinda Dwyer, Brian Domitrovic, Clay Nishi, Jeanne Sinquefield and Rex Sinquefield at Laffer Associates; Amy Baker, Georgiana Bristol and Bertie Hawkins at the Jobs Foundation; Nina Skero and Pushpin Singh at Cebr; Jonathan Isaby for proofreading the book for us; and Olivia Beattie, Suzanne Sangster, James Stephens, Mark Wallace, Nell Whitaker, Rosie Williamson and Ella Windsor at Biteback Publishing.

ABOUT THE AUTHORS

Dr Arthur B. Laffer, founder of Laffer Associates, is known as 'The Father of Supply-Side Economics'. He advised both President Reagan and Prime Minister Thatcher on fiscal policy. In 1999, *Time* named him one of 'the Century's Greatest Minds' for creating the Laffer curve. He received the Presidential Medal of Freedom in 2019, the highest civilian honour awarded by the United States, for his contributions to economics.

Matthew Elliott is one of the UK's foremost public policy thinkers, having set up numerous policy campaigns, including the TaxPayers' Alliance in 2003. He has overseen two successful national referendum campaigns – the NOtoAV campaign in 2011 and the Vote Leave campaign in 2016 – and convened two influential policy commissions. He is currently the co-founder and president of the Jobs Foundation, a charity which champions the role of business as a force for good. Matthew is also a member of the House of Lords, where he sits as Lord Elliott of Mickle Fell.

Michael Hintze is a financier and businessman. He has held positions in Credit Suisse First Boston, Goldman Sachs and Salomon Brothers, before founding CQS Investment Management and Deltroit Asset Management. He also served as an officer in the Australian Army. Lord Hintze's philanthropy spans contributions to the arts, religious charities, military charities and education. He was made a Knight Commander of the Order of St Gregory by Pope Benedict XVI and was subsequently elevated to the rank of Knight Grand Cross. He was appointed a Member of the Order of Australia in 2008 and was made a Knight Bachelor by Queen Elizabeth II. In 2022, he was granted a life peerage by King Charles III and sits in the House of Lords as Baron Hintze.

Douglas McWilliams sold the Centre for Economics and Business Research (Cebr), the economics consultancy that he had founded thirty-five years earlier, in autumn 2024 to a management buyout. Cebr has become well known, especially for its World Economic League Table published on Boxing Day each year. Before setting up Cebr, he had been chief economic adviser to the CBI and chief economist for IBM UK. Douglas had also chaired the Economics Committee of what is now called Business Europe in Brussels. While running Cebr, he was also the Gresham Professor of Commerce, and today he remains a member of the Growth Commission. Among his books, the best known are *The Flat White Economy*, about the emerging UK tech economy, and *The Inequality Paradox*, where he refutes Thomas Piketty's theory of exploitation.

INDEX